STUDIES IN EVANGELICAL HISTORY AND THOUGHT

Pentecostal Origins

Early Pentecostalism in Ireland in the Context of the British Isles

STUDIES IN EVANGELICAL HISTORY AND THOUGHT

A full listing of all titles in this series appears at the close of this book

STUDIES IN EVANGELICAL HISTORY AND THOUGHT

Pentecostal Origins

Early Pentecostalism in Ireland in the Context of the British Isles

James Robinson

Foreword by Neil Hudson

First published 2005 by Paternoster

Paternoster is an imprint of Authentic Media
9 Holdom Avenue, Bletchley, Milton Keynes, MK1 1QR, UK
and
PO Box 1047, Waynesboro, GA 30830–2047, USA

11 10 09 08 07 06 05   7 6 5 4 3 2 1

British Library Cataloguing in Publication Data
A catalogue record for this book is available from the British Library

ISBN 1–84227–329-9

Typeset by A.R. Cross
Printed and bound in Great Britain
for Paternoster

STUDIES IN EVANGELICAL HISTORY AND THOUGHT

Series Preface

The Evangelical movement has been marked by its union of four emphases: on the Bible, on the cross of Christ, on conversion as the entry to the Christian life and on the responsibility of the believer to be active. The present series is designed to publish scholarly studies of any aspect of this movement in Britain or overseas. Its volumes include social analysis as well as exploration of Evangelical ideas. The books in the series consider aspects of the movement shaped by the Evangelical Revival of the eighteenth century, when the impetus to mission began to turn the popular Protestantism of the British Isles and North America into a global phenomenon. The series aims to reap some of the rich harvest of academic research about those who, over the centuries, have believed that they had a gospel to tell to the nations.

Series Editors

To Mary
David, Peter and Stephen

Contents

Foreword

Jim Robinson is one of the growing number of people who have shown the interest and the necessary research skills to help us better understand the development of British and European Pentecostalism. This book, then, comes at a time when Pentecostal scholars are reminding people that there is no one homogenous Pentecostalism, but rather global Pentecostalisms, each with their own cultures, stories and heroes.

In the light of how Pentecostal denominations would develop within the United Kingdom, it is interesting that the central figure for the story in the pre-World War I period was the Rev. Alexander Boddy, a middle aged Anglican vicar. He towered amongst the European leaders as the focal point for the fledgling groups, the mediator between potential adversaries and the theological leader who helped Pentecostal groups to identify their distinctiveness. However, this book reminds us that the more radical aspects of Pentecostal theology and practice were being played out amongst the Celtic fringes in Wales, Scotland and Ireland.

This work takes us to the formation of one of the most effective evangelistic groups of the twentieth century. Led by George Jeffreys, the Elim churches developed out of their leader's central conviction that the Spirit had been given not merely to enhance worship, or to restructure church government (although this belief would become his own *bête noire* in later years), but for the central purpose of evangelism. This became his passion in the interwar periods, beginning from small beginnings in Ireland until eventually filling the largest auditoriums in Britain.

The other group that challenged the small Pentecostal movement was the emergence of the Apostolic churches. They believed that if the Spirit guided the church in biblical times, then he would do so again in contemporary days, and would do so in guiding people by the use of spoken, authoritative prophecy. This was a threat to the more restrained Pentecostalism that Boddy represented. Jim Robinson does a good job at showing this threat and how other groups reacted to it.

I want to congratulate Dr Robinson on his publication. He has brought our attention to primary source material that will be of longstanding help to all those wanting to take this research further in different directions. This is a story that has needed to be told for a long time, my fervent hope is that we will see the development of a group of competent historians, willing to take the vitality of Pentecostal spirituality seriously, able to applaud the leaders of the small groups for risking the opprobrium of religious groups they faced, whilst also recognising the mistakes that were made. In so doing we can open up the legacy of the past for future generations, in the hope that they learn to appreciate who they are, what their DNA involves, whilst also providing warnings against them repeating the mistakes of the past.

Rev. Dr Neil Hudson
Regents Theological College
Nantwich
England

Acknowledgements

In researching and writing this study I have incurred many debts. To come to the task of writing with an interest in a topic that threatens to exceed one's competence requires sizeable measures of encouragement and practical support. I have been singularly fortunate in receiving both. The Rev. Professor Finlay Holmes and the Rev. Professor Laurence Kirkpatrick, both of Union Theological College, Belfast, helped me in different ways. The former, in his final year before retirement from the chair of Church History at Union Theological College, Belfast, allowed me space to familiarise myself with a subject in which I had only a limited background. Professor Kirkpatrick prodded me into the way of writing and over a period of five years kept me steadily on course. Encouragement came from his enthusiasm for the project and a sustained interest in its findings as they slowly unrolled.

The name of Desmond Cartwright appears throughout these pages, usually in citations in footnotes. They reflect, in part, the immense amount of help he afforded me over the years. His knowledge of the history of British Pentecostalism, in particular, is vast, much of it garnered in his role as archivist of the Elim Church and the Donald Gee Pentecostal and Charismatic Research Centre at Mattersey, Nottinghamshire. Both in directing my attention to new source material and providing from his own large collection of otherwise unobtainable books, articles and photographs, he inspired me to share his passionate commitment to an empathetic, yet rigorous, treatment of Pentecostal history. At moments of hesitancy over facts or interpretations, I found it reassuring to know that he was never further than a phone call away.

Needless to say, my indebtedness extends to others. In my Bibliographical Note and the Primary Resource section of the Bibliography, I mention the names of those who offered specific help. I am especially beholden to all those named in the list of interviewees and those who loaned me original source material. Without exception, all were supportive of the project and were prepared to give me the time to probe memories and elicit opinions. The inter-library loan facility was exploited fully and Florence Gray of Queens University Belfast ensured a smooth and efficient service.

The substance of Chapter 3 appeared in 'Arthur Booth-Clibborn; Pentecostal Patriarch', *JEPTA*, Vol. XXI, 2001, pp. 68-90. I am grateful to the Association for permission to use much of the article. Such new material as has been added relates to the short, though significant, relationship between John Alexander Dowie and Booth-Clibborn. The background to their association has been made accessible recently by the publication in CD-ROM version of *Leaves of Healing*, the periodical edited by Dowie.

I am particularly grateful to Jeremy Mudditt and Dr Anthony Cross of Paternoster for their assistance in bringing this work to completion. Both were unfailingly supportive in giving of their time and advice, making it a pleasure and an education to work with them.

Completing a task such as this is a major learning process and when nearing completion I came across a sentence in A.T.Q. Stewart's latest book, [*The Shape of Irish History*, (Belfast: Blackstaff Press, 2001), p. 188] it resonated with my limited experience in the historical enterprise: 'Every historian should have two small notices on his desk, one reading "I do not know" and the other "Everything is older than you think it is"'. I would be pleased if in the course of this work I have demonstrated the latter and moderated, even if only slightly, the former.

Finally, I would wish to express my gratitude to my wife, Mary, for her constant support over the six years working on this topic and for her practical help in ways too diverse to specify. Fortunately, she is a person who keeps herself busy, otherwise she would have been forced to spend many lonely days and evenings. In appreciation of all she means to me, I dedicate this work to her and to the three sons she so lovingly nurtured to face the world.

Abbreviations

AFC	Apostolic Faith Church
AOG	Assemblies of God
ACM	Apostolic Church [in Ireland] Minutes
ACW	Apostolic Church in Wales
BEM	*Belfast Elim Minutes*
BIOLA	The Bible Institute of Los Angeles
BPA	Belfast Protestant Association
C&MA	Christian and Missionary Alliance
DUP	Democratic Unionist Party
ECONI	Evangelical Contribution on Northern Ireland
EE	*Elim Evangel*
EEB	Elim Evangelistic Band
EPA	Elim Pentecostal Alliance
EPAC	Elim Pentecostal Alliance Council
EEBM	*Elim Evangelistic Band Minutes*
INLA	Irish National Liberation Army
JEPTA	*Journal of the European Pentecostal Theological Association*
LH	*Leaves of Healing*
NIDPCM	*New International Dictionary of Pentecostal and Charismatic Movements*, ed. Stanley M. Burgess (Grand Rapids, MI: Zondervan, 2002)
PMU	Pentecostal Missionary Union
RT	*Redemption Tidings*
SPS	*Society for Pentecostal Studies*

Maps, Figures and Photographs

Maps

Figures

Photographs

Introduction

The truism that 'great oaks from little acorns grow' is compellingly demonstrated by the modern Pentecostal movement.[1] Starting virtually from scratch in the first decade of the twentieth century, the Pentecostal/Charismatic constituency by the year 2000 accounted for 8.7 per cent of the world's population, larger than the percentage of all Buddhists, and made up 26.7 per cent of all Christendom. The last figure is estimated to rise to 31 per cent. by the year 2025.[2] Peter Brierley has produced figures to suggest that most of this growth will take place in the Third World. Of the Pentecostal/Charismatic bloc in the year 2010, he estimated that 38% will be found in Latin America, 27% in North America, 20% in Africa, 11% in Asia, 3% in Europe and 1% in Australasia.[3] Harvey Cox saw this startling rise of Pentecostalism as nothing less than 'the reshaping of religion in the twenty-first century'.[4] Henry P. Van Dusen, who first applied the epithet 'Third Force' to Pentecostalism, held that it was the harbinger of 'a revolution comparable in importance with the establishment of the original church and with the Protestant Reformation'.[5] John A. Mackay feared that if the Protestant churches did not recover their dynamic, then 'the Christian future may lie

[1] The movement is commonly considered to have started with the Azusa Street, Los Angeles, revival in April 1906, though it is worth noting that Barratt puts the number of Pentecostal/Charismatics for the year 1900 at just below one million. (David B. Barrett, 'Status of Global Mission 2001', *International Bulletin of Missionary Research,* January 2001, p. 25.) Clearly definitions are not matching but his analysis provides a reminder that some forms of identifiable practice and belief-system found at the end of the nineteenth century tallied with the happenings at Azusa Street at the beginning of the twentieth century. For an account of nineteenth-century, pre-Azusa Street Pentecostal-type phenomena see Gary B. McGee, 'Pentecostal Phenomena and Revivals in India: Implication for Indigenous Church Leadership', *International Bulletin of Missionary Research,* Vol. 20.3, July 1996, pp. 112-17.

[2] Barrett, 'Status of Global Mission', *International Bulletin of Missionary Research,* January 2001, p. 25. By ecclesial bloc membership, Pentecostal/Charismatics are second only to the Roman Catholic Church. There are just over one billion Catholics and some half billion Pentecostal/Charismatics, though the two groups are not exclusive in that a sizeable number bracketed as Charismatic are members of the Catholic Church.

[3] Peter Brierley, *Future Church: A Global Analysis of the Christian Community to the Year 2000,* (East Sussex: Monarch, 1998), p. 124.

[4] This is the sub-title of his acclaimed *Fire from Heaven,* (Reading, MA: Addison-Wesley, 1995).

[5] The quote is from J. Rodman Williams, *A Theological Pilgrimage*, http://forum.regent.edu/rodmwil/tp03.html, Ch. 3, p. 3. Van Dusen (1897-1975) was an influential American Presbyterian theologian, prominent in ecumenical affairs.

with a reformed Catholicism and a matured Pentecostalism'.[6] Hendrikus Berkhof contended that 'the Pentecostals are basically right when they speak of a working of the Holy Spirit beyond that which is acknowledged in the major denominations'.[7] Despite these commendatory remarks, here all from ecumenists in the Reformed tradition, the twentieth century overall showed no easy acceptance of Pentecostalism. McDonnell writes that a commonly held view of it was, sometimes still is, that of a movement 'somehow psychologically disreputable, socially unwashed and theologically barren'.[8]

Everett Wilson conceded that there was some substance in the last charge: 'The fact is that while Pentecostalism started out without much to recommend it socially and ecclesiastically and still remains difficult to explain, it somehow made it across the Red Sea, surviving to become stronger and more influential than could ever have been imagined'.[9] The word 'imagined' is somewhat overdrawn in that the early Pentecostals were a people with high expectations who would have been disappointed with anything less than what the future proved to hold. Donald Gee made the point that 'the pioneers of "Pentecost" visualised a revival that was to touch and inspire every section of the Christian Church'.[10] What fanned their expectation was the eschatological conviction that they were living in the end times and theirs was the last revival before the Parousia.[11] Archer summarises the imperious claim of the early Pentecostals: they 'understood themselves as the prophetically promised eschatological community, who would bring about the unity of Christianity and usher in

---

[6] Williams, *Theological Pilgrimage*, p. 4. J.A. Mackay (1889-1983) was another leading Presbyterian churchman, President of Princeton Theological Seminary, 1936-59.

[7] Williams, *Theological Pilgrimage*, p. 8. Berkhof (b. 1914) was a theologian of the Dutch Reformed Church and a member of the Central Committee of the WCC (1954-75).

[8] Kilian McDonnell (b.1921) is one of the leading interpreters of the Pentecostal/Charismatic Renewal and is an intermediary between it and the Vatican. The quotation appeared in an article in the *Journal of Ecumenical Studies,* Winter 1968, p.128 where the author sought to answer the charge.

[9] Everett A. Wilson, 'They Crossed the Red Sea, Didn't They?', in Murray W. Dempster *et al.* (eds), *The Globalization of Pentecostalism: A Religion Made To Travel,* (Carlisle: Regnum/Paternoster, 1999), p. 91. Wilson was an American Pentecostal missionary.

[10] D. Gee, *Wind and Flame,* (Croydon: Heath Press, 1967), p. 2.

[11] See D.William Faupel, *The Everlasting Gospel: The Significance of Eschatology in the Development of Pentecostal Thought,* (Sheffield: Sheffield Academic Press, 1996). Faupel argues that the imminence of the Parousia in most Pentecostal teaching provided the dynamic to the movement's early growth. In this, it followed the nineteenth-century Holiness movement, though not its eighteenth-century Methodist parent.

the Second Coming of Christ'.[12] Their credo carried the conviction that they were the people on whom the end of the age had come. The second editorial in *The Apostolic Faith* set forth a heady reading of church history, as artless as it was breathtaking to those who accepted it.

> All along the ages men have been preaching a partial Gospel. A part of the Gospel remained when the world went into the Dark Ages. God has from time to time raised up men to bring back the truth to the church. He raised up Luther to bring back to the world the doctrine of justification by faith. He raised up another reformer in John Wesley to establish Bible holiness in the church. Then he raised up Dr. Cullis who brought back to the world the wonderful doctrine of divine healing. Now He is bringing back the Pentecostal Baptism to the church.[13]

Myland's pronouncement carried the same burden: 'No matter how often you said, "saved, sanctified, healed", you still need Pentecost'.[14]

Gee added a comment that, in part, provided the inspiration to embark on this book. He contended:

> One highly significant feature of the [Pentecostal] movement that distinguishes it in a striking way from most of those that have gone before [is that] it does not owe its origin to any outstanding personality or religious leader, but was a spontaneous revival appearing almost simultaneously in various parts of the world.[15]

One has only to juxtapose Gee's employment of the word 'spontaneous' to the revival with that of a modern scholar writing of the closing decades of the nineteenth century that 'popular Evangelicalism was indeed at the time but a hairs-breadth from Pentecostalism', to suspect that his assessment is, at least, open to question.[16]

---

[12] Kenneth J. Archer, 'Pentecostal Story: The Hermeneutical Filter for the Making of Meaning', *Pneuma: The Journal of the Society for Pentecostal Studies*, Vol. 26.1, 2004, p. 49.

[13] *The Apostolic Faith,* Vol. 1.2, October 1906, p. 1, col. 1. This magazine was started by William J. Seymour and was the mouthpiece of the Azusa Street Mission. Charles Cullis (1833-1992), a Boston physican, became well known for his 'faith work' or 'faith-cure', as the practice of divine healing was termed at the time.

[14] D.W. Myland (1858-1943) wrote one of the first definitive Pentecostal theological treatises, *Latter Rain Covenant,* (Springfield, MO: Temple Press, 1910), p. 61.

[15] Gee, *Wind and Flame*, p. 3. This observation should be seen as that of a first-generation Pentecostal historian who had to rely heavily on the writings of the early observer-participants, of whom Frank Bartleman (1871-1936) was to become the best known. It has taken the work of recent scholarship to uncover Pentecostalism's multi-source origin through study of the diverse streams that flowed together in the 1900s to give it its distinctive features. (See Joe Creech, 'Visions of Glory: The Place of the Azusa Street Revival in Pentecostal History', *Church History*, Vol. 65.3, 1996.)

[16] Donald W. Dayton, *The Theological Roots of Pentecostalism,* (Peabody, MA: Hendrickson, 1987), p. 176. In an earlier article Dayton saw the emergence of

This study has been undertaken on the basis that such a sweeping phenomenon as the Pentecostal movement, with its impact not confined to the Christian church, is one deserving of study as to its roots if one is to understand it better.[17] Pentecostal/Charismatic Christianity is advancing so rapidly that it is threatening to outpace its resources within scholarship, not least in its historians who in number are not commensurate with its march and are left puffing rather badly behind. If the maxim that 'those who do not learn from history are doomed to repeat it' has any validity, then the historian has a serious responsibility, not just to the past but also the future. Any proper understanding of a movement such as the Pentecostal—its ethos, dynamism, tensions and weaknesses—can only be gained by engaging with its past, especially so if one follows Hollenweger in maintaining that the heart and core of the Pentecostal reality is to be found in the first five or ten years of the movement.[18]

This study does not deal with the grand global scale but addresses itself to the island of Ireland. Whilst most Pentecostal activity by far was concentrated in what is now Northern Ireland, formed from six of the nine counties of the historic Irish province of Ulster, the vision of the pioneers was always to engage with the whole island.[19] Dublin and Monaghan, in their different ways, feature in the early history of Pentecostalism in Ireland. Dublin was the home base of two Anglicans, one a clergyman and the other a barrister, who made a considerable contribution to the movement in both Britain and Ireland. Monaghan, while not playing a major part in the story, nevertheless, has a large symbolic place in the heart of the members of the Elim Church. As for the province of Northern Ireland, despite its small size and population of

Pentecostalism as 'a natural development of forces that had been set in motion much earlier'. (D W. Dayton, 'Christian "Perfection" to the "Baptism of the Holy Ghost"', in Vinson Synan [ed.], *Aspects of Pentecostal-Charismatic Origins,* [Plainfield: Logos 1975], p. 52.)

[17] See Steve Brouwer (ed.), *Exporting the American Gospel: Global Christian Fundamentalism*, (London: Routledge, 1996). In this book, an interdisciplinary work of historical, sociological and religio-political analysis, the authors explore the intertwining of American Christian fundamentalism with US corporate imperialism and foreign policy. They argue that, in the long run, the most important American export may well prove not to lie in its economic/cultural dominance but in its indigenous religious culture that has become increasingly fundamentalist and Pentecostal-Charismatic. It is this religious culture that is the ultimate carrier of values and worldviews.

[18] Simon Chan, *Pentecostal Theology and the Christian Spiritual Tradition,* (Sheffield: Sheffield Academic Press, 2000), p. 6.

[19] At the partition of the island in 1920, three counties of the original nine of Ulster, *viz.*, Monaghan, Cavan and Donegal, became part of the new Irish Free State (Eire). The remaining six, *viz.*, Antrim, Down, Armagh, Tyrone, Londonderry and Fermanagh, became a constituent part of the United Kingdom of Great Britain and Northern Ireland.

just over 1.7 million, it has in matters religious managed to punch above its weight while at the same time presenting a side of its religiosity that has proved a source of embarrassment to its well-wishers and a cause of scorn to its detractors both inside and outside the province. It will be part of this study to uncover some of the ways in which Irish Pentecostalism has contributed to the wider movement.

As mentioned previously, this study had as its initial stimulus the desire to explore the historical interface between the popular evangelicalism of the latter-nineteenth/early-twentieth centuries and the early Pentecostal movement. Did the movement, in fact, emerge on the religious scene Melchizedek-like, without genealogy, as Gee rather implied? Such a question confines any discussion to the early years, hence the terminal point of 1925.[20] By that time, the movement had gained a reasonable toehold in the province and was largely self-generating. In 1925, two of the three largest British Pentecostal groups had been established in the province for at least five years and the third was in the process of being launched.[21]

With a core interest in discovering the theological streams that fed the nascent Pentecostal movement, this book devotes the first two chapters to the pre-Pentecostal stage and thereafter follows the development of the movement in the province in a broadly chronological sequence. Chapter 1 examines those influences, from within nineteenth-century American and British evangelicalism, that contributed to the making of the early Pentecostal movement in Britain. Chapter 2 takes a closer look at those theological currents that played a part in conditioning the minds of the first Pentecostal believers in Ireland to expect a move of God similar to that emanating from the much-heralded Azusa Street revival in 1906. Arthur Booth-Clibborn, son-in-law of General William Booth, is the subject of Chapter 3. From a Quaker and Salvation Army background, he was probably the first Irish person to come in contact with the new movement. He is representative of those people from the province who

---

[20] Any straying beyond this date will be to follow significant happenings that reach their *denouement* outside the allotted time span or to illustrate a point by a particularly apposite example drawn from the period shortly outside the boundary dates.

[21] The prosaic term 'group' is used here to draw attention to the problem of categorising the divisions that emerged early in the history of the movement. In sociological taxonomy such groups would be classified as sects rather than denominations. (See the influential paper by Bryan R. Wilson, 'An Analysis of Sect Development', *American Sociological Review*, Vol. 24, February 1959.) In general, it can be held that while Pentecostal groups had sect-like beginnings, they have now attained denominational status. Precise dating of the transition period is both debatable and elusive. The term 'denomination' is the preferred use in this work to refer to recognised bodies within the wider movement.

have contributed greatly to the wider movement. In his case, it was to the cause in Europe.

The Pentecostal message and experience first reached the shores of Ireland late in 1907 and up till 1913 was confined to a few small assemblies with few resources and minimal impact. Chapter 4 considers this pre-denominational stage. The movement in the province was given a sharp jolt with the arrival of the young Welsh evangelist, George Jeffreys, in 1915. His background and the influences that shaped both the man and his ministry are dealt with in Chapter 5. The next two chapters examine the growth of the Elim movement that in its first eight years was largely confined to the province. Chapter 6 deals with the years 1915-18 when the Elim Evangelistic Band was first established with Jeffreys spearheading the spread of the Pentecostal message through some sizeable campaigns. In 1918 the Elim Pentecostal Alliance Council was set up, a move that represented the first formal step in establishing a new denomination. Up till 1922 the headquarters of the Elim movement was in Belfast, but in that year it was transferred to London. From then on the centre of gravity of the denomination shifted perceptibly from the province. The years between 1918 and 1923 are surveyed in Chapter 7.

Ireland could not avoid the currents sweeping through the wider British movement and the formation of the Apostolic Church in Wales brought the first serious challenge to the hegemony of Elim in the province. Chapter 8 explores the nature and impact of this newcomer, with its radical ideas of church order, during the first five years of its existence in Ireland. In the Conclusion, a brief assessment is made of the movement and its place in the religious life of the province today.

Two considerations should be borne in mind in reading this work:

This is the first work of its kind in the study of British Pentecostalism. Denominational and biographical studies have been undertaken but none that specialise in a synoptic regional study. It is for others to attempt the same for other regions in the British Isles and for other periods within Ireland.[22]

This work aims to be primarily a historical study undertaken in the context of a distinctive theological position. It is not intended to be a treatise on Pentecostal apologetics. It takes most Pentecostal claims at face value and assumes the integrity of the witnesses whose story it tells. It is not so naive as to assume that the Pentecostal defining position is other than a minority one, and that hotly contested, nor that everything recorded is commendable or its adherents' interpretative framework unclouded. It does, however, work on the premise that Pentecostalism had,

---

[22] A helpful contribution, though understandingly thin on the Pentecostal side, has been made by Andrew Gibson, 'The Charismatic Movement in Northern Ireland against the Background of the Troubles', MTh thesis, Queen's University Belfast, 1987.

and will continue, to have something important to contribute to the wider church. Events on the ground allow for nothing less.[23] For that, much is owed to the mature direction of those men and women who feature prominently in these pages.

[23] World Pentecostalism is growing at present at the rate of 8.1% per annum, twice that of the remainder of the evangelical sub-set within Christianity. (Stan Guthrie, *Missions in the Third Millennium: 21 Key Trends for the 21st Century,* [Carlisle: Paternoster, 2000], p. 140.)

CHAPTER 1

The Roots of British Pentecostalism

1.1 Seminal People and Places

The Pentecostal movement has been called '*the* popular religious movement of the twentieth century'.[1] It developed from the merging of a number of distinct theological streams within popular evangelicalism in America and Britain in the late nineteenth century. A coalescence of ideas led some to the conclusion that, if believers are to enter into the fullness of their Christian inheritance, then conversion must be followed by a distinct and subsequent experience known as the 'Baptism in the Holy Spirit'.[2] Spirit-baptism was regarded as the basis of victorious Christian witness and the prelude to an expansive gifting of the *charismata*, as outlined in 1 Corinthians 12 and 14, within the wider church. Indeed, the only distinctively new teaching of the early Pentecostals,[3] the one that most nettled their fellow evangelicals and completely baffled outsiders, was that the incontestable proof or evidence for having received 'the Baptism' was the speech-act of 'speaking in tongues'.[4]

---

[1] Quoted from Peter Williams by Grant Wacker, 'Pentecostalism', in C.H. Lippy and P.W. Williams (eds), *Encyclopaedia of the American Religious Experience: Studies of Traditions and Movements*, 2 vols, (New York: Charles Scribner's and Sons, 1988), Vol. II, p. 933.

[2] Henceforth in this work it will most often be referred to as 'Spirit-baptism'.

[3] Pentecostal-type phenomena have featured throughout the entire history of the church. (See R.A. Knox, *Enthusiasm: A Chapter in the History of Religion,* (Oxford: Clarendon Press, 1950). In the course of the nineteenth century the term 'Baptism in the Spirit' was being bandied about in an ill-defined way with increasing frequency within Holiness circles. Only the Pentecostal distinctive of tying Spirit-baptism with *glossolalia* was new. With this emphasis Pentecostals ensured for themselves a distinctive identity by maintaining that the *charismata* were an essential component of the 'full gospel', as they termed it, partly because the sheer physicality often associated with their manifestation was so patent. In short, the issue would henceforth remain permanently on the agenda of debatable issues within the Christian church.

[4] Most Pentecostals make a clear distinction between *glossolalia* as an evidential *sign* of Spirit-baptism and a *gift*. Some are prepared to accept some other charism as serving as an evidential sign. In the case of the *gift*, it is the Spirit who distributes to each one individually as He wills (1 Cor. 12:11,31; 14:4-5). The gift is to be exercised both for

Pentecostalism usually traces its roots to the events in Topeka, Kansas, in 1901 with Charles Fox Parham (1873-1929) the leading figure.[5] It was Parham who first formulated the distinctive Pentecostal doctrine of 'speaking in tongues' as the initial evidence of the seeker having received Spirit-baptism.[6] However, historians of Pentecostalism single out two events as foundational to its origin. To Topeka, therefore, must be added the revival that began in 1906 at the Azusa Street mission in Los Angeles led by a black American, William J. Seymour (1870-1922).[7] While Topeka furnished the doctrinal distinctive, Azusa Street provided the thrust which impelled the new teaching to spread at such a rate that all continents, in varying measure, experienced similar phenomena with this new doctrinal understanding within two years of 1906.[8]

---

personal edification and for edifying the church as and when an utterance is interpreted. In the latter situation, the interpreted word can carry the force of a prophetic word.

[5] Parham was brought up a sickly child in a farm in Iowa. Early in life he felt a call to preach and for a short time held a supply Methodist pastorate before undertaking an independent ministry in Holiness circles.

[6] In September 1900 Parham returned to Topeka from a preaching tour of Holiness centres to establish a Bible School, Bethel College, to prepare prospective missionaries to seek and work for the outpouring of he Holy Spirit in power. He convinced his students that they had yet to experience true Spirit-baptism. Before leaving for a three-day campaign, he directed the students to read carefully Acts 2. On returning to the school on 30 December he asked the students for their findings: 'To my astonishment they had all come to the same story that while there were different things occurred (sic) when the blessing fell, that the indisputable proof on each occasion was, that they spoke in other tongues.' (R M. Anderson, *Vision of the Disinherited: The Making of American Pentecostalism,* [Peabody, MA: Hendrickson, 1979], p. 53.) One of the students, Agnes Ozman (1870-1937) was assured a place in Pentecostal history when she became the first person to speak in tongues, auspiciously so, on the first day of January 1901.

[7] William J. Seymour was born in 1870 in Louisiana to parents who were former slaves. During the period 1900-02, he came into contact with the Holiness Movement and accepted its emphasis on entire sanctification. In 1903 he moved to Houston, Texas, and enrolled in Parham's Bible School where he came to accept its teaching on Spirit-baptism. When Seymour was called to Los Angeles with a view to pastoring a black Holiness mission work, Parham felt that Seymour should remain in Topeka until such time as he received his personal Spirit-baptism. Little was Parham to realise that when he laid hands on Seymour before the latter set out for Los Angeles that he was passing on the foundational leadership of the movement to him.

[8] The revival at Azusa Street was to last for over three years and in that period services were held three times daily. However, within a very short time Azusa Street ceased to be the focal point of the Pentecostal movement as other centres replaced it. One of these was the hugely influential work established by William H. Durham (1873-1912) in Chicago after he returned to his North Avenue Mission from Azusa Street in 1907. It was at this church that Robert Semple (1881-1910), a young immigrant from County Tyrone was introduced to the Pentecostal experience in 1907, with an outcome that will be discussed in Chapter 4.

The link between Azusa Street and the British Isles was forged by Thomas Ball Barratt (1862-1940).[9] He has been described as 'the apostle of the Pentecostal Movement in Europe'.[10] Both Barratt and A.A. Boddy were strongly influenced by the Welsh Revival: the former played the key role in introducing Boddy to the Pentecostal experience, while the latter became the dominant figure in the formative years of British Pentecostalism. Both men developed a close friendship with Cecil Polhill who was to prove a generous benefactor to the movement and the driving force behind much Pentecostal missionary work. These three men were to dominate the British Pentecostal scene in its seminal years.

Alexander Alfred Boddy (1854-1930) was vicar of All Saints, Sunderland, when he received his Spirit-baptism, an event that was to enshrine forever Sunderland in the hearts of the early Pentecostal believers in Britain (Photograph A).[11] Boddy instigated and publicised the annual Whitsun Conventions in the town, starting in June 1908 until 1914. Donald Gee in his assessment of the impact of the Conventions stated:

---

[9] Barratt was born in Cornwall in 1862 and at the age of five his father was offered a position as manager of a sulphur mine on an island in the Hardanger Fjord, western Norway. Educated in England, he also studied music under Edvard Grieg. Barratt heard about the Pentecostal message while staying at the New York Mission Home of the Christian and Missionary Alliance (CMA). It was here that he learned of the revival at Azusa Street from its newspaper, *The Apostolic Faith*, first published in September 1906. After lengthy correspondence with Azusa Street and intense prayer and fasting, he had a heightened emotional experience on 7 October 1906, but his correspondent in Azusa Street informed him that it was tongues that were the indispensable evidence of Spirit-baptism. He eventually spoke in tongues at a meeting on the 15 November 1906.

[10] Barratt's contribution to the development of the Pentecostal movement in Europe is incalculable. All the countries in Western Europe in which the movement became established before World War I, with the exception of Holland and Italy, received the message from his adopted home of Norway, *viz.*, Sweden, Britain, Germany, Denmark, Switzerland in 1907 and Finland in 1911. Of all the European leaders, Barratt and the Swede Lewi Pethrus (1884-1974) were the most influential in their contribution to Pentecostalism in the British Isles.

[11] Boddy was born in 1854, the third son of James Alfred Boddy, rector of St. Thomas Church in the Jewish quarter in Manchester. Biographical details about Boddy can be found in Martin Robinson, 'The Charismatic Anglican—Historical and Contemporary: A Comparison of the Life and Work of Alexander Boddy (1854-1930) and Michael C. Harper', MLitt thesis, University of Birmingham, 1976. Before studying Theology at University College, Durham, he was articled for a short time to a firm of solicitors in Manchester. In 1881, he was ordained by J.B. Lightfoot, the scholarly Bishop of Durham, and, in 1884, was appointed curate to All Saints, Sunderland. After two years he was given full charge of the church where he was to minister for the next thirty-eight years. In 1891 he married Mary Pollock who was to prove a strong influence on him.

> From the point of view of the early history of the Pentecostal movement in the British Isles the Sunderland Conventions must occupy the supreme place of importance... Their importance...was not in their size but in their formative influence in attracting and helping to mould not only the immediate leaders of the multitudinous little Pentecostal meetings which were springing up all over the land, but the younger men who were destined to become the leaders of the Movement when it came to years of maturity.[12]

For a while Sunderland was the new focal point of religious interest in Britain. It was regarded by many fellow evangelicals with severe misgivings as a place of delusion, and by its supporters as the very gate of Heaven with all the promise of a spiritual renaissance that would break the mould of Christianity in the British Isles.[13] Failure in leadership at this moment could have aborted the movement in its embryonic stage. Boddy adopted two signal measures to protect and direct the new movement. Besides the Conventions, he published and edited the periodical *Confidence* which ran from April 1908 till 1926, 141 issues in all. The magazine quickly established itself as the authentic voice of the new movement in Britain. With articles presenting and defining Pentecostal teaching as well as full reports of conference sermons and snippets of news of events and personalities, it was an avidly awaited publication each month in the homes of many Pentecostal believers.[14] By these two means and his own dignified authority, Boddy bestowed a firm, though benign, leadership over the early movement.[15]

The importance of the leadership of Pentecostalism in the British Isles lying in the hands of Boddy cannot be over-emphasised. It meant that Pentecostalism did not come as some strange new cult associated with some charismatic guru-figure, but with a vicar of the Established Church. That by itself did not necessarily ensure it respectability, but it meant that it could not be easily dismissed. The distinctive tenets of the new movement were never tested as a doctrinal aberration in any court of the Church of England. The case against it could only have been mounted on

---

[12] Gee, *Wind and Flame*, p. 37

[13] One person who regarded the new movement with suspicion was the Holiness leader, Reader Harris (1847-1909), founder of the Pentecostal League, who was in Sunderland at the time of Barratt's visit.

[14] Gee recalled that copies were 'eagerly secured, and then highly treasured, by hungry hearts all over the land. I remember, as a young Congregationalist, finding my mother reading loaned copies of *Confidence* almost surreptitiously'. (Gee, *Wind and Flame*, p. 42.)

[15] William Kay writes that 'the formative years of the Pentecostal movement were providentially in Boddy's hands. What he taught, and the way he taught it, was to become normative and those problems which he faced were, by and large, similar to those that recurred in future years'. (William Kay, *Inside Story: A History of the British Assemblies of God,* [Mattersey: Mattersey Hall Publishing, 1990], p. 25.)

the highly disputable grounds that the cessationist position was the only orthodox one. When Boddy stated his mind that if the church 'will not receive this [Pentecostal] blessing from the Lord, or if it hinders me from spreading it abroad, then I shall consider my position as a member of the C. of E.'—he never had any serious cause to exercise such consideration.[16] If anything, in the final years of his ministry spent in the village of Pittington, his Anglicanism came to the fore more than his Pentecostalism. Without Boddy's standing, there was always the possibility that, between them, external hostility, fanaticism, low calibre leadership and doctrinal zaniness might have proved sufficiently damaging to kill off the young sapling. Theological aberration and behavioural excess were a constant threat. One such episode that provoked him to issue a warning was against 'a band of veiled women wearing peculiar apparel and claiming to speak in Tongues... Much harm has been done to God's Pentecostal work by visits from other lands of those not invited'.[17] Boddy with his legal and theological background proved a perfect foil to the excesses that threatened the infant movement. The magazine earned him such regard that the standing of *Confidence* as the unofficial voice of the movement in the British Isles remained undisputed for its first ten years.

It is unlikely that *Confidence* would have been financially viable if it had not been for the financial support provided by Cecil Polhill (1860-1938).[18] He received his Spirit-baptism indirectly through his missionary involvement with the China Inland Mission which brought him to Los Angeles.[19] With all concern for conventional dignity now cast aside,

---

[16] Robinson, *Charismatic Anglican*, p. 110.

[17] *Confidence*, 13 December, 1908, p.13. This group may have taken the concept of the Church as the Bride of Christ to the extreme of espousing celibacy for the married and forbidding marriage for the single. If that were so, it would have borne similarities to that of later 'eunuch life' teaching that held that only Christians living a celibate life would be prepared for the Rapture.

[18] Cecil H. Polhill was one of the Cambridge Seven, a group of young men who volunteered themselves as missionaries with the China Inland Mission (CIM) in 1885. In 1903 he inherited the family estate and became the squire of Howbury Hall. Polhill was unique among early Pentecostals in having high social status and inherited wealth. The use to which he placed his fortune made a vital contribution to the nascent movement.

[19] Writing of the period of the Welsh Revival, Polhill stated 'the Lord gave me one of His "touches", opening my heart afresh to spiritual influences and making me hungry for more of his life and love and power'. (Peter Hocken, 'Cecil Polhill: Pentecostal Layman', *Pneuma*, Vol. 20.2, 1988, p. 119.) Returning from a visit to China via Los Angeles on behalf of CIM, he purposely sought contact with the revival there. He was delighted to link up with George B. Studd, his old friend from Eton and Cambridge and brother of his former missionary colleague, C.T. Studd. As befitted an English gentleman, he received his Spirit-baptism while 'sitting at tea with dear George Studd'. This rather stiff and somewhat unimaginative man described the moment thus: 'Acting on a few simple

Polhill began to engage on a ministry which led him to pray, sing and preach on the streets of Bedford in the summer of 1908. His ease in mixing with all classes won over Donald Gee to the Pentecostal cause.[20] Polhill first met Boddy at the 1908 Whitsun conference in Sunderland and from that moment the two men, with their very different gifts and temperament, dominated the British Pentecostal scene until the Great War. Polhill helped to establish the movement in the Home Counties where he brought to it a degree of cohesion. Once the Sunderland Convention was terminated by the war, he took over the chairmanship of the annual Whitsun Conventions in London in the period 1915-24. In the course of his evangelistic travels around the country, Polhill was ever on the lookout for prospective young evangelists and missionaries and during a visit to South Wales it was he who recognised early the potential of the brothers Stephen and George Jeffreys.[21] Like Boddy he was to remain throughout his life a faithful member of the Anglican communion, a factor that contributed to the declining influence of both men once a new breed of leaders arose, most of whom identified with the new Pentecostal denominations. Donald Gee was one such.[22] Missen's stricture reflected some of the pained feelings of the younger leaders:

---

instructions given in the Spirit, combined with words of promise, I yielded my mouth, and gave my voice, in doing so, was twice filled with laughter and sent to the floor. Then the Lord spoke through me in a new tongue, making use of body and hands in gesture, for about a minute'. (Hocken, *Polhill*, p. 121.)

[20] As a young man Gee attended an all-night prayer meeting led by Polhill and observed his sharing of his well-worn copy of *Redemption Songs* with the kitchen maid. He commented: 'I was not used to seeing that kind of thing, and it made a deep impression'. (Donald Gee, *These Men I Knew,* [Nottingham: AOG Publishing, 1980], p. 74.)

[21] It was Polhill who urged George to leave the Co-Op store in Maesteg and provided the financial backing to enable him to begin studies with the Pentecostal Missionary Union (PMU) at Preston. The PMU was largely the brainchild of Polhill and reflected his enduring zeal for promoting missionary work. It was the recognition that missionaries required preparation and training for work overseas that led to the setting up of the first British Pentecostal Bible Schools, separately for men and women.

[22] Donald Gee (1891-1966) was one of the most balanced and influential teachers to grace the Pentecostal stage in the twentieth century. His history, *Wind and Flame*, remains one of the most accomplished accounts of the history of the movement, much of which he was to experience for himself at first-hand. He was converted under the ministry of Seth Joshua, a leading figure in the Welsh Revival. He received his Spirit-baptism in 1913, became a conscientious objector (1916-18) and from 1920-30 was pastor of a small assembly at Leith, the outport of Edinburgh. The rest of his life was given to a teaching ministry through conferences, editorials in *Pentecost*, the magazine published at the behest of the World Pentecostal Conference, editorship for a lengthy period of *Redemption Tidings* and as the Principal of the reorganised British Assemblies of God Bible School, Surrey (1951-64). His name will feature throughout this study. (See Brian

> It was easy for Mr Boddy and Mr Pohill, from the shelter of parsonage and country mansion, to suggest that their followers should be baptised in the Holy Spirit and remain in their churches. It was by no means so easy for those who had entered the Pentecostal blessing to follow their advice. The Movement met with almost universal ridicule and hostility. The resolute determination Mr Boddy and Mr Polhill to remain in the Anglican communion left the newly-established Pentecostal groups without any overall direction at a time when these meetings were beset with difficulties and problems.[23]

Martin Robinson, however, insists that Boddy's vision, one shared by Polhill, was always that 'of an interdenominational revival within the church... Their emphasis was always on Pentecostal mission abroad and Christian evangelical fellowship at home'.[24] Neither party could have foreseen the arrival of the Charismatic Movement in the latter half of the twentieth century when the Pentecostal experience once again breached the boundary of denominational confines.

1.2 Influences Shaping British Pentecostalism

Three significant influences will be examined in this section: Irvingism, the Keswick/Higher Life message and the Welsh Revival.

1.2.1 Edward Irving and the Catholic Apostolic Church.

Edward Irving (1792-1834)[25] was one of the more controversial figures in nineteenth-century Britain and not just in ecclesial settings.[26] He rose,

---

R. Ross, 'Donald Gee: In Search of a Church -Sectarian in Transition', DTh thesis, Toronto School of Theology, 1974.

[23] Alfred F. Missen: *The Sound of a Going,* (Nottingham: AOG Publishing, 1973), p. 6.

[24] Robinson, *Charismatic Anglican*, p. 121.

[25] Irving was born at Annan, near Dumfries, the son of a prosperous leather merchant and one of eight children. In 1815 he was licensed to preach in the Church of Scotland, and four years later he became assistant in Glasgow to Thomas Chalmers, the leading Scottish churchman of his day. In 1822 he accepted an invitation to become minister of the Caledonian Chapel in London and, when this proved too small, the church moved to a new and more spacious building three years later in Regent Square. From around 1828 Irving's reputation began to totter, primarily for his views on the Incarnation and his active encouragement of prophecy and *glossolalia* during public worship in Regent Square. After 1833, Irving and his supporters found their way into what was to become the Catholic Apostolic Church.

[26] In the mid-1820s Irving was by far the most celebrated preacher in the capital. He became part of the 'Albury set', a group first assembled by Henry Drummond MP (1786-1860), a wealthy English banker, at his country estate in Albury Park, Surrey, for eight days during Advent 1826. Their interest in prophecy, with Irving, became conflated with a bold charismaticism.

Icarus-like, on the wings of fame only to fall into the dark waters of rejection towards the end of his short life. He has been described as 'the first Reformed Pentecostal theologian' and 'the forerunner of the charismatic movement'.[27] While it is difficult to prove any direct link between Irvingism and the Pentecostal movement, there is little doubt now that Irving's writings anticipated the key theological insights of the later movement in a number of areas: *viz.*, hints of acceptance of speaking in tongues as evidence of Spirit-baptism—'the baptism with the Holy Spirit, whose standing sign, if we err not, is the speaking with tongues';[28] Spirit-baptism regarded as an overture to obtaining the other 'extraordinary' gifts of the Spirit; the *charismata* understood as a permanent possession of the Church, lost primarily through compromise and lack of faith; the wedding of charismatic and premillenial constructs. Strachan maintains that before the Irving period never had *glossolalia* occurred on such a scale in British church history and never since the first century, except for Montanism, had the phenomenon been set in a context of substantive theological understanding.[29] As early as 1827, three years before a charismatic episode in West Scotland,[30] Irving preached that he could see no reason why the work of the Spirit should not operate 'in all the ways recorded in the book of Acts and the apostolic letters'.[31]

In October 1831, the first occurrence of *glossolalia* erupted during the morning service at National Scotch Church in Regent Square, London. Thereafter, prophetic messages became more common during times of public worship, causing the church to become embroiled in public controversy. This formed part of the backdrop to the measures taken by the London presbytery of the Church of Scotland to remove Irving from his church on the grounds of his alleged heterodox views on the Incarnation. His followers, 800 or so, reconstituted themselves as the

---

[27] Gordon Strachan, *The Pentecostal Theology of Edward Irving,* (Peabody, MA: Hendrickson, 1973), p. 13.

[28] A quotation from Irving found in David W. Dorries, 'Edward Irving and the "Standing Sign" of Spirit Baptism', in Gary B. McGee (ed.), *Initial Evidence: Historical and Biblical Perspectives on the Pentecostal Doctrine of Spirit Baptism,* (Peabody, MA: Hendrickson, 1991), p. 49.

[29] Strachan, *Irving,* p. 18.

[30] In 1830 the lower Clyde region witnessed an outbreak of charismatic manifestations notably healings and *glossolalia.* In the words of Mrs Oliphant, 'a new miraculous dispensation was, to the belief of many, inaugurated, in all the power of Apostolic times, by these waters of the West'. (Mrs. Oliphant, *The Life of Edward Irving, Minister of the National Scotch Church, London,* [London: Hurst and Blackett, 1862 ed.], p. 290.) The locality attracted observers from England, Scotland, and Ireland. With the historical and cultural affinity between south-west Scotland and Ulster it is more than likely that among the visitors were interested observers from Ireland who, doubtless, on return added to the folk-memory tales of such dramatic events.

[31] Strachan, *Irving,* p. 55.

Catholic Apostolic Church, and he was appointed the Angel (pastor) of its first congregation in Newman Street. His authority in the church was considerably reduced as he became subject to the apostles who, in turn, were moved, though not controlled, by the utterances of the prophets. In effect, he became little more than a preaching deacon, reduced to the rank of an 'inferior minister'.[32] In what proved to be the final move, arguably to marginalise him, Irving was sent to Glasgow by the apostles in 1834, where he died in the same year from tuberculosis.

Back in London, J.B. Cardale was set to become the dominant apostle and it was he who almost single-handedly reshaped the liturgy of the church by combining Catholic and Orthodox elements to the extent that the church took on increasingly features matched by the contemporary Tractarian movement. Prophecy began to wane and by 1870 it virtually ceased in the British churches, though Philip Schaff reported that a friend and colleague of his at Union Theological Seminary, New York, had 'witnessed it [*glossolalia*] in 1879 in the principal Irvingite church at London'.[33]

Two congregations of the Catholic Apostolic Church were formed in Ireland, one in Dublin and the other in Belfast.[34] The Dublin congregation was formed either during or before 1836 and the one in Belfast at Cromwell Road, off Botanic Avenue, during or before 1851 (Photograph B). By that date the Catholic Apostolic Church had lapsed into a state of charismatic quietude and had become 'side-tracked into spiritual and evangelical sterility while they waited for the coming of the Lord'.[35] The location of the Belfast congregation, near Queen's University, in the then fashionable area of the city, says something about its social provenance. It was to be in the heartland of working-class Belfast, the Shankill area, that the city was to see, about thirty-five years later, its first Pentecostal mission hall. The future of the early movement was to lie more with the crudities of Azusa Street rather than the colloquies at Albury or the solemnities of Keswick.

1.2.2 The Keswick Convention

A convention has been held continuously since 1875 at Keswick in the Lake District, Cumbria. It was preceded by a number of similar large conferences convened at Broadlands in Hampshire and Oxford during

---

[32] See under his entry in *The Dictionary of National Biography,* (London: Smith, Elder & Co., 1908 ed.)

[33] Philip Schaff, *History of the Christian Church,* Vol. 1, Section 24,1886 ed., p. 203, on CD-Rom, AGES version.

[34] David Tierney, 'The Catholic Apostolic Church: a Study in Tory Millenarianism', *Historical Research*, Vol. 63, 1990, pp. 314-5.

[35] D. Gee, 'Instruction from Irvingism', *Redemption Tidings*, 29 August 1942, p. 5.

1874, and at Brighton in 1875, all with the aim of deepening spiritual life.[36] The inspiration behind this venue was Hannah Pearsall Smith, wife of Robert Pearsall Smith, both of them advocates of Higher Life teaching.[37] W.E. Boardman (1810-1886), an ordained American Presbyterian minister, participated with the Smiths in the English conferences. His ministry and writings, especially his book *The Higher Christian Life* published in 1858, were instrumental in popularising the teaching of the Holiness revival in non-Methodist circles.[38] While Keswick may have been activated by the American Higher Life movement, it soon fostered its own indigenous tradition, one that reflected a strong Anglican ethos.[39]

Keswick with its important role in British evangelicalism was to prove germinal for the nature of the early Pentecostal movement in Britain. Boddy stated that at Keswick in 1908 he was 'glad to see there faces we had looked into at the [first] Sunderland Convention'.[40] He mentioned that after lunch on the Wednesday of the Convention 'a happy Pentecostal party' went boating on Derwentwater.[41] He told of an

---

[36] Broadlands Park was the home of William and Georgina Cowper-Temple and former home of the deceased Prime Minister, Lord Palmerston.

[37] The debt owed by the early Pentecostal movement to the American Holiness movement in its Wesleyan mode was enormous, more so in America than in Britain and Europe. Donald Dayton, in his landmark study *Theological Roots of Pentecostalism*, set out to show the extent to which Pentecostalism is rooted in the Wesleyan theological tradition. On the other hand, Edith Blumhofer in her Harvard doctorate stressed the contribution of the Reformed/Baptistic tradition to Pentecostalism, a strand usually referred to as 'Higher Life' teaching to distinguish it from the Wesleyan Holiness tradition. Dayton's studies led him to the view that 'by the mid-1890s almost every branch of the Holiness and "Higher Life" movements of the nineteenth century, as well as the revivalism of the period in general, was teaching a variation of some sort or another on the baptism of the Holy Spirit, though with some significant differences in nuance and meaning'. (Dayton, *Theological Roots*, p. 107-8). *Glossolalia,* in a non-evidentialist sense, was anticipated by a number of American Holiness advocates as part of the end-time revival that was considered imminent at the turn of the century.

[38] Boardman held that Wesleyan perfectionism claimed too much if eradication of sin was seen as a possibility, while Reformed teaching claimed too little by accepting a position that 'could easily lead to low expectations of sanctifying grace altogether'. (D. Bruce Hindmarsh, *John Newton and the English Evangelical Tradition,* [Grand Rapids, MI: Eerdmans, 2001], p.140).

[39] The British and American wings of the Holiness movement were to develop different emphases which reflected their differing cultural milieux. The *eradicationist* view favoured by Pearsall Smith came to be deemed unguarded language in Keswick circles, to be replaced by the concept of *counteraction* by which was understood that in a fully consecrated life the power of the old nature of sin was *countered* by the presence of the indwelling Spirit, not purged as generally maintained by Wesleyan perfectionists.

[40] *Confidence*, August 1908, p. 13.

[41] *Confidence*, August 1908, p. 13.

acquaintance from Jersey attending the Convention who 'was telling those to whom the Lord led him, how he left Keswick for three days to visit Sunderland, and had there received a mighty deliverance, a Vision of Jesus and of his own nothingness, and the overwhelming Baptism of the Holy Ghost with the Sign of Tongues'.[42] However, indications of a creeping tension between the two movements could not be easily held in abeyance. At the previous year's Convention, Boddy had squared up, as he perceived it, to the inadequate spirituality of Keswick by distributing thousands of his pamphlet *Pentecost for England*. Shortly before, he had rather thrown down the gauntlet in stating that 'those who have "Tongues" will be present, and unable and unwilling to control them when moved by the Spirit'.[43] The disagreement of Pentecostals with Keswick teaching lay in the understanding of Spirit-baptism that for them was a *power* baptism that opened a way into a new spiritual dimension, one effecting 'a paradigm shift of such proportion that one spontaneously responds in tongues'.[44] Where Keswick majored on 'victory' and 'resting in the Lord',[45] Pentecostals took the more American Higher Life position that stressed 'power for service'.[46]

---

[42] *Confidence*, August 1908, p. 13.

[43] *The Apostolic Faith*, February-March, 1907, p. 1. In the event, nothing startling disturbed the Convention that year which was noted for its sense of spiritual unity. The future Archbishop of Melbourne rejoiced that 'the clash of creeds and strife of sects [yielded to] the tranquillising motto "All one in Christ Jesus!"' (J.C. Pollock, *The Keswick Story* [London: Hodder and Stoughton, 1964], p.130.)

[44] Simon Chan, *Pentecostal Theology and the Christian Spiritual Tradition,* [Sheffield: Sheffield Academic Press, 2000], p. 57.

[45] Evan Hopkins (1837-1918), a leading exponent of Keswick teaching, argued that 'nothing is more essential than restfulness if we would wait upon God. But many have so prayed for "the baptism of the Spirit" that they have completely wrestled themselves out of rest'. (Evan H. Hopkins, *The Law of Liberty in the Spiritual Life,* [London: Marshall, Morgan & Scott, 1952 ed.], p 124.) Hopkins advised seekers: 'See that you do not set your heart upon getting an experience—some extraordinary *afflatus*. Be willing to rest in God's will... One word as to evidences. Does anyone ask, "how shall I know I have the fullness of the Spirit?" You will be assured of this by knowing it' (pp. 124-5).

[46] George M. Marsden, *Fundamentalism and American Culture: The Shaping of Twentieth-Century Evangelicalism 1870-1925,* (New York: Oxford University Press, 1980 ed.), p. 79. Though Keswick owed much to American Higher Life teaching, there were differences in emphasis. Packer criticised what he saw as the logic of Keswick's position that forced its exponents 'to develop their doctrine of the Spirit's indwelling in a quietist direction'. (J I. Packer, 'Keswick and the Reformed Doctrine of Sanctification', *The Evangelical Quarterly*, July, 1955, p. 160.) Torrey spoke more for the American Higher Life view when he remarked of Spirit-baptism that it was not 'primarily intended to make believers happy or holy, but to make them useful'. (Grant Wacker, *Heaven Below: Early Pentecostals and American Culture,* [Cambridge: Harvard University Press, 2001], p. 2). Pentecostals, in general, came to take the line adumbrated in Torrey's

Pentecostals were frustrated by the woolliness of the 'teachers of the receive-by-faith school'[47] that Hopkins exemplified. Boddy after his remark that 'many of us thank God for Keswick in the past' went on to state that '[The Lord] is calling His people to "go forward"...to an experimental Pentecost, their Birthright because of the shed blood of Calvary'.[48] Adding to this portrayal of Keswick as stuck in a time warp, Thomas Mogridge attested to a new perspective after receiving his Spirit-baptism:

> I enjoyed many anointings and spiritual quickenings whilst among [the Holiness people], but never bedrock satisfaction until the full and scriptural blessing of Pentecost came on November 30th. 1907, at which time I came into soul-rest and perfect satisfaction... I went to Keswick and Southport once or twice after, but, oh, how cold, formal and lifeless it all seemed to be compared with the certain abiding presence of the Holy Comforter within. The very thing all these crowds of dear souls are in quest of year after year, but return home again disappointed.[49]

Gee, nevertheless, acknowledged that those who identified with the Pentecostal movement in its earliest days were Christians of mature spiritual experience who 'had tasted a previous experience of the Spirit's grace and power in connection with the Holiness and Keswick Movements'.[50] However, it was left to B.B. Warfield (1851-1921), voicing

---

remark. Like him, they tended to draw a distinction between holiness and a Spirit-baptism of power for service.

[47] Ian M. Randall, *Evangelical Experiences: A Study of the Spirituality of English Evangelicalism 1918-1939,* (Carlisle: Paternoster, 199), p. 208. The phrase was found in the *Elim Evangel*, 6 December 1926, pp. 297-8.

[48] *Confidence*, August 1908, p. 14. Here 'experimental' connotes an experience on the lines of 'a brother from Jersey' who visited Sunderland after spending three days at Keswick and who witnessed to receiving 'a mighty deliverance, a Vision of Jesus and his own nothingness, and the overwhelming Baptism of the Holy Ghost with the Sign of Tongues' (p.13).

[49] *RT*, June 1930, p. 7. Mogridge met up with Boddy at Keswick for which he had prepared a pamphlet *Pentecost and the Need of Keswick 1908*. The Southport Conference, established in 1885, was associated with the Wesleyan Methodist stream of the Holiness movement. It had strong links with Cliff College. (For the best short account of the British Holiness movement see David Bebbington, *Holiness in Nineteenth-Century England* [Carlisle: Paternoster, 2000].)

[50] Gee, *Wind and Flame,* p. 45. George Jeffreys, despite his reservations—'From one Christian Convention to another we went, always longing for an experience that would satisfy, and in each we were asked to receive in the same way'—continued to visit the Convention in the years after his split from the Elim Church. In so doing, he reflected the commonly held view among Pentecostals that while Keswick's message was always profitable, it was fundamentally incomplete. (Quotation from George Jeffreys, *The Miraculous Foursquare Gospel: Vol. 1 Doctrinal,* [London: Elim Publishing, 1929], p. 46.)

the concerns of Old Princeton Theology, to fire the most sustained salvos that aimed to destroy the theological rationale of Higher Life teaching and was equally dismissive of Pentecostalism. For him, the 'Welsh excesses' of 1905 were 'as nothing, however, to what befell...in the summer of 1907 *(sic)* when the so-called Pentecost Movement—the Los Angeles Revival—shook...with its full force'.[51]

1.2.3 The Welsh Revival

The part that the Welsh Revival played in fostering the nascent Pentecostal movement is a matter of some conjecture. Gee, from his insider perspective on the history of the movement, held:

> It is impossible, and would be historically incorrect, to dissociate the Pentecostal movement from that remarkable visitation of God's Spirit. Perhaps the most formative result was the creation of a widespread spirit of expectation for still greater things. Men justly asked 'Why Wales only?'...In this manner the spiritual soil was being prepared in the providence of God for the rise of the Pentecostal Movement.[52]

Other commentators have made their own assessment of the Revival. To Bruner, the Welsh Revival appeared to have been 'the last 'gap' across which the latest sparks of holiness enthusiasm leapt, igniting the Pentecostal movement'.[53] Edwin Orr likened Pentecostalism's relationship to the Welsh Revival to the emergence of the Baptist and Wesleyan movements from the evangelical stirrings of the seventeenth and eighteenth centuries.[54] Eifion Evans confined the distinctive emphases of the Pentecostal movement 'to [the] rarer occurrences and incidental features of the revival'.[55] Blumhofer is more categorical in her

---

[51] B.B. Warfield, *Perfectionism,* (Philadelphia: The Presbyterian and Reformed Publishing Co., 1971 ed.), p. 333.

[52] Gee, *Wind and Flame*, p. 6. For a man so spiritually questing as Boddy the Welsh Revival was a peak experience. When he heard of the Revival he travelled to Tonypandy and rejoiced in the privilege of being present 'at some of the most spiritual of the wonderful gatherings of the Welsh Revival and was in the pulpit with Evan Roberts'. (Robinson, *Charismatic Anglican*, p. 37.) On his return to Sunderland he plunged into a series of revival meetings and he initiated a prayer meeting in the All Saints' Vestry, where, in his own words, 'a little circle of earnest young men met night after night in prayer for further revival—for a great outpouring of the Holy Spirit' (p. 39).

[53] F.D. Bruner, *A Theology of the Holy Spirit: The Pentecostal Experience and the New Testament Witness,* (London: Hodder & Stoughton, 1970), p. 46.

[54] J.Edwin Orr, *The Flaming Tongue: The Impact of Twentieth Century Revivals,* (Chicago, IL: Moody Press, 1973), p. 128.

[55] Eifion E. Evans, *The Welsh Revival of 1904,* (Bridgend: Evangelical Press of Wales, 1987), p. 192. Evans acknowledged that there was a shake-up in the Welsh

appraisal: 'The Welsh revival and the Anglican/Keswickian heritage permanently influenced British Pentecostalism'.[56] Certainly, many of the defining features of the Revival were to continue in Pentecostal settings—prolonged singing; little structured preaching with sermons stirring the heart more than appealing to the mind; praying in concert; exclamatory, joyful outbursts; agonising conviction of sin; much talk of Spirit-baptism; dramatic claims to unmediated Spirit guidance and the power of the Spirit.[57]

The most defined link between the Revival and the Pentecostal movement as it emerged in Britain lay with the *Children of the Revival*, the term given to those converted in the Revival who maintained revival meetings additional to the usual services in their churches.[58] In the face of widespread defections, many sought to keep the revival fire burning in cottage prayer meetings run on cross-denominational lines. Over time churches developed from some of these nuclei. It was in South Wales that the Apostolic Church, the oldest of the extant Pentecostal denominations in Britain, was formed in 1916. Its founders were the brothers Daniel P. Williams (1882-1947) and William Jones Williams (1891-1945) who were converted during the Revival.[59] Other influential converts of the Revival

---

denominational scene after the Revival which saw the rise of new denominations, independent mission halls and Pentecostal/Apostolic churches

[56] Edith Blumhofer, 'The Welsh Revival', Stanley M. Burgess and Gary B. McGee (eds), *Dictionary of Pentecostal and Charismatic Movements*, (Grand Rapids, MI: Zondervan, 1998), pp. 881-2.

[57] In today's parlance, Roberts could be classed in the charismatic camp. He prepared nothing beforehand but waited on the Spirit's unction as to whether or not he should speak or be silent at any particular meeting.

[58] A report in *Confidence* in July 1912 captured the gusto with which the twelve Revivalists regaled the annual Sunderland Conference: 'They are the instruments of the second revival which is still going on... These brothers are a peculiar people. They do not have much inclination to give great speeches on teaching lines, but they are in their element when they are in the street and public places starting a fiery revival meeting; there they speak and testify, and sing and sing again. Their element is Revival! Revival!' (p. 134).

[59] Turnbull, in his insider history of the Apostolic Church, reported that Dan Williams had heard 'speaking with tongues in the years 1904-05, but because of the variety of supernatural manifestations at that time very little attention was given to this new phenomenon' before he experienced it for himself in 1909. (T.N. Turnbull, *What God Hath Wrought* [Bradford: Puritan Press, 1959], p. 18.) Despite this remark, some doubt has been expressed as to whether or not *glossolalia* were present in the Revival. Synan contends it was 'prevalent', citing *The Yorkshire Post* of the 27 December 1904. (Synan, *Pentecostal-Charismatic Origins*, p. 119) Williams, however, takes the reported happenings to be cases of *cryptomnesia* (the regurgitation of buried memories) rather than *glossolalia* or *xenolalia*. (Cyril G. Williams, *Tongues of the Spirit: A Study of Pentecostal Glossolalia and Related Phenomena,* [Cardiff: University of Wales Press,

were George Jeffreys (1889-1962) and his brother Stephen Jeffreys (1876-1943). Donald Gee (1891-1966), a founder member of the Assemblies of God, was converted through the preaching of Seth Joshua who exerted a powerful ministry during the Revival. In these ways the three classic Pentecostal denominations in the British Isles were influenced by the Welsh Revival.

News of the Revival began to filter through to small 'earnest and hungry groups of Christians' outside Wales.[60] It must have been such a group, to be considered in the next chapter, that invited Boddy to Belfast in 1905 to bring an eyewitness account of the Welsh Revival. Within three years of this visit the first Pentecostal meeting was held in Belfast.

1981], pp. 53-55.) Cartwright remains sceptical about the presence of *glossolalia* during the Welsh Revival and is of the opinion that, though Roberts himself spoke in tongues, he did not encourage *glossolalia* in his services.

[60] Gee's phrase for small groups throughout the British Isles who looked to Wales as the harbinger of a national revival. (Gee, *Wind and Flame*, p. 6.) For an account of the international impact of the Welsh Revival, see Noel Gibbard, *On the Wings of a Dove,* (Bridgend: Bryntirion Press, 2002).

CHAPTER 2

Proto-Pentecostal Currents in Ireland

This chapter considers those moves in Ireland that prepared the way for a welcome to the news emanating from Los Angeles. Two in particular are highlighted—the arrival of Holiness revivalism in the latter third of the nineteenth century and the invigorating effect of the Welsh Revival at the beginning of the twentieth century. The rapidity with which Pentecostalism spread to all continents can be attributed largely to the Holiness movement. In particular, the American branch with its global proliferation of mission stations and personnel provided the channel through which the Pentecostal experience spread within a few years of the Azusa Street outpouring. The Salvation Army, the Faith Mission and its wayward offspring, the Cooneyites, were among the more sizeable groups that identified with the Holiness cause in Britain. Its Keswick wing became identified with the Portstewart Convention and had an appreciable influence on the mainline denominations in Ireland. At the time of the Welsh Revival, the Zion movement in America, built around the towering figure of John Alexander Dowie, was making inroads in Ireland. All these movements were to prove significant feeder streams for the nascent Pentecostal movement.

2.1 The Arrival of the Holiness Message

The Holiness movement grew out of John Wesley's emphasis on Christian perfection as a possibility in this life subsequent to conversion. It was a state frequently referred to as 'perfect love' whereby the believer was freed from the disposition to sin. Wesley distinguished between an absolute sinlessness, unattainable this side of heaven, and a freedom that allows the believer to live without conscious, intentional sin, a clarification that makes due allowance for immaturity and ignorance. As a second work of grace, it is the goal of Christian spirituality and is normally experienced instantaneously, accepted by faith and confirmed by the inward witness of the Holy Spirit. With Methodism becoming increasingly respectable and 'worldly' in the nineteenth century, groups from within its ranks began to organise, often on an interdenominational basis, to recapture the earlier emphasis and terms such as 'entire sanctification', 'second blessing', 'full salvation' and 'baptism in the Holy Spirit' became commonplace in such circles. Holiness teaching from its beginning took on a revivalist stamp that became a marked feature of transatlantic popular evangelicalism in the nineteenth century.[1]

From 1835, Phoebe Palmer became one of the early advocates of Holiness perfectionism who through her writings and journeyings brought the attention of English-speaking Protestantism to the 'Higher Life' message.[2] Growing out of the 'Tuesday meeting for the Promotion of Holiness', held in her home town of New York, she developed a fast-track version of Wesleyan perfectionism. Her 'shorter way' played down the mainstream Methodist doctrine of sanctification that came to stress the continuous, progressive nature of sanctification and placed an emphasis on the instantaneous reception of entire sanctification by the genuine seeker, a veritable 'second blessing'. For her, holiness is the expected norm for Christian living rather than its apogee, and her presentation of the teaching made it both intelligible and accessible. Raser contends that her 'emphasis on Pentecost and the baptism of the Spirit and her interpretation of the early chapters Acts...laid the groundwork for much Pentecostal and charismatic thinking'.[3] The Tuesday meeting held in her home became a focal point in the upsurge of interest in 'entire sanctification' and expedited the trend toward lay activism among Victorian evangelicals.

The arrival of the Holiness message in Ireland owed much to the visit of the Palmers to the province in 1859 at the height of the Ulster Revival and again in 1862. It was probably through their influence that the converts of the 1859 Revival imbibed Holiness teaching. The Rev. D. Adams, the Presbyterian minister of the Ahoghill congregation, observed at the time: 'It is not uncommon to hear [some] say, "We have got *the glory!*"... Some of them have enthusiastically exclaimed—"Victory! Victory!" A few may, for a while *erroneously imagine* they are *already perfect...* Yesterday one informed me—"I now hardly have a sinful thought, and I feel myself every day growing more fit for heaven"'.[4] All this came as a completely new type of experience to the stolid Presbyterians of mid-Antrim. The reluctance within Reformed theology

---

[1] The best account of the period is found in Richard Carwardine: *Trans-Atlantic Revivalism: Popular Evangelicalism in Britain and America 1790-1865*, (Westport, CT: Greenwood Press, 1978).

[2] She married Dr Walter Palmer, a homeopathic practitioner who gave unflagging support to his wife in her more prominent ministry.

[3] H.E. Raser, 'Phoebe Palmer', in Timothy Larsen, (ed.), *Biographical Dictionary of Evangelicals*, (Leicester: Inter-Varsity Press, 2003), p. 503. For a fuller treatment see H.E. Raser, *Phoebe Palmer: Her Life and Thought*, (Lewiston, NY: Edwin Mellen Press, 1987).

[4] Rev. D. Adams, *The Revival in Ahoghill: Its Narrative And Nature With Suitable Reflections*, (Belfast: William McComb, 1859), pp. 26-7.

to reduce sanctification to special experiences and exaggerating its benefits, with an attendant proneness to subjectivism and perfectionism, precluded any teaching on Holiness lines among Presbyterians. Scott in his history of the 1859 Revival maintained that 'revival theology in Ulster had very little similarity to the modern Keswick doctrine of holiness... Apart from the Palmers, the doctrine of sanctification was that of the Shorter Catechism'.[5]

Palmer's ideas were promulgated by her books and journal, *The Guide to Holiness*, as well as her travels to Britain and Europe. Summer camp meetings were a popular venue for the promotion of her message. They had been introduced to Britain by the eccentric American evangelist Lorenzo Dow ('Crazy' Dow) during his visit to England during 1805-07.[6] Though dismissed by the main Wesleyan body as 'highly improper', they became a feature of the more revivalistic Primitive Methodist Connexion. It was to a camp organised on these lines that the Palmers paid a visit when they were in County Fermanagh, Ireland, in July 1862. The camp—'got up after the American fashion, which is no small rarity in these regions'—was held on the shores of Lough Erne.[7] For the Palmers the whole event 'was remarkably blessed of the Lord in the conviction and conversion of sinners, and in the *entire sanctification of believers*'.[8] Following the services on the middle Sunday, she was informed that 136 had 'professed to have found either the *blessing of* pardon or *purity* yesterday' and many 'having set themselves apart for God, had received the <u>gift of power</u>'.[9] At the conclusion of the camp meeting fortnight, the Palmers responded to the pleas of the ministers and people of Enniskillen to continue with meetings in the Town Hall. An average of forty to fifty responded each evening, 'some pleading for pardon, others for the <u>full baptism in the Holy Spirit</u>'.[10] Moving to Portadown, she laboured for two weeks in the Methodist church and

---

[5] Alfred R. Scott, *The Ulster Revival of 1859: Enthusiasm Emanating From Mid-Antrim*, (Ballymena: Mid-Antrim Historical Group, 1962), p. 165. James McWhirter, from Ballymena, who became a member of the Elim Evangelistic Band, stated that, in belonging to the Presbyterian Church, his seeking the Baptism was 'an entirely new and strange experience'. (*EE*, 19 June 1936, p. 394.)

[6] See John Kent, *Holding the Fort: Studies in Victorian Revivalism*, (London: Epworth Press, 1978), pp. 53-62.

[7] Palmer, *Four Years*, p. 584.

[8] Palmer, *Four Years*, p. 589. In the remainder of this paragraph the words in italics were recurrent Holiness themes and those underlined were to become key terms in Pentecostal discourse.

[9] Palmer, *Four Years*, pp. 590-91.

[10] Palmer, *Four Years*, p. 594.

during her stay many 'sought and obtained the *blessing of perfect love*'.[11]

In the latter decades of the nineteenth century the theology and practice of divine healing came to the fore among some Holiness groups.[12] One prominent advocate was Willam Edwin Boardman (1810-86), an American Presbyterian minister and evangelist, whose *Higher Christian Life* sold over 100,000 copies and played a major part in spreading Holiness doctrines in Reformed circles. Equally influential was his book *The Lord that Healeth Thee*, a work that ensured in his becoming an international advocate of divine healing. For Boardman and the radical healing movement in general there was no sharp doctrinal transition from depicting Christ as the saviour of the soul and sanctifier of the heart to Christ as the healer of the body. In a footnote in *The Lord that Healeth Thee,* he outlined an 'order of manifestations of Himself by the Lord to his child'.[13] After the disclosure of Christ to the believer as the 'pardoning Saviour', He comes as 'the Deliverer from all sin', then 'lastly, as the Deliverer from all the consequences from all sin, and from the heritage of sinful flesh—disease, etc'.[14] Carrying this message, Boardman spent the last years of his life in London and with the assistance of some local supporters, notably Mrs Elizabeth Baxter, established 'Bethshan' as a healing home in Highbury, north London. It was opened in 1882 'for those have been led to God to seek the Lord as their Healer in spirit, soul and body, that they, remaining for a short time, may attend the meetings of Holiness and Healing'.[15] A chapel was added at the rear of the home that seated 600 people and there Boardman and Mrs Baxter conducted healing services twice a week, while the practice of and teaching on divine healing operated on a continual basis in the home.

Mrs Baxter (1838-1923) whose husband, Michael, was the owner of the *Christian Herald*, was no less prominent in her role as editor of the bi-monthly magazine *Thy Healer*. She played a leading part in organising of the International Convention on Holiness and Divine Healing held in London in 1885. Among those who attended the Convention were five representatives from Ireland. Their spokesperson was Miss O'Hara who reported:

---

[11] Palmer, *Four Years*, p. 598.

[12] For the Holiness roots of divine healing see Nancy C. Hardesty, *Faith Cure: Divine Healing in the Holiness and Pentecostal Movements*, (Peabody, MA: Hendrickson, 2003), pp. 27-40.

[13] W.E. Boardman, *The Lord that Healeth Thee*, (London: Morgan and Scott, 1881), p. 11.

[14] Boardman, *The Lord that Healeth,* p. 11.

[15] Nathaniel Wiseman, *Elizabeth Baxter*, 2nd ed. (London: The Christian Herald), p. 87.

> There is no Faith Healing house like Bethshan in the whole of Ireland. Meetings for healing have been held in Dublin and Belfast. God has put it into the hearts of His children to have little private meetings there... There have been such meetings in Dublin, Blackrock, Kingston and Lisburn, and in the north. The Lord is held out to be the full Sanctifier and the Healer of the body and soul, and the poor Irish people are coming in and embracing the great salvation... We may add that God is doing a blessed work of healing at Bangor...through Mrs. Stewart, of Pond Park.[16]

That new Holiness initiatives continued to blossom was demonstrated by arrival of the Pentecostal League of Prayer in the last decade of the century. The League was founded by Reader Harris QC (1847-1909) in 1891 as an interdenominational mission and prayer fellowship to promote the Holiness message. Alexander Boddy was among those who gave support to the League in its earliest days which made Harris' later biting criticism of Pentecostals all the harder to take.[17] Harris launched the periodical *Tongues of Fire* in the same year. That divine healing, if not particularly stressed, was not frowned upon by the League is suggested in a brief obituary of a member. In *Tongues of Fire* a tribute was paid to Mrs F.W. Staveley who had been the founder in 1883 of the 'Berachah' healing home at Stockport, referred to as the 'Liverpool Bethshan'.[18] Differences between different Holiness groups occasionally outcropped. In 1895, Jessie Penn-Lewis, among other things the founder of Keswick in Wales, reported that leaders of the YWCA in Ireland had informed her that some of their members had joined Harris' new Pentecostal League and were holding separate meetings. They had expressed their concern that such meetings were disruptive of the unity needed to combat the widespread indifference to the Holiness message.[19]

In some ways the times could not have been more propitious for the advancement of Holiness teaching with its emphasis on the work of the Spirit in the life of the Christian. C.I. Scofield, of *Reference Bible* fame,

---

[16] *Record of the International Conference on Divine Healing and True Holiness, held at the Agricultural Hall, London, June 1 to 5, 1885*, (London: J. Snow, 1885), p. 156.

[17] Harris held meetings at Sunderland at the same time as Barratt's visit to the town in September 1907. He attacked the outpouring as a Satanic counterfeit and spoke of 'confusion, errors and immoral conduct, and the loosening of the marriage tie', to which criticisms Barratt gave a spirited response. (Gavin Wakefield, *The First Pentecostal Anglican: The Life and Legacy of Alexander Boddy*, [Cambridge: Grove Books, 2001], p. 9.)

[18] *Tongues of Fire*, February 1905, p. 5. Berachah (the 'house of blessing') was the name given to the first healing home opened by A.B. Simpson in New York in 1883. It was the forerunner of other similar homes opened by members of his C&MA (Christian and Missionary Alliance) throughout America and was a stimulus for establishing similar homes in Britain.

[19] Brynmor P. Jones, *The Trials and Triumphs of Mrs Jessie Penn-Lewis*, (North Brunswick, NJ: Bridge-Logos, 1997), p. 41.

though not a Holiness advocate observed that 'within the last 20 years more has been written and said upon the doctrine of the Holy Spirit than in the preceding 1800 years'.[20] In many evangelical circles there was a quickening of expectation that a new outpouring of the Holy Spirit was imminent as a prelude to the Second Coming. A.B. Simpson (1843-1919) concluded 'that we are to expect a great outpouring of the Holy Spirit in connection with the second coming of Christ and one as much greater than the Pentecostal effusion of the Spirit as the rains of autumn were greater than the showers of spring'.[21] One has only to look at the titles of the avidly read books written by the foremost evangelical spokesmen of the age to discern the air of expectancy. They include: D.L. Moody, *Secret Power* (1881); J. Wilbur Chapman, *Received ye the Holy Ghost?* (1894); Adoniram J. Gordon, *The Ministry of Healing* (1882) and *The Ministry of the Spirit* (1894); and Reuben A. Torrey, *The Baptism of the Holy Spirit* (1895).

In Torrey's book, he commented that 'in my early study of the Baptism with the Holy Ghost, I noticed that in many instances those who were so baptised "spoke with tongues", and the question was often in my mind: if one is baptised with the Holy Spirit will he not speak with tongues? But I saw no one so speaking, and I often wondered is there anyone today who actually is baptised with the Holy Spirit'.[22] He came later to decry any necessary link between the two but still maintained that Spirit-baptism 'is a definite experience of which one may know whether he has received it or not'.[23] A passage from another of his books has been described by Bruner as 'the most frequent quotation by a non-Pentecostal to be found in Pentecostal literature'. It reads: 'The Baptism with the Holy Ghost is an operation of the Holy Spirit distinct from and subsequent and additional to His regenerating work... *Every true believer has the Holy Spirit*, but not every believer has the Baptism with the Holy Ghost, though ever believer...may have'.[24] Though cautious on the

---

[20] Robert M. Anderson, *Vision of the Disinherited: The Making of American Pentecostalism*, (Peabody, MA: Hendrickson, 1992), p. 42.

[21] Edith L. Blumhofer, 'Restoration as Revival: Early American Pentecostalism', in Edith L. Blumhofer and Randall Balmer (eds), *Modern Christian Revivals*, (Chicago, IL: University of Illinois Press, 1993), p. 153. The 'Latter Rain' motif when taken up by Pentecostalism became one of the apologetic weapons to answer its critics who pointed to the dearth of historical precedents for the movement.

[22] Anderson, *Vision of the Disinherited,* p. 42.

[23] R.A. Torrey, *The Holy Spirit*, (Belfast: Ambassador, reprint, n.d.), p. 109. Torrey rejected evidential tongues on two grounds. Tongues were singularly absent throughout most of church history. Again, he interpreted 1 Cor. 12:30 ('do all speak with tongues?') in the negative, thereby, for Pentecostals, confusing tongues as 'sign' with that of 'gift'.

[24] F.D. Bruner, *A Theology of the Holy Spirit: The Pentecostal Experience and the New Testament Witness*, (London: Hodder and Stoughton, 1970), p. 46.

question of divine healing, he, nevertheless, accepted its biblical warrant: 'But in spite of all these gross and God-dishonouring errors into which people fall who over-emphasise Divine Healing,...let us not give up the precious truths of the texts...that the Gospel of Christ has salvation for the body as well as for the soul. It is the Church's forgetting this and not teaching this that left an opening for Mrs Eddy and for a host of other pretenders'.[25]

Such views may well have informed Torrey's preaching during his visit to Belfast in 1903. With numbers swelling, the halls and churches used at the beginning were found to be too small with the result that St George's Market, Cromac Square, was hired to accommodate 7,000 people. The leading sponsors of the visit were the Rev. Henry Montgomery, of the Presbyterian Shankill Road Mission and first chairman of the Portstewart Convention, and Dr Harry Guinness, the missionary son of Henry Grattan Guinness who was one of the gentlemen-evangelists prominent in the 1859 Revival in Ulster.[26] As will be shown, one of the first Pentecostal missionaries from Ireland, William J. Boyd, was strongly influenced by Harry Guinness.[27] Robert Ernest Darragh, from Bangor, County Down was another young man touched by Holiness teaching who was later to become the longest serving member of the Elim Revival Party. When Jeffreys attended his first Sunderland Conference in 1913 'he was accompanied by Brother Darragh [and] the early idyllic bond between [them] continued unbroken for the next 45 years'.[28]

For some, like Darragh, going beyond the Holiness understanding of Spirit-baptism to the Pentecostal one proved an emotionally taxing experience. In 1915, ten months after his conversion, Darragh attended some Holiness meetings for the deepening of spiritual life where emphasis was placed on the Baptism in the Holy Spirit. In response to the message, he and his companions sought the promised blessing: 'We were then told to rise from our knees and to praise God silently for the Baptism... This I did from all my heart—going a step further than some of the others, and in my bedroom went down on my knees and wrote in my Bible: "Baptised in the Holy Ghost" and the date'.[29]

He soon came to a realisation that he did not possess the power promised in Acts 1:7 and mentioned to some earnest Christian friends

---

[25] R.A. Torrey, *Divine Healing*, (Grand Rapids, MI: Baker, ed.1974), pp. 38-9. Christian Science was a *bête noire* equally for the early Pentecostals. Torrey would have confined the practice of divine healing to the elders of the local church, following Js 5:14-5.

[26] The famous Anglo-Irish Guinness family are said to fall into three branches—the brewing, banking and missionary.

[27] See Ch.4.2.3.

[28] John Carter, 'George Jeffreys—Apostle of God' in *RT*, 16 February 1962, p. 3.

[29] *EE*, 19 June 1936, p. 394

that he was seeking the Pentecostal experience. They warned him off on the grounds that he might get 'a wrong spirit'.[30] When he ceased wavering and got his 'feet once again on God's Word' he began afresh to wait upon the Lord. It was then laid on his heart that there were things he had to make right if he were to receive the baptism. The most daunting was his need, born of revived guilt, to apologise to a married couple for throwing a stone through their window years before in a boyish prank. Three weeks later, during a Sunday afternoon in the company of a few friends the heavens opened: 'What was it like? Right down in the innermost part of my being, rivers of water began to flow, rolling on and on until it came to my vocal organs and I spoke in other tongues and worshipped and magnified the Lord... Since then the rivers are still flowing as fresh as ever. I would not be without my heritage for worlds'.[31] Kärkkäinan speaks of Pentecostal-Charismatic Christians having a 'vivid, almost childlike enthusiasm of God's presence here and now'.[32]

Thanks largely to the cumulative impact of the 1859 Revival, mission halls and cottage meetings dotted the religious landscape of Ulster.[33] It was to one such mission hall in the Holiness tradition in Belfast that Alexander Boddy (1854-1930) and his brother-in-law, James Pollock, paid a visit in October 1905.[34] The meetings were held in Bethesda Hall, Landscape Terrace, a side street off the Crumlin Road, in the linen manufacturing district of west Belfast. Boddy's parish in Sunderland was a working class area so the dingy environs would not have been unfamiliar to him.[35] A shared involvement in Holiness spirituality must

---

[30] *EE*, 19 June 1936, p. 394. One of the most influential critiques of Pentecostalism was *War on the Saints* written by Jessie Penn-Lewis with Evan Roberts, first published in 1912. The titles of Ch.3 ('Deception by Evil Spirits in Modern Times') and Ch. 5 ('Deception and Possession') catch its burden.

[31] *EE*, 19 June 1936, p. 394

[32] Veli-Matti Kärkkäinan: *Pneumatology: The Holy Spirit in Ecumenical, International, and Contextual Perspective*, (Grand Rapids, MI: Baker, 2002), p. 134.

[33] The visit of D.L. Moody in 1874 fanned the embers of the 1859 Revival. Principal J.E. Davey wrote that as an outcome of the Moody mission cottage meetings were instituted in the neighbourhood of Carrickfergus. His father was converted at one of these at the age of seventeen and went on to become one of the evangelical luminaries of the Irish Presbyterian Church while his son became better known as a theological liberal who survived a heresy trial in 1927. (Joseph Thompson, 'D.L. Moody: A Centennial Study of the First American Evangelist to this Country and his Influence on Irish Presbyterianism', *The Bulletin of the Presbyterian Historical Society of Ireland*, May 1975, p.16.)

[34] *Belfast Telegraph*, 14 October 1905.

[35] In fact, Boddy made quite a play of the 'Buzzers', the factory horns of the nearby linen mills: 'In our town of Sunderland we are accustomed to "Buzzers", but they know when to stop'. Evidently they blared in Belfast 'like a great steam organ' for an hour on-

have drawn him to accept the invitation to Belfast a year before the events at Azusa Street supervened.

Four months before Boddy's visit Bethesda had advertised meetings under the banner headline 'BACK TO PENTECOST!' followed by the Holiness triad of 'Divine Life for Spirit, Soul And Body'.[36] When the pair arrived in Belfast their week-long special services were advertised as 'Meetings for Promoting Practical Holiness and Divine Healing' and at the meeting on the Tuesday afternoon Boddy was down to speak on 'What I saw of the Welsh Revival' and Pollock on 'My impressions of the Keswick Convention'.[37] The themes addressed were close to Boddy's heart—healing and holiness in the context of Keswick teaching—as they must have been for this small, independent mission in Belfast.[38] Both he and the Bethesda people were among those sensitive to their need for that deeper spiritual experience they had come to associate with the message of Keswick. Bethesda must have established contact with Boddy, possibly through the Pentecostal League, to invite him from Sunderland. They may have read some of his pamphlets in the series the *Roker Tracts*, one of which was titled *Health in Christ*. Boddy had come to accept divine healing in 1892 but added that he 'had not stepped out for myself or my family, as we were not then agreed'.[39] That changed with the healing of his wife of chronic bronchial asthma around 1900, and thereafter they carried on a healing ministry. Mary Boddy discovered she had the gift of healing and was often called upon to pray for the sick. Boddy did not have the gift but used the service of anointing the sick frequently.[40]

Thus, it can be seen that the Holiness message had taken hold in some quarters of the province, with women playing a not inconsiderable part in its furtherance, a shift furthered by such influential figures as Phoebe Palmer, Elizabeth Baxter and Salvationist, Catherine Booth. It has been said of the first of these three that 'while Palmer's teachings were directed to all Christians, they were particularly effective in offering spiritual

---

and-off, allowing him the whimsy that 'some people must sleep soundly, and needed a good deal of awakening'. (*Confidence*, July 1910, p. 156.)

[36] *Belfast Telegraph*, 3 June 1905.

[37] James M. Pollock became the curate at All Saints soon after Boddy's arrival during 1884 at Sunderland. It was through him that Boddy met his sister, Mary, whom he married in 1891.

[38] Boddy remarked that 'Keswick had been...a great help to me' in coming to an experience of what he came to recognise as 'a Baptism or Anointing of His Holy Spirit' in 1892. (A.A. Boddy, *A Vicar's Testimony*, [Sunderland, n.d.], p. 4.)

[39] Boddy, *Vicar's Testimony*, p. 6.

[40] Even in her last years when the Boddy's moved to the Durham pit village of Pittington, Mary Boddy ran a small Bible class for men in the vicarage, and though crippled by arthritis she saw many healings right up to her death in 1928.

empowerment to middle-class women'.[41] Even if the numbers attracted to Holiness teaching were small, they added to the tally of people in the province who were introduced to the need of a subsequent work of grace, separable from conversion, with a passion to proclaim divine healing as one of the fruits of the atonement. Theirs was a prospect that fed on the news from Wales. Had not Campbell G. Morgan reported it as 'Pentecost continued, without a single moment's doubt'.[42]

For many, at the time, news of the revival in Wales seemed to fit all the parameters of their expectation. The earnestness of desire for a move in Ireland similar to that in Wales is caught in an incident recorded by Archibald Irwin, a prominent Presbyterian layman, after he attended his first Keswick Convention in 1905. That evening after A.T. Pierson had preached movingly on 'The Reality of God', he went for a meditative walk and passing a hedge he heard voices: 'I listened and heard this petition repeated over and over again: "Lord, send the blessing of the Revival to Belfast". I peeped over the fence and saw on their knees three Belfast Presbyterian ministers, John Ross, Thomas Rodgers and James Hunter. I made their prayer my own'.[43]

2.2 The Impact of the Welsh Revival

The Edwardian period was the heyday of Belfast. The city was beginning to display the civic fruits of its great Victorian industrial heritage, based largely on its shipbuilding, engineering, tobacco and linen industries. Its prosperity rested on its export trade in these products, the entrepreneurial flair of its leading industrialists and the availability of an abundant and cheap labour force sucked in mainly from the surrounding rural counties in the second half of the nineteenth century. The migrants brought with them not only their aspirations but also their sectarian rivalries, only to replicate within the working class areas the tensions and violence of the Irish countryside. Periodic rioting throughout the period of rapid population growth led to a marked residential segregation of the Catholic and Protestant families. The segregation was most marked on the inner western side of the city where the linen mills by lining the main thoroughfares acted as a physical barrier separating the Protestant sector of the Shankill from that of the Catholic Falls and Ardoyne enclaves on

---

[41] William C. Kostlevy (ed.), *Historical Dictionary of the Holiness Movement*, (Lanham, MD: Scareceow Press, 2001, p. 197.

[42] Blumhofer, 'Restoration as Revival', p. 151.

[43] Archibald Irwin, *Lights Along The Way*, [Belfast: The Northern Whig, 1941], p. 119.

either side of it.[44] It was not so much the early segregation of the two groups that set it apart from other cities as the remorseless conflict that sustained it into the twenty-first century. The Shankill was the first area in the city to see a Pentecostal mission hall established in this Protestant enclave.

Belfast had the full plethora of religious activity which characterised the Victorian city—numerous churches, Sunday schools, tract distribution agencies, city missions, temperance and charitable societies, itinerant evangelists and open-air preachers. Nevertheless, all was not well in the bottom and widest layer of the social pyramid which represented 40% of the population of the city. The lowest-paid workers could not afford to buy a £3 plot in the city cemetery but had to be content with a public grave.[45] While labourers were sleeping off the effects of Saturday night indulgence, better-heeled artisans crowded on Sunday afternoons round the Custom House steps to sample such diversions as a Methodist choir, a rabble-rousing peroration from a speaker of the Belfast Protestant Association (BPA) or a humanist diatribe from a socialist orator. Crowds up to 10,000 would meet on Sundays to listen to the star turn, Arthur Trew, the BPA lay preacher, expatiate on the misdeeds of the Catholic Church.[46] In the inner city ward of Ballymacarrett, next to the shipyard where the *Titanic* was launched in 1911, only one in fifteen was estimated to attend church in 1908.[47]

Many evangelicals saw in the Welsh Revival an event to raise the spiritual tone of the city to match its social and economic advance. A sample of events drawn from Presbyterian and Anglican circles in Belfast provides the flavour and degree of involvement it evoked. In February 1905, the Belfast Presbytery met at a specially convened meeting 'at the suggestion of a number of brethren who thought that, in view of the widespread nature of the revival in Wales, some definite steps should be taken at the present time for prayer and conference in this city'.[48] The *Report on the State of Religion* presented to the General Assembly at the time recorded its thankfulness to God 'for the many tokens of blessing bestowed on the church as a whole, and several parts in particular, which

---

[44] For a detailed account of communal conflict in west Belfast see Catherine Hirst: *Religion, Politics and Violence in Nineteenth-century Belfast: The Pound and Sandy Row*, (Dublin: Four Courts Press, 2002).

[45] W. A. Maguire, *Belfast*, (Keele: Ryburn Publishing, 1993), p. 111.

[46] *Belfast Telegraph*, 10 April 1905, under the headline *Arthur Trew's Complaint*, reported that Trew had spoken from 3.15 pm till 4.45 pm.

[47] Sybil Gribbon, *Edwardian Belfast: A Social Profile*, (Belfast: Appletree Press, 1982), pp. 23-4. The Belfast figure is probably an underestimate in that numbers attending independent mission halls and cottage meetings under lay leadership were a feature of the city's religious life.

[48] *Belfast Telegraph*, 24 February 1905.

remind us in some measure of the marvellous Year of Grace, 1859... No such spirit of earnestness has been manifested since the Revival of '59'.[49] The report, while acknowledging a positive quickening of many churches, was careful to reiterate that there was no repeat of the dramatic sweep of 1859.[50] One Presbytery stated that two-thirds of its congregations had special services with encouraging results, although another was unable to record a single special effort.[51]

The fullest coverage in the local press of the reverberations of the Welsh Revival in Belfast was devoted to the services held in the Anglican Mariners' Church in the dockland area of Corporation Street, Belfast. In May 1905, the rector, Hedley Brownrigg, drew attention in the press to a letter he had received from 'a well-known clergyman of the Church of Ireland' in the hope that its contents would 'convince all God's people that Pentecost was not for a day but for a dispensation'.[52] His correspondent's account was all the more striking because it was written by a man who was 'no mere enthusiast or emotionalist but a sensible, hard-working clergyman of the practical sort'.[53] He quoted from the letter:

> If you are in earnest in coming to Wales to seek the fullness of the Holy Spirit, the power comes upon you and you become as 'mad' as everybody else. The 'Welsh fire' has so burned into my bones that I can't get away from it, nor do I want to... God gets into your life, that you can't help praying everywhere and always.[54]

Towards the end of the same month mission services were held in the Mariners' Church, conducted by the Rev. P.B. Johnson from Dublin with assistance from a Welsh choir.[55] The *Belfast Telegraph* report heralded it 'a novel experience for a Belfast audience to hear a preacher interrupted in the middle of his discourse by an outburst of praise in a foreign language [Welsh] coming from the seats under the pulpit'.[56] After the

---

[49] Orr, *The Flaming Tongue*, p. 31.

[50] The 1859 Revival in Ulster did not always go down well in some church circles at the time. A reaction set in against it in influential evangelical circles in the latter part of the nineteenth century registered by a determination not to let matters get out of hand again. (See Janice Holmes, *Religious Revivals in Britain and Ireland,* [Dublin: Irish Academic Press, 2000], especially Ch. 2, 'The British Response to 1859'.)

[51] Joe Thompson (alias 'Geneva'), *Repercussions in Ulster of the 1904-5 Welsh Revival*, Paul Memorial Prize, (n.d.), held in Union Theological College Library, Belfast.

[52] *Belfast Telegraph*, 3 May 1905.

[53] *Belfast Telegraph*, 3 May 1905.

[54] *Belfast Telegraph*, 3 May 1905.

[55] *Belfast Telegraph*, 3 May 1905. Johnson was in all probability the correspondent quoted.

[56] *Belfast Telegraph*, 22 May 1905, under the headline *Welsh Revivalists in Belfast*. Such displays of proto-Pentecostal behaviour accompanied the Welsh revivalists

preacher narrated some convincing conversion stories and before finishing his sentence 'the revivalists overcome with joy, burst forth into their national doxology...after which the preacher continued his discourse, apparently not in the least disturbed by the interruption'.[57] On the last evening of the mission the crowd was such that not everyone could be accommodated. At the end of the service 'for over an hour persons arose from all parts of the congregation and acknowledged having been converted, several as a result of that service. Shortly before 10 o'clock most of the congregation left, but in a short time the church was again filled, and another revival service was held at which many professed conversion'.[58] An advertisement in the press several days later gave notice that at the Sunday evening service at St Michael's Church, Craven Street, Shankill Road, the subject addressed would be 'The Power of the Holy Spirit' and that a mission would commence on 20 July conducted by the Rev. B.P. Johnson and the Welsh choir.[59]

Thus the Welsh Revival, in Belfast and in pockets throughout the province, saw a revitalisation of church life beyond the Principality that caused expectant Christian people to think in terms of a new Pentecostal outpouring, and not just in Ireland.[60] In north-east China, to take one example, there was a raised expectation of revival arising from the events in Wales. One missionary wrote: 'At last it has come, the "Revival" we have sought... We cast longing eyes on Wales no more'.[61] It is almost certain that the Irish Presbyterian missionaries in Manchuria were in contact with this major revival attended by unusual manifestations. In the years 1906-09, the spiritual awakening associated with the Canadian Presbyterian missionary, Jonathan Goforth (1859-1936), started there and then spread to six neighbouring provinces of China. The *Irish Presbyterian* in 1908 reported that the young members of the Christian Endeavour at Wellington Street Presbyterian Church were told that Wang, the Chinese evangelist whom they supported financially, 'had received a great blessing such as made him more enthusiastic and successful in his work'. A photograph had been received of a newly opened church in Manchuria that was the centre of a revival where Wang received 'a

---

wherever they went. In acting so, they were giving a lead and providing a pattern in worshipful exuberance. They saw it as almost mandatory that people should give evidence of being filled by the Holy Spirit by great bursts of noisy enthusiasm and emotion in contrast to the prevailing passivity of more conventional services.

[57] *Belfast Telegraph*, 22 May 1905.

[58] *Belfast Telegraph*, 1 June 1905, under the headline *Revival Movement in Belfast.*

[59] *Belfast Telegraph*, 10 June 1905.

[60] See Orr, *Flaming Tongues*, pp. 29-32 for an accessible source that relates the impact of the Welsh Revival in the province and beyond. .

[61] Daniel H. Bays, 'Christian Revival in China 1900-1937', in Blumhofer and Balmer, *Modern Christian Revivals*, p. 162)

baptism of the Holy Spirit, along with many others'.[62] Unbeknown to the writer of the article, a concept of Spirit-baptism that was alien to Reformed thinking was inserted with unsuspecting acquiesence. The 'great blessing' referred to was in all likelihood a discreet way of expressing some form of dramatic physical-emotional manifestation, selective in its subjects in that it was evidenced in some and not in others. Little wonder that Bays contends that 'all this was strong stuff for staid Scotch-Irish Presbyterian missionaries to countenance'.[63]

2.3 The Faith Mission

In 1905, J.G. Govan (1861-1927), the founder of the Faith Mission, delivered for his own organisation a verdict that was equally true for the Presbyterian Church in Ireland: 'Our work in Scotland and Ireland while we have as yet seen no general Revival, has been much influenced by the Welsh Revival... We have seen what might be called local revivals'.[64] The Faith Mission moved into Ireland from Scotland in 1891, five years after its beginning, and quickly established itself as a major source of Holiness teaching, owing more to the Reformed Keswick line than to the Wesleyan Holiness tradition. In the years 1892-94 it reached its peak conversion figure of 3,132 professions and by the end of 1894 about one-quarter of all its missions were being held in the province.[65]

The Mission became a significant force in the more rural areas with its conversionist preaching and fervent advocacy of 'full salvation', which embraced the Holiness emphasis on full surrender of the self to Christ as an explicit act for purity of life and effective witness.[66] In some rural pockets in both Scotland and Ireland, the Mission met stubborn opposition. Govan wrote of an Ayrshire village in 1886 that 'the people are very stiff, and seemed crammed with Calvinism, and the usual doubting, hoping, fearing, formalism and hypocrisy...but we shall have

---

[62] Thompson, *Repercussions in Ulster of the Welsh Revival*, p. 82.

[63] Bays, 'Christian Revival in China', p.164.

[64] I. R. Govan, *Spirit of Revival: A Biography of J. G. Govan,* (Edinburgh: The Faith Press, 1950 ed.), p. 134. The biographer was his daughter.

[65] T. Rennie Warburton, 'A Comparative Study of Minority Religious Groups, with Special Reference to Holiness and Related Movements in Britain in the Last 50 Years', (PhD thesis, University of London, 1966), p. 218.

[66] The Faith Mission is a good example of the tendency in the latter part of the nineteenth century to identify revivalism with Holiness teaching and outreach. Holmes, following Bebbington, points out that 'meetings with the intention of promoting holiness often bore a strong resemblance to traditional revival proceedings. The spontaneity, testimonies and emotionalism of holiness meetings made it difficult to tell the difference'. (Holmes, *Religious Revivals,* p. 193.)

the victory'.[67] In Ulster the pilgrims found conservative religious conviction stronger even than in Scotland, marked as it was by 'the staunchest kind of Presbyterianism, the most exclusive Episcopalianism and the animosity of the Roman Catholics'.[68] In 1894, in a village near Ballymena, depicted as 'utterly dead', the leader of the opposition to the two pilgrims criticised them on their use of 'human himes' [hymns] and the 'abominable after-meeting'.[69]

The doctrinal stance taken by the Faith Mission pilgrims, composed as it was by a blend of Arminian and Holiness theology, was unacceptable to those steeped in the Calvinist tradition. But even in such 'hard' places the dying embers of popular Protestant cross-denominational revivalism could be readily revived. One pilgrim reported: 'It is wonderful how people overflow their denominational barriers when they get filled with the Spirit, and are ready to have fellowship with all who are wholly the Lord's'.[70] Spirit-baptism terminology was a feature of the Mission's teaching and it shared with Pentecostalism the understanding of both the need for an experience of the Spirit subsequent to regeneration and its essential nature as an endowment of power for Christian living and service. Govan gave direction on such lines in stating 'I have been impressed with the necessity of every Christian to live a life pleasing to God and to be a power for Him on the earth, being baptised with the Holy Ghost and fire... So if you have not yet received the Holy Ghost since you believed, I would exhort you to put away every hindrance'.[71]

Coming as they were from the same stable, Govan had to give consideration to the startling events of the Welsh Revival and the rise of the nascent Pentecostal movement. When he was asked for his opinion about the manifestations accompanying the Welsh Revival, he replied that 'some disbelieve in and others dread visions, and anything that is supernatural, but a divine movement is *bound* to be accompanied by the supernatural'.[72] When questioned about the 'Tongues Movement', he replied, '[While there is] no reason why the gifts might not be restored, I have not the confidence in the latter-day [Pentecostal] Movement and do not feel they have kept to the Scriptures or to Paul's instructions. Consequently much of the work has not been helpful or for the glory of God, though I am sure there are good people among them'.[73]

---

[67] Govan, *Spirit of Revival*, p. 38.

[68] Govan, *Spirit of Revival*, p. 100.

[69] Govan, *Spirit of Revival*, p. 104. The after-meeting was most likely for those seeking, as the phrase goes, 'a deeper experience of God'.

[70] Govan, *Spirit of Revival*, p. 100.

[71] Govan, *Spirit of Revival*, pp. 68-9.

[72] Govan, *Spirit of Revival*, p. 132.

[73] Govan, *Spirit of Revival*, pp. 132-3.

As an interdenominational movement which required the acquiescence of mainline denominations, Govan was aware from the outset of the need to avoid all forms of extreme emotionalism in meetings, especially those where holiness teaching was promoted. The Mission, while firmly in the Holiness camp, confined this side of its teaching in the main to its annual convention meetings, though in Ireland the prevalence of lay evangelists brought a heightened tone to local Prayer Union meetings so that they often came to display more the intensified emotion of a convention service. One of the Mission's District Superintendents pointed out that 'the more emotional and enthusiastic behaviour of some of the movement's Northern Irish followers might be unacceptable to many of the more sober and undemonstrative Anglicans in the English districts'.[74] In a Faith Mission setting with its open acceptance of revivalism and its nineteenth-century legacy of grass-root interdenominationalism, the way was clear for a greater freedom of emotional expression that encouraged in many 'the need to experience a form of spiritual uplift at every meeting'.[75]

In the Irish countryside there were a few young men and women who were deeply influenced by the Faith Mission and who subsequently came into the Pentecostal experience and, in due time, leadership in the movement. Robert Tweed and Miss P.M. Thomson were two such. The latter first appeared in the list of Elim evangelists in the February 1922 edition of *Elim Evangel*. Before joining Elim she had laboured with the Faith Mission through which she was 'greatly used of the Lord in evangelical work in Wales'.[76] In May 1922, she married a fellow Elim evangelist, John B. Hamilton, and they laboured in the Lurgan assembly until they both resigned from Elim in November 1925.[77]

Tweed was born in 1899 near Ballymoney, County Antrim, with a small farm background. He was brought up in the Church of Ireland but owed his teenage conversion to a Faith Mission outreach conducted by two young women pilgrims in the local schoolroom.[78] The pilgrims 'were

---

[74] T.R. Warburton, 'The Faith Mission', in David Martin (ed.), *A Sociological Yearbook of Religion in Britain*, No. 2, (London: SCM Press, 1969), p. 91. The best-known Convention was and is that held at Bangor, Co. Down, since 1916.

[75] Warburton, 'The Faith Mission', p. 286.

[76] *Riches of Grace*, Vol. 4, 3 January 1929, p. 103.

[77] The Hamiltons were among the first leaders to have children born 'within Elim'. Financial stringency may lie behind their resignation.

[78] Robert Tweed produced when aged ninety-two a memoir in unpublished typescript form that provides a valuable background to the early days of Elim in the province, henceforth referred to as the *Tweed Memoir*. In it he gives a little of his religious background. In one passage he speaks of his drift away as a teenager from the Church of Ireland when he 'began to spend the Lord's Day cycling with those of the same age'. (*Tweed Memoir,* p. 5.) When he first heard the Elim evangelists, he detected differences

very well accepted especially by the Presbyterian Church'.[79] Their impact was such as to leave a mark on his own ministry: 'The Faith Mission pilgrims did not fill their sermons with profound words or high sounding ideas. Their message was not diluted but clear and simple and we could understand it. Years afterwards, having entered the ministry, I endeavoured to follow the example in preaching "the doctrine of the cross"'.[80]

He first came into contact with the Pentecostal movement in Rasharkin at the home of a prosperous farmer who had been influenced by George Jeffreys' campaign in Ballymena in 1916. The farmer had invited two of Jeffreys' co-workers to conduct a mission in one of the two Orange halls in the village.[81] The Faith Mission was holding a mission at the same time in the other Orange hall but started their meetings an hour earlier. This allowed Tweed to attend both services but it was to the Elim meetings conducted by R.E. Darragh and T.J. Logan that he felt the greater pull, drawn especially by the solo singing and leadership of the former and the spirited preaching of the latter. It was at the close of this mission that he first met Jeffreys and this led eventually in 1919 to his becoming a member of the Elim Evangelistic Band.

The crunch for Tweed came when he felt the time had come to sever his connection with the Faith Mission. He met with the two pilgrims at whose mission he was converted:

> The interview was stormy on their part. Miss Baxter, the senior, tackled me immediately about the speaking in tongues, which she said was 'of the devil' supporting the assertion with a story by one of their missionaries on the mission field. Being a linguist, he attended one of their meetings and heard the speaking in tongues, the interpretation of which he told them was blasphemous. Needless to

---

between them and the Faith Mission. The latter, for one, 'did not teach Divine Healing, but believed that God could answer prayer in that direction if it was His will and purpose to do so'. (*Tweed Memoir,* p. 7.) Elim impressed him with its vitality and challenge, enough to overcome the allure of the Sunday jaunt with his peers.

79 *Tweed Memoir*, p. 5. Tweed's was very much an outsider view that did not reflect the disquiet felt about the Faith Mission in some Presbyterian circles. The Ballymena Presbytery, stricter than most, had its attention drawn in 1904 to an 'office bearer', presumably an elder, who brought into his district 'a tent and lady preachers to conduct a mission which is thought uncalled for in a district of churches and Gospel ordinances'. (*The Irish Presbyterian*, October 1904, p. 160.) The Presbytery offered a stiff rebuke for such activities.

80 *Tweed Memoir*, p. 6.

81 One of the halls was owned by the Independent Orange Order and the other by the 'Old Orange Order'. A split in the Orange Order took place in 1903 with the formation of the Independent Orange Order. It was essentially a populist response to the unrepresentative nature of the early Edwardian Ulster Unionist Party over which the landlord class maintained considerable internal control.

> say, I left the mission... I am sure the lady preachers must have been very discouraged, for I think they may have entertained the idea that one day 'Robert' would enter their Bible College in Scotland.[82]

Such an episode in Tweed's life gives the flavour of the opposition towards the Elim movement in Ulster during its early days.

Other than *glossolalia* and its tie with Spirit-baptism and the radical charismaticism of Pentecostalism there was little that was otherwise distinctive from the doctrinal emphases of Holiness revivalism. The tensions between Elim and the Faith Mission exhibited, in Freud's phrase, something of 'the narcissism of minor differences'. The two movements had much in common—both were evangelistic bands with itinerant lay preachers; both had men and women workers who travelled in pairs largely in rural and small town settings and hired school rooms and Orange halls for their meetings; both sometimes came to an area at the behest of individual supporters who had been touched deeply by their ministry and who often had some standing in their community. The homes or even barns of such people could on occasions be used for meetings. Both put great emphasis on the quality of personal consecration and scriptural holiness with the acceptance of a distinct and subsequent work of the Spirit in the life of the individual Christian after regeneration. The appeal of the meetings was across the denominational divides and, in Elim's case during its early period, there was no determined intent to establish a splinter group.

2.4 The Cooneyites

Both the Faith Mission and Elim came to have virtually nothing in common with the Cooneyites, despite the latter's roots in Holiness teaching, other than to send forth their workers to labour 'on faith lines', as Tweed expressed it, citing Matthew 10:10 as their proof text.[83] It was the injunctions enjoined in this same chapter in Matthew that provided the Cooneyites (also known as Tramp Preachers, Go-Preachers, Irvingites, Pilgrims, Dippers, and No-Sect Preachers)[84] with much of their *raison d'être* and furnished the justification for adherents to support them sacrificially.[85] The Cooneyites developed from a split in the Faith Mission

---

[82] *Tweed Memoir:* p. 6.

[83] *Tweed Memoir,* p. 6. He was referring particularly to the ending of the verse, 'for a worker is worthy of his food'.

[84] There is a difficulty in the naming of the sect. From the beginning they maintained their movement would be nameless, hence the variety of names, many of them picked up by journalists. In France the movement was known as 'Les Anonymes' and in Germany as 'Namenlosen' ('the nameless ones'). 'Cooneyites' is the most familiar label in Ireland.

[85] D. and H. Parker, *The Secret Sect,* (privately published 1982).

around 1897 when William Irvine, a Scot from Kilysth, became disenchanted with the Mission while a pilgrim working in Ireland. His discontent had a radical, left-wing populist edge to it, allied to a strong anti-clerical streak.

There was something about the early Go-preachers that accorded with the levelling spirit of the 'sectaries' during the seventeenth-century Commonwealth period in England. A Go-preacher, in harking back to the earliest days, declared that 'we were fanatical and attacked the building of the cathedrals alongside the slums... We set out to form a brotherhood where all would be equal'.[86] One Methodist historian, R. Lee Cole, maintained that if the Cooneyites 'had been handled a little more wisely, they could have been made useful allies of the evangelical churches; they might have co-operated with the Methodists, because they laid stress on "the second blessing" which was in accord with the teaching of holiness proclaimed by John Wesley'.[87] Cole completely underestimated the radicalism of the Cooneyites in making this judgement. One of their preachers ventured that 'he would have been in hell with other Methodist preachers if his eyes had not been opened to God's true way'.[88]

The force and bluntness of Irvine's manner of speech, expressed with a cutting humour, won him admirers among young working class labourers and tradesmen.[89] As he saw it, an easy conversionism that showed little of the spirit of self-denial and personal effort was only too common among his converts. On studying Matthew 10:8-10 with one of his young preachers, John Long, they came to the conclusion, seized as of revelatory import, that the passage set the pattern for an unpaid, itinerant ministry. The sect taught that the 'Jesus Way', as they saw it set out on Matthew 10:5-42, was indispensable for salvation, an emphasis that came to tilt the balance in the works-grace debate towards the former. The doctrinal stress was very much on Christ as example, as demonstrated in the self-denying manner of the preachers themselves, less as Saviour and little as Redeemer.

One of the young men to take up the challenge was Edward Cooney (1868-1961), the son of a wealthy Enniskillen draper who, taking Irvine's teaching to heart in 1901, gave up his business interests and donated £1,300 to the sect.[90] He was educated at the prestigious local grammar school, Portora Royal School, in the period between the attendance there

[86] Parker, *The Secret Sect,* p. 26.

[87] R. Lee Cole, *History of Methodism in Ireland 1860-1960*, (Belfast: Irish Methodist Publishing, 1960), p. 101.

[88] Parker, *The Secret Sect*, p. 21.

[89] Parker, *The Secret Sect,* pp. 27, 29.

[90] *Belfast News-letter,* 10 February 1971, article under headline *Cooney: He Tried to Live Like Christ.*

of the internationally famed playwrights, Oscar Wilde and Samuel Beckett. From an Anglican background, Cooney was active in his church until leaving it at the age of thirty-four. Within the sect he was noted for his 'intense earnestness and burning zeal... He not only preached Christian communism, but earnestly practised it' and in time came to be seen as a leading contender for leadership against Irvine. As if to show their indifference to worldly concerns, Cooney and other preachers had so few changes of clothing that they earned a reputation for personal unkemptness. In its ways the sect challenged the prim religiosity and values of late Victorian Britain.

Of all the groups studied, the Cooneyites have a claim to be the only one to have its origin in Ireland. The movement for a while had an appreciable presence in the rural areas of Tyrone, Armagh and especially Fermanagh, though its early headquarters was in Belfast. Though germinated in the soil of the Holiness movement, the obfuscation of its doctrinal position, the exclusivist nature of its ecclesiology and the secrecy with which it handled its affairs drew puzzlement from outsiders.[91] Nevertheless, the impetus driving the sect was one familiar to many new movements, viz. a restorationist itch to recover the essence of primitive Christianity. Cooney was of the opinion that 'Irvine was a prophet raised up by God to lead back those in Christendom to the truth as it is in Jesus', but there is no indication of any clearly defined charismatic dimension to his prophetic role.[92] It was Irvine's conclusion that because for centuries long the church had fallen away from the practices of its first mission it had become apostate and ineffectual. In contrast to other movements, Cooneyites narrowed their practices down to the radical imperatives of Matthew 10 but at the expense of the wider ecclesiological implications of Acts and the Epistles. The charismatic dimension was muted, though Matthew 10:8 was taken as the warrant that some would be given power for healing and much stress was laid on the unmediated direction of the Holy Spirit. When Cooney came to resent growing organisational trends within the sect that led to his ostracism from the main body in 1928, he wrote: 'Thank God Wm. Irvine wasn't an organiser. You can never organise a person led by the Spirit... Workers need to know what it is to be checked by the Spirit, and to be led by the Spirit'. [93]

---

[91] The conventions organised by Irvine in the early days were modeled on the Keswick Convention. Both Irvine and Cooney visited the Keswick Convention in 1899 and in the same year conventions run on similar lines were held for the new movement in Glasgow, Belfast and Dublin. The Rev. George Grubb, a popular Keswick speaker at the time, was a regular speaker at some of the early conventions organised by Irvine. (Parker, *The Secret Sect,* p. 17.)

[92] Parker, *The Secret Sect,* p. 7.

[93] Parker, *The Secret Sect,* p. 74.

John Long, one of the earliest companions of Irvine in Ireland, was the most noted convert to Pentecostalism from the sect.[94] His life story was fairly typical of the early adherents of the Cooneyites. Born in Tipperary in 1872, he worked from the age of seven in the peat bog cutting turf in the summer, with schooling confined to the winter months. He received assurance of salvation in 1890 at a mission conducted by the Methodist evangelist, Gabriel Clarke. Shortly afterwards, he became a Methodist colporteur for about five years. He was aged twenty-five when he made his first contact with Irvine who at the time was conducting a Faith Mission gospel campaign in Ennis, County Clare. From 1897 to 1907 he was one of the tramp preachers until Irvine dramatically expelled him from the sect. Seven years later, Irvine was himself ousted for his increasingly autocratic ways and eccentric beliefs.[95]

While Long was preaching to a thousand people at the annual camp at Ballinamallard in July 1907, Irvine unsettled him with his audible asides and when Long sat down, proceeded to berate him on the grounds that Long

> was convinced that we were right and cast his lot with us. But he was not convinced that the Clergy were wrong, and there has always been a holding back in him. For years he has been dragging his feet on the ground to hinder our going on and we have decided to part company with him... All those stand up who believe that J[ohn] W[esley] is in Hell![96]

Long was one of the very few who refused to stand and the irascible Irvine was biting in his reaction. For a short period after his exclusion, Long was a member of the Elim Evangelistic Band but spent most of his long life as an independent, itinerant evangelist continuing in the tramp preacher manner of his former years.[97] He travelled into old age throughout the British Isles often by bicycle, depending on the leading of the Spirit and answerable to no organisation. He cut an idiosyncratic

---

[94] His son, John, has in his possession three bound manuscripts in the genre of a spiritual journal which his father kept.

[95] Parker, *The Secret Sect,* p. 62. With reference to the Second Advent, Irvine promulgated the belief that he had been divinely appointed to bring the message of Christ to the world before its judgement. This was coupled with the announcement of the imminence of the end in August 1914.

[96] Alf Magowan, *The History of an Unusual People,* (privately printed, n.d.), was a short play written by an early Go-preacher. The quotation is taken from the play and is almost certainly a faithful re-enactment of the original incident. It was shown previously that Fermanagh had a camp meeting tradition that went back at least forty years to the days of Phoebe Palmer.

[97] *Tweed Memoir*, p. 15.

figure in Pentecostal circles, familiar to many of the leading figures in the movement.[98]

2.5 The Christian Catholic Apostolic Church in Zion

Another movement to fish in the backwaters of Ulster Protestantism in the first decade of the twentieth century was the Christian Catholic Apostolic Church in Zion. A notice in the *Belfast Telegraph* in November 1905 announced a meeting to be held in Wellington Place, Belfast. The speaker advertised was Deacon A.C. Herring-Cooper and his address carried the theme 'Zion's Reply to her Enemies'.[99] The movement in question, referred to as 'Zion', was founded in 1895 by John Alexander Dowie (1847-1907). Dowie, a Scot, received a classical and theological education at the Free Church College of the University of Edinburgh without completing his degree. Around this time, DeArteaga maintains, though without substantiation, that he came under the influence of Irving's Catholic Apostolic Church.[100] Between 1872 and 1877, Dowie served as a Congregationalist minister. In 1882, he started the International Divine Healing Association and the following year he established the Free Christian Church in Melbourne where healing became a major concern.

Arriving in America in 1888, Dowie carried on an independent ministry that came to combine elements of Holiness teaching with healing revivalism. In 1896 he founded in Chicago the Christian Catholic Church which in 1904 became the Christian Catholic Apostolic Church. The slight change in title with the addition of 'Apostolic' signalled Dowie's self-declared status of 'First Apostle of the Lord Jesus, the Christ, in the Christian Catholic Apostolic Church in Zion, who is also Elijah, the Prophet of the Restoration of All Things'.[101] In 1900, he unveiled plans

---

[98] He would arrive unannounced at an assembly in Belfast on a Sunday morning, having cycled from Antrim town, some twenty miles away, and expect, if circumstances permitted, to preach at the morning and evening services. Sunday lunch and tea had to be hastily laid on. He was totally unselfconscious and spartan in his lifestyle—a veritable Pentecostal eccentric. (Personal recollection.)

[99] *Belfast Telegraph*, 18 November 1905, church notice.

[100] William DeArteaga, *Quenching the Spirit: Examining Centuries of Opposition to the Moving of the Holy Spirit*, (Lake Mary, FL: Creation House, 1992), p. 113. Faupel is of the opinion that it is most unlikely that Dowie would not be aware of the teachings of the Catholic Apostolic Church. He sets out five 'striking parallels' in the theologies of the two moments, one of which is the distinctive belief in the vital role for the 'Ministry of the Seventy', the Restoration Host. (Faupel, *The Everlasting Gospel*, p. 134.)

[101] The new order was ratified by the 7,000 who gathered in the sanctury in Zion. Dowie told them that the 'the Goal of Ecclesiastical Organisation (was) the Restoration of the Apostolic Office. Divine Order is Heaven's First Law. These are the times of Restoration. The key-note of this discourse is that the Church most get back to its

for a religious community shaped by a heady cocktail of biblical, utopian and modernist ideas.[102] Zion City, located on the shoreline of Lake Michigan forty miles north of Chicago, became the home of a community of over 6,000 people, enough to make it one of the more grandly conceived utopian settlements in modern American history. In Zion City he attempted to establish a theocratic society free of liquor, tobacco, pork and pharmacies. Along the sides of the assembly hall, Shiloh Tabernacle, a display of the letters 'S' and 'P' was erected, built from old cigar boxes. The two letters stood for 'stinkpot', Dowie's label for smokers. Even when he became publicly discredited, he could demonstrate the effectiveness of his message by mounting over the enormous platform of the Tabernacle crutches, casts, trusses, braces, orthopaedic shoes, pill bottles and wheelchairs of the healed. Where Dowie differed theologically from most other of his contemporaries who advocated divine healing, notably A.B. Simpson, was to place healing less in the Christological framework of soteriology and more in the distinctive Pentecostal pneumatology of gifts, power, signs and wonders.

In the course of his career Dowie was arrested over one hundred times for practicing healing without a license. He had a particular aversion to doctors and medical treatment. His inflammatory sermon, 'Doctors, Drugs and Devils', instigated a riot by medical students in Chicago in 1899. When in London in 1904, two medical students from St Bartholomew's hospital were each fined £10, having been charged with a breach of the peace when they threatened 'to hang him'.[103] The disturbance in London seems to have been aroused by Dowie's castigation of the philandering of Edward VII, though two of his sermons were 'Medicine, the Mother of Many Humbugs' and 'The Pharmacist, the Deadly "Cure-all" Humbug'. He described the monarch as 'a Masonic Baal-worshipper' and castigated 'his shameful life, a life of the vilest kind'.[104] Dowie's stridency, his distinctive views on divine healing, his proto-Pentecostal leanings, his bold vision and the later waywardness of his theology, all combined to make him an internationally known, though largely scorned, figure.

Primitive Order if it would have its Primitive Power'. (P.L. Cook, *Zion City: Twentieth Century Utopia*, [Syracuse: Syracuse University Press, 1996], p. 172.) As will be discussed in Ch. 8, such sentiments were to find their echo in the later Apostolic Church, particularly so in the use of the term 'Order'.

[102] See Grant Wacker, 'Marching to Zion: Religion in a Modern Utopian Community', *Church History*, Vol. 54, December 1985, pp. 496-511.

[103] *The Times*, 14 June 1904, p. 3.

[104] *LH*, 28 January, 1905, p. 474.

2.5.1 Zion Arrives in Ireland

The *Belfast Telegraph* occasionally carried snippets of news about Dowie, particularly of his more suspect activities. In April 1905, it hinted of chicanery in reporting that 'the "Profit" Dowie has been mortgaging Zion City properties'.[105] It was a charge that Bartleman upheld in classing Dowie among the 'spiritual charlatans, who have so severely abused and fleeced the flock of God, and come to a most disreputable and execrable end'.[106] In November, the *Belfast Telegraph* announced that Dowie had suffered a further stroke and, in December, it disclosed that a triumvirate would manage the affairs of Zion City to allow Dowie, described now as 'a nervous wreck', to recuperate in Jamaica.[107] Such barbs struck home to an extent that in making door-to-door visitation in Ulster the tiny band of Zion workers found any mention of the name Dowie evoked immediate hostility. Shortly after his arrival in the province in March 1904, Herring-Cooper wrote that 'the papers here, with one or two exceptions, have followed in the wake of the *American Cesspool* and misreported and misrepresented this good work in a shameful way'. Elizabeth Gaston, Ulster-born and converted to the cause of Zion while in America, reported some success in her house visitation: 'God has wonderfully used our testimony to change the minds of the people regarding Zion, and they will not believe the newspapers any more'.[108] In Lurgan, it was related that she and a co-worker met a man 'who had heard our beloved General Overseer [Dowie] in America [and who] was anxious to know if there was any truth in the newspaper reports about the bankruptcy of Zion. Deaconess Gaston, having been there during the difficulty, told him the truth, which he was pleased to hear'.[109]

On the grounds that all publicity is good publicity, the cause of the Christian Catholic Apostolic Church was hardly damaged in Ireland by such reports and warnings. In any case, 1904 was not the first foray of the movement into the island because in late 1900 Dowie had visited Britain and when he returned to Zion City he spoke of the success of his visit claiming that the Zion banner had been planted in Ireland, among other places.[110] In an address he gave in Zion in June 1901, he referred back his

---

[105] *Belfast Telegraph,* 10 April 1905, under the headline *Dowie's New Zion.*

[106] *Confidence*, April 1913, p. 79.

[107] *Belfast Telegraph,* 6 November 1905; 22 December 1905.

[108] *LH*, 20 August, 1904, p. 580. *Leaves of Healing* was Zion's weekly magazine and ran from 1894-1906.

[109] *LH,* 20 August, 1904, p. 580. In 1906 Dowie lost both his health and his control of Zion. In July 1906, a receiver was appointed pending a resolution of Zion's financial problems. That action did not prevent many individuals suffering severe financial loss. Zion soldiered on till 1935 under the leadership of Dowie's heir apparent, Wilbur Glenn Voliva, who retained control despite Parham's early attempts at a takeover.

[110] Cook, *Zion City,* p. 38.

meetings in Belfast, Ballymena and Londonderry, none of which ran smoothly. It is clear that, in quintessential Dowie manner, he wilfully stoked up animosity. Smokers, Freemasons and people who ate pork were among his targets. His treatment of the Levitical dietary laws as still applying was one expression of his making 'purity' an *idée fixe* .[111] In Ballymena, he told the packed audience in the Town Hall that he had come to the conclusion that St Patrick had cleared Ireland of snakes by getting the pigs to eat them, adding, 'My difficulty is that the Irish people are still eating the swine that ate the snakes; and the trouble is that when you eat the swine you eat the snakes too, so you are a compound of hog and snake!' There can be no surprise at the reaction to this verbal fusillade: 'Oh, how they howled!'[112] Opposed as he was to capital punishment, he added petrol to the fire in accusing the Orange Institution of allowing the death penalty as a sanction in its oaths. The furore aroused by such comments was such that 'it did not seem possible that we could get back to the hotel alive'.[113]

Arriving the following day at the Guildhall in Londonderry, he was told by the Head Constable that he expected disturbances and that his life was under threat, while reassuring him of protection at the risk, if needs be, to the policeman's own life. At the packed first meeting some students from Magee College, a Presbyterian foundation, raised a slight disturbance that was soon quelled. His sermon dealt largely with divine healing and only prompted a reaction of 'noises, groans and hisses' when he attacked tobacco smoking—'making yourself a walking stinkpot'—and cries of 'Rot! Bosh!' when he condemned eating pork.[114] The second evening he spoke on purity in 'Spirit, Soul and Body [that] opened up a new line of thought for most people; but they could take no exception to the teaching'.[115] At the end all who 'wanted to be free from sin and serve God' were asked to stand and 'the greater part of the audience arose'.[116] Indeed, fed by press reports, 'the people of Derry were bitterly disappointed because they could find no fault with the address'.[117] The healing of a young girl, Winnie Thompson, with a neck complaint was claimed and though considered 'a marvel to many', it did

[111] 'Citizens' Mid-Week Rally', Shiloh Grove, June, 1901, in *LH,* 15 April, 1905, p. 827. Dowie ensured that Zion City would permit no hog raising, selling or handling. Butchers in Zion perfected the technique for curing beef as an ersatz bacon. One of the slogans preached was 'Zion City, a Clean City for a Clean People'.

[112] 'Citizens' Mid-Week Rally', Shiloh Tabernacle, November 1903, in *LH,* 18 March 1905, p. 705.

[113] *LH,* 15 April 1905, p. 827.

[114] *LH*, 26 January 1901, p. 428.

[115] *LH*, 23 February 1901, p. 549.

[116] *LH*, 26 January 1901

[117] *LH*, 23 February 1901, p. 549.

not prevent the Thompson parents having to face 'opposition and persecution'.[118] Dowie was never slow to milk such incidents for dramatic effect in recounting them back in Zion.

Provocation and denunciation were his forte and from this myopic perspective his visit to Ireland must be counted a success in terms of publicity, something on which to establish a future work. With Dowie adopting such a confrontational *modus operandi*, listeners could sometimes be forgiven if what came across in his preaching was more the 'strong message of Zion' than the core themes of the gospel. Once when 30,000 cards, with their cover portrayal of 'Christ Knocking at the Door', announcing the services in London in 1904 ran out, they were replaced each week by 3,000 cards fronted by a 'beautiful photograph of the First Apostle in his priestly robes'.[119]

At the inauguration of the Christian Catholic Church in 1896, Dowie named Ireland together with Scotland and England as places where branches would be established.[120] By 1905, one 125 local groups had been established in the British Isles. A report in *Leaves of Healing* praised the efforts of H.E. Cantel, Overseer-in-Charge for Zion in the British Isles, who since his appointment in 1901 had organised 'the London Seventy of the Restoration Host', the 'London Company of Zion Guard, uniformed as in Zion City' and 'a Zion White-robed choir'.[121] The Restoration Host had been inaugurated in 1902 as the missionary arm of the movement. Volunteers vowed 'to proceed to any part of the world wherever he [Dowie] shall direct [and] that all family ties and obligations...shall be held subordinate to this Vow'. The Guards were first recruited to patrol the neighbourhood of the healing homes in Chicago around 1899 to prevent vandalism. They wore uniforms similar to that of the police. Their cap badge was a bronze dove with an olive leaf in its beak flying over flood-water across which the word 'Patience' was braided in gold letters. Bibles were carried in their holsters.[122] The London report observed that 'the need of this gallant band of defenders is often seen'.[123]

In the second half of 1904, the Restoration Host in the British Isles had visited 22,000 homes and distributed 67,000 invitation cards and printed sermons while the Guards had 'rendered efficient service'.[124] A statistical summary for the quarter ending December 1904 showed that six workers operated in Ulster and three centres were specified—Belfast, Londonderry

---

118 *LH*, 23 February 1901, p. 549.

119 *LH*, 18 March 1905, p. 710.

120 Faupel, *The Everlasting Gospel*, p. 131.

121 'Notes from Zion's Harvest Field', *LH*, 18 March 1905, p. 710.

122 Cook, *Zion City*, pp.145-6, 22.

123 *LH*, 18 March 1905, p. 710.

124 *LH*, 11 March 1905, p. 677.

and Cloughmills, the latter about twelve miles from Ballymena.[125] In Ulster over 5,200 houses had been paid a call, almost 500 saloon bars visited, 1,500 copies of *Leaves of Healing* sold and 8,000 copies of Zion literature distributed. That the work of the Restorationist Host was making some inroads is substantiated by two events. When five Zion missionaries were in Lurgan on Easter Monday 1904, they reported that 'there was a very strong feeling against our work because of a modern Demetrius, who preaches to the Orangemen against Dr Dowie, for he is greatly enraged at the way he speaks against secret societies, thereby bringing their craft into danger'.[126] Later in the year a warning was issued to the Presbyterians in Ballymena that 'a reverend disciple of the extraordinary disciple Dr Dowie is to visit [the town], and explain to those who are foolish enough to give audience to the principles of the Zionist movement'.[127]

The unnamed 'reverend disciple' was Harry Cantel who paid a visit to Ireland in October 1904 during which he baptized six believers in the Ormeau Baths, Belfast.[128] He spent two nights in Dublin where over 1,000 attended the 'limelight lectures', though the second one had to be cut short because of 'the ravings of lewd fellows of the baser sort', but not before hundreds filled in cards to receive literature.[129] Healing services were held on both afternoons. His visits to Ballymena and Londonderry in the course of four days 'were even more lawless, for the uproar centred in their Town Halls', though in Londonderry 'hundreds who had been cursed with the darkness of ignorance and prejudice saw by the light of the stereoptican the realities of Zion'.[130] However, when the party reached Belfast 'the haven of their desire had been reached at last. Vast audiences of teachable people gathered in the Exhibition Hall, both at the two limelight lectures and the Divine Healing services'.[131] The only disturbance came from 'a party of students from the adjoining Medical College' who calmed down enough to ask questions of Cantel who

---

[125] *LH,* 11 March 1905, p. 677.

[126] *LH*, 20 August 1905, p. 580.

[127] *The Irish Presbyterian*, November 1904, p. 176.

[128] Harry Cantel was born in France in 1865. After his arrival in America, he was appointed secretary of the YMCA in New Orleans in the late 1890s. He first met Dowie in 1899 and was ordained by him in the same year. His marked success in advancing the work in Britain earned him recognition as one of the leading assistants of Dowie. (For the Cantels, see Gordon P. Gardiner, *Out of Zion Into The World*, [Shippensburg, PA,: Companion Press, 1990], pp. 239-44.)

[129] The 'limelight lectures' used the stereopticon, a slide projector (magic lantern) that allowed one image to dissolve into another.

[130] *LH*, 18 March 1905, p. 710.

[131] *LH*, 18 March 1905, p. 710.

pointed them 'to the only Way of Healing'.[132] Harry Cantel and his wife Margaret were later to play a key role in British Pentecostalism.[133]

A picture of the beginning of the Zion movement in Ireland can be extracted from the pages of the *Leaves of Healing*. Fifteen months after Dowie's visit in 1900, Elizabeth Mackay started meetings in Belfast. The first Overseer was Daniel Bryant who baptised four believers in March 1904 before he was sent as Overseer to South Africa by Dowie later in that year.[134] He was succeeded by Anthony Herring-Cooper who had joined Zion through his healing from chronic constipation, having received encouragement to seek healing from reading testimonies in *Leaves of Healing*. Among the stalwarts of the work were Archibald McKane, Albert Osborne, Elizabeth Gaston and five members of the Mackay family, who together constituted the local Restoration Host. Elizabeth Mackay started meetings in Belfast some time in early 1903 so that when Herring-Cooper arrived in Belfast, he found 'a very loving, loyal, and faithful, though little, band of workers here'.[135] Of them all, Elizabeth Gaston was the longest-standing member of Zion. She was highly regarded by the Dowie family who had taken her under their wing when she first arrived in America and was one of the earliest Deaconesses to be appointed in the Zion movement.

Elizabeth Gaston grew up at Glarryford, County Antrim, near Cloughmills, which would account for the statistic of 119 homes visited and 247 copies of *Leaves of Healing* sold in that locality in the last quarter of 1904.[136] In conversation with a neighbour who knew her from childhood and who was concerned to read in the papers of people in Zion

---

[132] The only medical school in Ulster was that of Queens University of Belfast. The Exhibition Hall was most likely the Ulster Hall.

[133] In 1907, the year of his marriage, after hearing of the Pentecostal outpouring in Zion City promoted by Parham, Cantel crossed the Atlantic at once to investigate the new movement and as an outcome received his Spirit-baptism. Returning to London, he persuaded the majority of his group of the validity of the Pentecostal experience. Thus was formed by assimilation the first recognised Pentecostal assembly in Britain. The Cantels established for a time a residential home for divine healing. Harry died suddenly from peritonitis in 1910.

[134] Bryant played a formative role in the cause of Zion in South Africa out of which developed the present powerful African Zionist churches. Anderson speaks of 'the essential continuity between Zion and Pentecost in South Africa. [From 1908] Zion converts remained Zionists while adding Pentecostalism to their beliefs'. (Allan Anderson, *Zion and Pentecost*, [Pretoria: University of South Africa Press, 2000], p. 63.) Chidester maintains that 'the Zionist exchange between America and South Africa produced unexpected results that have been crucial to the formation of an African Christianity'. (David Chidester, *Christianity: A Global History* [London: Penguin Press, 2000], p. 464.)

[135] *LH*, 20 August 1904, p. 579.

[136] *LH*, 11 March 1905, p. 677.

suffering starvation, she was able to tell her 'of the beautiful, happy City where I had spent one year and seven months, and of my relatives and friends, and of their happy homes and sweet pure surroundings'.[137] Around 1896, when Lizzie Gaston was a very sick young woman, her interest in divine healing was quickened in reading testimonies of healing in *Leaves of Healing*. Accompanied by a cousin she travelled to Zion Healing Home in Chicago and was restored to health. She stayed on in Chicago to attend Zion College which had been established to 'prepare workers for service in the Master's Kingdom'.[138] She was one of the party of eleven that travelled with Dowie to Europe in September 1900. The visit included a short stay in Ireland that was part vacation, part reconnoitre, with the objective of opening a work in the island. It was largely in response to her plea that he came to Ballymena in November 1900. She returned again to Europe in January 1904 in the company of 'Overseer Cantel and party to do some special Restoration work in Ireland'.[139]

She remained in Ireland for much of 1904 working largely in Belfast, though she was directed at least once by Cantel to visit the branch in Londonderry. In the course of her stay she made contact with a family that were arranging to sell up and move to Zion City. There is no record of her future movements in the cause of Zion that, in any case, fell into a marked decline from 1906 onwards. The tumble in its fortunes owed much to the financial plight facing Zion City and increasing internal dissension, both of which were exacerbated by the deterioration in Dowie's health and his eventual death in 1907. How many of her Zion co-religionists then turned to Pentecostalism is the theme of the next section.

2.5.2 Zion and Pentecost

Dowie's message of divine healing and the slant of his millenarian views, both placed within the framework of a restorationist vision, made him one of the more important forefathers of Pentecostalism. David Harrell considers him 'the father of healing revivalism in America...the first man to bring national attention to divine healing in twentieth-century America'.[140] In the course of the twentieth century Dowie was to become the role model for some of the leading healing evangelists, not least in the

---

137 *LH*, 20 August 1904, p. 580.

138 Cook, *Zion City*, p. 128.

139 *LH*, 23 July 1904.

140 David E. Harrell, *All Things Are Possible: The Healing and Charismatic Revivals in Modern America*, (Bloomington, IN: Indiana University Press, 1975), p. 13.

flamboyance with which he publicised the healings under his ministry.[141] After Parham's visit to Zion in 1907, a considerable number of the community accepted the Pentecostal message and came to play a vital part in institutionalising the doctrine of divine healing as a permanent feature of the twentieth-century Pentecostal movement. Among them was Gordon Lindsay (1906-73), a leading figure of the post-war healing movement in America, who was born in Zion City where his parents had come as followers of Dowie. Parham claimed that Zion produced no fewer than 500 Pentecostal ministers and workers.[142]

Among the leaders influenced by Zion were three who feature in this study—Harry and Margaret Cantel and Marie Burgess, who married Robert Brown (1872-1948) in her parents' home in Zion City in 1909.[143] Brown was born in Enniskillen and migrated in 1898 to New York where he attended night classes and worked as a civil engineer until he was eventually ordained in the Wesleyan Methodist Church. He first met Marie in May 1907 who at the time conducted a Pentecostal storefront mission in midtown Manhattan. Won over to the Pentecostal position during a visit of Parham to Zion in 1906, she had accepted his advice and ventured into full-time ministry. They became the trailblazers of Pentecostalism in New York. Robert was to become a major figure in the American Assemblies of God. Donald Gee, who knew him well, said of his death, 'The whole Pentecostal Movement shared the bereavement. Pioneers like Robert Brown are irreplaceable'.[144] Once, when speaking of her upbringing in Zion, Marie Brown maintained, 'If it had not been for the truths of the Word of God as I learned them there, I would not be here today'.[145]

Dowie's restorationism at its best had a width of scope and grandeur unmatched by any other of his contemporaries. In Faupel's judgement, Dowie 'took the Keswick doctrine of sanctification and applied it on a cosmic scale'.[146] Unlike many others with a restorationist brief, he did not stress premillennial or dispensationalist schemes and offered 'no official

---

[141] Among the leading healing evangelists in the 1960-70s were William Branham, T.L. Osborn and Oral Roberts.

[142] See James R. Goff, *Fields White Unto Harvest: Charles F. Parham and Missionary Origins of Pentecostalism*, (Fayetteville, AR: University of Arkansas Press, 1988), p. 229.

[143] Edith L. Blumhofer, '*Pentecost in my Soul*', (Springfield, MO: Gospel Publishing House, 1989), pp. 191-217.

[144] D. Gee, *These Men I Knew*, (Nottingham: AOG Publishing House, 1980), p. 28.

[145] Edith L. Blumhofer, 'The Christian Catholic Church and the Apostolic Faith: A Study in the 1906 Pentecostal Revival', in Cecil M. Robeck, *Charismatic Experiences in History*, (Peabody, MA: Hendrickson, 1985), p. 140.

[146] Faupel, *Everlasting Gospel*, p. 134.

program of the future of an apocalyptical nature'.[147] Instead, to the consternation of some of his more perceptive followers, Dowie came increasingly to incarnate the end-time events in his own person when, in Wacker's epigram, 'he became entangled in the momentum of his own apotheosis'.[148] His millenarian vision became narrowly focused on Zion City and its mission to the world through his own strike force, the Restoration Host.

Dowie's restorationism carried within it a strong affirmation of the centrality of the charismatic element in the primitive church. At the founding of the Christian Catholic Church, he stated his purpose to make provision in Zion's church order for all the offices and gifts listed in 1 Corinthians 12 and 14.[149] In answer to a question if the gift of healing had been removed from the church, he responded:

> No, the 'Gifts of Healing' were never withdrawn, and never can be withdrawn from the true Church of God... There are nine gifts of God to the Church (enumerated in 1 Corinthians 12:8 to 11) and all these are in the Holy Ghost. Therefore as long as the Holy Ghost is in the Church, all the gifts must be there also. If they are not exercised that does not prove they do not exist, but that the faith to exercise them is lacking in God's servants. The gifts are perfectly preserved; for the Holy Spirit, not the Church, keeps them safely.[150]

However, Dowie was chary of any consideration that encouraged easy attainability of spiritual gifts throughout the whole body of the church. He hedged his teaching in this area—the gifts would only be given to those fully consecrated, as the Spirit wills, and at a pace and in a form consonant with the progressive growth in holiness and effectiveness of the church. His adage was 'that which is divine requires time to grow'.[151]

With the break-up of Zion, Parham captured part of its membership. He visited different branches of Zion taking advantage of its organisational infrastructure throughout North America and persuaded a sizeable number of Dowie's followers to accept the Pentecostal message. A similar shift took place in Britain. Polly Wigglesworth, eighteen years into her marriage to Smith Wigglesworth, was one of those baptised by Dowie in 1900.[152] Leeds and Manchester became the two most important regional centres in England. In 1913, the Leeds group invited George

---

147 Faupel, *Everlasting Gospel*, p. 127.

148 James R. Goff and Grant Wacker, *Portraits of a Generation: Early Pentecostal Leaders*, (Fayetteville, AR: University of Arkansas Press, 2002), p. 10.

149 Blumhofer, 'The Christian Catholic Church', p. 129.

150 *LH*, 1 December 1900, p. 178.

151 Blumhofer, 'The Christian Catholic Church', p. 133.

152 Jack Hywel-Davies, *The Life of Smith Wigglesworth*, (London: Hodder and Stoughton, 1987), p. 38. Polly was invited to become a Salvation Army officer without the customary training on the strength of her personal interview with General Booth.

Jeffreys to conduct meetings for them and was impressed sufficiently to form the nucleus of an Elim assembly.[153] After her husband's premature death, Margaret Cantel (1878-1926) exerted a marked influence on the young movement through the use of her newly purchased house at Highbury as a missionary guest home and meeting place.[154] It was in this setting in 1913 that Gee received his Spirit-baptism and preached his first sermon. Mrs Cantel was an accomplished speaker and attended at least one of the annual July camp meetings convened by George Jeffreys at Bangor, County Down.[155] The Zion incursion into Ireland raised the public profile of divine healing, possibly also the issue of the apostolic office, and may have eased the move of some to Pentecostalism. The Benjamin Fisher who was baptised by Herring-Cooper is almost certainly the person of the same name who played a notable part in the planting of the Apostolic Church in Ireland.[156]

For the most part most of these events were brushed off by the evangelical constituency in Ireland. Of more comfortable import to it was the inception of the Portstewart Convention in 1914 which brought directly the searching, albeit emotionally subdued, Keswick message to those in the province seeking a deeper consecration and experience of the Spirit. At the inauguration of the Portstewart convention, messages of welcome were read from the Lord Bishop of Down, the Moderator of the General Assembly and the vice-president of the Methodist Conference—all of which was a far call from the idiosyncrasies of Zion, the scuffles at Cooneyite baptismal services, the spontaneous outbursts of praise at meetings of the Welsh revivalists, the emotionally intensified atmosphere of the Faith Mission campaign and the raucous energy of urgent Belfast street preachers. To this list can be added the zeal of the Salvation Army as exemplified in the life and family of Arthur Booth-Clibborn, son-in-law of William Booth whose involvement in the early Pentecostal movement is the subject of the next chapter. It was to most of these groups that the Pentecostal movement had a closer affinity and

---

[153] Information provided by D.W. Cartwright.

[154] Margaret Cantel (née Fielden) was the daughter of one of Dowie's elders. In 1912, she moved to larger quarters at Highbury where there was a large drawing room that was large enough to hold fifty people. Gee commented that 'the presence in the home of a constant stream of missionaries and leaders passing through London ensured a rich supply of varied ministry'. (Gardiner, *Out of Zion*, p. 241.)

[155] A photograph of visitors to the Bangor camp meeting that included Margaret Cantel is found in Boulton, *Ministry of the Miraculous*, p. 60. The photograph was taken early in the second decade.

[156] *LH*, 27 January 1906, p. 400. Though the baptism took place in Barrow-in-Furness, England, that makes the conjecture all the more likely since Belfast and Barrow were major shipbuilding centres at the time with a tradition of migration of workers between the two. Fisher appears again in Ch. 8.

from them it was to draw some of its personnel. If Pentecostals were outside the camp, they were not entirely alone.

CHAPTER 3

Arthur Booth-Clibborn: Pentecostal Patriarch

3.1 His Introduction to Pentecostalism

Arthur Stanley Booth-Clibborn (1855-1939) was one of the most influential Irishmen to have an impact on the early Pentecostal movement. His story gives one of the sharpest insights into both the rigours faced and the exaltations experienced by the earliest Pentecostals. In his own person he combined the Quaker commitment to pacifism with the Salvationist search for the Holy Grail of 'entire sanctification' and the Zionist emphasis on divine healing—in all of which movements he played a leading part before taking up the Pentecostal cause in the mid-1900s. Donald Gee recalled Clibborn being present when he made his first attempt at preaching at the home of Margaret Cantel in London in 1913: 'I can remember old A.S. Booth-Clibborn beaming at me in his patriarchal way'.[1] At the Sunderland Conference in June 1911, he was described as 'a grey-haired gentleman of patriarchal appearance, with [the] leonine though kindly countenance of a veritable modern Moses. He frames his translations [of the German speakers] in beautiful language, delivered with soulful impressiveness'.[2]

According to his son, William, his father first came into contact with Pentecostalism at the home of Mrs Catherine Price who was the first person in England to receive the Pentecostal experience of speaking in tongues.[3] This event took place some six months before the arrival of T.B. Barratt in Sunderland in September 1907. During the summer of 1907 the Prices opened their home for prayer meetings that can justly be described as the first distinctly Pentecostal gatherings in the British Isles. Catherine Price and her husband, a bank manager, and three small children lived in Brixton, London, and it was at her home that a sick Booth-Clibborn, depressed over the events surrounding his dismissal from Dowie's movement, first arrived from Paris where he had been appointed

---

[1] Gee, *These Men I Knew*, p. 32

[2] *Confidence,* June 1911, p. 127.

[3] The date was the 9 January 1907. (*The Apostolic Faith*, April 1907, p.1.)

the Zion representative.[4] By 1909, Booth-Clibborn had become a recognised figure in the nascent movement. At a convention meeting in London in May 1909, he shared the platform with Boddy, Polhill and Barratt.

3.2 Early Life in Ireland

Arthur Clibborn, as then named, was born at Moate, County Westmeath, but spent his formative years in Bessbrook, County Armagh. The village was the creation of the Richardsons, a Quaker family that chose Bessbrook as the site of their new linen mill in 1845. John Grubb Richardson, a cousin of Arthur Clibborn, was an enlightened idealist who sought to form an exemplary community through the creation of a model industrial village.[5] Arthur's father, John Clibborn, was the co-founder of the linen mills at Bessbrook.[6] The Irish roots of the family lay with Colonel John Clibborn, an officer in Cromwell's army, who became an active Quaker after being impressed by the message and demeanour of the Friends whose meeting house he was called upon to raze by fire at Moate in 1657.[7]

Coming from a financially comfortable background, Arthur was sent at the age of thirteen to France and Switzerland for a private education and his formal education ended with the award of an honours degree from Lausanne University. He had a marked proficiency in languages, mastering five, and he was particularly fluent in French and German. On his return to Bessbrook, he trained for a period of six years in the family business. In the course of his training, he learnt the basic skills of spinning and weaving on the shop floor. On completing his apprenticeship, he became the manager of the spinning department where 800 people were employed with a view to taking up a senior position in due course.

Reflecting on his past, Arthur acknowledged that through 'living in Bessbrook...I had many spiritual advantages', not least because 'as a member of the Society of Friends, I was carefully and religiously brought up, [though] eighteen years of my life passed without anyone definitely speaking to me about my soul'.[8] He owed his conversion to a friend inviting him to a mission at Moyallon, near Portadown, held in the large

---

[4] Cornelis van der Laan, *Sectarian Against His Will: Gerrit Roelof Polman and the Birth of Pentecostalism in the Netherlands*, (Metuchen, NJ: Scarecrow Press, 1991), p. 65

[5] Gilbert Camblin, *The Town in Ulster*, (Belfast: Mullan & Son, 1951), pp. 99-101.

[6] Carolyn Scott, *The Heavenly Witch: The Story of the Marechale,* (London: Hamish Hamilton, 1981), p. 47.

[7] M.J. Wigham, *The Irish Quakers*, (Dublin: Historical Committee of the Religious Society of Friends, 1992), p. 23.

[8] Scott, *Heavenly Witch,* p. 50.

house where other Richardson relatives lived. A year later, in 1875, he received 'the life call of God' at the same time as 'an excellent prospect...opened up for him in the linen mill, though no clear direction came to him for another four years'.[9] During those years 'of cloudy Christian experience' he conducted meetings on board ships in dock, possibly in the nearby port of Newry, and in the surrounding villages. However, sensing increasingly a lack of fulfillment in his role as a recognised minister in the Society of Friends, he felt led to enlist in the Salvation Army for 'out and out work and, in doing so, go counter to the ideas of some older Christians'.[10]

3.3 The Salvation Army Years

The Salvation Army that Arthur Clibborn first encountered was in its phase of 'enthusiastic mobilisation', the period between 1878 and 1890 when it saw its most rapid and sustained growth.[11] A child of Holiness revivalism in Britain, the Army was to prove the most forceful of all the groups to bring the Holiness message to the province in the latter part of the century. Its coming to his area around 1881 was the catalyst to bring Clibborn's period of irresolution to an end.

> About that time I heard of the Salvation Army, and the rumours of its daring, desperate warfare and the glorious results made me feel that the mighty power of the Holy Ghost was there... I read Mrs Booth's books and longed for the full deliverance they spoke of... When one day Captain Edmonds came and held a meeting in Bessbrook, I saw and felt that he had got that something after which I was pining, and in an All-Night of prayer, with three others, he showed us how the blessing was received, and I entered by faith.[12]

A week later he took about thirty young male converts to Army Holiness meetings in Moyallon and was deeply moved as he 'looked upon the rows of officers, all dressed so simply, with faces that spoke of the deep restfulness, the peace and the power of "the life hid with Christ in God"'.[13] The impact of the occasion was such as move him to think 'Here is primitive Quakerism, primitive Methodism, primitive Christianity!'[14]

---

[9] Scott, *Heavenly Witch,* p. 51.

[10] Scott, *Heavenly Witch,* p. 52.

[11] The phrase is suggested by Roland Robertson, 'The Salvation Army: The Persistence of Sectarianism', in Wilson, *Patterns of Sectarianism,* p. 50. It was preceded by 'the incipient phase' (1865-78) and succeeded by 'the period of organisation' (c.1890-c.1930).

[12] Scott, *Heavenly Witch,* pp. 52-53.

[13] Scott, *Heavenly Witch,* p. 53.

[14] Scott, *Heavenly Witch,* p. 53.

In 1881 Arthur Clibborn made the difficult decision that changed the direction his life would take. From Captain Edmonds he learned that the Army was seeking helpers for its newly opened work in France. With his facility in the language and sense of call 'to go to work for souls upon the continent...and a conviction God would send me there ultimately', he offered his services to General Booth.[15] This apparently occurred during a visit by William Booth to the province when, in Booth-Clibborn's words, the General 'asked me to meet him, and as I knew French and German fluently, asked me to go out to the continent to take over the headquarters in Paris'.[16] From 1881 he assisted Catherine (Kate) Booth (1858-1955), the eldest and most naturally gifted daughter of her family, in consolidating the work of the Army in both France and Switzerland where she was known affectionately as 'La Maréchale' (the Field-Marshall). William Booth soon conferred on Clibborn the rank of Colonel and made him responsible for producing the first French edition of *War Cry*. Clibborn and Kate were married in 1887 and the freshly styled Booth-Clibborns continued their work that often involved them travelling apart.[17] They were a well matched couple though their relationship was not without its tensions, inherent in the fact that 'Colonel' Arthur, with 'the fierce pride of an Irish aristocrat',[18] was not the type of man to play second fiddle to his wife, 'La Maréchale' or not.[19] Both were strong-willed, single-minded and zealous soul-winners.

In a final tribute to her father, one of their daughters (Evangeline) described him as 'finely built and endowed with much physical strength... He for many years gloried in the early struggles of the Salvation Army, welcoming pain, persecution, and even physical injury,

---

[15] Scott, *Heavenly Witch*, p. 53.

[16] This is taken from a scribbled note in the *Booth-Clibborn Collection* on a certificate he was awarded for saving a man from drowning in France. The *Collection* is held by Mrs Ann Booth-Clibborn in Edinburgh whose late husband, Stanley Booth-Clibborn, was the former Bishop of Manchester and a grandson of Arthur Booth-Clibborn.

[17] General Booth insisted that his daughters on marriage retain the Booth name as part of their new name.

[18] From *Some Notes on the Life of Stanley Booth-Clibborn*, p. 2, written by himself and found in the *Booth-Clibborn Collection*. The Clibborns were more Anglo-Irish gentry than aristocracy. When Arthur joined the Salvation Army, 'he gave to the General a considerable fortune, made out of the Clibborn family's linen factories at Bessbrook' (p. 1).

[19] *Some Notes on the Life of Stanley Booth-Clibborn*, p. 2: 'We have come across many papers showing his hesitations before marriage on what his status would be, and his literalist clinging to Pauline texts on the man as the head of the woman. Catherine apparently dismissed these saying "Paul got it wrong, and when we get to heaven, I'll tell him!"'

for the furtherance of Christ's Kingdom'.[20] He was tall, handsome with a fine baritone singing voice that blended well in duets with Kate's clear soprano singing voice. He was a poet, writer, composer of hymns in French and translator of John Henry Newman into German. To his wife he was 'a mighty man of God, especially called and remarkably qualified' with all the disturbing intensity implied in that description, overwhelming in his enthusiasms and inflexible in matters of principle.[21] Physically courageous, he wore for years on his Army uniform the silver medal awarded to him by the President of France for saving while on holiday a man from drowning in the sea off Boulogne. Such was the impact of their work in France that when transferred to the Netherlands, they were welcomed by Queen Wilhelmina. Occasionally Dutch cabinet ministers were seen at their meetings.

By the mid-1890s the Salvation Army had left behind the first enthusiastic flush of its incipient phase and had entered its period of organisation when the processes of routinisation and formalisation became more evident. Kate was to say later, 'I was Territorial Commander of France, and I couldn't make a corporal a sergeant without permission from London'.[22] Routinisation, as deadening as it was inevitable, was a process that was to lead three of the Booth children out of the Army forever.[23] As early as 1891, Booth-Clibborn had written to the General requesting liberty to preach what he called the 'full, plain Gospel of the Sermon on the Mount', a plea that extended to three themes that challenged the Army's doctrinal position—pacifism, divine healing and premillennialism. The General refused the request and frustration was compounded in 1896 when the Booth-Clibborns were told to leave France, for which Kate had an abiding vision and passion, and take command in the Netherlands, a country for which she felt no particular affinity.

It was a testing time for an avowed pacifist like Booth-Clibborn to be in the Netherlands in the period between the two Anglo-South African [Boer] Wars. In 1898, conscription was introduced in the Netherlands and with rumours of war rampant Arthur took to writing on pacifist themes but was prevented from publishing anything by headquarters in London. The Booth-Clibborns' disillusionment with the Army finally reached a

---

[20] Catherine Booth-Clibborn, *A Poet of Praise: A Tribute to Arthur Booth-Clibborn*, (London: Marshall, Morgan and Scott, 1939), p. 33.

[21] Scott, *Heavenly Witch,* p. 197. This statement, addressed to her father, was written in her letter of resignation from the Salvation Army.

[22] Scott, *Heavenly Witch,* p. 198.

[23] Scott, *Heavenly Witch,* p. 179. The three were Catherine, Herbert and Ballington. The last set up the Volunteers in America in 1896. It was organised on lines similar to that of the Salvation Army. Ballington and his wife, Maud, resigned from the Army over the General's autocratic leadership.

breaking point when they ceased to dedicate the last of their ten children into the ranks. In 1900, defying the will of headquarters, they made representations to the Dutch government on behalf of pacifists in prison. His pacifism was the marker that the influence of his Quaker background ran deep. The 'Hallelujah Quaker', as he was dubbed on his first arrival in France, stuck with his vow of 1881: 'I stated that I could never forgo any of the essential truths of Quakerism, and I entered the work on that understanding'.[24]

3.4 Engagement with Dowieism

If pacifism owed much to Booth-Clibborn's Quaker background, his interest in divine healing was further stimulated by contact with John Alexander Dowie through *Leaves of Healing* and then by meeting him in London and Paris in 1900. Dowie's natural pugnacity was not curtailed during this visit. As Boddy said of him: He 'never minced matters, or watered down his language. At times it was coarsely pungent, but always commanded attention'.[25] His characterisation of the Archbishop of Canterbury as incompetent, his denunciation of the Prince of Wales' immoral life style, his own wife's taste for expensive clothes and their partiality for staying at the most expensive hotels, all combined to repel any support from evangelicals. It was, therefore, no surprise that churches refused him the facility of their baptisteries, forcing him to use public baths instead.

Observing the reception that Dowie received in London, Booth-Clibborn was challenged rather than dismayed. He, too, knew what it was to suffer sore abuse in his Salvationist work on the Continent. Anyone as passionate for pacifism and divine healing as Dowie had his respect. Earlier, in Holland, he had come to the conclusion that 'war only came into the Christian church when healing went out. Now healing comes in and war goes out'.[26] The fact that both anti-war protest and healing at the hands of Dowie were witnessed by Booth-Clibborn deepened his regard for Dowie. Shortly before, when he had met with Dowie personally in Paris, he had reservations about his mission, until '[Dowie] told me...some of his own personal experiences of the power of God, and the

[24] Scott, *Heavenly Witch,* p. 54.

[25] *Confidence*, February 1913, p. 36.

[26] *LH*, 21 June 1902, p. 289. Booth-Clibborn declared that he 'was led into the truth of the Second Coming...and the Scriptural character of Divine Healing in the Faith Home of Pastor Stockmayer' in Switzerland in 1882. (Nathaniel Wiseman: *Elizabeth Baxter*, [London: Christian Herald, 1928], p. 224.) He was on the platform when A.B. Simpson gave a famous address at the International Convention on Holiness and Divine Healing in London in 1885. The address was printed under the title of 'Himself' that by 1927 had sold over one million copies in many languages.

openings of the Kingdom of Heaven to him, and the return in his own life of apostolic powers and even apostolic manifestations'.[27] Now in London he had the opportunity to test the validity of this disclosure.

He was impressed by the fact that during the Sunday following the return of the City Imperial Volunteers from duty in the Boer War to be 'received in the streets and in St. Paul's with a frenzy of enthusiasm, the voice of John A. Dowie rang forth in the city, preaching the Everlasting Gospel. I noticed that this soldier of Christ was received in London with a passion of hatred only equaled by the passion of approval which met the soldiers of the City Imperial Volunteers'.[28] At the same time, he added:

> I noticed that a lady who had literally staggered through the streets to Dowie's hall, dying, half blind, crippled and blood poisoned through thirteen years of Bright's disease, pronounced as incurable by the best doctors had been instantaneously and perfectly healed when, after a tumultuous gathering, with thousands shouting in the streets for his blood, J.A. Dowie had laid hands on her and prayed.
>
> Instantly she felt a warm stream of life pass down her face and back. She put up her hand and found the great lump was gone from the back of her neck. She looked at her crippled finger; it was straight. She rushed down stairs full of a new life. In the omnibus, on seeing a clock in the street, she shouted, 'My eyesight is healed'. She has been in perfect health since then.[29]

It was an attack on Dowie in the *Daily Mail* that had drawn her to the meeting, for she said: 'If the world speaks so very badly of him he must be very good, and he may be a prophet of God'.[30]

Disillusioned and frustrated by the events surrounding his resignation from the Salvation Army, Booth-Clibborn found in Dowie some of the qualities of William Booth—vision, boldness, strength of character, personal charisma—and at this moment of stress, sick of heart, he was ready to follow another, though not blindly, and, time would show, not for long. It was, however, long enough to leave its mark on him and cast a blight on the ministry of his wife. One thing was certain, he was not the type to be put off by bitter opposition, having proved his mettle as a Salvationist in facing down the Nihilists in Paris on whose death list he appeared.[31] He spoke in a scribbled note in 1933 of 'having lain under

---

[27] *LH*, 26 July 1902, p. 463.

[28] *LH*, 21 June 1902, p. 289. The Volunteers were raised by the Lord Mayor of London and equipped by the City Corporation. They sailed for South Africa in January 1900 and returned in October of the same year.

[29] *LH*, 21 June 1902, p. 289.

[30] *LH*, 21 June 1902, p. 289.

[31] The Nihilists were Russian émigrés who fled to Paris. They rejected all traditional values including those of religion and the family. One of their slogans was 'What must be smashed, must be smashed'.

sentence of death from the anarchists of five continental lands for over 10 years'.[32] He had endured the hardship of jail in Geneva and expulsion by officialdom from Neuchâtel for disturbing the peace by street preaching. There was good cause for his being dubbed 'the apostle of abandonment'.[33] He said later in life of Dowie

> I looked upon [him] as a mighty man raised up. The fact that he never preached healing apart from conversion, and put the latter first, also impressed me. But I looked upon his declaration as the Elijah of Malachi, the Baptist of the Lord's Second Coming, as a woeful error and fanaticism. But [in Paris] I was deeply impressed by the spiritual experiences he related to me, and by the utter absence of any pressure or effort to win me to his cause. [34]

In November 1901, he detected a series of biblical coincidences that appeared to him to substantiate Dowie's claims and spent the next month in intense prayer and discussion with Kate about the direction of their future ministry. She had a particular distrust of Dowie and his methods, but, despite her reservations, at the end of the month he wrote to Dowie:

> I have decided to offer myself to you, dear Doctor, for Zion, and do so, firmly believing it to be the will of God, and his Great Gift to me in answer to years of prayer. I had thoughts of starting a separate Mission till I got light about the Elijah matter, as that was the great obstacle. It could only be either a gigantic error or a gigantic truth... I take it you are in the spirit and power of Elijah as the Herald of the Second Coming, the John the Baptist of the Millennial Dawn.[35]

Their resignation from the Salvation Army was announced in the *War Cry* at the end of January 1902 under the heading 'Our Loss in Holland'.[36]

In July they arrived in Zion City and stayed for four months. It was the beginning of a wretched time for Kate. Twice within the first month she defied Dowie publicly. She alone remained seated when the congregation rose to affirm Dowie as Elijah, the prophet and forerunner of Christ. When Dowie condemned William Booth for not reproving the rich, she rose and shouted that the allegation was a lie. The last sermon she was

---

[32] Hand-written note in the *Booth-Clibborn Collection.*

[33] Scott, *Heavenly Witch,* p. 47. His grandson said of him that 'he took up various causes with fanatical zeal'. (*Notes on the Life of Stanley Booth-Clibborn*, p. 1.)

[34] Scott, *Heavenly Witch,* p. 193.

[35] 'Our Loss in Holland', in *The War Cry*, 25 January 1902. This article broke the news of the Booth-Clibborns resignation from the Salvation Army.

[36] *The War Cry*, 25 January 1902. The resignation was announced in *The War Cry* by printing the letter from Bramwell Booth, Chief of the Staff, to 'our comrades and friends in Holland'. The reason for their resignation of the Booth-Clibborns was stated as their desire 'to obtain liberty to preach what they speak of as "a full Gospel" and a painful explanation of what they mean by a full Gospel is afforded by the announcement that the Commissioner has accepted the teaching of a person named Dowie'.

permitted to preach in Zion was to a congregation of 5,000 on the theme of David as a man 'after God's own heart', a riposte to Dowie's castigation of him as 'that dirty dog David'.[37] Yet, when she asked Dowie why he had not ordained her husband, he replied 'It is you I want and I will not ordain him without you'.[38] But, as she wrote to her close friend, the noted social reformer, Josephine Butler, 'I cannot give my ten beautiful children to this man'.[39] To another friend she wrote 'so much in him revolts me and violates the highest spiritual instincts I have'.[40] In a recently uncovered letter marked 'Private', written to a friend in England and addressed from Moody Bible Institute, Chicago, in 1913, she confided 'that no one has heard of the Dowie episode in the States. The Dowie community is very small and dying now and I am not going to have it published over here or in Canada'.[41] The reference seems to be to the biography of her written at the time by James Strachan, advance copies of which she had just received. Clearly, even a decade later, the whole Zion City experience still rankled.

When Strachan's biography was re-issued in 1966 there is no mention in it of the Dowie episode, only hints from her son Theodore that this period was for his mother 'a veritable *Via Dolorosa*'.[42] After spending only four months in Zion City, she prevailed upon her husband, against his will, to leave Zion City, though not the Zion movement. Arthur was appointed the Zion representative in the Netherlands. They lived in Amsterdam and Brussels for about two years and then moved to Paris for Arthur to take charge of the Zion work there in 1904. There is considerable uncertainty about their movements at this time and the exact status of Kate. Circumstances at that time were hardly propitious for her to engage in an independent ministry. Hurt by the fact that Salvation Army halls were closed to her and that her former comrades proved stiff in their dealings with both of them, she had resigned herself to never preaching again, fearing it would be interpreted as her setting up in opposition to the Army. In any case, she was hardly in a fit state, either mentally or physically, to engage in public ministry. She confided in her diary, 'depression, timidity, fear, and sadness, mark my character today'.[43]

---

[37] Scott, *Heavenly Witch,* p. 202.

[38] Van der Laan, *Sectarian Against His Will,* p. 65.

[39] Scott, *Heavenly Witch,* p. 203.

[40] Scott, *Heavenly Witch,* p. 203

[41] *Booth-Clibborn Collection*, letter is dated 1 December 1913 to Mr Callow. The words underlined are in the original.

[42] James Strachan, *The Maréchale: The Founder of the Salvation Army in France and Switzerland*, (London: James Clarke, ed. 1966), p. 201.

[43] Scott, *Heavenly Witch,* p. 205. This from one normally the most feisty of women. Her grandson described her as 'a woman of enormous practical ability and energy and

3.5 Transition from Zionism to Pentecostalism

It was during this period that Arthur, unbeknown to himself, was to make one of his most marked contributions to the Pentecostal cause in Europe. Gerrit Roelof Polman (1868-1932) began his ministry in the Dutch Salvation Army under the direction of Booth-Clibborn. Dowie's visit to Europe in 1900 had stimulated Polman to raise questions about divine healing and the Second Coming with his cadets in the Army's training school. Then the resignation of the Booth-Clibborns from the Salvation Army in January 1902 precipitated the departure of some key officers in the Netherlands, among them Polman. Two years later, through Booth-Clibborn, Polman made contact with Dowie in Zion City and stayed there until 1906 when he and his wife were sent back, as ordained messengers, to the Netherlands 'to make known the glorious Everlasting Gospel of Salvation, Healing and Holy Living'.[44] Stirred by reports of the Welsh Revival and Azusa Street, and particularly by reports of charismatic manifestations, the group formed round Polman became Pentecostal in 1907. Polman received his Spirit-baptism the following year at the first Sunderland Convention in 1908. The Polmans soon established themselves as leaders of the Dutch Pentecostal movement that from its earliest years established close links with the British movement. The first Dutch missionaries served with Polhill's Pentecostal Missionary Union. The Polmans hosted the International Pentecostal Conference in Amsterdam in 1920, the first occasion after the Great War for European leaders to meet together again. Booth-Clibborn was able on that occasion to meet again after many years his old Salvation Army protégé and former Dowieite colleague.

During their year in Paris, Arthur, dauntless as ever, preached in his usual provocative style on the streets, drawing the ire of inflamed mobs. In 1905 he was attacked with an iron bar which pierced his skin. Blood poisoning set in and the leg became gangrenous. At first, he refused medical help but was eventually saved from death by undergoing four operations. In submitting to surgery, he violated a cardinal principle of Zion and his discharge as 'Overseer Clibborn'[45] ensued when two emissaries from Chicago arrived to announce his dismissal. For the rest of his life he was crippled in his right leg and was subject to phlebitis in the same leg if he walked much and at times he needed the use of a bath

---

sheer nerve'. (*Notes on the life of Stanley Booth-Clibborn*, p. 1.) Richard Collier, writing of their Salvation Army days in Switzerland when the government forbade them to hold public meetings, commented that Kate's reaction was predictable: 'She would test the power of the decree by disobeying it'. (Quoted in van der Laan, *Sectarian against His Will*, p. 63.)

[44] Van der Laan, *Sectarian against His Will*, p. 86.

[45] Scott, *Heavenly Witch*, p. 210.

chair. He was never to be quite the same man again, more content to remain at home, writing poetry, composing over 300 hymns, playing his auto-harp and engaging in Bible study, largely in the more esoteric aspects of eschatology. His son William wrote of his father after he came to accept the Pentecostal position: 'In his studies he had come to the conclusion that God would in the last days of this age send a great revival that would restore the gifts of the Spirit in greater use in the Church, and whose main characteristics would be the Baptism in the Holy Ghost as received on the day of Pentecost'.[46] Yet, as late as 1927 Kate was to write, 'for the first time in long, long years, I notice how bravely he is ceasing to talk of the past and of the negative'.[47] The dark cloud of his disillusionment with Dowie is revealed in a letter he wrote in April 1908: 'I...see where I went astride...by joining Dr. Dowie and believing in his special mission. I was led into a labyrinth in that way which was not of God, and nearly killed by the devil, I lay in bed a year in Paris and barely escaped with my life'.[48]

When Booth-Clibborn arrived back in England in 1906 he was a sick man. He stayed first at the home of Catherine Price in Brixton and this probably afforded him the first opportunity he had to assess at first hand Pentecostal spirituality While boarding at the Prices' home, he gave a further insight into the nature of the earliest Pentecostal home meetings in Britain:

> God is doing a blessed work here in London. Seekers quietly slip in here for prayer in the evening in these consecrated Christians' sitting and drawing rooms, and some are receiving. The current here runs deep and pure and strong, the intense holy silence before Him into which He draws souls alone or together, reminds me of the days of early Quakerism, and of what one has known of the days of closest fellowship with the Crucified One.[49]

Meanwhile, Kate regained her confidence and became an independent evangelist drawing periodically on the assistance of her children as they matured. She never felt her divine vocation was revoked: 'To the masses I was sent, and my greatest blessings have come from that calling'.[50]

Kate never identified herself directly with the Pentecostal cause though occasionally she appeared with her husband on the platform at Pentecostal conventions. At a Pentecostal conference convened in January 1912 by Cecil Polhill in London, Kate, whose family had 'all received

---

[46] Van der Laan, *Sectarian against His Will*, p. 65.

[47] Scott, *Heavenly Witch,* p. 212

[48] Letter, 7 April 1908, *Cloud of Witnesses to Pentecost in India,* (No 6, 1908).

[49] Letter, 7 April 1908, *Cloud of Witnesses.*

[50] Scott, *Heavenly Witch,* p. 227.

blessing', was among those who gave 'helpful addresses'.[51] But by this stage Pohill in his inclusivist way was inviting to the platform clergymen such as E.W. Moore who 'while not "in the Movement", takes the deepest interest in every work of God, and has deep spiritual experiences'.[52] This, in all likelihood, mirrored something of the attitude of Kate herself towards the Pentecostal movement. She accepted elements of its spirituality more than its doctrinal singularities. But she could never again trust herself to any organised body. Having survived her 'years of hell', as she called the period after their resignation from the Salvation Army, years marred by the irreconcilable split with her widowed father. With the repercussions of the Dowie episode and the strain it put on their marriage as well as the trauma of a recent miscarriage, she was chary of engaging with any cause outside her own personal control. On her ninetieth birthday she confessed to her son Theo, 'I am still a Salvationist at heart'.[53]

3.6 The Pentecostal Experience in Family Life

Arthur Booth-Clibborn made a major contribution to the early Pentecostal movement by openly identifying himself with it. Of all the early leaders, he was the one with the highest public profile in British religious circles. His periods of illness meant that never again would he be the preaching force of his former days in Ireland and the Continent but, by his august and benevolent presence at public meetings and conferences, he encouraged the younger leaders and was a persuasive force in bringing a wider European dimension to the leadership of British Pentecostalism. The Booth name lent some degree of respectability to a sorely pressed movement living with the obloquy of charges of fanaticism and Satanic deception. The high profile of the name was demonstrated in press opinion at the time of his dismissal from Zion. When Arthur's salary ceased and the financial burden of ten children and doctors' bills had to be faced,[54] the satirical magazine, *John Bull,* printed a cartoon showing General Booth vigorously booting a football labelled 'Maréchale'.[55] The cartoon had the effect at least of making the General and his eldest son, Bramwell, when visiting France and anxious to avoid

---

[51] *Confidence,* February 1912, p. 37

[52] *Confidence,* February 1912, p. 37

[53] Scott, *Heavenly Witch,* p. 246

[54] Catherine wrote in a memorial tribute of her late husband that he 'never cared for money; indeed, not enough, for material burdens are very real when obligations are ever increasing. They must be carried by someone, and yet—and yet—if he was extreme on the one side, are not many of God's children extreme on the other?' In their case, she was the 'someone'. (Catherine Booth-Clibborn, *Poet of Praise*, p. viii.)

[55] Scott, *Heavenly Witch,* p. 150.

adverse publicity, pay a visit to the sorely pressed Booth-Clibborns. Such was the degree of family rupture that this was the last time Kate was to see of her father until she attended his deathbed seven years later. During the General's lying-in-state 150,000 people filed passed the coffin. On the day of the funeral offices in the City closed and 40,000 lined the streets. Queen Mary was among those who attended the funeral service.

It was through his influence on his own children and then in turn through their work in the movement that Arthur Booth-Clibborn made his most telling contribution to Pentecostal advance.[56] With Kate frequently campaigning away from home, a situation made all the more necessary by the need to provide financial support for the family, he played a major role in the parenting of the children in their teenage years. In November 1908, while preparing for exams to enter Cambridge University, William, the fifth born of their ten children, was pressed by his father to attend a weekend of meetings in London which, as it turned out, stretched till the following Wednesday. On the Saturday evening, father and son attended the small mission run by his former Zion colleagues, Harry and Margaret Cantel. The Cantels' mission, which according to William, 'looked very much like one of these small stores you see in some American towns', was his first experience of a Pentecostal meeting in a public hall.[57] The speaker that particular night was Moncur Niblock who testified that he had received his Spirit-baptism with tongues a few days before. The next evening, at a home in Plumstead with fifty people present, William received his Spirit-baptism.

> The relish and the ecstasy of that blessing have never left me, and the only sorrow was when they helped me to my feet and I realised, oh! with such pain, that I could not be with my Beloved, that I must walk this vale of tears and sorrow... Oh! I did want so to be with Jesus, I thought suffering and death would be nothing if only I could stay continually under the smile of his face forever, raptured to the throne of His Glory and never see this sinful earth any more.[58]

This experience is expressed in tones of sensuous intimacy, or in Martyn Percy's phrase 'sublimated eroticism', evocative more of a contemplative in the Catholic mystical tradition than in the gritty tone of most evangelical discourse.[59]

---

[56] Edward Booth-Clibborn said of his father: 'I am persuaded that if my dear father had not boldly taken me out of [boarding] school at this time, my experience would not have proved such an overwhelming initiation into the sphere and power of a Spirit-filled life'. (*RT*, 6 June 1929, p. 3.)

[57] *RT*, April 1929, p. 2

[58] *RT*, April 1929, p. 2

[59] Martyn Percy, *Power and the Church: Ecclesiology in an Age of Transition*, (London: Cassell, 1998), p. 141. In the mystical tradition, sexuality provided imagery for communicating the sublime nature of a spiritual climax, a task that drove writers to

It is to William as a teenager that the most intimate picture of family life in the Booth-Clibborn household is owed. He revealed the impact of the Pentecostal experience on the family in the earliest days when 'all, except one, of my brothers and sisters had received their Pentecost':[60]

> The news had spread that strange meetings were being held in our home. There was talk of countenancing spirits. You can well imagine with what consternation the report that we were speaking with tongues was received among our friends. Father stood like a rock. He refused to be moved, and if it had not been of his standing resolutely in the breach at the critical time, I do not believe we would not have been able to break through to victory in the whole family.[61]

The Booth-Clibborns must have been a puzzle to their neighbours at Westcliff-on-Sea, Essex. Their family worship sometimes continued till 2 am. Complaints from neighbours when the whole family came together for praise and worship in Pentecostal style were stemmed when Arthur fastened quilts and blankets over the doors and windows: 'Now we had a sound-proof room from which very little of the heavenly music could get through, so we sang yet more lustily and happily'.[62] William recalled the first meeting in their home after his mother returned from campaigning:

> Humbly she knelt with us, listening attentively to the heavenly choir, the speaking in tongues, and interpretations and watching us as we wept and prayed... She folded her hands, the tears were in her eyes. 'Willie', she said, 'pray with me too'... [This] revealed to me at once that she was hungry, that she wanted to share the general chrism of power that had fallen upon us all... She saw the change in me and the blessed effect in the whole home, and she pronounced this a work of the Holy Ghost.[63]

Besides William, two other of the Booth-Clibborn brothers were to identify with the Pentecostal movement: Eric (1895-1924) and Herbert became affiliated to the American Assemblies of God. Before becoming a missionary to Africa, Eric did pioneer work in Colorado. In 1924, he and his wife Lucille and baby daughter travelled as missionaries to French West Africa, the present Burkina Faso. William had warned him by prophetic revelation not to go, but Agabus-like, he overrode the warning.

---

the outer margins of metaphor. In St Teresa's words, 'one makes these comparisons because there are no [other] suitable ones'. (Filipe Fernandez-Armesto and Derek Wilson, *Reformation: Christianity and the World 1500-2000,* [London: Bantam Press, 1996], p. 51.)

[60] *RT,* June 1929, p. 3. This brother was probably Augustin who later became 'an artist and Bohemian agnostic'. (Scott, *Heavenly Witch,* p. 247.)

[61] *RT,* June 1929, p. 3.

[62] *RT,* June 1929, p. 3.

[63] *RT,* June 1929, p. 3.

Within nineteen days of their arrival he died of dysentery leaving a young widow expecting their second child, a son named Stanley, who later in life was to become Bishop of Manchester (1979-92). In 1917, Herbert published his book, *Should a Christian Fight? An Appeal to Christian Young Men of All Nations*, in which he argued that for Christians there was no alternative to pacifism. In this he was embracing his parents' anti-war stance, most notably articulated in Arthur's *Blood against Blood*.[64] His mother was equally opposed to bearing arms and one of Kate's nieces recalls her trying 'to convince us that you couldn't be a Christian—be saved as we say in the Army—if you were involved in war'.[65]

3.7 Pacifism and Pentecostals

While based in the Netherlands, Arthur, with the opportunity to read the war propaganda from both sides, wrote *Blood against Blood* as a remonstrance against the Anglo-South African [Boer] war (1899-1902). The first edition was published in the early part of the first decade of the century. The theme of the book was captured in its title. The book considers two kinds of bloodshed: one spilled by the use of weapons of warfare contrasted with the other shed in fighting for the cause of Christ with spiritual weapons. In Britain, where conscription was introduced in 1916, the book was banned and all copies were withdrawn from circulation—a reflection of the jingoistic fervour with which the war was pursued in its earlier stages. The Established Church was solidly supportive of the war. The Bishop of London called in the *Guardian* for the church to 'MOBILISE THE NATION FOR A HOLY WAR'.[66] The great majority of the 16,500 conscientious objectors were committed Christians and it was only from Free Church sources that some defence was mustered against their humiliating treatment.

The whole pacifist issue became a particularly searching one for Pentecostals in Britain and though there was no official line on conscientious objection among the various assemblies, nevertheless, in Donald Gee's words, conscription 'precipitated a personal issue of deep gravity for many young men among Pentecostal believers'.[67] While Boddy and Polhill 'manifested a strongly favourable attitude towards

---

[64] In the *Booth-Clibborn Collection* is a sworn affidavit drafted by Booth-Clibborn and witnessed by T.H. Mundell, solicitor and Honorary Secretary of the PMU. It was prepared on behalf of his son, Theodore, for consideration by a tribunal giving the reasons why Theo refused on grounds of conscience to enrol in the school cadet force.

[65] Scott, *Heavenly Witch,* p. 190.

[66] Adrian Hastings, *A History of English Christianity 1920-1990*, (London: SCM Press, 1991), p. 45.

[67] Gee, *Wind and Flame*, p. 101.

active participation in the conflict, Booth-Clibborn presented his own view in no half-hearted manner, and probably helped to influence many'.[68] The personal cost involved was commented on by Gee years later when he spoke of a young married couple who had been conscientious objectors visiting Margaret Cantel 'to seek counsel and comfort in their problems and trials'.[69] In his own case he could recollect 'the months and years of continual obloquy and petty persecution'.[70]

The pacifist issue had a longer-term effect on British Pentecostalism. The war had undoubtedly cast a shadow across the relationship between the recognised leadership and the young men who had suffered attack as 'conchies'. Polhill and Boddy were firm supporters of the war. It was not unexpected that the younger conscientious objectors began to look elsewhere for leadership and to question the wisdom of attempting to remain within denominational churches. They began to eye the advantages of being part of a recognised religious body, thereby gaining for it the civil privileges accompanying legal registration. As Allen concludes: 'Those who had felt the nakedness and exposure in the chill winds of militarism would henceforth seek to clothe themselves—albeit with some reluctance—in vestments of denominationalism'.[71]

3.8 Booth-Clibborn's Contribution to Pentecostalism

The one intriguing question surrounding Arthur Booth-Clibborn's Pentecostal attachment was whether or not he ever spoke in tongues. In *Confidence* (June 1911) it was reported that 'Mr. Booth-Clibborn said he had not yet spoken in tongues, and would not be satisfied till he did'.[72] In many of the early Pentecostal assemblies in Britain, the absence of *glossolalia* would have been taken as an indication of his not having received Spirit-baptism. This might account for his absence from the International Pentecostal Council that met in the years between 1912 and 1914.[73] The question as posed was answered by his son William in the

[68]Gee, *Wind and Flame*, pp. 101-2. Frank Bartleman was the primary chronicler of Pentecostal origins in Los Angles. Between 1912 and 1914 he visited Europe, including England, when it is almost certain he met with Booth-Clibborn. Most of his sermons 'were against the war spirit', which message, in an unfortunate turn of phrase, 'went down like a bomb in the camp' and perturbed the leader of the Conference [almost certainly Polhill]'.

[69] D. Gee, 'Snapshots of Highbury', in *RT,* 2 January 1939, p. 6.

[70] Jay Beaman, *Pentecostal Pacifism*, (Kansas: Mennonite Studies, 1989), p. 62.

[71] David Allen, 'Signs and Wonders: The Origins, Growth, Development and Significance of Assemblies of God in Great Britain and Ireland 1900-1980', (University of London, PhD thesis, 1990), p. 68.

[72] *Confidence,* June 1911, p. 128

[73] Van der Laan, *Sectarian against His Will*, p. 66.

postscript in the fourth edition of his autobiographical sketch, *The Baptism in the Holy Spirit*, where he stated, 'To the questions so often asked of me whether Father and Mother claimed this experience my answer is no. Yet all their sympathies were with the Outpouring, even from the beginning. How could it been otherwise when nine of their children had received their Pentecost'.[74] When visiting his mother shortly before her death in 1955, she remarked:

> William, I am convinced that the coming of Pentecost to our home made all the difference and it has proven so in your ministry. I have come to realize its effect for good upon Christianity everywhere. It was as a breath of God to revive true religion... Now if this Pentecostal blessing has been he means reaching uncounted millions with the gospel and if the movement's energies are turned more in that direction, it must succeed and prosper.[75]

There is no doubting the salient part Booth-Clibborn played in the early Pentecostal movement. The high public profile of his wife and the contribution of three of their sons to the wider international movement kept the Booth-Clibborn name to the fore in Pentecostal circles and beyond. His family background gave him a cachet unrivalled in the movement. In a note fitted round the certificate awarded with the life-saving medal by the President of France, he wrote that it had come through the British ambassador to the French government, Lord Dufferin. Frederick Blackwood, 1st Marquis of Dufferin and Ava (1826-1902) was one of the most distinguished diplomats of Victorian Britain whose roots lay in the family estate at Clandeboye, North Down. Booth-Clibborn, in his note, remarked, 'Lord Dufferin, by the way, knew my standing and that of my family and its various groups throughout all Ireland in some 15 centres'.[76] Above all, he was a benevolent presence at Pentecostal gatherings and a source of encouragement especially to young leaders. He had wider and more varied experience than any of the other British leaders. As he stated in the original preface of *Blood against Blood*, at the time of its publication he was 'living at the heart of things'.[77]

His pacifism influenced many young men, but not the Salvation Army which was a source of regret to him. It was his strong belief that acceptance of the pacifist and Pentecostal message by the Army would have returned it to its roots, to the time when it was a spiritual force in the nation before its growing involvement in social work. During the First

---

[74] William Booth-Clibborn, *The Baptism in the Holy Ghost: A Personal Testimony*, (Dallas, TX: Voice of Healing, 1962), p. 74.

[75] Booth-Clibborn, *The Baptism*, 74

[76] In the *Booth-Clibborn Collection*.

[77] A.S. Booth-Clibborn, *Blood against Blood*, (New York: Charles Cook, ed.1914), p. 3.

World War, he was an inspiration to the young conscientious objectors in their personal turmoil and by his advocacy of an ethic with elements of social radicalism that was a foil to the instinctive conservatism of the more acknowledged leadership. That such an ethic in expanded version did not transfer to the post-war years left the movement disengaged from the larger affairs of state and unimpressive to the many young men radicalised and disenchanted by their experience in the trenches.

Booth-Clibborn's internationalism contrasted with the essentially isolationist posture of the Pentecostal movement in the post-war period. It was he who responded for British Pentecostals to the Berlin Declaration of 1909 that issued from a conference of German evangelical Pietists and damned the Pentecostal movement as demonically infiltrated. It declared that the spirit of Pentecostalism is 'not from above but from below'.[78] The Declaration embodied a hostility towards the nascent German movement that Hollenweger holds made it 'the target of more harsh attacks than any other Pentecostal church in the world'.[79] Booth-Clibborn penned a lengthy article, published in *Confidence*, that set out to answer in broad terms the charges made against the movement. The article was written while he was visiting the Continent where he had just made contact with ten different centres which afforded him the opportunity to sound out opinion on the Declaration: 'From personal enquiry I *know* some of the signatories of that Declaration have not...examined it with the thoroughness which such a declaration required'.[80] He was the foremost among British Pentecostals to maintain a long-term involvement with the European scene. That made him familiar with events there and, in the case of the Berlin Declaration, drew from him a robust, if not entirely satisfactory, defence of the movement.[81]

There can, on the other hand, be little doubt that the Pentecostal movement did not see the best years of Booth-Clibborn. Those years belonged to his service in the Salvation Army. The culmination of circumstances surrounding the Dowie years threatened to leave him a broken man. A.E. Saxby, an early leader and fellow pacifist in the Pentecostal movement, recalled that 'when I first met him he was a scarred veteran, halting on his thigh... He was no longer the warrior in the

---

[78] Walter J. Hollenweger, *Pentecostalism: Origins and Developments Worldwide*, (Peabody, MA: Hendrickson, 1997), p. 337.

[79] Hollenweger, *Pentecostalism: Origins and Developments,* p. 337.

[80] *Confidence*, August 1910, p. 183. The word ordering in the sentence has been changed

[81] His line of defence was to make play with the charge that the Pentecostal movement was 'from below'. The following catches his drift: 'Brethren, is it not time something did come *from below,* from the dust, from the nothing; from our uttermost repentance and humiliation, from the midst of an absolute acceptance of despisal and death at the hands of the world'? (*Confidence*, August 1910, p. 184.)

sense that he was in the forefront of the battle but he was still the *man* who had made the *warrior*'.[82] One of his daughters observed that as the years passed her father 'seemed to retire more deeply into God and a very rare and lovely spiritual refinement began to take place which was felt by all who came near him. He became strangely removed from the earth, although he still followed with keen interest all the events of the day'.[83] He retreated increasingly to his study, devoting his time to arcane biblical research and writing, little of which ever entered the mainstream of Pentecostal literature.

Having weathered two authoritarian regimes, neither Booth-Clibborn parent cared to place themselves in a similar position again. Arthur could never again be cast in the role of a founder or leader and was, therefore, never able to exercise or enjoy the authority and prestige which accrue to such. He was content to state in the third edition of *Blood Against Blood* that 'the writer belongs to no particular Denomination of Christians, therefore none shares the responsibility of the views expressed'.[84] He was too focused on the single issue of anti-militarism to gain widespread popular support. He was no longer interested in exercising his personal charisma in the interests of building up a power base. As a freelance he had freedom of action but lacked the energy and desire to structure a future that would ensure the permanence of Pentecostal witness. Rather, he expressed himself strongly against any centralisation of the movement. He rejoiced that the new movement was exactly that and not 'a worldwide organisation. Every assembly is independent... Each group profits by the experiences which others have made through full and free development. Excesses and abuses are thus more easily detected and corrected... Were this revival to be organised or centralised, it would quickly go wrong, because carnal unity soon becomes a dead uniformity'.[85] The bitter experience surrounding his resignation from the Salvation Army and a certain idealisation of the Quakerism of his formative years combined to reinforce his wariness of institutional structures. Pentecostal advance had to wait the next generation of men of the stamp of George Jeffreys who felt the call to implement a revivalist strategy and thereon establish a denominational network as the foundation for future growth.

---

82 Catherine Booth-Clibborn, *A Poet of Praise*, p. 30.

83 Catherine Booth-Clibborn, *A Poet of Praise*, p. 33. The writer was his daughter Evangeline.

84 A.S. Booth-Clibborn, *Blood against Blood*, title page.

85 *Confidence*, June 1910, p. 145.

CHAPTER 4

The Pre-Denominational Phase in Irish Pentecostalism

4.1 The First Pentecostal Assembly

The Pentecostal movement in Ulster can trace its beginning to the visit Robert J. Kerr (1879-1959) and Joseph H. Gray made to Sunderland over the 1907 Christmas period. While there, they received their Spirit-baptism, as Pentecostal idiom has it, 'with signs following'. Donald Gee recorded that over the Easter 1908 period 'a few of these Irish friends visited Kilsyth, and caught the holy flame. Pentecostal meetings were soon established in the North of Ireland and a number were rejoicing in the fullness of the Spirit in 1908'.[1] Both Kerr and Gray by Easter 1908 were participants in a cottage meeting at the home of Mr and Mrs Samuel Finlay, 20 Cavour Street, off the Old Lodge Road in west Belfast. The house was not far from Landscape Terrace where Boddy had addressed a meeting on the Welsh Revival about two years previously though there is no evidence, either way, to confirm a link between the two events. Unless new evidence shows otherwise, it can be concluded that Kerr and Grey were the two who first introduced the Pentecostal message and experience to Ireland.[2]

Sam Finlay, a labourer, was one of the two from the small Belfast group to receive their Spirit-baptism when they attended the 1908 Easter Convention at Kilsyth, the other being 'Sister' Harbinson. When the small party returned from Kilsyth, Kerr informed Boddy that some more had 'received their Pentecost, [though] some have been a little frightened because of the bitter opposition from a most unexpected source. But we believe it will help to purify the work, and throw us more on the Lord... Some who were frightened from the meetings by those who were opposing, after waiting and watching were convinced that the work was

---

[1] Gee, *Wind and Flame*, p. 33.

[2] The information about the earliest days of the Pentecostal movement in Belfast is based on Bethshan *Tabernacle Belfast: Commemorative Brochure* (1972). Bethshan replaced the former Hopeton Street assembly and was destroyed by arson in 1968. It was rebuilt as part of inner-city redevelopment in 1972.

from the Lord'.[3] By May 1908 seven or eight people meeting in Cavour Street had received their Spirit-baptism. The intensity of their fellowship can be gauged by the frequency of their gatherings. In his letter Kerr continued, 'we meet every night at Brother and Sister Finlay's... Wed. nights 8 p.m. Lord's Day, 11.30 a.m., 3 and 7 p.m'.[4] This was a not uncommon schedule for many Pentecostal groups in their first flush. They felt themselves citizens of another kingdom intent of being ready for the summons home and left with no time for worldly distractions.

The next move of the Cavour Street group was to rent for a few years premises at 15 Riversdale Street. In the March 1911 issue of *Confidence*, under the title of 'Full Gospel Assembly', James N. Arnold, who was among those who had received their Spirit-baptism at Sunderland in 1907, announced a move to new premises at 7 Dover Street. He added the detail that elders and deacons had been installed, thus confirming its status as the first Pentecostal assembly in Ireland.[5] When the opportunity arose four years later to lease a house and hall, both redundant National School properties, at Hopeton Street, they took both at a rental of fourteen shillings (70p) a week. This move took place in the autumn of 1915.[6] All four premises were within a few streets of each other in the lower part of the Shankill Road.

When the hall in Dover Street was opened in 1911 the special guest for the occasion was Moncur Niblock who was quite a catch for the new fellowship in the heart of working-class west Belfast. Gee described him as a man of brilliant gifts and strong individuality who exercised a powerful influence within the movement for a short time.[7] Niblock is a good example of a Pentecostal leader who exercised an effective itinerant ministry among pioneer assemblies, helping them to assimilate into the wider movement. For such groups there was little in the way of any well-established precedent to guide them as they came to terms with new

---

3 *Confidence: Special Supplement,* May 1908, p. 3.

4 *Confidence: Special Supplement,* May 1908, p. 3. The stated meetings were probably the public meetings.

5 *Confidence*, March 1911, p. 61. The title 'Full Gospel' pointedly suggested the deficiency in other groups in their neglect of the charismatic element in doctrine and practice.

The *Belfast and Ulster Directory 1914* entry for the Dover Street premises would suggest they were shared with the Workers Union. The 1908 entry indicates the same building as occupied by Jas. Marshall, blacksmith, while 15 Riversdale Street is described as 'vacant'. It is likely that both properties were terrace houses that had fallen into disrepair and were then adapted for meeting purposes.

6 *Confidence,* November 1915, p. 214

7 Gee, *Wind and Flame*, p. 62. Niblock was principal of the PMU Bible College for Men when it was first established in London in 1909. As far as later Pentecostalism was concerned, he disappeared without trace.

doctrinal and behavioural distinctives. The Boddy era allowed free rein to roving freelance figures such as Niblock who experienced no curtailment of their personal freedom either by directives from headquarters or any requirement for financial accountability. At the same time, they fulfilled a vital role by giving a firmer sense of identity to small embryonic companies of Pentecostal believers. They ensured that the new Spirit-filled believers were made aware that they were part of a worldwide movement that fed on the expectation that the world had entered its terminal century. The report of the Dover Street opening ended on a high note: 'We are a happy band, having one desire only, the glory of Jesus and the hastening of His kingdom'.[8]

When Gee sought to portray an assembly that he considered a prototype of Pentecostal spirituality, he cited Kilsyth, near Glasgow.[9] It developed links with Belfast, acting as a kind of 'Scottish Sunderland', a place of pilgrimage where the new spirituality could be encountered at first hand. Thus, when the visitors from Belfast arrived for its 1908 Easter Conference, the Kilsyth Assembly was in the first glow of its Pentecostal initiation, making it all the more impressive as an exemplar.[10] Hutchison writes that at the Easter 1908 convention 'a number of Christians from [the north of] Ireland visited Kilsyth and on their return established a number of meetings there'—an unattributed remark which, if correct, would confirm that a number of unheard of little groups were in existence in the city at the time. In ways Kilsyth was closer to the sympathies of Ulster people than Sunderland. *The Apostolic Faith* pointed out: 'Scottish people know their Bibles. They are no fools, not carried away easily'[11]—an appraisal often made of Ulster Protestants with their close affinity to the Scottish religio-cultural tradition. In January 1910, *Confidence* published a letter from Kerr that told of a visit from Mr and Mrs Jack from Coatbridge, about ten miles from Kilsyth, who had conducted meetings in the Cavour Street fellowship.[12] Later, when the work became firmly established in Hopeton Street, Joseph Gray left Belfast to return to Kilsyth leaving Kerr in charge until the latter resigned in 1924.[13] Gray then returned from Scotland to renew his leadership role in Hopeton Street.

---

[8] *Confidence*, March 1911, p. 61.

[9] Gee, *Wind and Flame*, pp. 31-3 gives a potted history of what he called 'this fine assembly' and its 'famous outpouring of 1908'.

[10] See James Hutchison, *Weavers, Miners and the Open Book: a History of Kilsyth*, (published privately, 1986), p. 156.

[11] *The Apostolic Faith*, May 1908, p. 1

[12] It is more than likely that the Jacks visited all small, independent groups in the city.

[13] Gray had long-standing links with Kilsyth. Hutchison wrote that 'in the early years of this century a [Salvation Army] band was eventually established by such worthies as

That a three-stage Pentecostal-Holiness understanding of Spirit-baptism was accepted by the Belfast group is suggested in a letter Kerr wrote to *Confidence*.[14] Of the Jack meetings over the 1909 Christmas period, he reported:

> We enjoyed blessed fellowship together for ten days. It was a time of refreshing for us all. One brother professed *conversion*. A sister was healed of a sprained foot. Some sought and received the Lord as their *Sanctification*. A number were *baptised with the Holy Ghost* and with Fire, for which we give glory to God.[15]

This apparently anodyne report has a bearing on a major dispute, known as the 'Finished Work Controversy', that arose early in the Pentecostal movement in America over the issue of the normative stages in Christian maturation between those from the Wesleyan-Holiness tradition and those from the Reformed-Baptistic tradition. The former accepted a three-stage sequence of *conversion-sanctification-Spirit-baptism*. In other words, a clean heart was a prerequisite for receiving a baptism of power. The second group, following the Reformed view, saw sanctification as a lifelong process and, therefore, endorsed the two-stage sequence of *conversion-Spirit-baptism*. They saw the finished work of Christ on the cross as providing both for the forgiveness of sins and sanctification. Sanctification was the gradual process of appropriating the fruits of Calvary, not a second instantaneous work of grace subsequent to conversion, while Spirit-baptism was bestowed for the empowering of believers in their Christian service. When Boddy visited Los Angeles in 1912, he was dismayed that 'the Pentecostal people were just about tired of shaking fists at one another...and wonder how it came about'.[16] In America the split was to last for about thirty-five years as both sides adopted extreme positions. The controversy never reached this pitch in the British Isles. There were Pentecostals who did accept the three-stage pattern, particularly those who had a background in Wesleyan Holiness spirituality. Wigglesworth, for one, was adamant that 'there must be a purging of the old life. I never saw anyone baptised [in the Spirit] who was not clean within'.[17] However, Keswickian/Reformed/Higher Life teaching was too pervasive in British evangelicalism to allow the issue to stir dissension.

Jim Gibson and Joseph Gray, who became Corps Treasurer and Secretary, respectively, shortly after their arrival from Northern Ireland'. (Hutchison, *Weavers, Miners*, p. 147.) In the *Belfast and Ulster Directory 1916*, Gray is entered as resident at 4 Hopeton Street, the house rented with the schoolroom, and his occupation is given as 'labourer'.

[14] *Confidence*, January 1910, p. 23.

[15] See R.M. Riss, 'Finished Work Controversy', in *NIDPCM*, pp. 638-9.

[16] *The Latter Rain Evangel*, October 1912, p. 6.

[17] Hywel-Davies, *Smith Wigglesworth*, p. 60.

In a letter to Boddy, J.N. Arnold presented a rationale for the emphasis on sanctification in a statement that in an interwoven way set out the distinctive features of Pentecostal teaching:

> God is leading His dear ones right into the great preparation time for the coming of the Lord—the Bridegroom for the Bride. He is pouring out his Spirit upon all who are getting into line with Pentecost, that he may have a separate people, cleansed and purged and sanctified, ready for the translation to the marriage supper of the Lamb... I praise him for the gift of Tongues in which to adore Him in the heavenly language, and the songs of hallelujahs, as the Spirit gives me utterance. I believe every gift exercised by the New Testament Churches may be ours today, and will be ours when the Holy Spirit is recognised as supreme in the midst, and the Church humbles itself and comes back to a simple and implicit faith in the unchanging Word of God... I praise Him...that the Lord's hand is being stretched forth, and that signs and wonders are being done in the name of the holy Child Jesus.[18]

What is striking about this statement is the degree to which it accords with the core beliefs and spirituality emanating from the Azusa Street Revival. The swift standardisation of the package reflects both the pervasiveness of Pentecostal-Holiness ideas within some evangelical circles on either side of the Atlantic at the turn of the century and the ease by which they could be communicated in print and through itinerant teachers. The passage quoted above presents in a nutshell the trademark ideas that came together in a theologically coherent form at that time—a blend of Holiness emphases and premillennialist eschatology permeated by a restorationist charismaticism.[19] The teaching embraced an ecumenical vision of the church revived and equipped by the dynamic of the Spirit to usher in the soon expected Kingdom in all the graphic glory of its fulfilment. All of which bears out Faupel's contention that this eschatological anticipation remained, *par excellence*, the driving force behind the rapid growth of the movement.[20] Boddy, in his editorial leader marking the 1910 Sunderland Convention, reiterated the core theme of Pentecostal eschatology: 'We are more convinced than ever that this Pentecostal out-pouring of the Holy Spirit is at least *one*, if not the *last*, great call of God to the churches and world before the end of this age'.[21]

---

[18] *Confidence,* December 1909, p. 279.

[19] An illustration of an eschatological schema that owes much to Darbyite-Schofield dispensationalism is presented in *Confidence*, April 1914, pp. 70-1. However, Pentecostals differed in one significant point from the dispensationalist view presented in the Schofield Bible that took a cessationist view of the *charismata*. (*Confidence*, June 1910, p. 137.)

[20] See Faupel, *The Everlasting Gospel*, pp. 91-114.

[21] *Confidence*, June 1910, p. 137. Malcolm Taylor charts the premillennialist bent in British Pentecostalism as expressed in the pages of *Confidence*: 'Events such as the return of the Jews to Palestine, the outbreak of World War 1, the prevalence of natural

It was an emphasis taken from the Holiness movement and premillennial-dispensationalist fundamentalism, differing only in that, being a fuller revelation, it edged even closer the eschatological climax.

Other Christians regarded these claims as misguided and excessive, and thereby rendered them divisive. The humble origins and boisterous emotionalism of many Pentecostals opened them to the charge of fanaticism and added to the factors that led to the outright rejection of their position, enough to cause Arnold, for one, to 'stagger' at the opposition the movement faced from 'the professing Church of Jesus Christ'.[22] It is a recognition of the coherence of the new theological schema, though not necessarily its truth claims, that the original core tenets—Spirit-baptism accompanied by evidential attestation and the restoration of the panoply of spiritual gifts—have in general remained intact: the teaching of a distinct and separate work of sanctification and a premillennial eschatology have proved more disposable. The movement at the beginning of the twenty-first century could be said to differ more in style than substance from its stance at the beginning of the previous century.

4.2 Four Local Leaders: Their Background and Contribution

4.2.1 Robert J. Kerr

From what type of background did the early Pentecostal leaders in Belfast come? The short answer would point to people of solid and respectable background—certainly not the sort that would lend much weight to simplistic theories of social deprivation that set out to explain sect membership. Robert Kerr came from a farming family that worked land rented from the Dunleath estate at Ballywalter, County Down.[23] The family grave is found in the graveyard of Kircubbin Presbyterian Church. He moved to Belfast to serve his apprenticeship as a joiner at the firm of J.P. Corry in the dockland area of the city. He was soon appointed superintendent of the Sunday school at Newington Presbyterian Church.

---

disasters in the world, the upsurge of democracies, the amount of rainfall in Palestine, and even the physical measurements of the Great Pyramid [a whimsical obsession of Booth-Clibborn], were invested with apocalyptic significance and then manipulated to "prove" the imminence of the parousia'. (Malcolm J. Taylor, 'Publish and Be Blessed', [PhD thesis, Birmingham, 1994], p. 309.)

[22] *Confidence*, December 1909, p. 279. The full quotation is: 'The opposition to this great movement of the Spirit seemed to stagger me, especially when it came from the professing church of Jesus Christ... Never in my whole past Christian experience have I received more opposition and persecution than since God so graciously baptised me with the Holy Spirit... I have often been told this movement is not of God, and that I myself speak only gibberish'.

[23] Information on Robert Kerr was obtained from his second son, John Kerr, in a personal interview conducted on 23 May 1997.

When he was aged twenty-eight he first visited Sunderland in 1907 and seems to have struck up an easy relationship with the Boddys.[24] When his friend Joseph Gray returned later to Scotland, Kerr became the full-time leader of the assembly and lived for a time in the house in Hopeton Street adjacent to the rented hall. The hall was far from ideal being in a dilapidated state with few facilities but as one senior member reminisced, 'We were not interested in the building, only in the blessing'.[25]

Robert Kerr married in 1924 at the age of forty-five and this bore directly on his leaving the pastorate of Hopeton Street in the course of the same year. His fiancée, Mary E. Ferguson, came from Bangor, County Down, and was twenty years his junior. She had received an academic education that allowed her later to assist their eldest son with his Latin and French homework.[26] The Fergusons were a comfortable middle-class family and in time became prominent members of the Elim Church in Bangor. A difference of opinion over divine healing between the Ferguson parents, the twenty-year age gap between their daughter and Kerr and the uncertain financial prospects of the latter were factors in driving a wedge between them.

To support his young wife and growing family, Kerr became a partner with his brother in their building firm that specialised in the construction of quality houses. After his resignation from the leadership of the Hopeton Street assembly in 1924, he subsequently accepted honorary pastorates in a number of assemblies. With the formation of the Assemblies of God District Presbytery in 1927, he became and remained its chairman for many years. He was by temperament a man of composure, not in the least flamboyant, much given to prayer, dignified in manner and bearing and held in high esteem by his younger colleagues in the Presbytery. He was among the more formative figures in the new movement in Ulster in establishing a well-ordered assembly run on lines similar to Kilsyth.

4.2.2 Alex Ferguson

As stated, the question surrounding divine healing played a part in Alex Ferguson's difficulty in accepting the marriage of his daughter. It arose out of a disputable position on divine healing taken by some Pentecostals. Mary was the single surviving daughter of two Ferguson daughters, the first having died in childhood as a result of eating laburnum seeds. With

---

[24] John Kerr retains a personally inscribed copy of Boddy's travel book *With Christ in the Holy Land* given to his father by Boddy.

[25] *Bethshan Tabernacle Belfast: Commemorative Brochure*, 1972.

[26] Their eldest son, Edwin, was later to become a university lecturer in Mathematics and then the chief executive of the Council for National Academic Awards (CNAA), a position he held for fifteen years.

her sister's death, Mary as the only daughter of a comfortable middle-class home, carried an expectation that she would carry some domestic responsibility in the family home. Mary's marriage thwarted the triggering of this scenario. While the eldest of the Ferguson daughter's condition may not have proved amenable to medical help, it was certainly not helped by the delay in seeking it because of her father's conviction that divine healing could be claimed almost as a right for any illness through the exercise of faith.

The belief that medical assistance was the antithesis of the exercise of faith was often coupled with another—that divine healing was provided for all in the atonement. A.B. Simpson had been its leading advocate: 'Do not merely ask for it, but humbly and firmly claim healing as His covenant pledge, as your inheritance, as a purchased redemption right'.[27] It was a view that first began to receive some prominence in Irvingite circles and was further reinforced in the Dowie era.[28] Mrs Oliphant, in her life of Irving commented that 'the idea that disease itself was sin, and that no man with faith in his Lord *ought* to be overpowered by it, was one of the principles which began to be adopted by the newly-separated community'.[29] It came to be a conviction held in some Higher Life and Pentecostal circles though it was generally tempered with a note of caution by the British leadership. Boddy counseled readers of *Confidence:* 'WARNING—No one should give up the doctor or medicine unless fully convinced that the Lord not only can, but *has* healed. Giving up taking medicine, or dismissing the painstaking, skilful doctor, does not necessarily show perfect trust in Christ'[30] By some means, the more radical ideas surrounding the question of divine healing came to influence Alex Ferguson whose views on the matter proved unacceptable to his wife.

The Fergusons and Bangor played a significant role in the Pentecostal movement at this period. The very first issue of *Confidence* announced that '"Pentecost" with Signs has reached the north of Ireland, both at

---

[27] A.B. Simpson, *The Gospel of Healing*, (Camp Hill, PA: Christian Publications, ed.1992), p. 224. When Robert Tweed, in his early days as a member of the Elim Evangelistic Band, was laid aside by a tubercular hip condition, he recollected that he 'got great help on "this faith venture" from a book of divine healing by Dr. A.B. Simpson'. (*Tweed Memoir*, pp. 24-5.)

[28] Dowie in the 1890s insisted that the most dreaded disease of all was '*Bacillis lunaticus medicus*' which on the face of it seems to say more for his classical education than his common sense. (See Gordon Lindsay, *John Alexander Dowie: A Life Story of Trials, Tragedies and Triumphs*, [Dallas, TX: Christ for All Nations, ed. 1986], p. 15.)

[29] Mrs. Oliphant, *Edward Irving*, p. 373.

[30] Malcolm Taylor, 'A Historical Perspective on the Doctrine of Divine Healing', *JEPTA*, Vol. XIV, 1995, p. 59.

Belfast and Bangor'.[31] Three of the foundation members of the Elim Evangelistic Band—Margaret Streight, William Henderson and R. Ernest Darragh—all came from the town. The town became the convention and camp rendezvous for the early Elim work. From 1914 the annual camp was convened there during the holiday week in July when evangelistic outreach and services with baptisms in the sea were among the high profile events in the Elim's calendar. It was during this period the Fergusons, before their separation, entertained the young evangelists of the Band and the speakers. Many of their guests were missionaries among whom were William J. Boyd from Belfast and Alfred Lewer who set were both to work in China under the auspices of the Pentecostal Missionary Union. Others who attended the same conference included Arthur Richardson, James Salter and Alice Wigglesworth, daughter of the famous evangelist, who was later to marry Salter. The Salters were to engage in Pentecostal pioneer work in the Belgian Congo. Thomas Myerscough was also a speaker. He was the mentor of all the young male missionaries during their attendance at the PMU Bible School in Preston. Maintaining the missionary interest was another visitor, Margaret Cantel, whose Missionary Rest Home in London in Gee's words 'became one of the best known and loved addresses in the Pentecostal movement throughout the world'.[32]

Among the American visitors to the Ferguson household were Robert and Marie Brown from New York (Figure I). Robert was back to visit his native Ulster.[33] The Browns were among the first to bring the Pentecostal message to New York and were to minister there for forty years.[34] Robert's contribution to the Pentecostal movement in America was the greatest given by any native-born Ulsterman. It says much for the twenty-five year old George Jeffreys that he could have assembled from as early as 1914 such an array of people who played or were to play a key role in the global dissemination of the Pentecostal message. But then, two years earlier, Myerscough had written to T.H. Mundell, missionary secretary of the PMU: 'Jeffreys (Welsh student) has arrived a week ago and is a bright fellow and is enjoying the Bible studies. The Belfast student is expected next Wednesday'.[35]

---

[31] *Confidence,* April 1908, p. 15.

[32] Gee, *These Men I Knew*, p. 31.

[33] For Robert Brown see Ch. 2.5.2, n. 123.

[34] The Browns' work at the Glad Tidings Tabernacle established itself as the hub of Pentecostal witness in north-eastern USA. during the inter-war years. (See *NIDPCM*, p. 444.)

[35] Letter dated 21 November 1912. (Filed in the Donald Gee Pentecostal and Charismatic Research Centre, Mattersey, Nottinghamshire)

4.2.3 William J. Boyd

The 'Belfast student' was William Boyd who together with his wife Gladys worked for thirty-two years in the Yunnan province of southwest China under both the PMU banner and from 1925 with the British Assemblies of God.[36] In 1921, he was appointed superintendent of the PMU work in China. Reared in a working-class home in Belfast he, like R J. Kerr, was brought up in a Presbyterian congregation. His mother, Margaret, had been converted during the 1859 Revival at the age of twenty-four at Muckamore. She lived to see all her sizeable family converted. A tribute paid at her funeral held that her children were 'saved not through the eloquent preaching, which is to be found in Belfast so much, as through the godly and devoted life and practice of the mother in the daily Galilean life in the home'.[37] With the reputation of one who 'knew God', she was a decided influence on her son.[38]

It was at a service conducted by Dr Harry Guinness (1861-1915), eldest son of Grattan Guinness who had been a leading revivalist preacher in Ulster in 1859, that William Boyd made the decision, in his own words, 'to consecrate my life to Jesus Christ and His glorious service'.[39] He related that Guinness advised all the young converts 'to seek the fullness of the Holy Ghost...(and) other teachers came to Belfast proclaiming entire separation from the world and sanctification through the Spirit'.[40] Among such 'teachers' he would certainly have included the Torrey-Alexander team who in May 1903 conducted a series of meetings in Belfast.[41] Up to 4,000 converts were claimed for the Torry-Alexander mission. As Boyd indicated, it was conducted very much within the context of Higher Life teaching.[42]

---

[36] W.J. Boyd, 'Twenty-five Years a Missionary', *RT,* 10 April 1942, p. 4. The mission in China was closed in 1947 when the Communists seized power.

[37] *RT,* August 1928, p. 9: an obituary notice under the heading *The Late Mrs. Margaret Boyd: A Testimony from Belfast.*

[38] 'She was born in the fire, lived in the fire and died in the fire'. (*RT,* August 1928, p. 4.)

[39] *RT,* 10 April 1942, p. 4.

[40] *RT,* 10 April 1942, p. 4.

[41] For Charles Alexander it was a something of a return-to-roots visit because of the Scotch-Irish Presbyterian background of his parents. (See H.C. Kennedy and J.K. Maclean, *Charles M. Alexander: Romance of Song and Soul Winning*, [London: Marshall Brothers, c.1920].)

[42] At the welcome reception to welcome Torrey to Liverpool, Alexander taught the committee the chorus, ' O Lord, send the power just now and baptise everyone', that had such a profound effect as it was sung repeatedly that the mostly clerical company fell spontaneously upon its knees. Such an emphasis would have resonated with the young William Boyd every bit as much as it did later with Pentecostals.

William Boyd was to find in Pentecostalism the fulfilment of his Holiness-inspired yearnings. The exhortation of the visiting evangelists 'sank into my heart...for that anointing that would seal me forever as His! I was convinced from the Word of God that there was such a baptism of the Holy Spirit and Fire'.[43] He first heard of the events at Azusa Street and Sunderland in 1907:

> This blessed work was noised abroad and spread throughout the British Isles and my heart rejoiced at the news. In 1908 some of the Belfast Brethren visited Kilsyth... Those of us who could not visit these places at the time, tarried at home for the outpouring of the Holy Spirit... The Belfast brethren returned in the fullness of the blessing and when I shook hands with them, I knew immediately that they had been wonderfully blessed of God. A few nights later I received the baptism of the Holy Ghost in Brother Finlay's home. This blessed incoming was only the beginning; later it seemed as if one was submerged in a baptism of glory and fire.[44]

Exemplifying the Pentecostal understanding of Spirit-baptism as 'power for service', Boyd was emboldened to speak to his workmates in the shipyard at a regular lunchtime meeting. Though by temperament reserved, when he spoke 'the power and glory of God descended like a cloud upon me and gave me such liberty as I had never experienced in my life before. My voice rang out and was heard afar on the main road; my fellow-workmen were amazed and spellbound. The leader of the meeting said he trembled at the manifestation of the power of God'.[45]

On the Friday evening of the same week, he and a Presbyterian friend attended a meeting to hear 'a Mr. Wilson of Motherwell speaking on the baptism of the Holy Spirit'.[46] At this meeting Boyd was struck down and

> laid prostrate before Him [Christ] in adoration.... The only articulation I seemed to be able to make was 'JESUS IS THE LORD' until the close of the meeting, when the Spirit of the Lord took hold of my tongue and enabled me to preach to the unsaved at the meeting. From that moment I knew my calling—soul saving work for the Master.[47]

A Canadian woman visitor at the meeting reassured them by telling them that 'not to think that these demonstrations of His power are strange for they are happening over there in Canada'.[48] At the end of the meeting, 'I

---

[43] *RT,* 10 April 1942, p. 4.

[44] *RT,* 10 April 1942, p. 4.

[45] *RT,* 10 April 1942, p. 4.

[46] *RT,* 10 April 1942, p. 4. This was almost certainly Victor Wilson, an architect by profession, who had been present at the first Sunderland Convention and was instrumental in facilitating the first glossalalic outbreak at Kilsyth in 1908.

[47] *RT,* 10 April 1942, p. 4.

[48] *RT,* 10 April 1942, p. 4.

went up and down Sandy Row reminding people that Jesus the Saviour was also the Conqueror. At last my companions led me home, for I could have continued all night preaching JESUS to lost souls'.[49] Three and a half years later when alone in his own room 'the Lord appeared and called me to His service and even made it clear to me that He would send me to China'.[50] The next three years were spent at the PMU Bible School at Preston before sailing to China in 1915.

Boyd was typical of many young men in the first flush of the movement who felt impelled to work overseas. Indeed, Gee was of the opinion that there was a disproportionate emphasis in the early days on foreign mission work that was detrimental to the expansion of the work in the homeland.[51] One factor stimulating this trend was the fact that for many years the only Pentecostal Bible Schools existed almost exclusively for the training of missionary candidates. A wider consideration is that in the years leading up to the World War I missionary activity was in the latter stages of its expansionist phase, a chapter that was marked by the burgeoning of numerous faith mission societies, some of which had their origins in Ulster.[52] Thus there was a strong tradition within Ulster evangelicalism for committed young people, many shaped by Higher Life aspiration, to consider missionary service. That this impulse was strongly in evidence in the middle years of the first decade is backed by Edwin Orr's observation that one of the lasting effects on the Welsh Revival in Ulster was that 'it commissioned a host of candidates for the ministry and the mission field'.[53]

---

[49] *RT,* 10 April 1942, p. 4.

[50] *RT,* 10 April 1942, p. 4.

[51] Boyd and his fellow missionary colleagues in China, *pace* Gee's stricture, could barely have foreseen the day when, with the contemporary resurfacing of Christianity in China, 'the love and testimony of Christians and the power of the Holy Spirit manifested in miracles, healing and exorcism have played a part [in its resurgence]'. (Patrick Johnstone, *Operation World*, [Carlisle: OM Publishing, 1993] pp. 164-5.)

[52] Most of these movements sprang from the vision of Howard and Fanny Guinness in setting up their East London Training Institute in 1873. Their son, Harry, maintained the vision when, in 1889, he and Belfast-born John McKittrick established a work in the Congo Free State, now Zaire, that came to be known later as the Regions Beyond Missionary Union. (See Michele Guinness, *The Guinness Legend*, [London: Hodder & Stoughton, 1990], pp. 216-7.) From the same East Belfast mission hall in Island Street that McKittrick attended, Samuel Bill set out in 1887 to found the Qua Iboe Mission in south-east Nigeria, supported entirely by the members of Island Street assembly. (See Klaus Fiedler, *The Story of the Faith Missions*, [Oxford; Regnum Books, 1994] p. 217.)

[53] Orr, *The Flaming Tongue*, p. 32.

4.2.4 James N. Arnold

When the Boddys visited Belfast in June 1910, they found 'a Pentecostal party was awaiting us:—Brother Kerr, Brother Arnold, Brother Gillespie [either George or William] and Brother Grey *(sic)* with bright faces and hearty words'.[54] The couple spent the three nights of their stay at the home of the Arnolds, 'Glen Erin', Alliance Avenue. All the four men who greeted them had received their Spirit-baptism at Sunderland, Arnold in the Boddy drawing room in 1907.[55] In a letter to Boddy written two years after this event, he recounted that 'the anointing which I then received still abideth within... He laid His hand on me and took me aside with Himself, away from everyone, and taught me many precious lessons which He could not have done otherwise'.[56] He thanked Boddy for the copies of *Confidence* he had sent him which were 'so helpful and inspiring',[57] showing that the magazine was living up to its stated aim as set out in the first issue—'to be the means of grace and of mutual encouragement...to lonely ones and to scattered bands, to those who are attacked by doubt and difficulty, but longing to be loyal to the Almighty Deliverer'.[58]

Boddy provided some detail about his three days in Belfast, 21-23 June 1910. The public meetings were held in the centre of Belfast in the YMCA Minor Hall at the invitation of 'our Pentecostal friends'. Of the meetings, he reported:

> We were much encouraged by the earnestness of these dear people. At the close of the evening meetings...they came up and knelt in numbers at the front right across the hall—a solid line of seekers waiting to be dealt with and seeking the Lord's blessing... We felt that prejudice was removed and confidence established, and that Pentecostal blessing will spread in Belfast and the North of Ireland.[59]

He also added in a footnote that 'the other Centre hold their Pentecostal meetings at Frankfort Street School [in East Belfast] every Tuesday, Thursday and Saturday, at 8 p.m. and Sundays at 11.30 a.m., 3 p.m. and 7 p.m.'.[60] This information, tucked away in footnote, is a reminder that

---

[54] *Confidence*, July 1910, p. 156.

[55] *Confidence*, December 1909, p. 279.

[56] *Confidence*, December 1909, p. 279.

[57] *Confidence*, December 1909, p. 280.

[58] *Confidence*, April 1908, p. 3. Taylor submits that without *Confidence* the most likely outcome for the movement would have been that the small independent groups would have become increasingly introverted and would eventually have petered out. (Taylor, *Publish and be Blessed*, p. 343.)

[59] *Confidence*, July 1910, p. 157.

[60] The Frankfort Street meeting, assuming its continuity, was later to become one of the founder assemblies of the British Assemblies of God in 1927.

other similarly obscure groups may well have been meeting in the province in like manner, all within four years of the Azusa Street outpouring.

Evidence from the *Belfast Directory* throws some more light on Arnold. His occupation was given as 'merchant' against his address at Alliance Avenue.[61] At the time the Alliance Avenue district, sited on the western fringe of Edwardian Belfast, was part of a greenfield development of desirable, middle-class housing. The entry against his business address at 131 Donegall Street in central Belfast discloses that he ran a business trading under the name of the 'X.L. Clothing Company'.[62] His lengthy letter, written in an easy style, and printed in *Confidence* would indicate a man of some educational attainment. In it he quoted the hymn 'God moves in a mysterious way/His wonders to perform' which would point to a mainline denominational background. With this background it was not unexpected that the Arnolds acted as hosts to the Boddys during their short stay. Of the four men who greeted the Boddys, Arnold would have been the most financially secure. The other two not discussed so far were Joseph Gray and George Gillespie. The former may have worked in a linen mill at the time while the latter was a breadserver.[63]

The social distance as represented by Gillespie and Arnold is a reminder that the appeal of Pentecostal spirituality was wider than is generally appreciated. The Ferguson family travelled from Bangor to the Shankill Road to worship and it was through their attendance there that Robert Kerr first met his future wife. Alex Ferguson was described as 'of independent means' on his marriage certificate. This side of the early history of the Hopeton Street Assembly was recalled at the opening in 1972 of its successor building, Bethshan Tabernacle, when it was remarked that despite the unattractiveness of the old hall, 'the meetings attracted many fine people from all walks of life and professions'.[64]

To sum up this section, an observation of Gee is apposite. He made the point that the earliest seekers of the 'Pentecostal blessing' were experienced Christians and many of them were active workers.[65] They frequently had previous contact with Higher Life-Keswick teaching and this led them to put a premium on the place of sanctification in their personal life. Pentecostal Spirit-baptism was for many both a cause of anguished heart-searching as they grappled with the uncertainty of it all

---

[61] *The Belfast and Ulster Directory,1909.*

[62] *The Belfast and Ulster Directory*, 1909. The other occupants of the premises were an 'ice cream maker' and a 'carver and modeller'.

[63] *The Belfast and Ulster Directory*, 1909, has only one entry for a 'Joseph Grey'. The address, given as 154 Cupar Street, off the Shankill Road, though the different spelling of the surname makes identification not entirely certain.

[64] *Bethshan Tabernacle Belfast: Commemorative Brochure* (1972).

[65] Gee, *Wind and Flame*, pp. 44-5.

and, at the same time, an experience of exhilarating fulfilment, the culmination of a personal spiritual quest. In Ireland, the level-headedness of the four men considered here, connoted by their closeness to Boddy and the Sunderland Convention, curtailed many of the aberrations that tarnished the reputation of the movement in other places—witnessed not least in the decline to the point of virtual oblivion of the first British Pentecostal denomination.[66] In Wales, for instance, responsible leadership was deficient in many centres. T.M. Jeffreys, the minister of an English Congregational Church in whose study in December 1907 'Pentecost first broke out in Wales',[67] wrote two years after that event:

> In many centres deluding spirits have crept in: the gifts and manifestations have been exalted: strange doctrines and self-opinionated notions have possessed many, and sad havoc has 'the wolf' wrought among the little bands.
>
> The Welsh character lacks restraint... They need to be taught, for instance, that the wonderful emotions liberated in the soul by the Spirit of God, must needs also be controlled by the same Spirit, and not indulged in riotously to the mere gratification of the animal sense.[68]

In Ulster, the Presbyterian grounding, with its ingrained sense of reverence and emotional reserve, disposed many to be serious-minded in spiritual matters and to accept readily the Pauline injunction to 'let all things be done decently and in order'.

4.3 Spreading the Message

4.3.1 Robert and Aimee Semple

The spread of the Pentecostal message in Ireland was not entirely in the hands of locals. William Gillespie had been converted in 1907 through the preaching of an Irish American Pentecostal evangelist, William

---

[66] Malcolm Hathaway in telling the story of the leader of this denomination, the Apostolic Faith Church (see Ch. 8), concluded: 'The rise and fall of William Oliver Hutchinson and the Apostolic Faith Church is a cautionary tale of what happens when a Charismatic Movement abandons the Reformation principle of *Sola Scriptura* and the universal creeds of the Christian Church. It is a tale that must be told'. (Malcolm R. Hathaway, 'The Role of William Oliver Hutchinson and the Apostolic Faith Church in the formation of British Pentecostal Churches', *JEPTA*, Vol. XVI, 1996, p. 56.)

[67] *Confidence*, April 1908, p. 14.

[68] *Confidence: Special Supplement,* April 1909, p. 1. In chairing the Cardiff Conference, the first of its kind for Welsh Pentecostals, Jeffreys 'lovingly but firmly denounced the ecstasies of the flesh which some were indulging in, and also to silence one or two brothers, who were giving vent to vehement ejaculations of Tongues, manifestly not of God'.

Anderson.[69] But, undoubtedly, the most colourful Pentecostal visitors were Robert Semple and his young wife, Aimee, who in 1910 were on their way from America to China as missionaries (Figure II). The Semple parents ran the general store in Magherafelt, County Tyrone, where 'everything from boots and shoes to granite dippers and outing flannel for baby garments was sold'.[70] They were a Presbyterian family and Robert was a singular young man in the fervency of his devotion.[71] His mother, meeting her daughter-in-law for the first time, showed her the loft in the barn where he 'would always be out...crying to God to use him'.[72] Their first stop was Ireland to allow Robert, after twelve years, to meet his family and to introduce his young wife, now pregnant, to them.

In her autobiography, *The Story of My Life*, Aimee recollected:

> While in the north of Ireland, Robert was asked to preach in Belfast. The meeting was a glorious success, and the altars of the great hall were crowded. We received an invitation from the Lord Mayor to visit him in the City Hall and were presented with the key to the city. I was awed with his pompous robes, golden chains, and gleaming medals. Robert stood very straight and tall among the crowd that had gathered on the marble steps for the ceremony.[73]

According to Blumhofer, 'between forty and fifty received the baptism of the Holy Spirit...and the little assembly [in Belfast] warmly welcomed the visitors'.[74] Aimee's recollection is, to say the least, implausible. The high honour of freeman status of receiving the symbolic key of the city is not given to obscure, impecunious evangelists, with the wife barely out of her teens. The only person to be made a freeman of the Belfast in 1910 was

---

[69] Desmond W. Cartwright, *The Great Evangelists: The Lives of George and Stephen Jeffreys*, (Basingstoke: Marshall Pickering, 1986), p. 39.

[70] Aimee Semple McPherson, *The Story of My Life,* (Waco, TX: Word Books, ed.1971), p. 42.

[71] Robert Semple (1881-1910) emigrated to America at the age of seventeen. He found work in a department store in Chicago. While working there he first came in contact with Pentecostalism probably at the Baptist mission on North Avenue pastored by William H. Durham (1873-1912). It was there that he received his Spirit-baptism. By late 1907, Semple, proving an eloquent speaker, launched out into an evangelistic ministry that often took him into Canada. There he met Aimee Elizabeth Kennedy who was converted under his ministry. They were married in 1908 in a ceremony conducted by a Salvation Army officer. In January 1909 Durham ordained Semple, seeing in him a young man who carried the 'anointing' which in Pentecostal circles was the *sine qua non* for ministry. Italians in the mission provided the initial backing, supplemented by offerings from Canadian supporters raised at the valedictory services they attended before embarking for Europe.

[72] McPherson, *The Story of My Life,* p. 43.

[73] McPherson, *The Story of My Life,* p. 44.

[74] Edith L. Blumhofer, *Aimee Semple McPherson: Everybody's Sister,* (Grand Rapids, MI: Eerdmans, 1993), p. 87. No source is given for this statement.

Andrew Carnegie, the seventy-five year old American industrialist and philanthropist. She may have confused this incident with a Lord Mayoral reception when she returned for a brief visit to Belfast in 1926 at the invitation of George Jeffreys. Press photographs show an impressive array of councillors and aldermen as part of the reception party, but by that stage Robert had been dead sixteen years (see Photograph F). As she told the story it enhanced his standing and endeared her memory of him and that is conceivably the subliminal motivation of her recollection. Blumhofer recognised Aimee's 'proclivity for investing stories with symbolism and drama and for transforming ordinary events into watersheds'.[75]

At the end of their stay in Ireland, the Semples travelled to London and there met Cecil Polhill.[76] During their stay Robert conducted services for his host and Aimee had her first experience of addressing a public meeting when Polhill surprised her by suggesting that she should bring the message at the meeting that night.[77] On leaving London, they reached China in June 1910 but within weeks of their arrival Robert died of malaria on 19 August 1910. Their daughter, Roberta, called after her father, was born a month later. Aimee returned to New York and in 1911 married Harold McPherson but retained her first husband's name in choosing to be known as Aimee Semple McPherson.[78]

By 1926, Aimee had achieved star rating on the Pentecostal stage. She was a colourful and controversial figure, in Wacker's phrase, 'a Pentecostal barnstormer'.[79] She was the most extraordinary woman leader

---

[75] Blumhofer, *Aimee Semple McPherson*, p. 83.

[76] The newly-weds stayed for a week at Polhill's elegant London home, long enough to bedazzle the young, incurably romantic Aimee. She was captivated by trappings of wealth. Among those she met were the butler ('elegantly uniformed with an impressive John Bull tummy'), a gold-braided doorman, maids, a chauffeur to drive her and Polhill's personal secretary to show her around London. All this was in a setting of only dreamed-of elegance: 'such gorgeous furniture and such a massive four-poster I had never seen before'. (Blumhofer, *Aimee Semple McPherson*, p. 45.)

[77] McPherson, *The Story of My Life,* p. 47. A tremulous Aimee was faced by an audience of 15,000 (her estimate) which packed the Royal Albert Hall (maximum capacity 9,000). C.M. Robeck wryly observed that it was not like Aimee to underestimate anything. When her showpiece Angelus Temple in Los Angeles was built, it was the Royal Albert Hall that provided the blueprint.

[78] She became a national figure when her Angelus Temple, Los Angeles, with seating for 5,300, opened in 1923 and reached celebrity status in 1926 when she claimed, in still unresolved circumstances, to have been kidnapped for a period of over a month. This incident occurred a month after she had visited both London and Belfast at the invitation of George Jeffreys and the Elim Alliance.

[79] Grant Wacker, 'Searching for Eden with a Satellite Dish', in Richard T. Hughes, (ed.), *The Primitive Church in the Modern World,* (Urbana, IL: University of Illinois Press, 1995), p. 147.

the movement produced in the whole of the twentieth century.[80] In the making of Aimee Semple McPherson, her first husband played a key role as defined by Blumhofer:

> Robert awakened her emotions, defined her spirituality, and took her off the farm and around the world, all before she was twenty years old... Robert Semple's shadow loomed over the rest of Aimee's life: he—and what he stood for—never really left her, or perhaps she opted not to let go of him. He was the only man whose influence she acknowledged in her recitation of her life story... Everything within her had vibrated in response to Robert.[81]

In life and death it was the young Ulsterman, together with her mother who proved the most formative influences on one of the most flamboyant and intriguing evangelists of the twentieth century and plausibly the greatest woman evangelist of the twentieth century.[82] He was the dominant partner in their short marriage and introduced her to the Pentecostal experience.[83] In an interview she gave during a weekend visit to her in-laws at Magherafelt, County Londonderry, in November 1928, she stated that 'her conversion and all her success were due to the influence of her first husband' and that the 5,300-seater Angelus Temple at Los Angeles was erected to his memory, as was another church in the course of erection in Hong Kong.[84] Gee's overall assessment of her ministry is fair: 'She needs putting against her own proper background of the city she made her home—the city of Los Angeles and the dramatic'.[85] Epstein

---

[80] 'She became, in the 1920s and 1930s, such a celebrity that the press publicly thanked her for having given work to so many journalists'. (Daniel Mark Epstein, *Sister Aimee: The Life of Aimee Semple McPherson*, [NewYork: Harcourt Brace, 1993], cover blurb.)

[81] Blumhofer, *Aimee Semple McPherson,* pp. 92-3.

[82] Minnie Kennedy was a Salvationist and one of the early so-called 'Hallelujah Lasses' who 'used the broad gestures and dramatic effects of popular commercial entertainment to dramatise their spiritual vision'. (Pamela J. Walker, 'A Chaste and Fervid Eloquence: Catherine Booth and the Ministry of Women in the Salvation Army', in Beverly Mayne Kienzle and Pamela J. Walker, eds, *Women Preachers and Prophets through Two Millennia of Christianity*, [Berkeley, CA: University of California Press, 1998], p. 297.) Minnie 'firmly believed Aimee was the reincarnation of Catherine Booth (mother of Kate Booth-Clibborn), destined to be a great evangelist'. (Walker, 'A Chaste and Fervid Eloquence', p. 299.)

[83] The foyer of her home beside the Angelus Temple was bathed in light from a window on a winding staircase. The window carried a family coat of arms which she designed herself. On the upper left quadrant was a harp, representing all the young Ulsterman meant to her as a spiritual mentor and husband. It can only be a matter for speculation as to whether or not she would have achieved so much fame, opponents would say notoriety, if Robert had not died at the age of twenty-nine.

[84] *Belfast Telegraph*, 6 November 1928.

[85] Gee, *Wind and Flame*, p. 120.

observed that Aimee 'brought to Los Angeles her own brand of fantasy... She would prove no less inventive than Zukor and Lasky, and as energetic as Goldwyn and Fox—and these giants of the cinema admired her'.[86] Charlie Chaplin advised her on her stage sets at the Angelus Temple and Anthony Quinn played the saxophone in the pit.

4.3.2 Jacob Nathan

Documentary material from the first decade relating to other, if less glittering, visitors to Ireland is absent with the exception of a piece printed in *Confidence* in September 1910. Under the heading 'A Hebrew Christian at Belfast' was printed a letter from Jacob Nathan sent from Ilford, Essex.[87] Some background information about him was provided. He had received his Spirit-baptism at Sunderland in 1907 and visited Boddy's church whenever business duties, which involved his travelling throughout Britain, permitted. His story was added to in a London daily that reported on the Sunderland conference: 'A Jew, he spoke of an aching heart, breaking in exile. He said he came to the meetings for enlightenment, and just when the light seemed to be at hand darkness settled on his soul, and all but smothered it in despair. His was a story that roused the men and women who listened to a frenzy of enthusiasm'.

His work had brought him to Belfast in July 1909 and one Saturday evening, while listening at an open-air meeting, he stated that two young men 'came directly to me and straightway began to talk. They were Protestants. Was I one?'[88] The young men invited him to the mission hall in the Holiness tradition situated in Campbell Street that lay in the warren of streets between the Shankill Road and the Old Lodge Road. On the following Thursday he was given the chance to speak and 'with heart and soul I gave them the Story of Sunderland and its Pentecostal Blessings'.[89] Describing an after meeting held the following Sunday, he recounted:

> The Holy Spirit pressed upon us. Numbers gave themselves up fully to the service of God. Two young men promised to give up smoking, and asked for full sanctification. I found myself kneeling by these two brothers, and when I would pray the power of the Gifts of Tongues fell upon me. These young men shook and trembled under the power of the Spirit and were filled, their faces shone with glory. I met them day after day, and they told me the same tale—a flow of energy, a desire, a burning to work for Christ: a peace, a knowledge that God had taken them unto

---

[86] Epstein, *Sister Aimee*, p. 252.

[87] *Confidence*, September 1910, p. 219.

[88] In the oft-rehearsed Belfast joke if he had answered that he was a Jew the inevitable riposte would have been, 'Yes, but are you a Protestant Jew or a Catholic Jew?'

[89] *Confidence*, September 1910, p. 220.

> Himself. *These brothers each gained converts to Christ during* the last week I remained in Belfast.[90]

During his final meeting on the third Sunday the typical pattern of emotional ebb-and-flow imposed itself on the evening. Voices raised in praise were succeeded by 'a great spirit of awe [falling] upon us all, and we remained silent before God. Then hymn after hymn arose, and one knew of a surety that at last the work was all of God, and this little flock were ripe for the Pentecost'.[91]

For a people 'ripe for Pentecost' it was only fitting that after the meeting 'we marched the streets through the slums of the town'.[92] Such intense zeal to reach the outsider comes through in the few accounts of early Pentecostal witness in Ulster. J.N. Arnold, the most venturesome and confident of the local leaders, in a letter published in *Confidence* in May 1913, revealed something of the sheer energy he continued to put into the cause without any apparent backing. It was sufficient to him to know that divine leading entailed divine enabling: 'The Lord has led me to open a large hall one night in the week [Thursday]... I have also started an open-air Meeting every Sunday night at 8.15 on one of our best public squares. Hundreds stand until the end. I give full Pentecostal testimony, and the Lord is present in giving great help and blessing'.[93]

The pattern of diffusion of the early Pentecostal movement in Ireland was paralleled in most other places. As Blumhofer noted those who accepted the Pentecostal logic about Spirit-baptism sometimes embraced the idea, became ardent in their desire to have it, and even proclaimed it earnestly before they themselves had received the evidential sign of tongues.[94] Those who did so receive felt an even stronger urge to proclaim the message. Although in its first phase the movement attracted those evangelicals drawn to a 'deeper life' experience, it would soon attract new converts like Jacob Nathan. The movement extended through networks of people who often knew each other, as well as through the energy of countless lay people who felt the impulse to witness and engage in evangelistic outreach. In this way interrelationships emerged that gave an informal unity to the movement marked on the surface more by the diversity of its adherents in terms of class, culture and church background than by any natural affinity.

---

[90] *Confidence,* September 1910, p. 220.

[91] *Confidence,* September 1910, p. 220.

[92] *Confidence,* September 1910, p. 220.

[93] *Confidence*, May 1913, p. 100.

[94] Moncur Niblock and Arthur Booth-Clibborn were cases in point.

4.4 Preparing for Advance

A sense of belonging is a critical element in the commitment of members of new movements. But equally, visible growth and a salient collective identity are important, otherwise the sense of mission and destiny begin to fade and morale wavers. The need to mobilise resources—whether financial, social or spiritual—to achieve a sense of legitimacy calls for a deliberate, more formalised structuration. In short, initial wonderment and personal empowerment are not enough to sustain a movement. The succeeding stage is critical. Little did James Arnold realise that the seeds of that stage were being sown in Ireland when he wrote a letter to *Confidence* in 1913. It carried information that had considerable implications for the Pentecostal movement in Ireland and beyond. In the letter he stated, 'I was asked to go to Monaghan, where a band of earnest seekers were tarrying, and the Lord graciously baptised four, and witnessed through two other dear souls that they had previously received the Baptism. It was a time never to be forgotten. The glory of the Lord filled the place'.[95]

There can be little doubt that among the 'band of earnest seekers' were numbered the young men who were to invite George Jeffreys to conduct a mission in Monaghan town a few months later in July 1913. That event was the beginning of Jeffreys' personal engagement with Ireland and marked Monaghan as the birthplace of the Elim movement. When Arnold and William Gillespie attended the 1913 Sunderland Convention it was the first opportunity they had to hear and be impressed by the young Welsh evangelist. After the Conference Gillespie wrote to Jeffreys and invited him to his home in Pine Street, Belfast, for a break and enclosed thirty shillings for his fare.

Jeffreys was to prove the major force in giving shape and direction to the movement in Ireland in its next stage. He took the movement from the early days of little assemblies that grew up around the personality of some individual leader(s) with the limit of their evangelistic zeal confined to open air preaching and a devotion to missionary work. Such impassioned Christians in their small and intimate meetings, while rejoicing in the release of an expressive spirituality were, in Gee's words, often inclined 'to suffer from an unhealthy selfishness and smallness of outlook... A handful of kindred spirits could make a happy little company to enjoy fellowship among themselves; but it scarcely seemed to be realised that there was a complete lack of ministry sufficiently powerful to attract and move the masses outside. There was a genuine desire to do so, and much prayer and zeal, but little else'.[96]

---

[95] *Confidence*, May 1913, p. 100.

[96] Gee, *Wind and Flame*, pp. 89, 63.

Jeffreys was to radically change that and it was in Ireland that he did much to hone his skills as an evangelist and Pentecostal leader that would bring both him and his message to the wider British public and then to the wider world.

CHAPTER 5

George Jeffreys: Background and Role

5.1 George Jeffreys: Profile

In 1935, Rom Landau, a *littérateur* of Polish extraction, produced a curious book that gave short pen-pictures of some 'modern mystics, masters and teachers'. The book, *God is My Adventure*, proved a bestseller and was reissued at the height of the war in 1943, an occasion that gives a measure of its appeal at that critical time. The later edition made reference to the reasons why readers took an initial interest in the first edition: 'Many other people, disillusioned by the churches, were only too willing to delve into the ways and methods of unorthodox schools of thought'.[1] Landau saw his subjects as spiritual pathfinders with the potential to introduce spiritualities or ideologies capable of catching what Adrian Hastings termed 'the central tide of English thought and culture in the 1930s', a flow he visualised as advancing in one general direction—'from irreligion to religion, from liberal and modernist religion to neo-orthodoxy, and from Protestantism towards Catholicism'.[2]

Landau had on his list of spiritual gurus just one Briton, George Jeffreys.[3] Landau's interest in Jeffreys was aroused by the billboards displayed throughout London inviting passers-by to meetings in the Royal Albert Hall on Easter Monday, 1934. Having previously attended emotionally intense services at Harlem, New York, that left him feeling rather disconcerted, Landau reluctantly succumbed to his curiosity to witness at first hand 'a religious movement powerful enough for its supporters to hire the Royal Albert Hall year after year'.[4] Contrary to the

---

[1] Rom Landau, *God Is My Adventure,* (London: Faber and Faber, ed.1943), p. 7.

[2] Adrian Hastings, *A History of English Christianity 1920-1990*, (London: SCM Press, ed.1991), p. 289.

[3] Among other individuals featured in the book were: Krishnamurti (1895-1986), Indian theosophist and acclaimed 'Messiah' in 1925 by fellow theosophist Annie Besant; Rudolph Steiner (1861-1925), Austrian social philosopher and educationist; Frank Buchman (1878-1961), American founder of the 'Moral Rearmament'movement as it was known from 1938 onwards .

[4] Landau, *God Is My Adventure,* p. 119. The annual meetings ran in the Royal Albert Hall from 1926 to 1939.

nature of his research into the other ideologues, he recognised that this visit was to an event 'that seemed organised for people with very little critical faculty'.[5]

When Landau arrived at the venue on the Monday morning he was surrounded by 'a jumble of taxis, bath chairs and even ambulances in the street outside. In the crowd there were people on crutches, men and women with deformed limbs or with bandaged heads or eyes, mothers with sick children in their arms'.[6] The 10,000 people who filled the huge arena had come primarily to listen to one slightly built man in his mid-forties. When Jeffreys mounted the platform, Landau recorded:

> I saw through my opera glasses a strong face with a rather soft mouth, dark curly hair and a fine presence in which there was nothing calculated to play upon the emotions. He possessed none of the characteristics that I had expected of a revivalist movement. Had I not seen Mrs Aimee McPherson...preaching in this very hall, and equipped with all the tricks of an ingenious stage technique? Smiles, golden curls, searchlights and trumpets crowded my recollections.[7]

> The moment Jeffreys began to speak the impression of impersonality disappeared... The voice was strong;...it was baritone, and full of the melody which we are accustomed to find in a Welsh voice... I did not doubt that the strong and sincere tone of the voice of Jeffreys was responsible for much of the veneration which his followers held him... The whole philosophy of Jeffreys was neither emotional nor intellectual—it was just biblical... It seemed that the Scriptures had become the very life blood of George Jeffreys.[8]

John Carter, who as a young man worked under Jeffreys in Ireland saw him in action often and drew a similar picture: 'What a striking figure he was! Those fine features, their clear whiteness accentuated by a shock of curly black hair, deep velvety brown eyes, slim, graceful figure, expressively musical voice, arresting gestures, intensely serious delivery, and, above all, an anointed ministry; all combined to draw the multitudes'.[9] Hollenweger is equally affirmative of both Jeffreys brothers: '[They] possessed extraordinary natural talents, such as the Pentecostal movement, in Europe at least, has scarcely ever produced since. These talents did not consist of "American gimmicky". By simple, powerful and logically structured addresses they captured the minds and hearts of audiences thousands strong'.[10]

---

[5] Landau, *God Is My Adventure,* p. 119.

[6] Landau, *God Is My Adventure,* p. 120.

[7] Landau, *God Is My Adventure,* p. 122.

[8] Landau, *God Is My Adventure,* pp. 122, 123, 124.

[9] 'George Jeffreys: An Apostle of God', *RT*, 16 February 1962, p. 3.

[10] Walter J. Hollenweger, *The Pentecostals,* (London: SCM Press, 1972], p. 199.

Landau concluded his chapter with this assessment of the impact of Jeffreys' handling of a healing service in one of London's smaller public halls:

> It seemed as though the presence of God really filled the hall. And there was nothing miraculous in it... What Jeffreys did [for the people there] was to compress their consciousness of God, to vitalise it, to force it into a concentration that was more powerful than any state they were able to achieve by themselves. Jeffreys forced their God to emerge from the shadows of their longings, and manifest himself to their conscious feelings. He made Him their living God.[11]

5.2 The Making of a Pentecostal Leader

George Jeffreys (1889-1962), the eighth child of a miner, Thomas Jeffreys and his wife Kezia, born and reared in Nantyffylon, Maesteg, South Wales, was born into a large, respectable but impoverished family. His mother was the daughter of a Baptist minister, though the family belonged to the Welsh Congregational Church. Like many miners at the time, his father, Thomas, died from a lung disease when George was six years old. The deprivations of their upbringing played a part in the fact that only three of the sons lived beyond their thirties. The three favoured with relative longevity—Stephen (1876-1943), George (d. 1962) and William (d. 1945)—all became preachers. Stephen became an outstanding evangelist, though of a different stamp from George, being extrovert and passionate where George was reserved and self-contained.[12] George had many devotees but no real confidants with the exception of William Henderson, whose death in 1931 at the age of fifty-two left him

---

[11] Landau, *God Is My Adventure*, p. 139. Landau's portrait of Jeffreys is all the more valuable because of the external observer status of the writer who brought to his task the refinement of a cultured intellect. His was an outsider's view which captured in print some of the spellbinding attraction of Jeffreys at the height of his powers in the 1930s, a assignment now made the more necessary to counterbalance the doctoral study by Hudson that carries a fuller, more critical evaluation of the evangelist. (Neil Hudson, 'A Schism and its Aftermath: A Historical Analysis of Denominational Discerption in the Elim Church, 1939-1940', (PhD thesis, London, 1999). In Andrew Walker's view, Jeffreys turned out to be 'probably Britain's most successful evangelist and healer of the twentieth century'. (Andrew Walker, *Restoring The Kingdom: The Radical Christianity of the House Church Movement*, [Guildford: Eagle, ed.1998], p. 262.) As a rider to this assessment, Walker added that Evan Roberts may be able to claim greater success as an evangelist, but he was no healer.

[12] E.C.W. Boulton said of Stephen that 'there was something almost vehement and volcanic in his personality and preaching. The truth poured forth in a torrential stream which swept all before it'. (Edward Jeffreys: *Stephen Jeffreys: The Beloved Evangelist*, [Luton: Redemption Tidings Bookroom, 1946], p. 67.)

bereft of the one colleague on whose counsel he most relied.[13] He never married but had an easy rapport with children who were drawn to him by his gentle manner.[14] His most dutiful colleague who acted as his long-time pianist, chauffeur and secretary, Albert Edsor (1909-99), told Landau that 'people worship [George] because they feel the divine presence in him; and yet he is as simple as though he were no one in particular'.[15]

George and Stephen were converted during the Welsh Revival in November 1904. George was fifteen years old at the time and worked in the local Co-operative Store as an errand boy. With his frail frame and health, his mother was determined that he would not go down the mine where the more robust Stephen worked. Both brothers were converted under the preaching of their own minister, Glasnant Jones, whom George described as loveable and indefatigable. Jones was to him the father he never knew. The minister recalled that the young George was always at his side in the open-air revival services: 'I was privileged to give him his early religious tuition and a splendid scholar he was. Superior to the other lads, there was character in his face: I knew he was a "chosen vessel"'.[16]

Pentecostalism came to the Welsh valleys through the visit of Moncur Niblock to the English Congregational Church in the Ebbw Vale district. The minister of the church, the Rev. T.M. Jeffreys (no relation) and some of his members came into the experience in December 1907. By Easter 1909, there had been sufficient growth for T.M. Jeffrey's to convene a conference in Cardiff. Around 150 representatives were in attendance, representing the many little centres in Wales that had experienced a personal Pentecost. One of the noticeable features of the movement at the time was the number of children who received their Spirit-baptism with accompanying tongues. Among them was Edward Jeffreys, the ten-year-old son of Stephen and nephew of George, who entered the Pentecostal experience when on holiday.[17] The Rev. T.E. Hackett stated that both

---

[13] In a tribute to his late colleague, Jeffreys wrote: 'Whenever I was called upon to face a crisis, to go through an ordeal, or contend with a difficulty, I waited, whenever possible, upon Henderson first; for I knew the value of his strong advice, the certainty of his unbiased opinion, and the power of his fervent prayers'. (*EE*, 26 January 1934, p. 58.)

[14] In a letter to the Wilkinsons in Monaghan, who hosted him in his first evangelistic meetings in Ireland in 1915, he wrote: 'I am sure of one thing that I shall miss very much, the sweet and happy company of the darling children, and whenever Monaghan will come before my mind's eye, I will most certainly think of "Gra-am's pig". The way in which dear little Reg[g]ie pronounced that will never leave my memory'. (Mattersey archives.)

[15] Landau, *God Is My Adventure*, p. 132.

[16] Boulton, *A Ministry of the Miraculous*, p. 11.

[17] Edward recounted in his biography of his father that, on returning home, one of the leaders who convened the holiday meetings called to explain to his parents what had

Stephen and George were at first deeply opposed to the new movement but like many other 'Children of the Revival',[18] feeling their lack of spiritual power, the two brothers with young Edward present prayed passionately:

> 'Lord, baptise us with the Holy Ghost', when to their utter astonishment, [Edward] began to speak in tongues of manifestly 'divers kinds', and followed at great length in Welsh with a wonderful and quite unwonted use of Scripture. A few days later...George found himself one Sunday morning singing in tongues though, but a short time before, he had publicly preached against it as from below. They confessed they were wrong, and solemnly asked the Lord to forgive and make them more careful as to His Word.[19]

This event seems to have taken place in 1910 in the old Duffryn Congregational Chapel, up-valley from Maesteg, the mining village where a former Baptist minister, W.G. Hill, had started Pentecostal meetings. In Jeffreys own testimony written for the Christmas edition of the *Elim Evangel* in 1929, he wrote of the 'the thrill of the baptism of the Holy Ghost...received according to Acts 2 in the old Duffryn Chapel building'.[20]

Despite the explicit nature of Hackett's account, an air of mystery hangs over Jeffreys' Spirit-baptism. Malcolm Hathaway takes the view that Jeffreys probably received his Spirit-baptism during a visit to Bournemouth.[21] This town was the home of the first Pentecostal *denomination* in Britain, the Apostolic Faith Church (AFC). The church grew out of a work established there by William Oliver Hutchinson (1864-1928).[22] Having been stirred by a visit to Wales at the height of the

---

happened and 'this made my father and mother, also an uncle of mine, think seriously concerning this wonderful blessing'. (Edward Jeffreys in *Bethel Messenger,* December 1931, quoted in Hudson, 'A Schism and its Aftermath', n. 178.)

[18] This was the name given to those converts of the Welsh Revival who sought to preserve their fervency, often by meeting for prayer in cottage meetings, some of which became the nuclei of new churches.

[19] *Confidence*, April-June 1918, pp. 19-20. Hackett was reporting on Pentecostal meetings in Belfast conducted by George in 1918. This Irish clergyman's background is related later in this chapter.

[20] *EE,* 25 December 1929, p. 529.

[21] Hathaway, 'Role of William Oliver Hutchinson', p. 52.

[22] Hutchinson was a former sergeant in the Grenadier Guards who joined the army at the age of nineteen. He was invalided out as a result of injuries sustained during the Boer War. On discharge he found employment in Bournemouth. with the NSPPC (National Society for the Prevention of Cruelty to Children). From a Primitive Methodist background, Hutchinson served for a short time as a Methodist lay preacher until he came to embrace adult baptism, at which point he joined the local Baptist church. He became attracted to the Holiness message through a visit of Holiness leader, Reader Harris, and his

Revival, Hutchinson launched out on an independent ministry. In 1908, he responded to an invitation to attend the first Sunderland Conference and there received his Spirit-baptism. On his return to Bournemouth, he opened the first purpose-built Pentecostal church in Britain in November 1908 in the Winton district of the town. In January 1910, he launched the magazine *Showers of Blessing* which he edited for the rest of his life. By 1911, the magazine, distributed free, consisted entirely of original material written by contributors from a network of churches that looked to him for leadership. *Showers of Blessing* in 1914 listed fourteen assemblies that formed a loosely-knit fellowship of which eleven were in Wales, seven in England and four in Scotland. In 1911 the fellowship adopted the name Apostolic Faith Church (AFC).

In 1910, James Brooke, a city missionary with the Brethren who prior to that had served as pastor of a Baptist church in Winton, changed his allegiance to the AFC. He was directed by Hutchinson to accept the pastorate of Belle Vue Chapel, Swansea, which by that time had become one of the churches within the Winton network. George Jeffreys was a regular attender at the Saturday evening services at Swansea and it was there through Brooke that he made his first contact with Hutchinson. In August 1910, Jeffreys wrote Hutchinson a letter, later published in *Showers of Blessing*, that is difficult to reconcile with other views as to the timing of his personal Pentecost:

> Since I have been at Bournemouth, 'All things have become new—Old things have passed away'. Hallelujah! I have been saved, sanctified, baptised in the Holy Ghost (with the scriptural sign of tongues) and healed of sickness. This is the Lord's doing and Marvellous in our eyes... I have the gift of 'tongues and interpretation' but the latter gift must still be developed... Now comes my testing time. I am going home to Wales, and this is but the beginning of a mighty battle.[23]

Hathaway argues that these events probably took place at Winton, making it a singularly formative influence on him, while Cartwright, following Hackett, contends that they took place prior to his visit there. On the face of it, this is but a quibble, but Hathaway's construal, supported by Hudson, carries significant undertones that reveal something about Jeffreys and his part in shaping the future direction of mainstream British Pentecostalism.[24] Hathaway argues that Jeffreys later in his career removed all traces of his involvement with Hutchinson as he saw the need to distance himself and the Elim movement from the

---

Pentecostal League to Bournemouth and entered there into the experience of a 'clean heart' before God.

[23] Quoted in Hathaway, 'Role of William Oliver Hutchinson', p. 52.

[24] Hudson sees Hathaway's interpretation as the most natural way of reading the above letter.

growing heterodoxy of the AFC and the personality cult that began to develop around Hutchinson.[25] Within the AFC new teachings began to be promulgated that increasingly sidelined core evangelical beliefs, the substance of them often coming through prophecy. Most of the 'revelations' were expressed in opaque language but, behind the ambiguity, there was a seemingly unstoppable drift towards placing Hutchinson on a transcendental pedestal.

The progressive drift into heterodoxy within the AFC, if it had caught on, had all the making of a Dowie-type *denouement* that would have reduced the early Pentecostal movement in Britain to the status of a bizarre, ephemeral cult. Like Dowie's Zion movement, when the end came, the AFC collapsed dramatically, though not completely, releasing many of its remaining adherents to form the secessionist United Apostolic Faith Church in 1926. However, by that stage many key members had left it. Two were to become leading figures in the Elim movement, E.C.W. Boulton, the first biographer of George Jeffreys, and W.G. Hathaway who became its Field Superintendent. Neither of these two men ever made public reference to their former involvement with the AFC. Hathaway, made wary by his experiences, warned of 'Montanist extremes', cautioned that 'in this dispensation God does not give new revelation beyond that contained in the Written Word'.[26]

Jeffreys' links with Bournemouth had ceased long before the questionable trends surfaced. In fact, at the time of Jeffreys' Spirit-baptism, the AFC was regarded as a model of decorum. Thomas Myerscough, for one, was a regular visitor to the yearly convention held over the August Bank Holiday weekend. There is clear evidence that George Jeffreys was first ordained in 1912 in a church with AFC sympathies. Some detail of this ordination is preserved in an extant copy of the Certificate of Ordination issued for the occasion which recorded that he was 'first ordained on 13th November [1912] to the regular work of the Christian ministry by the independent Apostolic Church known as Emanuel *(sic)* Christ Church in the town of Maesteg'.[27] The ordination may well have involved Hutchinson and/or other AFC ministers but as a step it never featured in his life story, such was his urge to screen his past

[25] Malcolm R. Hathaway, 'The Elim Pentecostal Church: Origins, Development and Distinctives', in Keith Warrington, ed., *Pentecostal Perspectives*, (Carlisle: Paternoster Press, 1998), p. 10.

[26] Hathaway, 'Role of William Oliver Hutchinson', p. 54. The quotation is taken by Malcolm Hathaway from his grandfather's book, W.G. Hathaway, *Spiritual Gifts in the Church,* (London: Elim Publishing, 1933), p. 61.

[27] Desmond W. Cartwright, 'Some Evangelists: The Life and Ministry of George Jeffreys and P.S. Brewster in the Formation of the Elim Pentecostal Church', (MA dissertation, Sheffield), p. 11.

association with the AFC. Jeffreys was to seek ordination again five years later in Belfast.

Though Ireland has not featured so far in the story of the AFC, there is some evidence that at least one assembly was part of the Winton network. At the start of the War, Hutchinson told readers in *Showers of Blessing* about the congregation in Belfast which he indicated was standing true to doctrine and unity in spite of Pastor Hardie being called up for war service.[28] The next report of Hardie was that he had appeared on his local church platform in the uniform of a Seaforth Highlander and had achieved the rank of Corporal, an indication that as a former soldier, Hutchinson, unlike the pacifist wing of the Pentecostal movement, held little truck with conscientious objectors.[29] Hardie's name next appeared in a report of special meetings in Belfast in 1916. He had been discharged from the army on account of blindness. Sightless, he continued to minister for three Sundays. Then, in a meeting, a prophetic word was given that commanded him to read the Bible. He stood up and in attempting to read found his eyesight restored. At the same meeting two elders and a deacon were called and anointed to office.[30]

In November 1912, Jeffreys enrolled at the PMU Missionary Training School at Preston under the tutelage of Myerscough. Any links with the Apostolic Faith churches were quickly dropped. With the cold shouldering of the AFC by the rest of the movement from 1915 onwards, Jeffreys could not afford to expose himself or Elim to guilt by past association. As Hudson observes, he 'was very conscious of the vulnerability of his public image and the need to be constantly aware of the possibility of attack..If that entailed him obscuring his own past, then he was willing to do so'.[31] In a letter as late as 28 September 1928, sixteen years after his first ordination, he instructed E.J. Phillips, the secretary-general of Elim, 'not refer to [it] to anyone. I have purposely kept it out of my book... Be sure and deal with the ordination question so as to keep me clear before the public'.[32]

From his early childhood Jeffreys carried a consciousness that he was 'called to preach the Gospel... There was no other purpose in life for me

---

[28] James E. Worsfold, *The Origins of the Apostolic Church in Great Britain*, (Wellington: Julian Literature Trust, 1991), p. 122.

[29] Worsfold, *The Origins of the Apostolic Church,* p. 127.

[30] Worsfold, *The Origins of the Apostolic Church,* p. 143. It is possible that Hardie later represented the independent assembly in Dromore at the meeting held in September 1927 to consider the formation of a presbytery of the Assemblies of God in Belfast and District. The relevant line reads, 'Brothers Hardie, Mulligan, Weir from Dromore Assembly'. (*Minutes of the AOG Belfast and District*, 21 September 1927.)

[31] Hudson, 'A Schism and its Aftermath', n. 189.

[32] Letter Jeffreys to Phillips, 28 September 1928, quoted in Hudson, 'A Schism and its Aftermath', n. 315.

if I could not preach'.[33] However, he had to face a seemingly intractable barrier that threatened to thwart his calling. He suffered since birth from a facial paralysis as well as a speech impediment. He later spoke of his complete healing one Sunday morning at 'exactly nine o'clock' while praying with Stephen's family:[34] 'I received such an inflow of Divine life that I can only liken the experience to being charged with electricity... From that day I have never had the least symptoms of the old trouble'.[35] The healing was for him the outward confirmation of his call and provided for him 'a witness within to the faithfulness of God's word'.[36] As he saw it, if his calling was to be an evangelist, then he would be a healing evangelist with a passionate conviction born out of his own deliverance: 'The difficulty with opposers to this truth [divine healing] is that they consult people about these experiences who have never known them'.[37]

Jeffreys also faced the problem of finding denominational recognition if he was ever to fulfil his call. Some of his personal turmoil is captured in his later musings when, writing of himself in the third person, he described the problems he had to face in considering a future in the ministry:

> I have seen the young Jeffreys grappling with the seeming insuperable difficulties that lay in the way of his cherished hope to enter the regular ministry... The responsibility of the old home is now upon your shoulders, and you cannot be a true minister of the Gospel and not provide for your dear old mother. On the other hand, if you cut out some of these controversial subjects, such as the Baptism of the Holy Ghost and Divine Healing, it will be an easy matter for you to enter the ministry, for the door is already open, and the financial needs for yourself and home are assured.[38]

His growing identification with the Pentecostals and his very public act of undergoing baptism by full immersion in the local river in April 1911 made the conventional denominational training that would have given him financial assurance an increasingly remote eventuality. This may have lain behind his decision to apply for entry to the PMU Training School. It was made possible by Cecil Polhill who, ever on the lookout for promising candidates, on a visit to South Wales met Jeffreys and urged him to leave the Co-op. store and provided the financial backing for him to do so.[39] A note in *Confidence* reported that Jeffreys had been accepted

---

[33] George Jeffreys, *Healing Rays*, (Worthing: H.E. Walter, ed.1985), pp. 56-7.

[34] Jeffreys, *Healing Rays*, p. 57.

[35] Jeffreys, *Healing Rays*, p. 57.

[36] Landau, *God Is My Adventure,* p. 134.

[37] Jeffreys, *Healing Rays*, p. 58.

[38] *EE*, 25 December 1929, pp. 529-30.

[39] Hocken, 'Cecil Polhill', p. 124.

at Preston 'as a candidate for foreign service'.[40] It turned out that he was not to stay at Preston more than a few months, if even that, because in response to a call for help from his brother Stephen he returned to Wales. Stephen had been conducting a mission at Cwmtwrch in the Swansea Valley but as the mission lengthened to seven weeks, he found himself stretched and began to run out of both stamina and sermons. He needed help immediately and his brother was the obvious choice.

This mission was to have a profound effect on the direction of the brothers' lives. It brought them to the notice of the wider evangelical constituency. The *Life of Faith*, the mouthpiece of the Keswick Convention, in its 5 February 1913 issue ran an article under the heading 'WALES IN THE DAWN OF REVIVAL' which printed a selection from different sources of first-hand reports of the meetings. Mention of *glossolalia* and specific healings were included and the success of the meetings held the prospect for one writer that 'in a week or two, possibly, Stephen Jeffreys will be considered another Evan Roberts'.[41] A correspondent writing to Boddy described the form of the meetings which suggested they were much in the mould of the 1904-05 Revival: 'The meetings are left perfectly free and open, and the Holy Spirit just seems to bear us along—prayers, singing and speaking all interspersed... We all do as we are moved and yet there is no confusion, no extravagance'.[42]

The publicity given to the missions held early in 1913 began to lend recognition of the two Jeffreys brothers at national level. It led to numerous requests for them to conduct missions throughout Britain and lifted them from the parochialism of the Welsh valleys onto the wider national stage. After 1913, Jeffreys rarely preached again in Wales and began to conduct missions in a variety of geographical and denominational settings. Among them were missions at Emmanuel Baptist Church, Plymouth, Croydon Holiness Hall, the Welsh Wesleyan Methodist Church, City Road, London, with the concluding meetings held in Arundel Square Congregational Church. While in London he stayed at 'Maranatha', the missionary guesthouse run by Margaret Cantel. The constant demands of conducting missions meant that George had to absent himself from the PMU School, which was a matter of some

---

[40] *Confidence,* October 1912, p. 237.

[41] *Confidence*, February 1913, p. 28.

[42] *Confidence*, February 1913, p. 28. A writer in the *Life of Faith* considered that 'the fervour of the meetings is as great as 1904... Sometimes several will be testifying and praying at the same time, and then one more fervent still will keep on'. (*Confidence*, February 1913, p. 29.) The writer was John Owen Jenkins, a Quaker magistrate and gentleman farmer. So impressed was he by what he observed at Cwmtwrch that he invited the brothers to conduct a mission in the Friends Mission House in the heart of rural Radnorshire.

concern to the Council. It was recorded in the Minute Book that it would be 'very desirable for him to return to Preston...and it was resolved that Mr Polhill see G. Jeffreys hereon'.[43] There is no clear indication that George ever studied at the School again. He was, in effect, an autodidact in biblical and theological matters, a circumstance that probably contributed to the assurance and conviction that marked his preaching and his tenacity in matters of principle and private judgement.[44] He was not schooled to engage in scholarly equivocation.

The *Life of Faith* articles led to the initial contact between Jeffreys and Alexander Boddy. Elated by the reports from South Wales, Boddy set out in February 1913 to visit the next mission conducted by the Jeffreys brothers at Penybont, a remote hamlet near Llandrindod Wells, Radnorshire. He arrived unannounced at the evening meeting and introduced himself for the first time to the brothers. The next day he had a 'long heart-to-heart talk'with them and learned that 150 people had been converted at their previous mission at Cwmtwrch and about forty had received their Spirit-baptism.[45] Boddy intimated: 'They feel that the Lord needs evangelists in Pentecostal work today. There are many teachers and would-be teachers, but few evangelists. The Lord is giving an answer through this Revival to the criticism that the Pentecostal people are not interested in Evangelistic work, and only seek to have good times'.[46] At the evening service Edith Carr gave testimony to her healing, the first of the many noteworthy miracles that marked the ministries of the two brothers.[47] In the next issue of *Confidence,* George related that as an outcome of the Ponybont mission, 'ministers are now earnestly seeking the Baptism of the Holy Ghost'.[48] Before leaving them, Boddy issued the brothers an invitation to attend the next Sunderland Conference.

5.3 The Influence of Jeffreys' Background on his Future Ministry

The concern of this section turns to assessing the extent to which his future ministry was foreshadowed in these early days. The suggestion is

---

[43] *Confidence*, February 1913, p. 16.

[44] A.W. Edsor told Landau that Jeffreys 'only reads books on religious subjects. Practically only the Bible, which he studies constantly. He is not interested in the theatre, art, politics. At least I have never heard him talk about them in the six years that I have been with him. His spiritual mission occupies all his attention, all his thoughts'. (Landau, *God Is My Adventure,* pp. 135-6.)

[45] *Confidence*, March 1913, p. 48.

[46] *Confidence*, March 1913, p. 48.

[47] She had been lame with a diseased bone in her foot and, after prayer, was able to walk with scarcely any help. The mission with its healing emphasis attracted great interest in the district, both lay and clerical.

[48] *Confidence*, April 1913, p. 78.

that at least three facets of his ministry were prefigured in the period before he arrived in Ireland where his efforts in the years 1915-23 launched the Pentecostal movement into its first truly expansionist stage in the province and laid the foundation of the Elim Church.

First, it is clear that before he came to Ireland his calling as an evangelist was firmly established and it was one that was to be pursued with Pentecostal conviction. Bryan Wilson's contention that the Pentecostalism of Elim 'was not evident in its revival activity' is overstated, conclusively as far as Jeffreys was concerned.[49] A typical report of a mission that he conducted at Coulsdon, Croydon, in late 1914 in his pre-Elim days informed readers of *Confidence* that 'souls were *saved*, *backsliders reclaimed*, and many *baptised* in the *Holy Ghost* with *Bible signs*'.[50] When Elim became established, few were left in doubt about the Pentecostal pedigree of his message, certainly not any stray visitors who may have attended the newly opened Elim Church in Lurgan in May 1923. The *Elim Evangel* reported that 'at the close of every meeting, souls were led to Christ, and many were healed and baptised in the Holy Ghost with signs following'.[51]

A second feature of Jeffreys' ministry was his preference for working in collaboration with others. It started in the first place with his brother Stephen who at the beginning was the dominant partner. Boddy painted for readers of *Confidence* a word-picture of the two brothers at ease with each other at Penybont: 'Stephen and George...are sitting by the fire, reading their bibles, or *Confidence* and other papers, or meditating and praying'.[52] Within a short time of his arrival in Ireland Jeffreys started to

---

[49] Bryan R. Wilson, *Sects and Society: The Sociology of Three Religious Groups in Britain*, (London: Heinemann, 1961), p. 35.

[50] *Confidence*, December 1914, p. 233. Italics in the original. Pastor Inchcomb of the local Holiness Mission submitted the report.

[51] *EE*, September 1921, p. 55. In the days of his mature ministry, he often referred to the 'Foursquare gospel' in which Christ is proclaimed as Saviour, Healer, Baptiser [in the Spirit] and Coming King. This 'Foursquare' *leitmotif* was first coined by A.B. Simpson in 1890 to convey the distinctives of his Christian and Missionary Alliance. Elim followed the precedent set by Aimee Semple McPherson in incorporating the motto in the name of the Angelus Temple—the 'International Church of the Foursquare Gospel'—except that she had replaced Simpson's reference to 'Sanctifier' with 'Baptiser [in the Holy Spirit]'.

[52] *Confidence*, April 1913, p. 48. Such cosiness was not to last. From 1925 onwards the relationship between the two brothers became frosty, though at his brother's funeral, George spoke of 'our heart to heart talks during latter years'. (Edsor, *'Set Your House In Order'*, p. 144.) In the biography of his father, Edward Jeffreys rued the loss of the dream of the two brothers accomplishing in the twentieth century 'what John and Charles Wesley did in the 18th century'. (Edward Jeffreys: *Stephen Jeffreys*, p. 37.) Yet, in the same work, no mention is made of his uncle playing any part in the Cwmtwrch and Penybont missions. George was virtually written out in the book, possibly in an attempt to redress the perceived imbalance of esteem in which the two brothers were held, and

build up a team of young men and women to form the Elim Evangelistic Band (EEB), from among whom were to be drawn his closest colleagues and travelling companions in the Revival Party once he began to engage in mass evangelism. It was a feature of his ministry that was to persist throughout his active years. He may have been reserved by temperament but he was not a loner. He evoked strong loyalty from his colleagues in the Revival Party, some of whom were to remain, like himself, lifelong bachelors.[53] Those who did marry usually left the Revival Party.

As befitted a Welshman and 'a child of the Revival', music was to play a major role in Jeffreys' evangelism. It also made it necessary to engage others to assist him in this aspect of his itinerant evangelism. Singing was a major feature in his services with R.E. Darragh acting as song leader.[54] Like all the members of the party, Darragh carried a variety of other responsibilities within the group. A.W. Edsor joined the Revival Party as pianist/organist in 1928 and acted in that capacity for thirty-four years, succeeding Fred Bell who, like Darragh, came from Bangor, County Down. Bell was one of the young men who left the Revival Party after his marriage and subsequently emigrated to America. It was Darragh and Edsor who were responsible for the music at the meetings at the Crystal Palace which Landau attended in 1934 as part of the congregation of 20,000. He commented: 'The singing was an outstanding feature of all the meetings... They sang the glory of God and they no doubt believed every word of their hymns; but they also shouted at the top of their voices, revelling in the physical enjoyment of "letting themselves go". This primitive form of self-realisation is an important factor in mass movements'.[55] The Revival Party were not the first revivalists to act upon

more to favour his father. Edward in the 1930s became an Anglican clergyman disillusioned by what he saw as Pentecostal excesses. (See Randall, *Evangelical Experiences*, p. 220.)

[53] Such is the current climate of suspicion and innuendo that a sentence like this, as regrettable as it is inevitable, raises the question of Jeffreys' sexual orientation. Walker is adamant that 'despite occasional whiffs of scandal surrounding his sexuality, there is not the slightest historical evidence that Jeffreys was a homosexual... [N]o charismatic leader escapes the rumour machine'. (Andrew Walker, *Restoring the Kingdom: The Radical Christianity of the House Church Movement,* [Guildford: Eagle, 1998], p. 251.)

[54] At the mission at Cwmtwrch, the *Life of Faith* report noted that the two brothers were 'good singers, and there is a good deal of singing in the meetings'. (*Confidence,* February 1913, p. 29.) The brothers followed the example of the major Higher Life evangelists who pioneered the use in their services of music that was characterised by simple lyrics and melodies that could be memorised in two or three singings. In the Welsh Revival many of the individual numbers sung were from this same source and the manner in which the same songs were routinely repeated over and over again persisted in Pentecostal meetings.

[55] Landau, *God Is My Adventure,* p. 128

the maxim that a singing audience is less bored and critical than a subdued one.

The third characteristic of Jeffreys' ministry that was basically resolved in his own mind before his arrival in Ireland related to the nature and ethos of his ministry. It revolved round the question as to what kind of evangelist he sought to be. Noel Brooks, a ministerial colleague who stood by him at the time of the split within Elim, observed:

> One cannot be long in [Jeffreys'] company, whether privately or in the great public meetings,...without realising that he is indebted to the Welsh Revival not merely for his conversion but also for this dominating vision and passion for religious revival. The scenes which his boyish eyes witnessed have ever burned within his memory as a pattern towards which he must work... He burned to make an impact upon the Christless masses. The new discovery of Apostolic gifts was already wedded within him to the older flaming vision of mass revival which he had inherited from Evan Roberts.[56]

Hudson agrees with this assessment and adds that indeed some of the seeds of the split that forced Jeffreys out of Elim in 1940 can be traced back to the Welsh Revival in that his success as a revivalist could not be matched by those Elim pastors who had to cope in more humdrum settings where the fear of failure was a recurrent concern. He is clear that this contrast was a factor that stored up future troubles: 'He actively encouraged this distinction... This led to a distancing between Jeffreys and the body of ministers which was exacerbated when Jeffreys suggested changes in church government procedures [after 1934]'.[57]

As was described earlier, the meetings at Cwmtwrch manifested a high degree of spontaneity and overt emotion, reminiscent of the 1904 Revival. A report in the *Life of Faith* suggested that 'the fervour of the meetings is as great as 1904'.[58] It could hardly be otherwise. It is Hudson's contention that Jeffreys' 'experience of revival was that it had spectacular effects upon all who encountered it; his experience of church life was dominated by a stress on spontaneity and lack of clerical control'.[59] In a letter to Boddy, outlining his programme in London in March 1913, Jeffreys referred back to a meeting at Penybont at which 'the people were sobbing and crying aloud'.[60] Yet, by the end of the letter, a note of caution can be detected in his praying that 'God may call out a people to lead in all wisdom, and to avoid extravagance in this

---

[56] Noel Brooks, *Fight for the Faith and Freedom*, (London: Pattern Bookroom, 1948), pp. 22, 25.

[57] Hudson, 'A Schism and its Aftermath', p. 62.

[58] *Confidence*, February 1913, p. 78.

[59] Hudson, 'A Schism and its Aftermath', p. 47.

[60] *Confidence*, April 1913, p. 78.

wonderful outpouring of God'.[61] Even at this early stage, a note of wariness about emotional overreaction was being aired just when he was becoming increasingly confident that he was the answer to his own prayer. By the time he arrived in Ireland he was clearly disposed to present the Pentecostal message within an ordered and restrained framework. Edsor, who observed Jeffreys over many years, remarked 'although he did spectacular things, he was never flamboyant, upholding the dignity of his calling as a minister. In his public preaching he never attempted "to play to the gallery", but pressed home his messages with authority and power. He exercised remarkable control over meetings'.[62]

Even with their limited experience of evangelism in 1913, the Jeffreys' brothers were mindful that individual localities reacted differently in their response to the message. The Welsh Revival was not the sole model of revival and the mission in Ponybont carried its own lessons. It was in an English-speaking district in the Welsh Marches and, as Boddy gingerly expressed it, in rural Radnorshire 'there was not the abandonment of South Wales'.[63] The fact that the Penybont mission was held in a Quaker meeting-house, led by a well respected magistrate, may also have contributed to the sense of constraint. If Jeffreys' policy was to be one of order and restraint, then it was not because emotion was dismissed but more that it was not to run to self-indulgence and reach levels where it became vacuous and unseemly. In the first statement of doctrine that Jeffreys wrote, the fourth article was worded, 'we can expect the onslaught of the enemy to be furious, in his seeking to counterfeit and to produce extravagances, which we must be careful to avoid, by continuing steadfastly in God's precious word'.[64] In the section dealing with church discipline, the justification for the rules laid down for members is stated as 'not to bring saints into bondage, but to preserve order'.[65] In later years the masthead of the *Elim Evangel* carried the watchword, Elim 'condemns extravagance and fanaticism in every shape and form. It promulgates the old-time gospel in old-time power'.[66] Jeffreys, in the course of employing an extended nautical metaphor, concluded that church history taught the lesson that 'the once powerful spiritual liner [of

---

[61] *Confidence*, April 1913, p. 78.

[62] Albert W. Edsor, '*Set Your House In Order': God's Call to George Jeffreys as the Founder of the Elim Pentecostal Movement*, (Chichester: New Wine Press, 1989), pp. 42-3.

[63] *Confidence*, March 1913, p. 48.

[64] The doctrinal statement was titled *What We Believe* and was drawn up by Jeffreys in 1916 at the request of the oversight of the first Elim assembly, Hunter Street, Belfast.

[65] *What We Believe*, p. 7.

[66] See, for example, *EE*, 25 December 1929, p. 547.

revival can] become a wreck upon the rocks of excrescences and extravagance and the end means disaster to all'.[67]

Jeffreys' approach from the beginning of giving priority to evangelism reaching a mass audience conjunctive with an emotionally controlled Pentecostalism was one that commended him to those Ulster audiences that were well accustomed to incisive gospelling and yet were temperamentally wary of fanaticism.[68] Thus, a key objective for Jeffreys throughout his ministry was the ever-pressing need to establish the credibility of the Elim movement. He maintained this in a number of ways, two of which are exemplified here from events that belong more in his mature years. They were, nevertheless, clearly adumbrated in his stay in Ireland as will be shown when the part played by John Leech and the Rev. Thomas Hackett in the Pentecostal movement is considered.

In the first place, Elim invited outside its own ranks only those speakers who held some appeal to the broader evangelical constituency. Among them were Hugh Redwood, author of *God in the Slums* and distinguished Fleet Street journalist, who testified at one of the Easter Monday meetings, and Gladys Aylward (1902-70). In the post-war period, Jeffreys urged Martyn Lloyd-Jones, unsuccessfully as it turned out, to share a meeting at the Royal Albert Hall which he believed they 'would fill to capacity'. [69] Aimee Semple McPherson was another of the few 'outsiders' engaged to preach at Elim's big events. In 1926, she shortened her visit to the Holy Land to stay in London for four days to speak at the Easter Convention in the Royal Albert Hall. Even so, when she visited London again, the media attention she attracted caused Elim considerable discomfiture. In Hathaway's opinion, the relationship with McPherson 'undoubtedly emboldened Jeffreys for the more dramatic occasions. However, the media love for her more sensational style caused Elim embarrassment when she visited again'.[70]

---

[67] George Jeffreys, *Pentecostal Rays: The Baptism and Gifts of the Holy Spirit*, (Worthing: Henry E. Walter, ed.1954), p. 148. Is it a coincidence that the nouns 'excrescences' and 'extravagance' were used in Boddy's article on the history of Pentecostalism in the British Isles in *Confidence* August 1910, p. 196?

[68] William Arthur (1819-1901, b. County Antrim) was a Methodist leader, the author of *The Tongue of Fire* (1856) which had great influence in Holiness-Pentecostal circles when it was republished in America in 1891. When he visited his native province at the start of the 1859 Revival he expressed the puzzlement of many when highly dramatic and emotional manifestations erupted among a normally staid people: 'What occurred could not have found a people less likely to welcome anything boisterous, or forms of worship less likely to fan wildfire, than among the "Cold Presbyterians", as they were so often called'. (W. Arthur, *The Revival in Ballymena and Coleraine*, [London: Hamilton, Adams & Co., 1859], pp. 3-4.)

[69] I.H. Murray, *Martyn Lloyd-Jones: The Fight of Faith 1939-1981*, (Edinburgh: Banner of Truth, 1990), p. 482.

[70] Hathaway, 'The Elim Pentecostal Church', p. 18.

However, another and darker side of this policy of caution was that members of Elim, when faced with declining numbers in their sometimes struggling gatherings, became unduly dependent on the evangelistic prowess of Jeffreys to solve their problems. It was a situation that neither Jeffreys nor the leadership of the movement faced squarely and, in time, became a factor contributing to the split in Elim that came to a head in 1940. Hudson maintains that Jeffreys refused to allow others in the Elim movement to engage in an itinerant healing ministry because he drew a sharp theological distinction between the ministry of the evangelist and the pastor. The former could seek validation of the message by 'signs following' the preaching of the gospel regardless of the moral standing of the seeker but, within the church, meaningful observation of sacraments and commitment to the fellowship along with evidence of godly living were to be sought in those seeking healing.

Another, and more highly charged explanation, for Jeffreys' restrictiveness is also given. Hudson considers Jeffreys may have been anxious lest his own opportunities were damaged by too many Elim evangelists. During 1925, he expressed concern to Phillips that his name had not been placed sufficiently prominently on a revised letter heading. He complained that there was nothing 'in the eyes of the public that links me with Elim except as an ordinary worker and any work run on these lines will not succeed'.[71] Jeffreys, in the last sentence, may well have been making a perfectly valid point. It is hard to resist the conclusion that the growth of the Pentecostal, and certainly the Elim, movement in these islands would have been more sluggish without his ministry. Kay points out that, after 1935, new Elim churches were small and therefore unable to contribute a surplus to the general funds which formed the financial stay of the denomination. Only the big campaign-funded churches could do so.[72]

A second means for bolstering the credibility of Jeffreys' ministry, and by extension the standing of the denomination, was the taking of measures to permeate both with an aura of respectability. On the face of it, this may seem at odds with the ethos of a denomination whose membership was largely working class. The opportunity to hire the largest and grandest auditoriums in the land—for example, the King's Hall, the Ulster Hall and Wellington Hall in Belfast—shored up the self-esteem of the adherents of Elim and heralded a people who had every reason to think they had arrived. Landau commented on the applause in the Royal Albert Hall at the Easter Conference in 1934 when a telegram from the King's private secretary, sent in reply to a loyal message from

---

[71] Hudson, 'A Schism and its Aftermath', n. 150.

[72] William K. Kay, *Pentecostals in Britain*, (Carlisle: Paternoster, 2000), p. 26.

the Conference, was read out.[73] A variation on the same theme was the courting of prestigious sympathisers of Elim. Jeffreys was not against cultivating friends in high places. Early in the formation of Elim in Ireland, he persuaded John Leech and the Rev. Thomas Hackett to become members of the first Elim Council of Reference. The former was a King's Counsellor and the latter a retired Church of Ireland clergyman and brother-in-law of J.W. Crozier, the Primate of All Ireland in the period 1911-20. When his book *Healing Rays* was reissued in its third edition in 1952 it carried an appreciation written in 1947 by Sir Douglas Savory (1878-1969). Savory had been Professor of French and Roman Philology from 1909 to 1941 at Queen's University, Belfast. From 1940 to 1955 he represented the University as a Unionist member of the Westminster parliament. In the appreciation Savory congratulated Jeffreys on his book which he 'found most fascinating; above all, from its profound knowledge and interpretation of scripture; and next, owing to the charming style and choice of the most perfect vocabulary'.[74]

Jeffreys, like Donald Gee, belonged to that first generation of Pentecostals who had experienced the effects of the Welsh Revival, the archetypal revival of the twentieth century, and had lived through the early phase of the movement before the lines of denominational demarcation had become sharply drawn. Jeffreys knew what it was to have been influenced by godly denominational ministers, like Glasnant Jones, and to be invited to preach in churches of differing denominations.[75] Once, during the mission at Penybont, 'eleven ministers of various denominations, and from different parts of the country, were present'.[76] The fact that the Pentecostal movement preceded the Pentecostal denominations made it easier for people like Jeffreys and Gee to envision the possibility of the Pentecostal distinctives permeating the

---

[73] Landau, *God Is My Adventure*, p. 123.

[74] Savory's autobiography, *From the Haven into the Storm*, provides no clue as to why or how the contact with Jeffreys was made. In an interview with A. W. Edsor, then aged eighty-seven, in his home at Mitcham, London, 16 April 1997, he recalled visiting the Savory home at least twice with Jeffreys. The maid who served tea was called Primrose. It is likely that the Savorys attended some services in the first Elim assembly at Hunter Street, Belfast. One possible link between the two men might have been Leech who moved in the same social and political circles as Savory. The latter may have been sympathetic to British-Israel teaching, of which Leech was a leading proponent. Edsor and Jeffreys describe both men in similar terms. Edsor spoke of Savory as a 'staunch Protestant Christian' (Edsor, '*Set Your House In Order'*, p. 151) and Jeffreys of Leech as 'a staunch Protestant, a people's man' (*The Pattern*, mid-August 1942, p. 4). Again, for an academic linguist like Savory whose particular interest was Phonetics, the opportunity to hear *glossolalia* would have presented its own *frisson*.

[75] He described Jones as 'loveable and indefatigable', who gave him 'paternal advice and able instruction'. (*EE,* 25 December 1929, p. 529.)

[76] *Confidence*, March 1913, p. 49.

churches. As Gee expressed it in 1947: 'Before we became so movement-conscious we thought more often of the Pentecostal Revival as a means of grace to quicken whomsoever the Lord our God should call. Denominational loyalties were a secondary consideration. Let them remain such'.[77]

This broader conception of the Pentecostal experience as a generic blessing sanctioned Jeffreys to invite Hackett and Leech to act in an advisory role to the young movement. Both men had received their Spirit-baptism at Sunderland, yet neither joined the Elim Church but continued as staunch members of the Church of Ireland. The young Jeffreys was to some extent the protégé of two Anglicans, Boddy and Polhill. These two men had ties of friendship with the two Irishmen, a mutual regard facilitated by their membership of the Anglican communion.

5.4 Two Influential Anglican Irish Pentecostals

Thomas Edmund Hackett (1850-1939) was the son of the Rev. John W. Hackett (1804-88) and Jane Hackett.[78] His mother was the daughter of Henry Monck Mason, LLD, Librarian of King's Inns, Dublin, John Hackett was born in County Tipperary, the son of John H. Hackett who, in being described as a 'gentleman', was clearly a person of independent means. Thomas had five siblings, two brothers and three sisters. One brother was knighted and became a member of the Legislative Council of Western Australia; the other was appointed Dean of Waterford. The eldest daughter became the second wife of Dr W. Packenham Walsh, Bishop of Ossory, and Anne, the youngest daughter, was married in 1897 to Dr John Baptist Crozier (1853-1920) who was Primate of All Ireland from 1911 until his death in 1920. The Crozier's son, and nephew of Thomas, was appointed Bishop of Tuam in 1938. Thomas Hackett graduated in Classical Studies from Trinity College, Dublin, in 1870.

Hackett was ordained to the ministry of the Church of Ireland in 1875 and served as curate in three different churches in the south Dublin area before becoming the incumbent of St James, Crinken, Bray, in County Dublin in 1883. There, he followed in the steps of his father who was the first incumbent of the church from its foundation in 1840 till 1883, when his son succeeded him. In an unusual reversal of role, the father became curate to his son for the last five years of his life and died in harness aged eighty-four. Thomas retired in 1903, a confirmed bachelor, and for the

---

[77] D. Gee, 'Are we too "Movement" Conscious?', *Pentecost*, December 1947, editorial.

[78] Details of Hackett's background are found in J.B. Leslie, *Biographical Succession: List of the Clergy of Dublin Diocese*, Vol. I. (Used with permission of the Representative Church Body, Dublin: RCB Library MS 61/2/4/1.)

next twenty-five years continued to live in Bray where he was a 'familiar and picturesque figure...as, with truly apostolic zeal, he cycled to and fro to look up friends of the church, new and old; and ever with one purpose—to win or keep them for Christ'. [79] When the break-up of the family home, Crinken House, took place in 1929, he moved to Old Colwyn, North Wales, and lived there until his death in 1939. He was buried in the family vault in Mount Jerome cemetery, Harold's Cross, Dublin—the last member of his family to be interred there.

The Hacketts belonged to the privileged Anglo-Irish Ascendancy that from the constitutional settlement of 1691 enjoyed almost complete control of the instruments of power and influence in Ireland, subject only to the crown and government in London. They identified strongly with the established and, from 1869, post-disestablishment Church of Ireland, a church to which the extended Hackett family made a salient contribution. They were part of a social grouping that saw a sizeable number of its members spiritually quickened during the period of evangelical revitalisation that characterised the Church of Ireland in the years c.1845-95, and to which, indirectly, St James, Crinken, owed its existence.[80]

With such a high-profile background, it is easy to see the influences that predisposed Thomas Hackett to continue as a lifelong member of the Anglican communion and to identify strongly with its evangelical wing. That he should be one of the first people in Ireland, if not the very first, to receive the Pentecostal experience and to advocate it so publicly is not so readily explained. The fact that he had retired from active ministry and had no close family commitments made it easier for him to side with the new movement. His alignment with a movement that shunned clerical domination, spiritual restraint and formalism to allow a new freedom for the Spirit was not without precedent in Ireland. During the years of quickening in the Established Church in the nineteenth century, people of as high social standing as Hackett left it to become part of the newly formed Brethren movement.[81] True to the radicalism of its early days, some in the new movement were even prepared to consider the question of spiritual gifts. A.N. Groves, for one, 'feeling the diversity of languages

---

[79] The story of the church is told in St. James Crinken 1840-1990, a booklet written to commemorate its 150 years of history.

[80] The origin of the church at Crinken owed much to the evangelical sympathies of Lord and Lady Powerscourt. Lady Powerscourt was the key figure in the organisation of the prophetic conferences in the early 1830s at which Edward Irving and J.N. Darby were participants.

[81] Coad has pointed out that the early Brethren movement in Ireland 'made quick headway, but the headway was largely among the Anglo-Irish, and particularly in their upper classes'. (Roy Coad, *A History of the Brethren Movement*, [Exeter: Paternoster Press, ed. 1976], p. 84.)

to be a great barrier to missionary work, raised the question whether the gift of tongues would be among the gifts poured down in the latter days'.[82]

Hackett gave an account in an article written for *The Elim Evangel* of how he came to be involved with the Pentecostal movement. News surrounding the Azusa Street event first alerted his interest: 'I had known much of what transpired in the United States and Canada in 1906'.[83] An insight into his spiritual state at the time was given in a sermon he preached at the 1912 Sunderland Convention. In arguing that 'not till heart purity is reached through simple faith in the name of Jesus, then, and not till then, we are ready for the reception of the Holy Ghost'[84]—a view that more or less petered out in British Pentecostalism in the second decade—he referred to a critical moment in his life in the period 1906-07. At that time he seems to have experienced a Holiness/Keswick-type crisis: 'Not till that wonderful day for me in Geneva was it presented so clearly that I was able to recognise that my old man was crucified with Christ'.[85] Many of the first generation Pentecostals who had imbibed Higher Life teaching and some had similar moments of intense spiritual exultation. Boddy recounted such a moment at his 8.40 am service of Holy Communion on 21 September 1892 when 'the Holy Spirit in infinite love came upon me... It overwhelmed me; my voice broke, and tears were in my eyes. I knew he had come, and that I was "fulfilled with his grace and heavenly benediction"'.[86]

In August 1907, Hackett was brought into contact in London 'by very directly providential leadings' with Mrs Catherine Price, 'the first apparently in England under this mysterious power... [Her] life history and character with which I became ultimately acquainted confirmed the conviction that it was a true working of God's Spirit. When she had spoken in public, almost all in that crowded hall at Lewisham were as a result on their knees or faces before God'.[87] In September 1907, he attended the Sunderland Conference at which T.B. Barratt was first introduced to a Pentecostal audience in Britain. It was at a gathering in

---

[82] Harold H. Rowdon, *The Origins of the Brethren 1825-1850*, (London: Pickering & Inglis, 1967), pp. 78, 81. A similar openness to the charismatic was evidenced in G.V. Wigram (1805-79), author of the *Englishman's Greek Concordance of the New Testament*. He maintained that the graces and gifts of the Spirit should continue and added, 'I will not listen to any argument which denies this, for he that advances it, has made God a liar'.

[83] 'The Nearing Advent of our Lord: Convictions and Experiences', *EE*, June 1921, p. 43.

[84] *Confidence*, July 1912, p. 157.

[85] *Confidence*, July 1912, p. 157.

[86] *Confidence*, April 1909, p. 98.

[87] *EE*, June 1921, p. 43

the Parochial Hall after a mission meeting that he joined those who stayed to 'earnestly wait...on their God, seeking the fuller power of the blessed Spirit'.[88] A young man kneeling beside him, after breaking into a prolonged period of glossolalic utterance, spoke in English for the first time in his hearing that evening:

> He sank lower and lower on his knees, and then these words came slowly, softly and yet most clearly...TELL-THEM-I-AM- COMING-SOON. I felt it to be as a voice from heaven intended very directly for myself—almost the only hearer of the words—giving me this Advent message as a sacred charge. What else could be done but bow low at his side and receive it as from my Lord Himself![89]

This account provides no definite confirmation that Hackett received his Spirit-baptism at those particular meetings in Sunderland, though with his expectancy so highly pitched there is a strong likelihood that he did. If that were so, then he would have been the first person of Irish extraction to speak in tongues in classical Pentecostal understanding. Three months later R.J. Kerr received his Spirit-baptism.

The best vignette of Hackett in action was that given by Donald Gee. Gee had every reason to remember Hackett. In 1939, he recollected dashing to a Pentecostal meeting in Margaret Cantel's drawing-room in Highbury, London, in March 1913. When he entered the room 'a venerable minister of the Church of Ireland was still in the middle of his message... That night the young organist received his own personal "Pentecost" as a result of a simple talk with the man of God, Thomas Hackett, who had been preaching'.[90] In an earlier article Gee elaborated on this incident which reveals a more robust side to Hackett:

> After [the meeting] concluded, the brother who had been conducting it, a respected minister from Ireland, put me through a sort of catechism. 'Was I saved?' Yes. 'Was I baptised?' Yes. 'Was I baptised in the Spirit?' No. 'Then why not?' I explained my aversion to the apparently weary 'waiting' times. He electrified me by telling me they were not essential. Opening his Bible he read me Luke 11:13, and then Mark 11:24, and then asked me if I believed those verses.[91]

---

88 *EE*, June 1921, p. 43.

89 *EE*, June 1921, p. 44. The prophetic element in this passage raises the question how soon is 'soon' to be interpreted and the nature of the 'coming'. If Hackett misconceived the import of the message, or the message was not of divine inspiration, does that automatically invalidate his subsequent experiences? The issue, of course, is wider than this particular case. The Pentecostal cause since Irvingism has been largely predicated on the imminence of the Lord's return, as Faupel has shown. How Rev 3:11 ('Behold, I come quickly') should be interpreted may be of some guidance on this issue.

90 *RT*, 2 January 1939, p. 5.

91 *RT*, 30 July 1930, p. 3.

Gee makes a rather intriguing remark about Dublin that would undoubtedly have involved Hackett and John Leech in some capacity. He mentioned that, while Pentecostal meetings were quickly established in Ulster in 1908, 'there is also mention of a Pentecostal interest in Dublin'.[92] Gee may have gleaned this information from the subscription lists printed in the early editions of *Confidence*. The lists do not identify persons directly but an initial letter is given against the name of the subscriber's home town together with the sum sent to help cover the costs of the magazine. The first mention of Dublin is in the subscription list in the June 1908 issue and thereafter the city featured quite often in the monthly lists. Eight different initials appeared over the years 1908-18 and it is probable, almost to the point of certainty, that the inital is the first letter of the surname of the subscriber. In that case the identifiable ones are 'L' for Leech with four mentions in all, 'H' for Hackett, four, and probably 'P' for Eva Purden, one. The most recurring unidentifiable initial is 'G' with eleven mentions and some of these are smaller sums acknowledged on the same date that would suggest she was responsible for handling the subscriptions of a number of people.[93]

Other evidence would support the view that some sort of fellowship existed in Dublin. In 1910 Boddy wrote an article outlining the short history of Pentecostalism in the British Isles that allowed him to state that 'extravagances and excresences are dying down'.[94] In it he gave a list of the all centres that were known to him, most of which would have had some connection with Sunderland. In Ireland, there were two such, Belfast and Dublin. The following year at the Whitsun Conference it was reported that 'Miss Eva Purden (Dublin) praised her God for the Baptism of the blessed Comforter. He had come to her the previous evening soon after arriving in Sunderland'.[95] Later in the year *Confidence* carried a piece about David Millie, from Stirling, who in his tour of Ireland had spoken at meetings in Dublin, Belfast and Bangor: 'At Dublin the Pentecostal work has been greatly quickened and several baptised in the Holy Spirit'.[96] Two years later, meetings were still being held in the city. In a reference to a meeting held in Dublin 1913 'a lady worker in an important mission said an address in Dublin...on the Promise of the Spirit had deeply impressed her'.[97] In an account of his visit to Ulster in 1917,

[92] Gee, *Wind and Flame*, p. 34.

[93] Averaging out the amount of the total of the subscriptions sent gives the following amounts, expressed in today's currency: L = 82p; H = 55p; M = 46p. The figures would seem to correlate crudely with the surmised purchasing power of the three.

[94] *Confidence*, August 1910, p. 196. See text referred to in n. 67 above.

[95] *Confidence*, June 1911, p. 130.

[96] *Confidence*, October 1911, p. 235.

[97] *Confidence*, November 1916, p. 176. The worker may have been Florence Vipan who will be met in Ch. 7 conducting Elim missions in Ulster. In *Confidence* September

Hackett mentioned that on special occasions meetings held in the Hunter Street Elim hall in Belfast, visitors from Dublin and Monaghan were among those 'abundantly refreshed'.[98] It is likely that with the growing constitutional crisis leading to the partition of the island and the sizeable migration of Protestants from the south that ensued, the work in Dublin was disrupted, if not terminated.

The story of John Leech in that period illustrates the tensions of the time. John Leech (1857-1942) was an Ulsterman who turned out to be a more formative and controversial figure within British Pentecostalism than Hackett. Leech was the son of Charles Leech, QC, and Sarah Frances, the daughter of Major George Hudson Greaves. Both he and his brother, Hunt, followed in their father's footsteps in practising law. [99] John scaled greater professional heights than his brother did after he graduated from Trinity College, Dublin. As a student at Trinity he won glittering prizes in the form of First Honoursman and Plunket Gold Medallist for Oratory (Legal Debating). He was called to the Irish Bar in 1881 becoming a member of the Bar of Ireland, a King's Counsel and Bencher of the Honourable Society of King's Inns. He joined the northwest circuit and was appointed Senior Crown Prosecutor for County Longford in 1920, a position that he was unable to retain after the partition of the island a year later. Forced to leave Dublin, he moved north to the newly constituted Northern Ireland where he was appointed a member of the judiciary.

Leech was soon appointed Deputy Recorder of Belfast and Judge of the County Court, Antrim, but the next stage in his legal career proved far from smooth when he failed to be appointed Recorder. According to James McWhirter, Leech was deprived of the post 'by a political manoeuvre and offered a less important appointment, which he indignantly refused... Sufficient to say that the issue was clear-cut discrimination against a man of God by a political party; ironically enough, they were Protestant loyalists'.[100] The reasons for his being refused preferment were not disclosed by McWhirter who stated that 'the details would not make edifying reading'.[101] One possibility is that Leech was denied advancement at the time because he was regarded in high

---

1916, p. 154, mention is made of 'Miss Vipan (Dublin)' as a speaker at the August convention at Heathfield, Sussex. As an experienced 'lady worker', Florence Vipan would have been a capable speaker.

[98] *Confidence*, April-June 1918, p. 21.

[99] Hunt was described in an obituary notice as 'the veteran Coleraine solicitor'. (*Belfast News-Letter*, 28 July 1942.)

[100] James McWhirter, *Every Barrier Swept Away*, (Cardiff: Megiddo Press, 1983), p. 36. McWhirter, whose story will be recounted in Ch. 6, was told of this episode after Leech had retired and had become a member of the church in London of which he was the minister.

[101] McWhirter, *Every Barrier*, p. 36.

legal circles in Ulster as an *arriviste*, a virtual outsider from Dublin attempting to overtake insiders on the track?[102]

Leech and Jeffreys met for the first time at the Sunderland Convention in 1913. In his foreword to Boulton's history of the early Elim movement, Leech wrote of himself 'as one who has observed this work commenced by George Jeffreys from its small beginning to its present wonderful development'.[103] In 1916, he took part in Jeffreys' summer mission in Ballymena shortly after both he and Hackett were invited to become advisory members of the Elim Evangelistic Band Council.[104] Reporting on the Christmas Convention in Ballymena Town Hall in the same year, *Confidence* stated that Leech's 'deep spiritual teaching which he gave throughout the convention...made a lasting impression, and...brought the people into a place where they had never been before'.[105] Jeffreys, in an obituary tribute to Leech, commented on the blending of natural and charismatic gifts in his ministry:

> In addition to his vast store of knowledge, Mr. Leech had given to him by the Holy Spirit the frequent manifestation of the supernatural word of knowledge, and his wealth of natural wisdom was frequently augmented by the miraculous spiritual gift of the word of wisdom. He applied his classical knowledge to the study of the Scriptures and was an eminent expositor of the Word of God.[106]

The regard in which Leech was held in some government circles within the newly constituted state can be gauged by the task he was invited to undertake. Leech was a nominee of Dawson Bates, a Belfast solicitor and Home Secretary of the new administration, who had the reputation of being the least enlightened member of the cabinet. In Alvin Jackson's view, Bates was 'an apparatchik of somewhat limited calibre'.[107] He was

---

[102] Or does Jeffreys offer another clue? In a foreword to Leech's pamphlet in support of British-Israelism, he referred to the author's 'firm stand for the inspiration of the Scriptures, *in* and out of the Law Courts'. (John Leech, *Israel in Britain; Point by Point Reply to W.F.P. Burton's ' Why I do not Believe the British-Israel Theory'*, [published privately, 1940], emphasis added.) Was Leech's Protestant fundamentalism and/or advocacy of British-Israelism, never mind his association with 'tongues people', too risky in a situation where politico-religious sensitivities were such that the appointment of someone with 'extremist' views would have been regarded as unduly risky? Or, was it simply that he was regarded as tainted by having worked in 'the South'? It is unlikely that the facts of the situation prevailing at the time will ever be uncovered.

[103] Boulton, *Ministry of the Miraculous*, p. iii.

[104] *Minutes of the Elim Evangelistic Band: Fourth Informal Meeting*, 24 April 1916.

[105] *Confidence*, March-April 1917, p. 20.

[106] *The Pattern*, mid-August 1942, p. 4.

[107] Jackson, *Ireland 1798-1998*, p. 336. The stamp of Bates and the mood of the times can be gauged when, as minister of Home Affairs in the new Stormont government, he made it clear to his permanent secretary that he did not want even the 'most juvenile clerk

also something of an *éminence grise* of the Ulster Unionist Council, of which he had been secretary for fifteen years and, as such, was ideally placed to influence the preferment of his acquaintances. When the new cabinet at Stormont decided to abolish proportional representation in local government elections and replace it with a first-past-the-post system, Leech accepted the task of chairing the commission to consider the rearrangement of local government boundaries in areas of dispute. This entailed the holding of public enquiries in those areas, mostly in Tyrone and Fermanagh, where any potential changes in electoral boundaries were likely to lead to internecine party squabbling.[108] In effect, the Leech Commission was deciding the future shape, literally, of the two Irelands. Jeffreys alluded to another of Leech's high-profile duties about the same time when he spoke of him having 'to adjudicate upon claims amounting to many millions of pounds stirling arising out of the disturbances in Belfast'.[109]

This period in Leech's life was referred to by Joseph Smith, the Divisional Superintendent of Elim in Ireland, in the obituary he wrote for *The Elim Evangel* in 1942:

> I greatly appreciate all he did for the people of Belfast and Ulster in the dark and troublous days of some twenty years ago. In those days Mr Leech put his life in his hands because as a judge he stood for the right, and ignored the threatenings of those opposed to justice. Although it meant that his house had to be guarded by the officers of the law, and he himself had to be protected, yet he never swerved from the path of duty.[110]

This passage when taken with the comments from the nationalist *Irish News* that Leech's duty was to do nothing 'but look wise, accept the schemes, and maps, and boundaries prepared in advance by the local agents of Toryism', reflects the smouldering incomprehension that both sides continued to have of each other's evident fears.

---

or typist, if a Papist, assigned for duty to his ministry'. (Chris Ryder and Vincent Kearney, *Drumcree: The Orange Order's Last Stand*, [London: Methuen, 2001], p. 43.)

[108] See Thomas Hennessey, *A History of Northern Ireland 1920-1996*, (Dublin: Gill & Macmillan, 1997), p. 47. The first public inquiries were held in 1923 but the exercise was impaired by the boycotting of the proceedings by the leaders of nationalist opinion who feared that to participate would jeopardise their claims for the transfer of swathes of border areas to the southern state. The demarcation of the national boundary of Northern Ireland was a matter for the Boundary Commission but its report was not to be published for another two years in 1925. The nationalist *Irish News* declared: 'Bluntly, Mr. Leech's mission is that of a gerrymander'. (Eamon Phoenix, *Northern Nationalism: Nationalist Politics, Partition and the Catholic Minority in Northern Ireland, 1890-1920*, [Belfast: Ulster Historical Foundation, 1996], p. 274.)

[109] *The Pattern*, mid-August 1942, p. 4.

[110] *EE*, 10 August 1942, p. 380.

One other comment of Smith throws light on Leech's broad religio-political stance: 'I remember those talks we had about some of the hard fought battle-fields in his experience, and how he took his stand in defence of Protestant liberties and rights'.[111] Leech became a recognised spokesman for the evangelical cause within the Church of Ireland to which end he sought to use his forensic talents for the maintenance of its Protestant and Reformed tradition. On matters of principle he was unflinching, a trait he used as a tease with a knowing Ulster audience when he told them at the Christmas Convention in Belfast in 1921 that he was a 'bigot' and encouraged them to be so as well—'bigots for Salvation, Divine Healing and the Baptism in the Holy Ghost'.[112]

Leech's ability was quickly recognised from the beginning of his engagement with Pentecostalism.[113] Around 1915 there was talk of him going to India as superintendent of the PMU, a position that Polhill was keen to see filled.[114] No appointment was made despite the prior decision not to send any more missionaries to India until oversight in that particular field had been provided. He maintained a close friendship with Boddy who warmed to his preaching ability. Boddy announced in *Confidence* in May 1913 that Leech 'by the special and willing sanction of the Bishop' would preach at his evening service on Whit-Sunday and then printed the full text of the sermon, entitled *Friendship with Christ*, in the July issue.[115] Then in September he held a ten-day mission in Boddy's church, assisted by Mrs Leech who addressed the Women's Meeting. Two years later he and Polhill conducted a weeklong

---

[111] *EE*, 10 August 1942, p. 380. One of the 'battle-fields' where he played a leading role in maintaining the Protestant cause was on the floor of the General Synod of the Church of Ireland, notably when it met in Dublin in 1910. On that occasion he was foremost in voicing a concern that Anglo-Catholic teaching and practice were infiltrating the Divinity School of Trinity College, Dublin, where most of the clergy of the Church of Ireland were trained. (Synod debates in *Belfast News-Letter*, 8 and 9 April 1910, p. 5.)

[112] *EE*, February 1922, p. 18. That this was a bit of a tease is in keeping with his character. Jeffreys said of him: 'He was one of the most upright, contented and happiest Christians I had ever known. He was a genial personality, an Israelite in whom there was no guile. Children loved Mr. Leech wherever he went'. (*The Pattern*, mid-August 1942, p. 4.)

[113] How and when that came about is not known. Edsor recalled hearing that Leech was baptised in the Spirit in England (Sunderland?) and at the time 'fell from his seat'. (Personal interview, 16 April 1997.) Leech first became a regular speaker at Sunderland Conferences from 1912 onwards sharing with Jeffreys in the preaching at the 1913 and 1914 Sunderland Conventions. Before that he had spoken at the Heathfield Convention, Sussex, in August 1910 with Harry Cantel and Moncur Niblock. Assuming 'L' is Leech, his earliest subscription was recorded in the July 1909 issue of *Confidence*. By 1912, therefore, he was a seasoned Pentecostal.

[114] Peter Hocken, 'Pentecostal Missionary Union', in *NIDPCM*, p. 971.

[115] *Confidence*, May 1913, p. 94.

evangelistic mission in Westminster Central Hall (Lesser Hall) in October 1915.

At the age of sixty-nine Leech relinquished his legal career to devote himself full-time to the cause of the British-Israel World Federation. He had long championed British-Israel teaching and was regarded as one of its most able and indefatigable advocates in the British Isles. He had been responsible for organising the youth work of the Federation before becoming its General Commissioner in 1926 and then its chairman. Significantly for this study, he played a major part in influencing George Jeffreys, over thirty years his junior and lacking his mentor's impressive formal education, to accept the British-Israel position around 1919, though it was not till 1925 that this became public knowledge.[116] On the occasion of Leech leaving Ireland to take up the position of General Commissioner in London, Jeffreys was fulsome in his praise of him and his wife: 'Since the inception of the Elim work, he had found these true and loyal friends of Elim to be a source of strength and encouragement to him under all circumstances'.[117]

The close friendship of Boddy, Polhill, Hackett and Leech was cemented primarily by their Pentecostal experience and shared engagements. They developed a mutuality of regard through defending a heavily criticised minority position, a task that tested both character and mental resource. Their compatability was sustained also by a shared churchmanship and social class—a background that became increasingly under-represented as the revivalist impulse in the movement quickened with a consequent widening of its appeal to those lower down the social scale. Joseph Smith's tribute to Leech was heartfelt: 'In those early days, when we were but few in number, and very few in the religious world were willing to identify themselves with us in the smallest way, Mr. Leech not only identified with Elim, but also shared the burden with us'.[118]

While Jeffreys and Leech shared a commitment to their respective denominations, neither was entirely comfortable with the constraints that imposed.[119] Their expectation and experience accommodated a wider

---

[116] Letter Jeffreys to Phillips, 1 December 1934: 'My attitude towards B.I. today is what it has been for fifteen years'. (Hudson, 'A Schism and its Aftermath', n. 602.)

[117] 'Meeting in the New Elim Temple', *EE*, 15 July 1926.

[118] *EE*, 10 August 1942, p. 380.

[119] Though he spread his talents widely over many church, charitable and missionary committees, Leech remained a lifelong member of the Anglican communion where his preaching ability was appreciated in some circles. For instance, during the absence of Dr Stuart Holden (1874-1934) in America, probably in the early 1930s, Leech was invited to occupy the pulpit of St Paul's, Portman Square. (*The National Message*, 19 August, 1942, p. 135.) Though Jeffreys in many ways *was* Elim, Kay reminds his readers that initially it 'was set up as a revivalist agency with ecumenical intentions towards other free churches and evangelicals'. (Kay, *Pentecostals in Britain*, p. 21.)

embrace than those who had little or no experience of anything other than an exclusively Pentecostal ambience and were thereby less attuned to finding accommodation with fellow evangelical believers and churches. Even those who sought the Pentecostal experience and chose to remain within their denomination were soon made conscious of their minority position. As late as 1930 an article appeared written from Belfast that spoke of a small independent group of believers who were either enjoying or seeking their personal Pentecost though still remaining 'members of the Presbyterian, Baptist, and Episcopal Churches'.[120] The group met in a friend's home and had been enthused by a recent visit of William Booth-Clibborn to the city. The writer, related that 1929 had seen a move of the Spirit in the city, but that it had provoked a reaction in the form of 'certain well-meaning ministers of various denominations [setting out] to prove that these miraculous and supernatural gifts were not of God. Literature of every description by writers antagonistic to Pentecostal work were much in evidence in bookstalls and shops... [I]gnorance, superstition, and I am sorry to say opposition, [were] displayed by so many Christians, and especially Pastors who should have known their Bible better.'[121] Their antipathy had led him to write a pamphlet under the title *Are Tongues & Miracles Scriptural?* The conundrum of how to put charismatic new wine into denominational old bottles only began to be resolved constructively towards the latter third of the twentieth century.

This chapter has shown that in the short period November 1912—May 1913 a dramatic transformation took place in the fortunes of George Jeffreys. At the age of twenty-four he found himself lifted from the obscurity of mining village life in South Wales to centre stage at the shrine of British Pentecostalism at Sunderland. Within a few short months of the visit by Boddy to Penybont, George Jeffreys was addressing the annual International Pentecostal Conference over the Whitsun period in Sunderland. With Boddy in the chair, he gave brief gospel messages each evening following the other speakers who included John Leech, Smith Wigglesworth, Jonathan Paul and Gerrit Polman. The latter two were the founder-leaders of German and Dutch Pentecostalism respectively. Within a period of six months, he was to meet the leaders of the international movement as well as fellow students at the PMU School at Preston who would come to be numbered among the next generation of leaders. They included pioneer missionaries, W.F.P. Burton, James Salter and W.J. Boyd and two who would later join him in the Elim movement, R.E. Darragh and E.J. Phillips.

---

[120] *RT*, February 1930, p. 6.

[121] *RT*, February 1930, p. 6.

From the perspective of the future of the movement in Ireland, two visitors to the 1913 Sunderland Conference were destined to play a key role. The role of John Leech and William Gillespie in the evolution of the early Elim movement will be examined in the next chapter. In Jeffreys' formative years Leech and Hackett, as professional men of affairs, gave him the necessary support and recognition which helped to hone his natural refinement into a ministry capable of appealing across the boundaries of social class. Time would reveal that Leech's influence in the induction of Jeffreys to British-Israelism would provide British Pentecostalism, and the Elim movement in particular, with one of the most traumatic episodes in its short history.

CHAPTER 6

The Early Years of Elim (1915-18)

6.1 Events and People Related to Monaghan

Why George Jeffreys should have made Ireland the settled base for the first six years of his evangelistic and healing ministry in Ireland is easier posed than answered. That it was a decision not easily reached is clear from an observation of R.E. Darragh that at the time of his first association with Ireland, Jeffreys 'stood at the cross roads'.[1] One voice called from America carrying the assurance that a positive 'response would mean no financial worry, but a life of ease and personal comfort'.[2] Another voice called from Ireland: '[Jeffreys] knew it was the voice of God. Nothing was promised...except a hard, uphill fight and only difficulties that God could take one through. As he waited in His presence, the Lord said "Ireland" and so one morning a lonely figure stepped on to Irish soil with his message. Surely it was born of God'.[3] Written in 1934, this passage could be posited as a founder-myth, a genre which lends to factual details a symbolic quality that presents the founder as an heroic figure resisting the allure of ease and overcoming all odds. From about 1934, the first indications of the distancing of Jeffreys from Elim were beginning to show so any reaffirmation of his role as founder was a salutary reminder to the movement of his place within it, especially one coming from Darragh, one of his closest friends.

Jeffreys had no previous close personal or family links with Ireland nor does he seem to have arrived with the glint of some great evangelistic strategy in his eye. If he had, he would have been quickly disabused. His first visit in 1913 when the intention was to conduct a mission in the town of Monaghan was to prove a non-starter, despite Hudson's contention that it was a success. Cartwright takes the first view and Hudson, following Boulton, the second. Cartwright is clear that the mission had to be aborted, but Hudson, when he cites Boulton to suggest the success of the mission, seems unaware that Boulton was quoting verbatim from a report

[1] *EE,* 26 January 1934, p. 53.

[2] *EE,* 26 January 1934, p. 53.

[3] *EE,* 26 January 1934, p. 53.

of Jeffreys printed in the August 1915 issue of *Confidence* that clearly had been written shortly before publication and therefore referred to a mission subsequent to the one aborted in 1913.[4] Robert Mercer, one of the local promoters of the 1913 mission, later recollected that the campaign 'did not then materialise'.[5]

If Jeffreys had come to Ireland with a fully worked out strategy, and there is little evidence that he did, then he might have figured that Ireland could offer certain advantages for a new movement. Ulster Protestantism carried within it a strong evangelical ethos, manifested in its vigorous mission hall tradition, and a spirited acceptance of lay initiative. As far as Pentecostalism in the British Isles was concerned, Ireland was a fertile but as yet largely uncultivated field. Up to the First World War, the English Pentecostal scene was dominated by Boddy and Polhill. In Wales, the Apostolic Faith Church under Hutchinson looked for a short period as if it could play a unifying role, while Scotland had a fair proliferation of independent assemblies in the central industrial belt. Outside Belfast, with the exception of Bangor, there was little Pentecostal witness and numbers were small and impact barely perceptible. The province had no one with the formal authority of Boddy or the prophetic charisma of Hutchinson and nothing to match the diffusive energy of Kilsyth and like-minded assemblies.

What Ulster had was a ready reservoir of Christians with a strong drive to engage in aggressive outreach. The whole island presented an accessible but daunting challenge with its four-fifths Catholic majority. The young men who met in Monaghan in January 1915 set their agenda for the future in no uncertain terms. Their initial coming together was for nothing less than to deliberate 'the best means of reaching Ireland with the Full Gospel on Pentecostal Lines'.[6] The fact that Jeffreys himself was neither from the 'black North', nor English but came from another Celtic Fringe country and presented a youthful, non-threatening and well-mannered persona raised the potential for his appeal.

When William Gillespie returned from the 1913 Sunderland Convention to his home in Pine Street, off Donegal Pass, Belfast, he discussed with his brother George the prospects of inviting to the province the bright young preacher who had created such a favourable

---

[4] *Confidence,* August 1915, p. 156.

[5] Albert W. Edsor, *George Jeffreys—Man of God: The Story of a Phenomenal Ministry*, [London: Ludgate Press, 1964], p. 26. When the group first met on Thursday 7 January 1915 to discuss 'the best means of reaching Ireland with the full gospel on Pentecostal lines', the first item discussed was 'the reason why the arrangements for the Gospel Mission which was to be held in the Methodist Hall, Monaghan was (sic) broken down'. For convenience, these minutes and all subsequent ones are henceforth referred to as the *EEBM* (*Elim Evangelistic Band Minutes*).

[6] *EEBM*, 7 January 1915.

impression at the Conference. Joseph Smith, from Carrickmore, who was later to become a member of the EEB provided some detail relating to Jeffreys' earliest days in the province: 'Before the foundation of the Elim work was laid in Ireland, Mr. George Jeffreys visited the home of my parents in Co. Tyrone for a time of rest and recuperation... Mr Jeffreys was then invited by my cousins, George and William Gillespie, to come and live in their home at 14 Pine Street, Belfast which he did in company with Mr. R.E. Darragh'.[7] With their invitation the Gillespie brothers enclosed three ten shilling notes to pay the boat fare, a demanding enough expense for someone like George who was a bread-server. When they sought to hold meetings in Monaghan town, they were refused the use of the Methodist Church hall once it was discovered that they were Pentecostals. It was a real setback as the leaflets advertising their mission had already been printed.

This rebuff recalls Wesley's first visit to the town in 1762 when he was threatened with arrest 'as a person of questionable designs'.[8] Unlike Wesley, the Jeffreys party did not carry commendatory letters written by such prestigious figures as the Bishop of Derry and the Earl of Moira. The reference to Wesley is not irrelevant because two years later when he returned to Monaghan to conduct a tent mission in the town, Jeffreys wrote to Boddy that 'Monaghan is a place situated almost in the heart of Ireland, where John Wesley was imprisoned for preaching the same gospel which I am now privileged to proclaim'.[9] Jeffreys was never averse to pointing to parallels between the itineraries of himself and well-known evangelists, a reflection, perhaps, of his own budding sense of destiny.

In true Pentecostal fashion the call of God to Jeffreys to a wider work in Ireland was confirmed in a vision given to an unnamed 'sister' who at the time knew nothing of the plans proposed in Monaghan.

> The vision consisted of a large golden ring, out of which came a dazzling brightness brighter than the sun at noonday, and out of the ring ran many other rings in all directions. She prayed to God for the interpretation and it was given: 'The large ring is the first Elim Assembly, and out of it shall come many other assemblies'. To her...it was a vision given by God, one...which was meant to be actually fulfilled.[10]

When Jeffreys wrote this passage in 1920, he could, with some justification, declare that the vision had come to pass with fifteen permanent assemblies and twenty-five workers in the field to prove it.

---

[7] *EE*, 17 February 1962, p. 105.

[8] C.H. Crookshank, *History of Methodism in Ireland,* (Clonmel: Tentmaker Publications, ed.1994), Vol. I, p. 148.

[9] *Confidence*, August 1915, p. 156.

[10] *EE*, December 1920, pp. 5-7.

Wilson's inference that the early revival party intended to evangelise only in the north of the island is overstated.[11] The all-Ireland element in the aspiration of the group was tested in a mission in Galway but the times in Ireland at the end of the second decade were not propitious as the political situation surrounding the Home Rule issue created severe communal tension.

Because of the paucity of documentary material the sequence of events that led up to the first meeting of the ad hoc committee in Monaghan town on the 7 January 1915 can be put together only in a fragmented and somewhat speculative way. The following orchestration of events carries elements of conjecture.[12] Though Jeffreys suffered a reverse in Monaghan in 1913 he continued to hold meetings in other places in the province. Robert Ernest Darragh from Bangor, who was to prove a life-long colleague, first met him that same year. It is likely that the paths of the two men had crossed fleetingly in late 1912 at Preston when they both attended the PMU Bible School. According to Edsor, Darragh was stirred early in 1913 by reports of the Cwmtwrch mission in the *Christian Herald* and prayed to see a similar move in his own land.[13] On learning from a local newspaper that Jeffreys was to visit Ireland, he attended one of his meetings. Through the laying on of hands he was healed permanently of throat trouble, a deliverance that enabled him to act for forty-four years as song-leader of the Revival Party.

For the next eighteen months until the middle of 1915, Jeffreys pursued an itinerant ministry. He held successful missions in Plymouth and Croydon, campaigns that ensured him a growing reputation among Pentecostal people. In a letter to Boddy, dealing mainly with the dramatic impact on the town of Llanelli of the first Pentecostal Convention there, Jeffreys drew attention to his 'making arrangements for special Camp Meetings in Bangor, Ireland, during July and August [1914]'.[14] The Bangor summer camp was probably an initiative of Alex Ferguson that was subsequently taken over by the Jeffreys party. The source of this conjecture lies in the fact that Jeffreys purchased a tent for £20 from Ferguson which, in his words, took place 'at the end of [the Ferguson] meetings' in July 1914.[15]

---

[11] Wilson, *Sects and Society*, p. 35.

[12] The problem of dating lies largely on having to rely quite often on the written memoirs of older men in recalling the events of their youth. The only sure dating is that based on contemporary reports in *Confidence* and the first minutes of the EEB from 1915 onwards.

[13] Edsor, *'Set Your House In Order'*, p. 37. The word 'early' is suggested because contemporary reports appeared in the February 1913 issue of *The Life of Faith*.

[14] *Confidence*, August 1915, p. 156.

[15] *Confidence*, August 1915, p. 156

Jeffreys was invited to be a speaker at the 1914 Christmas Convention in Dover Street, the year before the assembly moved to Hopeton Street. The Convention was attended for the first time by Robert Mercer and William Henderson, both of whom travelled to Belfast from Monaghan where they both worked. Mercer came to spend Christmas with relatives in Belfast and attended the convention with his aunt who was a member of the Dover Street assembly. It was shown earlier that J.N. Arnold had made contact between Dover Street and Monaghan in the first half of 1913, so it is possible that the Mercer family connection may have facilitated the link between the two places. This strengthens the claim of the Dover/Hopeton Street assembly to be regarded as the foundation assembly of the Pentecostal movement in Ireland. Mercer added: 'At the close of the service George Jeffreys came down to Mr. Henderson and I (sic) for a chat. From the other side of the aisle Mr. Darragh walked over to us and joined the little group. That was my first meeting with these two servants of God. It was as though God was thus bringing us all together'.[16]

Robert Mercer later stated that he was one of the young men among the 'three of us who were taking our stand for Pentecost in Monaghan, namely, Messrs. A. Kerr, George Allen and myself'.[17] The fact that he omitted mention of Henderson, Farlow and his brother John, would suggest either a lapse in memory or that the latter three joined the original three later, possibly some time after the aborted 1913 mission in Monaghan but before the Christmas Convention in 1914.[18]

In 1920, George Jeffreys, reflecting on the origins of Elim, wrote: 'I regard the county town of Monaghan...as being the birth-place of this work', to which he added that he had crossed to Ireland from England in January 1915 'for the purpose of conducting a mission in that town'.[19] It is, therefore, inconceivable that Jeffreys did not discuss such a mission during the Dover Street Christmas Convention before travelling back to England and then returning in time for the 7 January 1915 meeting in Monaghan. This means that Robert Mercer, Henderson, Darragh and, almost certainly, the Gillespie brothers would all have been in the picture of the meeting in Monaghan a fortnight hence.[20] Those who did attend

---

[16] Edsor, *George Jeffreys,* p. 26.

[17] Edsor, *'Set Your House In Order',* p. 32.

[18] Mercer's account appears to have been written later in life as a recollection, as Edsor put it, of what 'Pastor Mercer had...to say of those early pioneer days'. So facts may well have been forgotten or misplaced in time sequence.

[19] *EE,* December 1920, pp. 5-6.

[20] That the Gillespies were involved comes out in a comment of Mercer: 'Mr William Gillespie came up for a week-end [to Monaghan] and it was then decided to open up the Elim work in Ireland'. (Edsor, *'Set Your House In Order',* p. 32.) It is not possible to date

the 7 January 1915 meeting in Monaghan, an event that can be rightly regarded as the birth of the Elim movement, were local men Albert Kerr, George Allen, William Henderson, Robert and John Mercer, and Frederick Farlow, besides Ernest Darragh and George Jeffreys.

Jeffreys said of the January meeting that 'a number of young business men discussed the question of how to reach their country with the full gospel for Spirit, Soul and Body, and to spread the news of the Pentecostal outpouring of the Holy Ghost', adding that 'at this time not one had received the experience [of Spirit-baptism] in the town, but they had seen the truth in the Word'. [21] This comment is something of a puzzle in that it that appears to fly in the face of Arnold's statement made in 1913 that of the 'band of earnest seekers...the Lord graciously baptised four after the laying on of hands'.[22] Nor does it accord with Mercer's recollection that at the time of the invitation going out to Jeffreys to conduct the aborted mission in the Methodist Church in 1913, 'there were three of us who were taking our stand for Pentecost in Monaghan'.[23]

A number of clues may help in resolving this discrepancy. In an earlier report sent in by Jeffreys to *Confidence* that was almost contemporaneous with the July 1915 mission in Monaghan, his assertion that some young men had 'quite recently' received the outpouring of the Holy Ghost suggests a time scale more flexible than if he had said, or implied, 'very' recently which would almost certainly have pinned the event to 1915.[24] As for Mercer's point, the possibility, remote as it is, exists that by 1913 they may have taken a stand on the teaching but had not come into the experience to which it bore witness. Farlow's account of his Spirit-baptism is not of great help on the issue since it is undated. Nevertheless, it carries no hint that Jeffreys was present at his Spirit-baptism. Priority must be given to Arnold's version because it is contemporaneous with the events it describes and is thereby definitive about the timing. The record, on balance, points to the Pentecostal experience of Spirit-baptism coming to Monaghan from Sunderland via Dover Street and not as a direct result of the Jeffreys mission. Jeffreys, in other words, came to a small but enlivened band of Spirit-baptised young men who sought his help to 'reach their own country' with the Pentecostal message. With the men sharing this wider vision for the island and they, themselves, not having deep roots in the town, it was inevitable that Monaghan would not be the limit of their vision nor could it be the base for a work of any ambitious

---

this 'week-end' visit. The January meeting was held on a Thursday and Gillespie's name in not among the eight who attended.

[21] *EE,* December 1920, p. 6.

[22] *Confidence*, 13 May 1913, p. 100.

[23] Edsor, *'Set Your House In Order'*, p. 32.

[24] *Confidence*, August 1915, p. 156.

sweep. Its rurality and geographical peripherality to both post-Partition states added to its unsuitability.

There can be little doubt that the unnamed 'band of earnest seekers' in Monaghan that Arnold met, especially those who could witness to Spirit-baptism, included the three reported by Robert Mercer as taking their stand in Monaghan, viz. Kerr, Allen and himself. The latter's nephew, W.R. Mercer, has provided the only extant story of Pentecostalism in Monaghan in the period leading up to Jeffreys' return to the town in 1915.[25] His memoir provides cameos of six young men who lived in the town and established a Pentecostal witness there. Most of them seem to have been employed in the retail business. Some attended the Methodist Church and were active in the Christian Endeavour movement.[26] The small group took the motto of the Endeavour movement, 'Ireland for Christ', with great seriousness, possessed as they were 'with a burning passion for the evangelisation of Ireland, especially the Roman Catholic South'.[27]

None of the constitutional turmoil that disturbed pre-partition Ireland, with its profound implications for everyday living, was hinted at in any literature emanating from the Pentecostals at the time.[28] For them, the battle was on a different front and, in an ill-defined and simplistic way, they deemed revival to be the answer to Ireland's problems. An article published in 1918 in *Confidence* and written by Thomas Hackett concluded 'that it is as true as ever that the ONE CURE FOR IRELAND'S WOES is the Gospel of Christ. Only let it be a full Gospel,

---

[25] W.R. Mercer, *Memoir*, (typescript, 1996): henceforth *Mercer Memoir*. It was written in his old age in Canada where he resided for many years.

[26] Francis E. Clark founded the Christian Endeavour in America in 1881 with the purpose of integrating young people into the total life of the church.

[27] *Mercer Memoir*, p. 13. In this drive they shared a feature endemic in Ulster evangelicalism which retained much of the mindset that energised the nineteenth-century Protestant Crusade, or Second Reformation, which sought nothing less than the mass conversion of the Catholic population to Protestantism in Ireland. Such zeal was driven, in part, by a subliminal expectation that the conversion of the Irish Catholic would in some indeterminate way make easier the contested constitutional lot of Ulster Protestantism.

[28] The political situation in Monaghan could not have been more tense for all who lived in the town at the time. At the meeting of the Monaghan branch of the Ulster Women's Unionist Council, held in the town's assembly rooms in February 1914, one local speaker concluded by saying: 'If Ulster is excluded from Home Rule, it seems that Monaghan will not be included in Ulster (sic). The prospect before us...is that of being placed under a Dublin Roman Catholic Parliament which will be under priestly influence and dominated—and this I fear most—by Mr. Devlin's anti-Protestant Ancient Order of Hibernians'. (Jonathan Bardon, *A History of Ulster*, [Belfast: Blackstaff Press, 1992], p. 446.)

such as our brethren [of the EEB] know and preach as a living experience'.[29]

The six young men were largely outsiders to Monaghan though William Henderson may well have been brought up in the town.[30] He was the manager of a furniture-hardware business. Aged thirty-five, he was the oldest and most mature of the group and would have been its natural leader. Robert Mercer and his brother John were both Methodists and had come to Monaghan to augment their business experience. John was trained in the same furniture and hardware firm that Henderson managed and Robert worked in the boot and shoe business. Their father had worked with the Irish Evangelisation Society and travelled throughout Ireland holding summer mission services in a portable construction with a canvas roof, a structure similar to one that came to be used by the EEB. When John left Monaghan, he moved to Portadown and was an elder in the Elim Church there for over fifty years. Frederick Farlow came from the neighbouring county of Fermanagh. Of these four, John Mercer was the only one not to enter the full-time ministry of Elim.

The remaining two young men were George Allen and Alex Kerr. Allen was a deeply committed Methodist who had a thorough knowledge of and a deep love for the *Journals* of John Wesley, insights from which he was keen to share with others. He remained throughout his life in the grocery business and eventually moved to Ballymena from where, after his marriage to Jeffreys' former housekeeper, he moved to Belfast. He was ordained an elder in the Ballymena Elim Church and later joined the Bible-Pattern Church in Belfast. Little is known about Kerr, other than he may have been a postman. One clue explaining his obscurity may lie in a copy of a brief testimony written by Farlow recounting his Spirit-baptism. Assuming it was written in the 1930s, the passage could be interpreted as follows:

> Two of those young men are [now] ministers of the Elim Foursquare Gospel Alliance [Robert Mercer and Farlow]. Two are businessmen and members of Elim Assemblies [John Mercer and Allen]. One is telling the glad story of a Saviour's love in the

---

[29] *Confidence*, July-September 1918, p. 53. The aftermath of the 1859 Revival allows no such easy solution to a complex problem. In Ian Paisley's analysis, 'the revival of 1859 strengthened Ulster in her stand against Roman Catholic agitation and without doubt laid the foundation which enabled Ulster under the leadership of Lord Carson to preserve her Protestant position'. (I.R.K. Paisley, *The Fifty-Nine Revival*, [Belfast: Martyrs' Memorial Free Presbyterian Church, 1958], p. 202.) A strengthened Protestantism was never likely to produce a weakened Catholicism or a debilitated Irish nationalism.

[30] His younger sister, Adelaide, who was later to become an Elim missionary, was born in Monaghan. (*EE*, 17 February 1962, p. 105.) She was Presbyterian so it is likely that this was the family affiliation.

> Belgian Congo [Kerr?], and one has gone to his eternal reward [Henderson, d. 1931].[31]

One immediate problem the group of friends faced was that, as single men living away from home, it was the custom for them to 'live in' on the employer's premises which meant that part of their remuneration was received in the form of board and lodging. Also, in the age of labour paternalism they were expected to attend the church of their employer. When they became convinced of the truth of Pentecostal teaching, they approached the minister of the Methodist Church in the town with a view to seeking his support. His response to their testimony that they had searched Scripture to corroborate the Pentecostal experience was in a tone of curt dismissal that 'it's a pity it's there'.[32] He forbade them to teach any Pentecostal doctrine within the church. They were now left with the problem of whether or not to leave the Methodist Church, knowing that no other church in the locality would entertain them and also they were putting their employment at risk. Robert Mercer seems to have taken the lead in reaching the decision to make a clean start that led to their seeking out a place in which to worship.

After a protracted search, they found a room above a stable. After applying a few coats of whitewash and providing a small number of backless forms, they began a prayer meeting. Adelaide Henderson gave a slightly different setting to the room. She recalled that 'at the rear of a small hotel in Monaghan there stood a dingy, unattractive-looking bottling store. Above this store there was an empty loft, which five young men...hired for prayer meetings, calling it the Upper Room'.[33] There is no easy way to reconcile the discrepancies in the two accounts, especially as Farlow's description in the next paragraph, is quite specific about the presence of horses, though Adelaide Henderson was equally firm about it all happening 'above the bottles in that dingy loft'.[34]

One night, while praying fervently, three of them received their Spirit-baptism. Farlow, in ways the most intense of the group, described the occasion:

> Some may say it was excitement or emotionalism. No, there was nothing in that room to excite the emotion. Walls unplastered, openings in floor and windows through which a cold wind was blowing, down below we could hear the horses eating their fodder. Then suddenly it seemed as if we were transported into heaven

---

[31] On an undated sheet, but must have been written after Henderson's death in 1931 but before the schism around 1940. (*Mattersey Archives*.)

[32] Unquestionably 'the final solution' to every hermeneutical problem! Quote is from *Mercer Memoir*, p.14. Such a reaction may lie behind the aborted 1913 mission.

[33] *EE*, 17 February 1962, p. 105

[34] *EE*, 17 February 1962, p. 105.

> itself, and the place that once was dark, damp, cold and dismal became filled with the glory of God, and all we could say was, 'This is that' [Acts 2:16 AV]'.[35]

Farlow continued to speak in tongues all night and well into the next day. His experience was so overwhelming that he found difficulty in carrying on his work for a day or so. It was no surprise that the whole episode 'caused rather a sensation and many and varied were the comments made'.[36] Adelaide Henderson added that 'many, many more were added to their number...and a new experience from God shook the little Irish town... where spiritual life...was at a very low ebb'.[37] 'Madness' was all the talk of the town in Monaghan in 1915.[38] Farlow went on to assert that 'those young men went forth from that upper room with a new power and vision... It was heaven upon earth... Some said we were mad, but little did they know the joy that filled our souls'. Farlow's admission that speaking in tongues caused something of a 'sensation' takes on a more elevated complexion when it is placed within the wider theological framework of Welker's work on pneumatology. Welker poses the question as to why the Pentecostals regard *glossolalia* not merely as a subordinate gift of the Spirit but rather as a central and thus indispensable one, a claim that he personally regards as a mistaken evaluation. In answering his own question, he provides a rationale for the movement in its gestation stage: 'The centring on *glossolalia* is to be...taken seriously as an effort to respond to faith's need for concretization and as a protest phenomenon... Here speaking in tongues, as a phenomenon that diverges with particular clarity from the normal forms of experience, offered the very kernel around which a *countermovement could crystallise*'.[39]

On the assumption that the events outlined above took place before January 1915, it is now opportune to look at the outcome of the meeting that took place in Knox's Temperance Hotel in the centre of the

---

[35] *Farlow Typescript* (*Mattersey Archives*). Chan makes the point that 'what the early Pentecostals experienced was not just a new surge for witness, but also a new sense of the nearness of the triune God, and it is such an experience that they claimed was evidenced by their speaking in tongues'. (Simon Chan, *Pentecostal Theology and the Christian Spiritual Tradition*, [Sheffield: Sheffield Academic Press, 2000], p. 46.)

[36] *Farlow Typescript.*

[37] *EE*, 17 February 1962, p. 105.

[38] *Farlow Typescript.* Michael Welker, Professor of Systematic Theology at Heidelberg, makes a perceptive comment that treats an experience such as Farlow's with conceptual finesse. For Welker, one outcome of *glossolalia* lies in its public impact: 'It...opens up depth dimensions of the capacity for feeling and expression that go beyond all standardisations and typologies... It is essentially a process that...*generates and binds...public attention*'. (Michael Welker,*God the Spirit*, [Minneapolis, MN: Fortress Press, 1994], p. 270, emphasis added.)

[39] Welker, *God the Spirit*, pp. 268-9, emphasis added.

Monaghan.[40] The drift of their strategic thinking, such as it was, was captured in the minutes:

> We believe it to be the mind of God that evangelist Jeffreys...be invited to take up permanent evangelistic work in Ireland, and that a centre be chosen by him for the purpose of establishing a church out of which evangelists would be sent into the country towns and villages, and that a tent be hired, for the purpose of holding a Gospel mission during the month of July to commence the work in Ireland.[41]

Events moved rapidly from this point. By the end of 1915, the mission in Monaghan had been completed, a tent purchased from Ferguson, a mission held in Galway, the first members of the evangelistic team brought together and premises found in Belfast to act as a centre for the new work. Jeffreys was clearly a man in a hurry with a personal authority that encouraged the group to entrust him with the choice of a site for their headquarters. Already, they were pinning their expectation of success on God working through him—a portent of things to come. That he was controlled with a light hand is revealed in the number of minuted meetings when the group met—three in 1915, two in 1916, once in 1917 and twice in 1918. The hand-written minutes rarely extended much more than one side of quarto. At the beginning of his ministry in Ireland, Jeffreys was very much his own man with little accountability to a central body with teeth. As Wilson attests, 'In these years George Jeffreys *was* Elim'.[42]

The mission in Monaghan was held in the first fortnight in July 1915. The local weekly paper, *The Northern Standard*, reported that meetings were held in a tent in a field adjoining North Road: 'On each occasion there was a good attendance. Mr Jeffreys was accompanied on his tour by Miss Stevens (sic), who also takes part in the meetings'.[43] In a report of the mission sent to *Confidence*, Jeffreys was more upbeat than the local press: 'From the first of the meetings, God has been saving souls, and sinners have been trembling under conviction of sin... People come from great distances, and the hunger for revival is such that people come from miles around, and the cry is everywhere, "Come over and help us"'.[44] While there was no specific mention of healing, he referred to a young man 'stricken down from his seat by the power of God...and immediately

---

[40] *EEBM,* 7 January 1915.

[41] *EEBM,* 7 January 1915.

[42] Wilson, *Sects and Society*, p. 37.

[43] *The Northern Standard*, 24 July 1915. 'Stephens' is the correct spelling.

[44] *Confidence*, August 1915, p. 156.

delivered from sin. Next morning he burnt a number of cigarettes, although no one had spoken to him about them'.[45]

It was at the start of mission in Monaghan that the organising group came together for their second informal meeting on the 3 July 1915. This time they met at the home of Jack Wilkinson located on the side of North Road opposite the town park where the tent was erected. The Wilkinsons hosted Jeffreys during his visit to their home town. Wilkinson lived in one of the more substantial houses in Monaghan and was probably a building contractor. His comfortable life style and grandparent status meant that he was considerably older and experienced in the ways of the world than the band of young men. Jeffreys retained a high regard for him and, at his funeral in 1943, paid this warm tribute:

> From the moment our beloved brother saw the truth of the Pentecostal message, he never wavered, he stood solidly by me in the bitter opposition that came against me from every quarter. But truth prevailed and the stream of truth that found its source in Jack Wilkinson's home town has reached many people and places far away from dear old Monaghan.[46]

Wilkinson would undoubtedly have been the stalwart in the continuation of the Elim work in the town, especially when the younger men moved away, three of them to become full-time members of the EEB.

The second meeting of the committee in Monaghan was convened just before the mission commenced in July. It was minuted that Jeffreys informed the meeting that 'God had already answered our prayers and had given a definite call to R.E. Darragh and Miss M. Streight, of Bangor, Co. Down, to work in connection with the Band of Evangelists which we had claimed by faith for the Pentecostal movement in Ireland. Mr. Darragh had kindly accepted the invitation to act as secretary pro tem'.[47]

---

[45] *Confidence*, August 1915, p. 156. Not that the young man needed to be told as dropping the habit was expected of converts. A.T. Pierson remarked that one feature of Keswick spirituality was 'the abandonment of tobacco, not because its use can be conclusively shown to be inherently sinful, or because of any direct pressure brought to bear by speakers; but because, where used, not as a medicine, but for indulgence of a liking, it exalts self to the throne'. (A.T. Pierson, *Forward Movements in the Last Half Century,* [New York: Funk and Wagnall, 1905], p. 156.) A letter from Jeffreys to Hutchinson in Bournemouth, written probably after his own conversion, suggests why he identified so strongly with the young man in Monaghan as to mention him: 'This is the Lord's doing: God has taken the cigarette from between my lips, and put a Hallelujah there instead'. (Cartwright, *The Great Evangelists*, p. 26.)

[46] Edsor, *'Set Your House In Order'*, p. 33.

[47] *EEBM*, 3 July 1915. The heading of the minutes was 'Second Informal Meeting of Pentecostal Workers at Monaghan, July 3rd. 1915'. The signatories were Jeffreys, Henderson, Farlow, Darragh and A.S. Kerr. Although the use of the term 'Elim

The third meeting of the committee was held in 'the Hall, Hunter Street, Belfast' that had recently been acquired.[48] There was rejoicing that God had given them a building as a base 'for sending out Spirit-filled workers', while pleasure was expressed at 'the success that had attended the ministry of Pastor Jeffreys since he had taken over the pastorate of Elim Church in the city of Belfast; many souls had been saved and accepted into membership, while lives and homes had been transformed'.[49] To the list of the signatories was added the new name of Margaret Montgomery Streight.

6.2 The Role of Women

That a woman should have been among the first two recruits to Jeffreys' evangelistic team should not be a surprise. Zeal engendered by the imminence of the parousia, the emphasis on Spirit anointing as against formal ordination and the centrality of views on the priesthood, indeed prophethood, of believers—these all shaped the understanding of Christian ministry in the early Pentecostal movement. Spirit-emphasising movements have tended in their first flush to give women a high, though rarely equal, status in ministry, while it was an exceptional circumstance in mainline denominations until the latter third of the twentieth century.[50] From the beginning women were included as full members of the EEB. By 1924, of the thirty-four members of the EEB in the regular work of the ministry, twenty-two were men and twelve women, a proportion matched by few other denominations at the time.[51] Any of these women could be called upon to serve at any one time either as a deaconess, evangelist, missionary or acting pastor.

Evangelistic Band' is anachronistic at this stage, it can be seen from the minute that the germ of the nomenclature was present.

[48] *EEBM*, 24 December 1915. The minutes were headed 'Third Informal Meeting of Pentecostal Workers'.

[49] *EEBM*, 24 December 1915.

[50] Even the Free Churches only accepted the ordination of women in a very hesitant way towards the end of the nineteenth century. In some Higher Life circles, A.T. Pierson and A.J. Gordon, argued that the prophecies in Joel 2 supported women's right to engage in evangelism but stopped at any advocacy of ordination. In Ireland, the 'Protestant Nuns', as the women pilgrims with the Faith Mission were dubbed, were a familiar enough sight throughout the countryside visiting, in pairs, farmhouses and conducting missions. Photographs of Margaret Streight show her wearing a bonnet with chin ribbon similar to the headdresses worn by Salvation Army and Faith Mission women on active duty. The equivocal nature of New Testament texts on this issue gives us, a Blumhofer observes, 'both daughters speaking their visions and women keeping silence'. (Edith L. Blumhofer, *Restoring The Faith: The Assemblies of God, Pentecostalism, and American Culture*, [Chicago, IL: University of Illinois Press, 1993], p. 176)

[51] Figures based on EEB membership as recorded in *EE,* October 1924.

Margaret Streight and Adelaide Henderson, the first two women accepted into the EEB as full members, hailed from Bangor, County Down. Robert Tweed, who knew Margaret Streight well, spoke of her leaving 'a good home and a prospective business position to take the step of faith'.[52] Speaking of Jeffreys' choice of her as pastor of the Ballymoney Elim assembly for a short period, Tweed commented that he could not have made a better choice: 'Her cheerful uplifting disposition, her ability as a speaker and leader of the open air and indoor meetings made her a very popular and delightful person to be in charge of the young church'.[53] As will be shown, Tweed here presents a side of her that was not always recognisable. Adelaide Henderson was converted under the ministry of Jeffreys in 1915 in Hunter Street, where she must have been among the first of the converts in the newly opened Elim hall. She was a teacher who for a short time served as a missionary to the Belgian Congo with the Congo Evangelistic Mission. In Africa, she and her friend, Elsie Brooks, were both stricken by malaria and when her colleague died within three months of arrival she was forced to return to Ireland.[54] Subsequently, she was appointed Missionary Secretary to the wider Elim movement. Alice McKinley, who married Robert Tweed in 1926, took charge of five churches in the period 1923-26 after she became a member of the EEB and before becoming an assistant to her future husband in Belfast.[55] Despite the regard with which such women were held, as central control in Elim grew stronger in the 1920s, new rules were introduced and many pastors were re-ordained, an option not open to women, though those in post retained the prerogative to be in charge of a church and were permitted to conduct weddings, funerals and baptismal services if a suitable male pastor could not be found.[56]

Margaret Streight was a preacher of some eloquence and bluntness and developed a reputation in her later ministry for sharpness of tongue and manner: 'Streight by name and strait by nature' was a quip that summed up her martinet qualities. In fact, before joining the Band, she had applied to the PMU but had been rejected as 'too fanatical'. On one occasion she protested 'We'll have no more of that!' when a woman who was having

---

52 *Tweed Memoir,* p. 14. Robert Tweed was an early member of the EEB. His unpublished memoir was written c.1991 when he was aged ninety-two. While it is disjointed and opaque in places, it is, nevertheless, an invaluable source of otherwise unavailable opinion and information.

53 *Tweed Memoir,* p. 13

54 *Tweed Memoir,* p. 35

55 *Tweed Memoir,* p. 34.

56 D.W. Cartwright, '"Your Daughters Shall Prophecy": The Contribution of Women in Early Pentecostalism', p. 9, a paper delivered at the Society for Pentecostal Studies Conference, Maryland, November 1985.

an affair with a married man started to speak in tongues.[57] After remonstrating with two girls for being talkative during a service and then publicly dismissing them from the hall, she called on the congregation to 'pray for those two sinners', displaying in this case the traits more of an amazon than a paragon! She kept her emotions and her meetings under firm control and was rigorous in 'sticking to the Word', a combination that led some to suggest that 'she would have made a good Brethren!' and Tweed to remark of her marriage to Robert Mercer that it 'came to us as a very great wonder and surprise'.[58] In fact, the question of marriage did not feature strongly within the early Band, partly as a consequence of the parlous state of the Band's finances when the cost of providing married quarters became a vital consideration.

An incident in Margaret Streight's life corroborates her reputation for being singularly gifted in what most Pentecostals would regard as the 'word of knowledge'. John Carter (1893-1981) was a member of the EEB from 1919-21.[59] In a memoir he narrated the following incident:

> When [Miss Streight], Jeffreys and Darragh were conducting the mission in Ballymena in 1916, she lodged in accommodation on the other side of the town from the two men to prevent any talk of a scandal-mongering nature. The two men were burdened by the financial needs of the campaign but did not wish to disturb their colleague with the problem. When the two men were conversing about the situation, Margaret Streight, while praying some miles away heard their voices distinctly and was made immediately aware of the problem. Next morning, much to their astonishment she confronted her two colleagues with the news that she knew exactly how things stood and told them the exact state of the finances. [60]

Doubtless, they saw in the incident shades of Elisha's overhearing the plans of the king of Syria (2 Kings 6:8-9.) and were confirmed in their Pentecostal conviction.

6.3 Resource Problems

Establishing a new movement is a demanding task that requires commitment from those who espouse it and a resource base to sustain it. In this section it is the latter that will be examined.

---

[57] A reminiscence of Mr J. Towell, aged seventy-nine, given in an interview on 19 December 1996.

[58] *Tweed Memoir*, p. 14.

[59] He and his brother, Howard, were to become leading figures in the British Assemblies of God.

[60] *British Pentecostal History,* typescript memoir [n.d.], pp. 17-8.

6.3.1 Finance

The time-honoured ways to meet financial commitments are by increasing income and keeping costs low. Increasing income was a struggle for a new movement like Elim that had no traditional body of support on which to call. The one plus the movement had was the received view that a tithe of one's income was the norm for Pentecostals. It was an expectation laid on all members who joined the Band, even with their meagre income. For the rest, Elim had to rely mainly on working-class people, most of whom were forced to struggle on low incomes. Unusually, George Jeffreys, as the residuary legatee of a Mrs Jane Rees, was led to believe that he would be the beneficiary from her estate to the sum of £5,000. Being a windfall, it was as surprising as it was welcome. However, the Rees family contested the will and, in the event, only about £1,000 was forthcoming. One consequence of the episode was that the first formal step in the denominationalisation of the movement was hastened. As the money had been left to Jeffreys personally, legal advice was given that it would be better if it were transferred into a charitable trust. In 1918, under the title of 'Elim Pentecostal Alliance Council', this property holding body was set up and this, in effect, prompted the mutation of the Elim Evangelistic Band into the Elim Pentecostal Alliance.

The Band just about managed to survive by keeping costs and overheads down. The major saving was in salaries. Hackett made the point in *Confidence* that 'this work is full of promise, yet is seriously hampered for lack of funds... These people and workers long to go forward, they are alive and aflame for God, but have not much of this world's goods'.[61] The first meeting in Monaghan placed on record: 'We agree that God promises to supply the temporal needs of every Evangelist that would be called by him into the work, and that through prayer and faith in his promises, He would prove Himself to be to each one Jehovah Jared'.[62] The working on 'faith lines' had become well established by this time. Jeffreys would have seen the principle in operation at first hand at the PMU School at Preston. Polhill had modelled the PMU on the lines of his beloved China Inland Mission with its core principle that workers were not guaranteed any fixed amount of support, only a fair distribution of whatever funds were available. Though Hudson Taylor is often considered the father of the 'faith mission' concept, it is arguable that its theological underpinning owes more to Edward Irving for whom it was all of a piece with his later charismatic orientation.[63]

---

[61] *Confidence*, April-June 1918, p. 21.

[62] *EEBM*, 7 January 1915.

[63] In an address to the London Missionary Society in 1824, Irving declared that today's missionaries should take their lead from the apostles and go forth 'destitute of all visible sustenance, and all human help'. The apostles were 'men of Faith, that they might

Privation, at times bordering on destitution, was endemic within the Band. Robert Mercer recalled seeing the earliest workers on their knees in prayer and, observing the state of their soles, was moved to provide them with new shoes. Margaret Streight's culinary resourcefulness was called upon for those occasions when she had 'to thin the sausages' to feed the workers in the University Street headquarters.[64] W.R. Mercer remembered Miss Streight, his aunt, telling him how she carried a letter in her pocket for six weeks because she did not have the penny necessary for the stamp.[65] It was clearly in the interest of the Band to engage mostly young, single people and this was a consideration in the pervasive culture of singleness-late marriage that marked the early work.[66] For one, accommodation was more difficult to obtain for married couples and allowed for less flexibility in stationing.

At a meeting of the EEB convened at the beginning of 1917, it was agreed that from the following April collecting boxes would be distributed only to supporters, and 'not from collecting from the public at large'.[67] Out of the money brought in by this means, all the initial expenses of the evangelists were paid and a tenth was set aside for foreign missions. It is likely that the PMU was the main beneficiary of this tithe. The remainder was placed in a fund together with all private gifts and the total divided, presumably equally, among the then six members of the Band at the end of each quarter. The communitarian idealism behind this scheme lasted only a year and had to give way to a more pragmatic distribution that matched needs and means by giving Jeffreys the final voice in the allocation of funds. A 1918 minute recorded that the money left after the tithe had been deducted and the expenses of missions met was 'to be divided by the Superintendent as the needs arise in the different parts'.[68] This last change consolidated Jeffreys' authority over the Band and recognised the unreserved trust they had in the sensitivity informing his judgement of financial needs. Jeffreys was left with the responsibility of determining the income of the young evangelists, a task made all the more daunting by the sacrificial commitment they had all made, notably Henderson. The latter, according to Tweed, 'had given up a lucrative position as a business man to become an Elim evangelist'.[69] That he earned the trust and affection of his colleagues is clear from the

---

plant Faith, and Faith alone'. (D.W. Bebbington, *Evangelicalism in Modern Britain*, [London: Unwin, 1989], pp. 93-4.)

[64] Interview with Mr J. Towell.

[65] *Mercer Memoir*, p.16.

[66] Of the members of the EEB who worked largely in Ireland in the period 1919-20, three were married couples and seventeen were single.

[67] *EEBM*, 4 January 1917.

[68] *EEBM*, 2 January 1918.

[69] *Tweed Memoir*, p. 19.

tributes paid to Jeffreys by former colleagues. John Carter said of his time with the EEB: 'We were like one great family; no one was paid a salary, all lived by faith. When he knew I was having a hard time financially in one place, the Principal slipped a 10s. note into my hand. No wonder we all admired and loved him'.[70]

Robert Tweed had every reason to respect the memory of Jeffreys. Shortly after joining the Band, he became crippled with tuberculosis of the left femur which left him in excruciating pain. The first indication of his condition occurred when he attended the summer camp at Bangor. Unable to join the others in their holiday activities, Jeffreys took Tweed as pillion passenger on an old motor cycle he had been given. He recounted that 'I never forgot that ride. It cheered me up greatly and I saw in Pastor Jeffreys a kindly, considerate, and helpful man not to be kept at a distance, but accepted as a friend'.[71] As Tweed's condition worsened to a complete breakdown in health, Jeffreys arranged for him to be taken care of by the Gault family at their farm near Ballymena.[72] Referring to the Gaults, Tweed added 'they were not being paid so far as I personally was concerned for my upkeep care and attention'.[73] That would have been a matter between them and Jeffreys who was doubtless relieved that the generosity of the Gaults had spared any financial burden falling on the Band.

6.3.2 Premises

With limited financial backing, travelling light with minimum overheads was the key to building up a presence in the province. Meetings were convened in low cost premises or were hosted by well-disposed supporters. Orange Halls, dotting the Ulster landscape in rural areas wherever a sizeable Protestant community existed, were frequently hired. They are to be found in most villages and in the open countryside where many stand in unprepossessing yet defiant isolation. The halls formed a focal point in the social and religious life of many in the Protestant community. Tweed first heard the Pentecostal message in one of the two Orange Halls in Rasharkin in 1918 and recorded that at the end of that mission an offering was taken to support the evangelists, R.E. Darragh and T.J. Logan in their next venture planned for Ballymoney. 'The Orange Hall had evidently been booked in advance, and that was a remarkable achievement and must have [had] the goodwill of the members of the Orange Order, for the various denominations were

---

[70] *RT*, 16 February 1962, p. 3.

[71] *Tweed Memoir*, p. 22.

[72] James Gault had accepted in 1916 the Pentecostal message at the Ballymena mission led by Jeffreys and was among the first elders of the Elim Church in the town.

[73] *Tweed Memoir*, p. 24.

opposed to any new venture under the name of religion or of anything of that nature outside their "inner circle"'.[74]

An existence where one mission was called upon to support the next one was an indication of the parlous state of living on a knife-edge. The Ballymoney assembly when it first started had 'just sufficient to keep things going for the weekend services'.[75] The situation demanded that the evangelists had to be appealing in every sense. A few years later, Tweed, together with another Band colleague, conducted a mission in Ahoghill where they found 'members of the Orange Order...very favourable towards the preaching of the gospel'[76]—a reminder that, as a mass movement, the strength of Orangeism lay in late Victorian evangelical piety. At the same time, there were other forces in Protestantism, well represented in the professional middle-class, not least among a sizeable proportion of mainline clergy, that were deeply antipathetic to the Order, hence the greater likelihood of a more favourable reception from Orange committees than church manses.

In addition to Orange Halls, other types of venue were used. For example, the hall in Lisburn owned by the Good Templars, a Protestant temperance counterpart to the Catholic 'Pioneers', was rented. The YMCA hall in Ballymena was used in 1916 for the first short summer campaign and the old Town Hall for the following Christmas Convention. The Town Hall continued to be hired for special meetings up to 1919 when it was destroyed by fire, allowing one wag to remark that 'the holy rollers kept singing "Let the fire fall". Well, their God answered them and burned the building as well!'[77] In Hackett's record of his visit to Ballymena in 1917, he developed the symbolism of fire in his description of a Saturday evening prayer meeting convened before a group of thirty set out to hold an open-air meeting: 'Well might one present at that hallowed scene say "There is fire here". Yes, fire indeed! "The Holy Ghost and fire"—a holy fervour burning throughout the room. The prayer of a young girl who had received the Baptism, "May burning desire for souls fill our hearts", simply voiced the desire and prayer of all'.[78]

There is no evidence that Jeffreys preached in any mainline church other than in the Parish Church in Ballymena. Hackett was probably instrumental in the invitation being issued through contact with a clerical

---

[74] *Tweed Memoir*, p. 8.

[75] *Tweed Memoir*, p. 11.

[76] *Tweed Memoir*, p. 8.

[77] Montgomery, *Elim in Ballymena 1916-1986*, p.18. 'Fire', indeed, was one of the potent images favoured by Pentecostals with its connotations of John the Baptist's promise that the Messiah 'will baptise you with the Holy Spirit and fire' (Luke 3:16) and the 'divided tongues as of fire' (Acts 2:3) that sat on each of the disciples at Pentecost.

[78] *Confidence*, July-September 1918, p. 54.

colleague.[79] Another factor possibly encouraging the invitation rested in the sympathetic attitude of the vicar. Jeffreys reported in *Confidence* that a woman resident of the town had told of a visit she had made in 1909 to Sunderland during which she 'heard of great blessing in a Vicarage'.[80] When in England, she related that 'a longing came into my heart that the blessing might reach my home in the North of Ireland. I made my desire known to the vicar and his wife, and we knelt down together and asked God to send the blessing to Ballymena... I do praise God because I am privileged to see the answer'. [81] Pentecostals, as here, sometimes found themselves knocking on a door that was quarter-open such as the woman whom Darragh recorded who was similarly expectant. She had been a Christian for over twenty years and suffered from a heart condition that had prevented her from attending church for seventeen years, and 'had often prayed that God would again restore the gifts of the Holy Ghost to the Church'.[82] He rejoiced that she had been healed and baptised in the Spirit, 'the Spirit speaking through her with new tongues, and giving her the interpretation, which was praise and thanksgiving to God'.[83] Both women came from the Ballymena area, substantially the Presbyterian heartland of the 1859 Revival, where the folk memory of the Revival had become idealised within the older generation.[84] For them, the Jeffreys campaign recalled those halcyon days and now, as he reported, 'How they praise God for a touch of the old time power'.[85]

The *Tweed Memoir* draws attention to another group that exemplifies the penetration of the Pentecostal message before the arrival of Elim. During 1918, at the first Elim mission he attended at Rasharkin, Tweed was introduced to a Mr Fulton. Fulton lived a short distance outside Ballymoney and together with some friends supported the Rasharkin effort. In Ballymoney, he was the leader of a small group of about six who met each Sunday in a house in a back street 'for the purpose of "breaking bread" and the exercise of spiritual gifts'. While working in Scotland, Fulton in 1908 had come in contact with Pentecostalism, very probably at Kilsyth. On his return to Ulster he formed a small group, which were branded as the 'tongues people' and generally shunned. It

---

[79] The address for the occasion focused on Acts 1:3, 5, 11, from which Jeffreys drew attention to Calvary (the starting point), Pentecost (the pathway) and Parousia (the goal) of the Christian race.

[80] *Confidence,* August 1916, p. 130.

[81] *Confidence,* August 1916, p. 130.

[82] *Confidence*, March-April 1917, p. 19.

[83] *Confidence*, March-April 1917, p. 19.

[84] Janice Holmes makes the point that in the latter part of nineteenth century, with few signs of a revival on the lines of that in 1859, there was a tendency to promote 'the idealisation of the 1859 Revival'. (Holmes, *Religious Revivals*, p. 177.)

[85] *Confidence*, August 1916, p. 130.

was Fulton who first raised the issue of adult baptism with Tweed, later baptising him in the River Bush, as well as pressing him on the matter of Spirit-baptism.

Some of the halls used were fairly basic and in a few cases makeshift. The Orange Hall at Ahoghill was lit by fickle oil lamps and the seating there and in similar settings 'as a rule [was] without backs, so people did not attend for comfort'.[86] Barns were even less comfortable. Tweed conducted a mission in the barn at Eskylane, near Ballymena, that belonged to the Gault family who were founder members of the Ballymena church. He later led another mission in a barn belonging to the McWilliams family at Lisdrumbrocus, about three miles south of Armagh city. It was at this mission that Tweed first met his future wife. She was one of a party of young people that E.J. Phillips, the pastor of the Armagh church, brought with him to support the mission. Sometimes a sizeable farmhouse provided hospitality for smaller meetings, as at the end of the first mission in Rasharkin. The farmer had most likely been converted during the mission that Jeffreys conducted in Ballymena in 1916. It was there that Tweed first met Jeffreys in the 'Big Farm House' to which a blacksmith's forge was attached, both indicators of the well-to-do lifestyle of the owner. Pentecostals, no less in Ireland than other parts of the British Isles, were not entirely drawn from the lower social classes and this was as true of the farming community as the urban.[87]

During August 1917, Margaret Streight with an unnamed colleague arranged to hold a meeting in a large farmhouse in the Braid Valley under Slemish Mountain. Hackett outlined the sequence of events:

> The owner at first refused to attend, owing to strong prejudices, excited by another mission formerly at work there. A little later he came in. The meeting seemed so hard and dry that the young lady [Margaret Streight] proposed prayer... In a few moments she was under the mighty Power of God in tongues. Prejudices were dispelled; the work was at once seen to be of God. Nineteen were brought to Christ in a fortnight, nine in a later fortnight. The tongues had fulfilled the Divine purpose...had awakened attention, solemnised the hearers, demonstrated the near presence of our God, and made room for the mighty work of the Spirit.[88]

The final sentence demonstrates something of Hackett's theological acuity in summarising the purpose of tongues. He later formalised his views in a widely distributed tract *The Baptism in the Holy Ghost & Gifts*

---

[86] *Tweed Memoir*, p. 27.

[87] Class is, arguably, less of a social divide in Ireland than in Britain. In Ulster, sectarianism has fostered a protective cohesion within the two major communities. With the preservation of the Union as the sacred cow of political Unionism, there has been a strong commonality of interest across all social classes.

[88] *Confidence*, July-September 1918, p. 54.

of the Spirit—Why Now?[89] Boddy affectionately referred to Hackett as 'our beloved brother, [who] is deeply taught in the Word. His scholarly knowledge of the original is lit up by the blessed Spirit and made useful to God's people'.[90]

Apart from farmhouses, other workplaces were used for meetings. Once the Darragh/Logan mission ended in Ballymoney, the home of the Livingstones in Henry Street became the meeting place for the Elim nucleus. The Livingstones were friendly with the Fulton group and may even have been part of it. It was they who had introduced Tweed to Fulton in the course of gathering support for the earlier Rasharkin mission. As numbers increased in Ballymoney, the company moved into the large 'Garden Shed' where Livingstone had earlier carried on his stonemason business.[91] Just as unpretentious was the building purchased in 1919 for the new assembly in Cullybackey. In 1917, Henderson had conducted a mission in the village and since no public hall was available, he obtained an empty shed which had been fitted out by a young American inventor as his workshop. When the time came to start a new assembly, the American was approached with a view to purchasing the structure.[92] Not only was the transaction completed but the young man became a Christian. The building was re-erected in Pottinger Street and officially opened as an Elim Church by Jeffreys in 1919.[93]

Elim began with a tent mission in Monaghan. Of all the structures used, the tent proved the most versatile, though limited to summer use and even then, with the Irish climate, it could not always be guaranteed to provide protection. At a mission in the linen mill village of Milford, about three miles south of Armagh, the tent was destroyed beyond repair in a gale. Some locals saw in the loss the judgement of God on the mission. The purchase of a tent for £20 from Ferguson provided a 275-seat facility. The June 1916 mission in Ballymena lasted for five weeks with the tent filled most evenings and, occasionally, three were seated to every two chairs with others standing in any available space. At the meetings on Sunday, the sides were lowered to let the overspill crowd participate. Jeffreys reported that 150 conversions had taken place over the previous five weeks:

> Many have received the baptism in the Holy Ghost... One sister was baptised in the street after leaving the meeting one evening, while another received during the

---

[89] Reprinted in *EE*, September 1920, pp. 10-11.

[90] *Confidence*, October 1911, p. 235.

[91] *Tweed Memoir*, p. 12.

[92] *Diary of Events in the Irish Work Since 1915*, a typescript account compiled possibly by E. J. Phillips (c.1936) in the Mattersey Archive Collection.

[93] W.L. Spence, *Elim in Cullybackey 1919-1989*, (Cullybackey: Elim Pentecostal Church, 1989).

> dinner hour in the business place. Some who have been faithful Christians for years are now seeking and are very hungry for the fullness... On Wednesday evening about 150 Christians publicly testified that they were consecrating themselves to God that they might receive the Pentecostal Baptism.[94]

Temporary and impermanent meeting places brought the benefits of cost-cutting and flexibility but, as minuted in June some weeks before the commencement of the tent mission in Monaghan in 1915, there was an expressed intention to establish 'a church on Scriptural lines...from which the full Gospel should be sent into Ireland'.[95] The resolve to establish a headquarters church was swiftly realised when the local leaders, the Gillespie brothers, found premises fairly close to their home at 22 Pine Street, off Donegall Pass. It was a badly dilapidated building in Hunter Street, off the Donegal Road, that had been used previously as a laundry. According to Farlow, the premises were situated in one of the worst streets in the city, 'the name of which had to be changed several times, owing to the sinfulness of its inhabitants'.[96] Children used the lamp-post at the front door for swinging around, an irritant to all who entered. The local youths made it impossible to keep a pane of glass intact in the building. Money, in any case, was so short that replacement was out of the question so they had to make do with filling the openings with old rags. Tweed recalled how he and Henderson spent time on their knees 'praying that God would send the money for a larger and better place of worship'.[97]

Located not far from the Protestant heartland of Sandy Row, Hunter Street was placed in a setting every bit as unprepossessing as the Azusa Street mission was in Los Angeles or the working-class environs of All Saints, Monkwearmouth, Sunderland. The building was secured on a three-year lease with George Jeffreys and William Gillespie named as the tenants and George Gillespie and David A. Graham appointed as guarantors. Considerable work was required to make the premises suitable for meetings and the labour was provided largely by Jeffreys and Henderson. In June 1915, Jeffreys accepted the call to become pastor-in-charge, though the title carries a hint of the frequent absences that were inevitable as he fulfilled what was recognised as his primary task, the call to engage in an itinerant Pentecostal evangelistic ministry. In fact,

---

[94] *Confidence*, August 1916, p. 130.

[95] The minutes were headed '*Report of Meeting in connection with the forming of Elim Christ Church*' which most likely met in the home of the Gillespie brothers. All the minutes of this group will be referred to as *BEM* (*Belfast Elim Minutes*). The *BEM* deal with the affairs of the Hunter Street assembly and its successor from 1919, the Melbourne Street assembly.

[96] Cartwright, *The Great Evangelists*, p. 45.

[97] *Tweed Memoir*, p. 18.

provision was made for such a contingency since it was agreed that Miss A. Stephens from Shrewsbury, who had assisted Jeffreys at the mission in Monaghan, would deputise when Jeffreys honoured engagements elsewhere. The fact that he was in Ireland exempted Jeffreys from conscription, an eventuality in which Hackett discerned 'God's precious providence [that] enabled him to continue the good work without interruption'.[98]

6.4 The First Elim Constitution

The first meeting to agree a constitution for the new church in Belfast was held in Pine Street on the 23 August 1915 when William Gillespie, David Graham, Ernest Darragh and George Jeffreys came together. They reached agreement on the following points:

1. The name of the church to be Elim Christ Church.

2. No member of any other assembly to be asked to join the church.

3. A free-will offering box to be placed at the door and an offering would be collected only at the Sunday morning service.

4. W. Gillespie, Graham and Darragh to fulfil the office of deacon. [Three others including G. Gillespie were added a few months later.]

5. Jeffreys to draw up a doctrinal statement *What We Believe* for submission at the next church meeting.[99]

It is worth examining in some detail each of these points as they did much to capture the course and ethos of all subsequent Elim work.

6.4.1 Elim Christ Church

The name 'Elim' was taken from the episode recorded in Exodus 15:27 when the Israelites on their migration to the Promised Land were refreshed in their desert journey at the oasis of the same name.[100] With his

---

[98] *Confidence*, April-June 1918, p. 20. In April 1918 the British government sought to impose conscription in Ireland, an attempt that only succeeded in further alienating nationalist Ireland.

[99] *BEM*, June 1915

[100] The designation was common enough in American Holiness settings. For example, the Elim Faith Home in Rochester, New York, was opened in 1887 by the Duncan sisters in connection with their Holiness and healing ministry. When they accepted the Pentecostal message in 1907 they had already established a church, the Elim Tabernacle as well as Rochester Bible Training School.

Welsh background, Jeffreys was familiar with local churches adopting biblical names such as 'Carmel', 'Ebenezer', 'Shiloh' and 'Bethel'. To these can be added 'Elim' which was seen as 'a fitting symbol of a movement with a message that gives refreshing health and hope to soul and body'.[101] The *Elim Evangel*, first published in December 1919, carried on its cover the sketch of an oasis beside the relevant text. When he was a student at the PMU school at Preston, Jeffreys preached on a number of occasions in the Elim Mission at nearby Lytham. He told its founder, Henry Mogridge, that if he ever opened a new work, he would call it Elim and so when the opportunity arose, he implemented his desire.[102] The name proved popular and was adopted as the formal title of the Evangelistic Band from July 1916.[103]

Others were less impressed by the name, including the Presbyterian author of *The Elimites,* who indulged in a little drollery at its expense:

> Why this particular name was selected is difficult to understand... There is no evidence that the Israelites ever regarded the oasis as anything more than a useful halting place on the way to Canaan... [O]ne might ask if the Elim Church, like the Elim grove, can only temporarily, and in a very limited way, satisfy the forward moving life of man, and if advancing beyond Elim is not more important than reaching it? [104]

In taking this tack, the writer was following the line taken in 1928 by Harold Barker in a Brethren periodical. In pointing out that the oasis was only a respite stop and not Canaan, he submitted that Elim needed to move on to true spiritual maturity. Its followers were too concerned with their own needs and forever talking of their 'wonderful experiences...till one gets weary... The teaching of the *Elim Evangel* and the "testimony" of its adherents are but the prattle of children wading in the shallows'.[105]

The name 'Christ Church', besides sounding uncharacteristically grand for a back-street mission, was intended to make a point. For such a building, 'Church' would not have been the first term to come to the mind of a well-heeled visitor as, indeed, was the case when Mrs John Leech referred to the Elim 'Mission' and the Elim 'Hall' in two consecutive paragraphs in a report she contributed to *Confidence*.[106] The

---

[101] 'Observer', *Who Are They?: The Elimites*, (Belfast: Sabbath School Society, c.1950), p. 3. This pamphlet, of Presbyterian provenance, was one of a series that took a hard look at different 'sects' which, besides Elim, included Jehovah's Witnesses, the Brethren, and the Communists. The writer obtained the quotation from the Elim publication, *Labourers with God,* only to pour cold water on the claim.

[102] Cartwright, *The Great Evangelists*, pp. 45-6.

[103] *EEBM*, 8 July 1916.

[104] 'Observer', *The Elimites,* p. 4.

[105] *The Witness*, 1928, p. 432.

[106] *Confidence*, May 1916, p. 81.

term 'Hall' was also used in a notice in the local press advertising the Easter Convention in 1916.[107] In using the term 'Church', Jeffreys and the deacons were making a statement of their status ambition and their orthodox and evangelical credentials, aiming above all to allay any suspicions of being a cult or exclusivist sect. Pentecostal Christians of the stamp of Jeffreys were ever keen to press their deeply traditional evangelical identity from the beginning. As for the use of 'Christ' in this context, Carl Brumback makes a perceptive observation. He maintained that there was a shared problem facing the movement, one that Jeffreys with some degree of awareness addressed in naming the church: 'Early Pentecost was in danger of too much emphasis upon the distinctive truths which God restored to the Church through them... When sincere inquirers recognised the movement to be Christo-centric, rather than Pneuma-centric or charisma-centred, many of them made their decision to accept the Pentecostal message.[108]

6.4.2 The Proselytism Issue

Caution needs to be taken not to see the minuted statement—'No member of any other assembly be asked to join the church'—as a strict non-proselytising policy. Though the early years of Elim have been described as the era of 'ecumenical evangelisation',[109] as evidenced by Leech and the Hackett agreeing to become advisory members of the EEB, it is likely that the term 'assembly' referred in effect to other Pentecostal or sympathetic fellowships in Belfast. It is most unlikely that there were any strong feelings of inhibition about transfer growth. Once the process of denominalisation started, the ideal of convert-only growth became virtually unsustainable. Nevertheless, in their capacity as advisory members, Leech and Hackett, by remaining within the Church of Ireland, helped to ensure, on paper at least, that with the setting up of the new legal body in 1918, the Elim Pentecostal Alliance (EPA), Elim would remain an open fellowship. When Leech, Hackett and Jeffreys met in January 1918 the following resolution was passed: 'That members of all churches who are born again and who stand for the Full Gospel can

---

[107] *Belfast News-Letter*, 29 April 1916.

[108] Carl Brumback, *Suddenly From Heaven: A History of the Assemblies of God,* (Springfield, MO: Gospel Publishing House, 1961), p. 46. It will be recalled as well that Jeffreys in his AFC days was ordained in Emmanuel Christ Church, Maesteg. It is possible that this had a bearing, even if subliminal, on the naming of the Belfast centre.

[109] A term used by Wilson, *Sects and Society,* p. 43. He added that even when Elim had a clear denominational identity 'many Elimites still regarded themselves as more generally Pentecostal, or evangelical, rather than specifically Elim'—a statement made possible by Jeffreys, for the most part, operating more as an evangelist than the builder of a denomination.

become members of the [EPA] without leaving their own churches, the aim of the Alliance not to be that of encouraging members to leave their own denominations'.[110]

This formula ensured the continuance of Leech and Hackett on the advisory committee of the EEB, though it changed nothing on the ground. Hathaway is of the opinion that the non-proselytising ordinance 'eased the high tension a new movement causes'[111]—a view born possibly more of wish than fact. He also takes as evidence of Jeffreys' 'irenic, if not ecumenical, spirit' his long association with Hackett and 'with other denominational leaders'.[112] As far as Ireland was concerned there is no documentation of who such 'other leaders' might be. Hackett was a special case. He had come into the Pentecostal experience before Jeffreys and was as dedicated to the Pentecostal cause as the latter, going as far as to be baptised by total immersion by Jeffreys in the Elim Tabernacle, Melbourne Street, Belfast.[113] Other than in Ballymena, there is no evidence of contact, even less fraternisation, between the Band members and mainline denominational ministers, certainly in Ireland. The evidence is to the contrary. The policy did nothing to reduce the animosity the movement aroused which was one of the reasons for creeping denominationalism. At Jeffreys' funeral service, Robert Tweed spoke feelingly of

> the price Principal Jeffreys and his faithful band of workers had to pay in those early pioneer days... The Baptism of the Holy Spirit, Divine Healing, and the Second Advent of Christ were considered 'new doctrines' and many of the religious denominations were in bitter opposition to this teaching, sometimes calling those who believed in it by names that were by no means complimentary.[114]

He indicated that the pressure to form new churches lay often with those strongly influenced by Jeffreys' ministry. Even though during the mission in Ballymoney in 1918 'there had been no denunciations or preaching against the established churches, Catholic or Protestant, [yet] at the close of the mission, problems arose'.[115] Converts and those persuaded of the truth of the Pentecostal emphases 'made it clear that they would have to separate themselves from whatever denomination they belonged, and form a group of like-minded believers who would continue to enjoy the blessings they had experienced... George Jeffreys

---

[110] *Minutes of the Special Meeting of the Advisory members of the EEB*, 7 January 1918 at the home of John Leech in Dublin.

[111] Hathaway, 'The Elim Pentecostal Church', p. 13.

[112] Hathaway, 'The Elim Pentecostal Church', p. 13.

[113] Edsor, *'Set Your House In Order'*, p.31.

[114] 'A Tribute by Pastor Robert Gordon Tweed', *The Pattern*, April 1962, p. 12.

[115] *Tweed Memoir*, p. 9.

was no wrecker of churches, but he well knew that when "Pentecostal power fell"...that a spiritual home would have to be found after each mission'.[116] Edsor came to a similar conclusion: Jeffreys 'established churches for the converts believing these fundamental truths [Pentecostal distinctives] because, as a general rule, they were not preached wholly in other denominations. Hence the inevitable formation of the Elim movement under his leadership in 1915'.[117]

6.4.3 Finance

Finances were undoubtedly stretched to cover the expenses of the Hunter Street assembly. The members had to meet the running costs and Jeffreys' salary. The minutes hint that the Gillespie brothers generously supported the work in every sense. They were thanked for 'their practical sympathy with the church at the commencement of the work'.[118] This was followed by a recommendation that at the next full meeting of members 'the needs of the church' should be put before them. The 'needs' in all likelihood encompassed the church's financial situation which was always prone to be precarious considering its particular setting. Mrs Leech commented on the location of the church: 'Elim Hall is situated in a very poor populous district, truly a light in a dark place! Thousands of the people around *never* enter a place of worship'.[119] When Jeffreys was called to visit a dying man living in a house nearby, he witnessed at first hand the ravages of deprivation. The banister rails and balustrade had been used as firewood and Jeffreys had to use a rope to climb the stairs to talk and pray with the man while downstairs two women were busily engaged in a drunken brawl.[120] In his obituary tribute to Leech, Jeffreys said of him and his wife who had died before her husband in 1931: 'When I founded the Elim movement in the North of Ireland, both threw themselves unreservedly into the work and were not ashamed to be identified with its humble beginnings in a back-street mission hall in the city of Belfast'.[121] James McWhirter gave some background to Leech's pre-Pentecostal days in Dublin that reveal his familiarity with inner city conditions: 'When he was the "youngest father of the barristers in Ireland" he was also a "chucker-out" at a slum mission in Dublin—a

[116] *Tweed Memoir*, p. 9.

[117] Edsor, *'Set Your House In Order'*, p. 42.

[118] *BEM*, 1 November 1916, in Hunter Street.

[119] *Confidence*, May 1916, p. 81.

[120] Compensating for the dismal surroundings of Hunter Street was the reality in 1916 of the city enjoying one of its periods of economic boom and low unemployment. However, wartime inflation only allowed living standards to be maintained by working extremely long hours.

[121] *The Pattern*, mid-August 1942, p. 3.

tough gentleman who saw off the "baser sort" when they would have broken up gospel open-air meetings'.[122]

6.4.4 Church Government

The sorriest episode in the history of Elim was the departure of George Jeffreys in the early 1940s from the denomination he founded. It grew from a controversy fought largely on the issue of church government which centred on the role and powers of the local oversight vis-à-vis the authority of the central body. As the number of Elim churches increased, Jeffreys pressed for a system of strong central and ministerial control established over all local churches. It was a position that was bound to arouse dissent where there was an independent-minded eldership, especially in Ulster that had such a tradition. Elders, notably those drawn from Presbyterian or Brethren backgrounds, were not likely to take easily to outside *diktat* such as came increasingly from the headquarters in London from the mid-1920s onwards. Whereas it could be said that the typical convert in Ulster was a church attached layman, in England it was a mill girl. Consequently, the type of church government that was likely to prove acceptable in Ulster was one that cultivated a self-governing ethos in the local church within a framework of greater regional autonomy than that provided for the rest of the movement. That, in fact, was how it panned out more or less after the split, though the pressure for such an outcome had been building up steadily in the 1930s. In England, by contrast, the often youthful pastors had to exert direct personal control over church affairs and they, themselves, were the target of directives from an ever increasing administrative machine masterminded by a headquarters that was in the efficient hands of E.J. Phillips from 1923 onwards. Events were to prove that there could be no going back to the heady, less structured ways of the movement's origins.

Then, from around the middle of the 1930s, Jeffreys did a complete *volte face* and dubbed the system of central control which he had established, 'pagan Babylonish', a switch that has intrigued commentators ever since. It will always carry an air of mystery insofar as the weight that should be given to Jeffreys' psychological and medical state is an imponderable.[123] His obsessive absorption with a matter that 'diverted his attention away from his God-appointed task of winning multitudes to

---

[122] *The Pattern*, April 1942, p. 4.

[123] Around the time of the split, Jeffreys had a breakdown in his health. In January 1938, his physical condition was giving 'cause for grave concern'. (Cartwright, *The Great Evangelists*, p. 142.) He was never again to recover his robust good health and was not helped by the onset of diabetes. The thick files in Elim archives of his various schemes to decentralise Elim's decision-making procedures point more to a fixation than a rational reform.

Christ' was one of the distressing outcomes of the situation.[124] The vehemence with which the dispute was carried out is startling to modern ears. Its flavour is captured in the first paragraph of a pamphlet, *Fight For The Faith And Freedom*, that Jeffreys published in 1944: 'The division in the Elim Movement...has sounded the alarm against organising the members of Christ's Body after the Pattern of a Limited Company, with Churches like chain-stores throughout the land. It has demonstrated the fact that Local Churches born in revival can be...enslaved by a legalised system of central Church Government that is decidedly Babylonish'.[125]

What is of concern to this study is how this sorry episode is related to the early history of Elim.[126] With the benefit of hindsight, Jeffreys wrote forty years later on the origins of the problem as he saw it:

> It was 'Then'—back in 1915—that we in Elim made the big mistake that shaped the destiny of the movement. *We did not establish the Scriptural sovereignty of the local church in the first Elim Church.*[127]

> If there is one thing I regret more than another it is that I allowed the Elim churches I had founded to be without Elders and Deacons... I could never forgive myself this lack, if it were not for the fact that my busy life was so taken up with extensive campaign work that there was little time and strength left for church government'.[128]

These assertions throw the origins of the conflict right back to the earliest years of the movement in Ireland, starting with Hunter Street and followed by the opening of the next two churches in Ballymena in 1916 and Lisburn in 1917.

Do these declarations represent little more than a *post factum* malaise? The reply of Elim to his charge presents an entirely different perspective:

---

[124] This is the view of Cartwright. (Cartwright, *The Great Evangelists*, p. 139.) Jeffreys provided an answer to this type of charge: 'I have come to see that the Scriptural sovereignty of the local church is of paramount importance. Christ is not only the Saviour of sinners, He is also the Architect of his Churches'. (Edsor, *'Set Your House In Order'*, p. 86.)

[125] *Fight for the Faith and Freedom,* an eight-page pamphlet issued in May 1944.

[126] In the leaflet published by Elim around the time of the split, entitled *'The Right of the Local Church: George Jeffreys Eight Points Analysed'*, p. 1, the writer commented that the whole contention had 'divided homes, broken hearts, split churches, in discouragement to many dear children of God, and worse still, in shame and reproach being brought on the work of the Lord'.

[127] His emphasis. Quoted in Edsor, *'Set Your House In Order',* p. 85.

[128] *The Right of the Local Church*, p. 2.

> Mr. Jeffreys has always concerned himself with church government... When Elim was started in Ireland, Mr. Jeffreys appointed elders in the Irish churches as also he did in the early Elim churches in Great Britain. The trouble was that, when these elders wanted to have some say in local church affairs, he disapproved, and subsequently abolished lay elders and substituted personal control by the minister under his authority.[129]

The evidence supports this view as against that of Jeffreys. Tweed, who followed Jeffreys into the Bible-Pattern Fellowship, maintained that the 'churches in the early days had lifetime eldership' and it was only in the case of 'some big discussion or dissension' that Jeffreys became involved.[130] When the Hunter Street assembly moved to Melbourne Street in 1919 the work began there 'with a solid membership, and a number of elders with Bible qualifications [who were] all men of great spiritual stature'.[131] As for directives from headquarters, he recalled that when he was pastor of the Tullynahinion Church for two years in the early 1920s he received 'only one letter that savoured of officialism [and that] was from Mr Phillips...which to me was quite in order and necessary'.[132]

In fact it would have been astonishing if the Hunter Street assembly had not had a strong local leadership, considering that it was born of their initiative, as had the work in Monaghan before it. It is noteworthy that the first office bearers were not termed elders but held the subordinate office of deacons. Their entitlement to the office of elder would have been more appropriate. After all, it was from their number that the initial call had been issued to Jeffreys to work in Ireland and then to accept the pastorate of Hunter Street. The chairman of the oversight meetings was always one of the deacons. Jeffreys was probably younger than most of them. On the many occasions when Jeffreys was absent conducting missions or attending conventions, the deacons carried a major responsibility both for the practical and spiritual side of the work. There is no evidence that Miss

---

129 *The Right of the Local Church*, p. 2., penned, most likely, by Phillips.

130 *Tweed Memoir*, p. 29. Tweed, like many who moved with Jeffreys out of Elim at the time of the split, seemed to be quite oblivious to the fact that it was Jeffreys, admittedly with the support of Phillips, who was pressing for greater centralisation..

131 *Tweed Memoir*, p. 37.

132 *Tweed Memoir*, p. 29. When E.J. Phillips became a member of the EEB in 1919, he may well have had doubts about accepting Jeffreys' invitation to join the Band because years later he wrote that 'my ideas on church government at that time were not altogether in line with those of Pastor Jeffreys'. (*EE*, 15 November 1969, p. 765.) If the differing attitudes of the two men were true to type, then Phillips would have been pushing for a more centralist polity. If that were so, it would confirm that Jeffreys, in the early period, held quite flexible views on this issue which he then came to sharpen in favour of strong central control, only to change tack once again, in effect reverting more or less to his original position.

Stephens, his short-term co-pastor, played any significant part in the life of the Hunter Street assembly.

It is probably best not to read too much into the deacon-elder distinction at the early stage in the history of Elim. The constitution of Christ Church referred simply to 'the leaders' and gave them wide powers: 'All members must be submissive to the leaders, in the Lord, esteeming them for their works' sake and for the office in which God has placed them (1 Thess: 5 vv. 12-12)'.[133] The Ballymena assembly from the beginning appointed elders. At the induction service of Robert Mercer, Jeffreys gave the church 'a never-to-be forgotten exhortation, warning them of the dangers of lawlessness and rebellion, and urging them to recognise the authority of those put in charge of them by the Lord'.[134] The fact that the body of deacons associated with the former Hunter Street after the move to Melbourne Street changed their title to that of 'elder' in 1922 does not suggest a downgrading of office, if anything its opposite. It is easy to see that the rather informal organisational arrangements of the earliest years could have been irksome to Phillips with his leaning to bureaucratic tidiness.

On the other hand, as a man of administrative tidiness, Phillips would have approved of the stringency of the disciplinary codes that were framed to counter what the Elim Christ Church saw as a persistent danger—'the onslaught of the enemy...in his seeking to counterfeit and to produce extravagances, which we must be careful to avoid, by continuing steadfastly in God's precious word'.[135] This again demonstrated the misgivings Jeffreys had of 'extravagance', the avoidance of which was for him a major preoccupation. Phillips considered that Jeffreys' 'call was to conserve the results of his evangelistic efforts by establishing Pentecostal churches free from the fanaticism and extravagances which were all too common in the early days of the Pentecostal movement'.[136] Throughout Jeffreys' leadership, every effort was made to forestall unseemly and unruly behaviour, which, as more churches were added, contributed to an ethos of control that unfolded itself in the organisational structures of Elim.

It is difficult to deny Wilson's contention that centralised organisation had come into being 'not at [Jeffreys'] instigation, but rather by force of circumstances'.[137] The early days when Jeffreys had, in Wilson's words, 'the spontaneous, unorganised and naïve desire to convert the nation', could not last: 'Unbeknown even to himself, Jeffreys was fighting a social process—that of instituitionalisation, although he only saw the

[133] *Jeffreys, What We Believe,* p. 6

[134] Boulton, *Ministry of the Miraculous*, p. 69.

[135] Jeffreys, *What We Believe*, p. 2.

[136] *EE*, 17 February 1962, p. 104.

[137] Wilson, *Sects and Society*, p. 43.

symptom—the changed locus of power'.[138] The concatenation of events that led to the formation of Elim churches made it difficult for the denomination to settle for a loose federation of independent churches. A congregationalist polity would only have been an option where contrasting conditions prevailed. That this was not ruled out can be seen in the events leading up to and during the conference held in Sheffield in May 1922 called to promote a greater unity among British Pentecostals, though the Apostolic Church was not involved.[139] The Conference was promoted strongly by Jeffreys and William Burton. The final recommendations were communicated to all the invited assemblies, under the heading *Constitution of the General Council of the Assemblies of God in Great Britain and Ireland*. The proposals appear to assume the independence of the participating assemblies, though clause VI carried tones too ominous for many. It recommended that the proposed General Council be empowered 'to exercise any needed discipline as required by Scripture over the recognised workers of the assemblies in fellowship and assist all local assemblies'. It is likely that the phrase 'exercise any needed discipline', if interpreted as a threat to local autonomy, would have scared off many. Nevertheless, the episode shows that Jeffreys was more accepting of a looser organisational structure for a unified Pentecostal movement than he came to promote within Elim.

Gee recognised the inevitability of the centralist polity that unfolded in Elim: 'The majority of Elim Assemblies came into existence through the instrumentality of one man's spiritual gifts, and looked to one personality as their founder. To them, therefore, a unified form of central government was natural, logical, acceptable and successful. It seemed to indicate the way by which the blessing had brought them to birth could be perpetuated'.[140] Joseph Smith, on more pragmatic grounds, sided from the first with the centralist line that Jeffreys began increasingly to take.[141] He expressed with some feeling the skirmishes leaders like him had to

---

138 Wilson, *Sects and Society*, pp. 58; 50. The concept of *the routinisation of charisma* was formulated by the German sociologist, Max Weber (1864-1920), and provided a conceptual framework in Wilson's study of Elim. (See Margaret Poloma, *The Charismatic Movement: Is There a New Pentecost*?, [Boston: Twayne Publishers, 1982], p. 38.)

139 Wilson, *Sects and Society*, p. 58. See also Ch. 3 entitled *The abortive Sheffield Conference May 1922*, in Richard D. Massey, '"A Sound and Scriptural Union": An Examination of the Origins of the Assemblies of God of Great Britain and Ireland during the Years 1920-1925', (PhD, Birmingham, 1987), for a full account of the conference proceedings.

140 Gee, *Wind and Flame*, p. 130.

141 Smith joined the Band in 1920 and had some ministerial experience, probably gained in America. He received his Spirit-baptism in Philadelphia in 1915 sitting at his office desk.

face in independent assemblies: 'Before I came into Elim I was a member of a Pentecostal church where doctrinal matters were judged by the local assembly and I know how the church was rent asunder because of that very thing... Conference is the place to settle disputes—a church is a place to worship God'.[142] Jeffreys was well acquainted with the congregational form of church government from his own upbringing within Welsh Congregationalism. Perhaps a youthful disenchantment with church sessions in the valleys made him cool at times towards the idea of elders, fearing their ability to stultify a move of the Spirit through wranglings and spiritual atrophy. In a letter to Phillips, Jeffreys complained of Irish church officers as 'monuments...strutting about in the churches, a stumbling block and a positive hindrance to any progress in the church'[143]—an echo, perhaps, of a commonplace lament from his early chapel days.

Gee's observation can be teased out a little further. A case could be made for the view that Jeffreys, though reserved and private by nature, had as a side to his nature a need to exert control. A.W. Edsor recollected that it was not unusual for Jeffreys to summon him in a quite peremptory manner to drive him to South Wales to visit his sister, journeys made all the more inconvenient by the considerable distances involved.[144] However, unravelling the contradistinction between a charge of Jeffreys' being highhanded and a view of him as man fulfilling his destiny, with due allowance made, is too knotty to permit an easy answer. For Phillips, however, who was hardly a neutral observer on this question, there was little doubt as to where he saw the balance lying. His exasperation was expressed in some unpublished hand-written notes he used to give a talk at the Ministerial Conference in Ireland in 1941:

> G.J. knows the power of his personality and builds up the whole of his methods on it...never happy unless in absolute control. [He] insisted on always being made much of, demanded photo in every *Evangel*, & healings thro[ough] other Pastors in small type. Stopped campaigns when reached point of success. Often wrote up his own meetings and praise of himself... We partly to blame for making him the idol of the Elim people.[145]

Others seemed unaware of this side of Jeffreys and painted a less jaundiced picture. When John Carter wrote that Jeffreys 'was a born

---

[142] *EE*, Vol. 22 1941, pp. 267-8.

[143] Letter dated 23 October 1933, cited by Hudson, 'A Schism and its Aftermath', n. 507.

[144] Personal interview conducted 16 April 1997 at Mitcham, London.

[145] Hudson, 'A Schism and its Aftermath', Appendix 3, with some rearrangement of sentences.

leader',[146] it summed up his overriding impression gained by working for fifteen months with him in the EEB in Ireland during 1919-20. He added that 'although very little older than most of us and younger than some members of the Band, he was the acknowledged Captain'.[147] Another military metaphor came to mind in Tweed's portrayal Jeffreys in action: 'The church in Hunter Street at first was like a battlefield from whence Pastor Jeffreys as commander-in-chief sent forth new recruits into different parts of the country'.[148] Such was the dominance of Jeffreys, boosted by the success of his evangelism, that it was inevitable that the stamp of his personality would be pressed on the Elim movement. It showed itself in little ways. For instance, the cover sheet of the Elim Christ Church pamphlet setting out the articles of faith, *What We Believe*, carried his name alone even though the document required the approval of the diaconate of Hunter Street and expressed the doctrinal stance of the church as a whole.

The fact is that Jeffreys had very few internal restrictions placed on him in matters of overall policy and strategy. The Hunter Street diaconate was preoccupied with running the church and coping with Jeffreys' intermittent absences. Formal, minuted meetings with both the diaconate and the EEB were few. The Hunter Street oversight met eight times between June 1915 and December 1918, on average about once every six months. In the same period the EEB met six times. In neither situation, of course, was informal discussion precluded such as to prevent effective business being transacted but it did mean that, as the work was gaining momentum, Jeffreys operated virtually with a free hand. Such freedom for a leader of Jeffreys' gifts and vision allowed for a flexibility that fostered the growth through a diffuse array of operations—a state of affairs that had certain advantages at the start but was to prove quite unsustainable in the long run. Once issues arose that were concerned with the purchase of property, the appointment and stationing of Band members and matters of financial control surfaced, then 'the exigencies of a recurrent situation demanded efficient and routinised central direction'.[149]

That change can lead to concentration of power is illustrated by the move of the work in Hunter Street to Melbourne Street, an operation first mooted at the oversight meeting in October 1917. The lease for the Hunter Street site was originally only for three years but pressure was

---

[146] *RT*, 16 February 1962, p. 3.

[147] *RT*, 16 February 1962, p. 3.

[148] *Tweed Memoir*, pp. 20, 15. Tweed added a cameo of Jeffreys redolent of a field commander engaged in an exercise in logistics. He recalled that 'supplying the young churches with weekend ministry was a great problem that Pastor Jeffreys had to contend with and being with him when making up the lists, it is marvellous how God undertook'.

[149] Wilson, *Sects and Society*, p. 43.

building for the use of larger premises to accommodate the swelling numbers. At the meeting of the deacons in May 1918, it was minuted that 'after failing to procure a place in the Donegal Road district, an effort should be made *by the Pastor* to secure the disused church premises situated in Melbourne Street'—a task that in the case of the Hunter Street premises had been undertaken by the deacons.[150] At the next meeting, the oversight was faced with a number of debatable issues. William Gillespie was brought to the point of resigning from the diaconate, a situation that might well have been brought to a head by a decision taken at the meeting:

> [Agreed] to take upon ourselves the name of the 'Elim Pentecostal Alliance' for the purpose of uniting into one, the different branches, viz., 'Elim Churches', 'Elim Mission' and the 'Elim Evangelistic Band' and we, therefore, acknowledge *a representative body of control with plenary powers* and known as the Council of 'The Elim Pentecostal Alliance' and approve the following as members of the said Council—John Leech, Esq. KC, Rev Thos. Hackett, Pastor Geo. Jeffreys, Wm. Henderson, R.E. Darragh and Pastor S. Jeffreys.[151]

This administrative set-up placed considerable power in Jeffreys' hands, despite the appearance it gave of shared responsibility and built-in accountability. Three of the members of the new Council were not resident in Ulster. Stephen Jeffreys was based in South Wales and the advisory members of the Band, Leech and Hackett, who together with Jeffreys could come together as an inner decision-making triumvirate, resided in the Dublin area. The latter two, by not burning their bridges with their denomination, showed their commitment was more to the Pentecostal experience than any particular denominational expression of it. Darragh and Henderson were loyal colleagues of Jeffreys and chosen by him to join the Band. The questions now remains, did Gillespie see in this move an inevitable downgrading of the local diaconate?

When it came to the purchase of the property at Melbourne Street, then it is plain that the initiative behind the new venture had passed completely from the diaconate to the new Elim Pentecostal Alliance Council (EPAC). When the purchase was at the point of being agreed, the oversight of Hunter Street which remained unchanged in its composition, passed the following resolution which more or less underscored its governmental nullity:

> That we render thanks to God for opening the way for the Elim Pentecostal Alliance Council to secure the premises and agree to help the Council in every possible way to further the interests of the Kingdom of God in the acquired premises and that a

[150] *BEM*, 14 May 1918. Emphasis added.

[151] *BEM*, 8 October 1918. Emphasis added

> meeting of church members be called to put before them the need and to pass a vote of confidence in the Council in their undertaking such a step.[152]

In their approval, there is a perceptible shift on the deacons' part from having been leading players to amenable followers. A dependency culture was here in the making. It hinged on Jeffreys' drawing power to raise the money to launch his own initiatives which was, in effect, a major factor in the concentration of power in his hands. The personal sway of Jeffreys was made complete when the debt burden on the church was lightened by the promise of the proceeds of the legacy left to Jeffreys by Mrs Jane Rees. It was recorded in the minutes of December 1920 meeting that 'all the deacons expressed thankfulness to God for the prospect of a legacy bequeathed to the Pastor coming to clear off the debt of the Tabernacle'.[153] In the event, the Rees legacy was paid years later in September 1925 and amounted to £901 plus £150 in shares.[154] The whole episode was an adumbration of the future direction of Elim and is illustrative of Wilson's observation that Jeffreys' evangelistic success led inevitably to a situation where 'he was extending the area which the [later] permanent administrators of Elim needed to control'.[155]

That not all were overly impressed by the direction being taken in Elim's internal affairs and the growing dominance of Jeffreys within the movement is revealed in the overtures made by the EPAC to the Hopeton Street assembly to become part of a unified Pentecostal witness.[156] In this episode there was a foreshadowing of the discussions between Elim and those representatives of independent assemblies in Britain desirous of greater unity in the Pentecostal movement in the period 1922-24, out of which the Assemblies of God in Great Britain and Ireland came to be formed. In both cases it became clear that there was a resolute resistance to becoming sucked into a larger more centralised organisation with a consequent loss of the freedoms peculiar to independency.

At the meeting of the oversight of the Hunter Street Church in October 1918, correspondence between Jeffreys and R.J. Kerr was discussed and it was agreed that 'the deacons of each assembly...meet and discuss the following: first, origin of Elim work; second, difficulties and differences and, third, unity'.[157] At the next meeting, the following motion was passed:

---

[152] *BEM,* 3 April 1919.

[153] *BEM*, 9 December 1920.

[154] Desmond W. Cartwright, personal communication, 10 April 2000.

[155] Wilson, *Sects and Society*, p. 43.

[156] This story has to be set in the context of the 1922 Sheffield Conference, the purpose of which is dealt with on p. ... above.

[157] *BEM*, 8 October 1918.

> That we...consider that only by uniting into one alliance can real unity be realised and therefore submit the said [EPAC] rules to their [the Hopeton Street oversight] consideration, and that they as an assembly come in under the Alliance as part of it and like every other centre work under the supervision of the Elim Pentecostal Alliance Council...and that the leader in Hopeton St. becomes one of the recognised workers in the Alliance.[158]

Nine months later there had been no formal response to this proposal and the only further minuted contact between the two parties related to a disciplinary matter involving a member of the EEB.[159] To the Hopeton Street oversight, the attitude conveyed in any discussion undertaken must have been interpreted as nothing less than a blatant take-over bid. It is not surprising that the Elim proposal was turned down and the matter rumbled on for a number of years

A certain *hauteur* on the part of Elim towards the Hopeton Street assembly comes out in a letter sent by its oversight most likely to E.C.W. Boulton as the secretary of the 1922 Sheffield Conference. It will be recalled that Jeffreys and Burton were the prime movers in the calling of the Conference. Of the thirty-eight people in attendance, Jeffreys and Henderson were the only representatives from Ireland. Jeffreys was clearly in a position to have a strong say in any decision relating to Ireland. The letter is dated the 19 May 1922, just four days before the Conference started. In it the Hopeton Street oversight expressed their surprise at a letter they had received from Boulton which withdrew an invitation to them to attend the Conference 'on account of an alleged serious division between the Elim Alliance and the Full Gospel Assembly [Hopeton Street]'. An extract from the letter in response to Boulton reads as follows:

> We are not aware of any serious division existing among us. There are a few minor items of difference which could easily be put right if Mr. Jeffrey (sic) would consent to meet us in frank conversation... When Mr. W. Burton was in Belfast at Christmas 1921, Mr. Kerr [at Mr. Burton's suggestion] consented to meet Mr. Jeffrey in friendly conversation, but this he refused to do stating that a letter which Mr. Kerr had agreed to read before the Full Gospel Assembly [Hopeton Street] had not been read, but he would meet him when this letter had been read.

They then went on to state that the letter referred to from Jeffreys had not been read at Hopeton Street because Kerr had been seriously ill for some months.[160] They then added that the Jeffreys' letter had been read at the

---

158 *BEM*, 23 January 1919.

159 This matter related to Logan and will be dealt with in the following chapter.

160 Kerr's illness was the result of a shooting incident associated with the 'Troubles'. His condition must have been common knowledge in Pentecostal and wider circles in Belfast. At the height of 'the Troubles' in Belfast, Kerr found himself within range of

Hopeton Street Annual Meeting in February 1922 and Jeffreys had been apprised of this. Though Jeffreys had acknowledged receiving the information, he had 'taken no steps to meet us in conversation'. The oversight requested Boulton that the Conference appoint 'two or three brethren to come over and inquire full into the matter'. It was just the type of situation that the draft constitutional proposals agreed by the Sheffield Conference sought to address. The oversight put forward Thomas Myerscough and James Tetchner as suitable names to adjudicate in the dispute, the nature of which was not specified but it is not unreasonable to surmise that Hopeton Street would have been fearful that their independent status would be compromised by overtures from Elim.

Though no official record of the Sheffield Conference was kept, Massey has pieced together some of the matters raised in debate. He notes that Burton in an address 'concluded with a reference to the Belfast assemblies [note plural] and George Jeffreys, indicating presumably that discussions had gone on between himself and Jeffreys, and that perhaps the Elim Pentecostal Alliance in Ireland was another possible model for an initiative in Britain'.[161] It is not unreasonable to postulate that the 'model' was the one formulated in the letter to the Hopeton Street oversight, viz., that 'an assembly come under the Alliance as part of it and like every centre work under the supervision of the Alliance'.[162] If 'supervision' was taken to imply 'control', then that pinpoints the reason why many of the Pentecostal independent assemblies in Britain grew suspicious of any closer engagement with Elim. If, at the time, Jeffeys had conveyed what he came to articulate some twenty years later as his rationale for Pentecostal unity, then the issue becomes one of wider consequence and bears directly on the whole destiny of Pentecostalism in Britain and Ireland. In 1943, he wrote,

> Had we, and others, who were called of God to serve as pioneers and leaders of the Pentecostal Movement, seen the vision of one body, with its members gathered together in free, self-governing Churches as our dear Pastor Lewi Pethrus, of Sweden, had seen it, [then] the history of the Pentecostal Movement in the British Isles would have been vastly different. There would have been one great Pentecostal Movement instead of different sections.

---

random bullets fired by a Republican sniper from the top floor of the Woolworth Building in High Street in the city centre. In running from the scene he tripped and suffered a head gash. The wound became septic and on admission to hospital he was left for dead and taken to the mortuary the next morning. His flock, unaware that he was technically dead, called a prayer meeting that evening. When morning came he was found to be conscious and, on recovering his full senses, he wanted to know what all the fuss was about. (Information from interview with his son, John Kerr, 23 May 1997.)

[161] Massey, 'A Sound and Scriptural Union', p. 29.

[162] *BEM,* 23 January 1919.

> Pentecost has demonstrated that it is far too big for sectarian frontiers, and that its leaders, clothed with power and graced with gifts, are called to fields of service far beyond the narrow confines of any one particular sect.[163]

It is doubtful if such 'AN INSPIRING VISION', the title of the article, was conveyed to the Hopeton Street oversight and, even if it had, it is unlikely it would have been embraced. Events suggest otherwise. The assembly later joined the Assemblies of God in Great Britain and Ireland (AOG), a body organised on congregationalist principles, and even then it showed a characteristic chariness. The leadership dragged its feet for four years and the assembly only became a member of the Irish Presbytery four years after the Presbytery was first established.

None of the considerations discussed so far answer the question as to why Jeffreys stated as a matter of regret that he allowed the first Elim churches in Ireland to be without elders and deacons when in actual fact both offices were operative. When he made this statement, around 1940, it might have helped to advance his case for local church government to have got his facts right. He could then justifiably have made the point that his mistake lay simply in not retaining the right of the local churches to be self-governing. In saying so, he might have come to a greater understanding of his case at the time of the split. However, events had moved on and in 1937 Jeffreys claimed a revelation of the divine mind in which he was mandated to 'Put your house in order'.[164] The situation leading up to the split was further muddied by the belief of many in the Elim leadership that Jeffreys' arguing for a decentralist polity was a gambit to cover his real intention which was 'to use his outstanding rhetorical gifts to persuade rank and file members to adopt British Israelism as a normative belief'.[165] In 1934 the Executive Council considered the influence of John Leech on Jeffreys a baneful factor in his urging the movement to be more amenable to the advocacy of British-Israelism in those churches over which it had direct control. The Executive went as far as suggesting that photographs of Leech be no longer printed in *Elim Evangel*. Jeffreys, ever in awe of Leech, reacted furiously to this suggestion, seeing it as 'an affront to a true and tried

---

[163] Edsor, *'Set Your House In Order'*, p. 144. The mention of Sweden is apposite because it one of the highest percentage of Pentecostals in Europe—4.2%, making it the third largest denominational grouping in the country after the Lutheran and Catholic Churches. It publishes its own daily paper, runs its own Folk Schools and 12% of Swedish parliamentarians are Pentecostal.

[164] This was the command of the prophet Isaiah to Hezekiah as recorded in 1 Kings 20:1. A.W. Edsor chose the text as the title of his glowing account of Jeffreys' ministry.

[165] Neil Hudson and Andrew Walker, 'George Jeffreys, Revivalist and Reformer', in Andrew Walker and Kristin Aune (eds.), *On Revival: A Critical Examination*, (Carlisle: Paternoster, 2003), p. 147.

brother and friend of Elim of twenty years standing'.[166] There was a real fear that the adoption of a decentralist policy would have allowed Jeffreys to win round individual Elim churches to British Israelism and effectively neuter Conference in any decisions it might come to on the subject.[167]

Answers to the question posed at the beginning of the previous paragraph can only be speculative. The simplest is that the *ad hoc* organisational structures of the early days in Ireland registered little with him. As for his part in sanctioning strong executive control in the 1920s, he was in a state of denial as he found it increasingly difficult to come to terms with the unintended repercussions of the policies that he himself had earlier endorsed. By the very nature of his itinerant ministry, Jeffreys at the height of his powers could be less engaged in organisational affairs than Phillips. The Revival Party in spearheading major evangelistic advance were in ways virtually hermetically sealed from the workaday world of local assembly life. On tour, they moved from place to place towing a specially adapted four-berth caravan that was usually parked in the field of some obliging farmer. The cooking was done in a small tent, usually by Darragh, as the jest went, with his Bible in one hand and 'Mrs Beeton' in the other. All this goes some way to explain his growing alienation from the movement in the mid-1930s. It is not difficult to appreciate how institutional change could creep up insidiously on a inspirational leader at the same time as the administrator-bureaucrat begins, perforce, to take control of the reins of power: 'The qualities fitted for the propagation of the work were not those necessary to its continuance'.[168] It is in his analysis of this transition that Wilson is at his most perceptive in his major academic study of Elim.

6.4.5 Belief and Practice

It comes as no surprise that the oversight of Hunter Street accepted 'the Doctrines, Ordinances and Church Discipline as drawn up by Jeffreys in *What We Believe*'.[169] The larger part of the short pamphlet was given to stating those truths accepted by the majority of evangelical Christians with relevant proof texts provided. The most distinctly Pentecostal article is

---

[166] Hudson, 'A Schism and its Aftermath', n. 605

[167] Another major concern was that British Israelism tended to become the hobby horse of those who accepted it, an endorsement that might lead the churches to pay less attention to evangelism and play down Pentecostal emphases. Divisions over the teaching had the potential to split local assemblies and widen the gap between Elim and the mainstream denominations. At the 1934 Annual Conference attended by around 130 delegates, only 13% voted as accepting British Israelism, 56% rejected it and the rest were 'neutral'.

[168] Wilson, *Sects and Society*, p. 50.

[169] *BEM*, 20 January 1916

found in Section II.IV: 'We believe that God is again restoring the gifts of the Holy Ghost to His Church on earth. They were distributed among the saints at the commencement of this dispensation, and as we believe we are nearing its end, we can fully expect to witness the demonstration of all the gifts, which shall remain until the coming of our Lord'.[170]

This statement is one to which almost every Pentecostal body would have subscribed, yet one that estranged it from other Christian bodies, some dismissing it out of hand and others expressing serious reservations. Two other beliefs follow from the thrust of the above statement of belief: 'We believe that when our Lord Jesus Christ died, he bore our sicknesses as well as our sins... We do not believe in any one-man ministry; the Holy Ghost working through each member, will fit every one into the place that He Himself has designed'.[171] The conviction behind the first of these statements remains a matter of keen debate among Pentecostals and has prompted serious thinking among theologians in the modern movement.[172] The essential thrust of the second is now generally accepted in most denominations, and some credit for this wider acceptance must go to the post-war Pentecostal-Charismatic Renewal movements.

What is noteworthy about the articles of faith is the absence of any mention of *glossolalia* as the initial evidence of Spirit-baptism. The term 'initial' in any case was probably first coined in the American Assemblies of God's *Statement of Faith* in 1916 and would have taken some time to become common currency.[173] Jeffreys view on this issue was explicated later in his *Pentecostal Rays*: 'When we come to the Samaritan revival (Acts 8:1-25) the Scripture *positively* declares that the converts received the Holy Spirit by the laying on of the Apostles' hands, yet there is no mention of the sign of speaking in tongues... But...there was undoubtedly some kind of physical manifestation...for Simon saw the effect of the laying on of the Apostles' hands'.[174] For Jeffreys any one of the supernatural gifts of the Spirit should be recognised as evidence of Spirit-baptism. This remains the position of the Elim Church and on this issue it finds itself closer to many in the Charismatic Renewal Movement in Britain than to other classical Pentecostal groups.

---

170 Jeffreys, *What We Believe*, pp. 3-4.

171 Jeffreys, *What We Believe*, pp. 3-4.

172 Representative works include: J.C. Thomas, *The Devil, Disease and Deliverance: Origins of Illness in New Testament Thought*, (Sheffield: Sheffield Academic Press, 1998); David Petts, 'Healing and the Atonement', (PhD, Nottingham, 1993). The issue is addressed directly in Keith Warrington, 'Major Aspects of Healing within British Pentecostalism', *JEPTA*, Vol. XIX, 1999, pp. 41-3.

173 McGee, *Initial Evidence*, p. 110.

174 Jeffreys, *Pentecostal Rays,* pp. 34-5.

6.5 Jeffreys in Action

6.5.1 The Ballymena Mission

While matters of church government and doctrine provide a necessary framework for the work of any church or denomination, they are not ends in themselves. What happens on the ground is paramount and it would be remiss, before concluding this chapter, not to relate a few incidents that highlight the distinctive contribution that Jeffreys' ministry made to the Pentecostal cause during his first three years in Ireland. That the penetration of the Pentecostal message was limited and patchy is the fairest assessment of the effort made in this period. Many hundreds, possibly reaching the low thousands, sat under the ministry of members of the EEB with Jeffreys proving the biggest crowd-puller. His greatest success was at Ballymena, which proved to be something of a prototype of later great citywide missions.

Jeffreys first came to Ballymena at the invitation of a group of people of whom the most prominent were James and Agnes Gault. The meetings were held in the old YMCA in Wellington Street in February 1916. The Band returned in June 1916 for over five weeks when the 275-seater tent was packed every evening with people coming from the town and surrounding area. There were at least 120 conversions and preaching on the theme of Spirit-baptism was not muted. In a letter printed in *Confidence*, Jeffreys recounted:

> Many have received the Baptism...with signs following...and they all testify to the power they have received to witness for God. One sister was baptised in the street, while another was baptised during the dinner hour in the business place... There are hundreds of Christians in Ireland who are praying for a deeper experience of God and they have never heard the Baptism of the Holy Ghost, according to Acts 2:4, proclaimed.[175]

Six months later the *Ballymena Observer* carried this insider report of the 'Convention for the Deepening of Spiritual Life' held in the old Town Hall over the New Year period:

> The convention...was a great success. It attracted a very large and representative gathering from all denominations, and the interest which was evidenced from the beginning until the final meetings when the hall was not large enough to accommodate all who came. The speakers, Mr J. Leech, KC, MA, and Pastor George Jeffreys, clearly demonstrated by the way in which they held the attention (for periods spell-bound) of those assemblies for over two hours, and yet showing no

[175] *Confidence*, August 1916, pp. 130-1.

> signs of restlessness, that the power of God was with them and that a great revival spirit was abroad.[176]

At the Sunday afternoon service of the Convention the service opened with the singing of the Old Hundredth Psalm, words that continue to carry a stirring resonance within Ulster Protestantism. The impression conveyed by the press report and the nature of the chosen topics is that the meetings were of interest to serious-minded people of evangelical persuasion and there was little of the emotional froth that came to be associated with some Pentecostal meetings.[177] Leech had a Finneyesque capacity to press his case with the artistry of a leading lawyer. In dealing with the Second Advent, 'he produced evidence from the Scripture that God had given legal proof that Christ was to return'.[178]

The emphasis on revival was of particular interest to an audience in Ballymena, the town and hinterland most closely identified with the beginnings of the 1859 Revival. It was set in a locality that epitomised much of the ethos of Ulster Presbyterianism, such as might be expected of an area with a legacy of centuries-old Scottish settlement. Gee made the point that Jeffreys in his first foray into Scotland in 1927 with a mission in Glasgow did not at first get a ready response: 'The stiffer Presbyterian soil did not prove so immediately responsive to the somewhat emotional and spectacular characteristics of Foursquare Gospel campaigning, and it took several weeks of steady logical preaching of the Word before the people finally became gripped with its power in the Spirit of God'.[179] By comparison, mid-Antrim was more amenable to the Jeffreys' message and style. The reverberations of the 1859 Revival on Ulster Protestantism go some way to explain the difference.[180]

Jeffreys, commenting on the summer mission in the town, wrote that he had 'spoken to many of the old inhabitants who were in the revival of 1859, and it is a real treat to listen to their testimonies. They speak of seeing many at that time prostrate under the power of God, while others would lose their powers of speech for many days, and also of seeing

---

[176] Montgomery, *Elim in Ballymena,* pp. 13-15.

[177] The topics were: The Infallibility of the Scriptures; Holiness, and the deliverance from the penalty and power of sin; The Baptism and Gifts of the Holy Spirit; The Pre-millennial return of Christ; Jehovah-rapha—'The Lord that healeth'; The need, preparation, experience and results of a religious revival.

[178] *Ballymena Observer*, 19 January 1917, quoted in Montgomery, *Elim in Ballymena,* p. 15.

[179] Gee, *Flame and Fire*, p. 140.

[180] As a result of the 1859 Revival in the Ballymena district, two new churches were built—West Church, which became the fourth Presbyterian church in a town of under 6,000 people, and Second Presbyterian Church in the nearby village of Broughshane.

lights and visions in the heavens'.[181] Nothing quite so dramatic, to the point of the melodramatic, as these wonders characterised the Jeffreys' mission, though Darragh reported that many cases of healing had taken place.

Two of the topics considered at the convention were distinctly Pentecostal in emphasis while the other four were the standard fare of evangelicalism. Jeffreys' stance on the Bible, in particular, went down well with his audiences. When, in the course of explaining the purpose of his mission during one of his first meetings in the YMCA, he declared his faith in the Bible from cover to cover, this drew a hearty 'Amen' from a woman in the body of the hall. The response came from Mrs Matthew McWhirter, the mother of James McWhirter, who was deeply concerned about the spiritual welfare of her son who was a boy soldier. Mrs McWhirter may well have come in contact with the Pentecostal message at the mission conducted by Margaret Streight in the farmhouse near Slemish mountain. Her son wrote that his 'godly mother' at the age of fourteen 'was a Sunday School teacher at the foot of Mount Slamish' (sic).[182] He related that when she was aged twenty-one and expecting her first child, she read in her Bible that 'the firstborn is the Lord's' and that led her to pray, 'Lord Jesus, please accept this child for your holy service'.[183] His father, who died when the boy was young, was equally devout and prayed, 'Lord, make my first-born to think, say and do only Your Will for Your Glory alone'.[184] McWhirter later wrote of the family memory of his grandfather hearing 'speaking in tongues' in the 1859 Revival.[185]

The young James McWhirter was never a conformist and his boyish rebelliousness was a cause of concern to his widowed mother. He later confessed:

> Since in my youth I failed to find answers to all the questions bothering me in my little world at Sunday School, I refused to join any of the auxiliary weekday

---

[181] *Confidence*, August 1916, p. 130. Visions and claims to sightings of lights have been a feature of some twentieth century revivals, notably during the Welsh Revival and the Revival in the Isle of Lewis, Scotland. (See J. Vyrnwy Morgan, *The Welsh Religious Revival 1904-5*, [CD-ROM, Welsh Revival Library, ed. 1909], p. 119, and Colin and Mary Peckham, *Sounds from Heaven*: *The Revival on the Isle of Lewis 1949-1952*, [Fearn: Christian Focus, 2004].)

[182] McWhirter, *Every Barrier*, p. viii.

[183] McWhirter, *Every Barrier,* p. vii.

[184] McWhirter, *Every Barrier,* p. ix.

[185] McWhirter, *Every Barrier,* p. 74. There is a distinct possibility that susceptible folk memory would eliminate the subtle distinction between ecstatic babble and genuine tongues. Pentecostals would probably accept that *glossolalia* devoid of its biblical-theological context can hardly be accorded the same significance as belongs to the phenomenon in the post-Azusa era.

> societies of the church. That was the only way I could make protest against that with which I disagreed. The first Great War ultimately provided a way of escape. During the next few years I was unchurched.[186]

His parents' prayerful solicitude was answered when he was converted at the age of nineteen under Jeffreys' ministry in Belfast. Though of limited formal education, he proved to be a quick learner and his promise was recognised by Jeffreys in extending an invitation to join the Revival Party the following year 1920.

With his Presbyterian youthful background, James McWhirter is one of the few Ulster people met with in these pages who does not appear to have been influenced by contact with Holiness teaching. On first hearing of the novel teaching of Spirit-baptism, he began to find his seeking for it so began to pall on him that he resolved to give up the quest. However, having heard singing in the Spirit—'something beyond compare'—the desire was revived and kept him seeking for seven months. Throughout his years as a member of the Revival Party, he discovered,

> The power of the Holy Spirit found expression in my life in the ordinary work of organisation. When weary and tired out I often realised the quickening and vitalising power of the Spirit. As a minister of the gospel I would say it means more to me than anything else. In my private worship I have practised meditation, creative silence and contemplation and I have derived much benefit from the discipline and practice of those different attitudes of mind and heart and spirit, but must say I have received more power and inspiration, so far, by the exercise of unknown tongues.[187]

These words, written in 1936, reveal that wider range of sympathies and a venturesomeness towards a more inclusivist spirituality that were to come increasingly to the fore in his later years.

6.5.2 Hunter Street Convention

The new headquarters church in Hunter Street began to live up to its purpose as envisaged by the young men who met in Monaghan in 1915, viz., a centre 'out of which evangelists would be sent into the country and towns'.[188] Within a short time Hunter Street had become too small for the numbers attending, necessitating a search for new premises. Most of the converts were young people who would have entered into the spirit of that most joyous of occasions in Pentecostal circles—the convention season.[189] Convention periods coincided with the major public holiday

---

[186] McWhirter, *Every Barrier,* p. 11.

[187] *EE*, 19 June 1936, p. 394.

[188] *EEBM*, 7 January 1915.

[189] An observation of Mrs Leech, *Confidence,* May 1916, p. 81.

periods—Christmas-New Year, Easter, Whitsun, and in Ulster the 'Twelfth Fortnight' in July. They were particularly important for those who worshipped in small assemblies who were relieved of their isolation and fragility for a few days, as was exemplified in a study of one such convention in Manchester.[190]

In 1971, Walker and Atherton made an ethnographic study of a convention held in 'Bethshan', the large AOG church in Manchester where Nelson Parr ('dressed in a colonial lightweight suit and eighty-four years old') was the senior pastor. Conventions in the 1970s were as much ritualised occasions as they had been from the beginning of the movement. They had as their desideratum the 'receiving of a blessing' that for some was often the occasion to seek their Spirit-baptism. The 'blessing', while usually recounted as 'wonderful', could not be pinned down to any clearly defined outcome but as something intimately tailored through 'experiencing the Lord, or being met by Him in a marvellous way'.[191] Conventions were also major social events that encouraged the participants to enjoy the major 'blessing' of fellowship. New choruses were learned and new worship styles encountered, providing something different to be attempted in the home assembly. New speakers, selected for their quality and 'liveliness' or more travelled ways, were introduced to inject an exotic element to break the routine of familiar fare. A couple of quotes from participants in the article gives the flavour of the Manchester convention:

> Some of us who never normally clap in our own assembly when we get into a crowd like this have the audacity to clap. It's surprising what we do in convention meetings that we never normally do.
>
> Convention meetings are wonderful, aren't they? We meet old friends and make new friends, and somehow in these times of meeting together there is a feeling of revival.[192]

In their conclusion the authors noted that though a good time was had by all, it was assessed in a very personal, unreflecting way: 'Attempts to get people to explain their blessings led to resentment, and also surprise at such stupid questions seemingly coming from believers'.[193]

How did the 1916 Easter Convention sponsored by Hunter Street compare with that in Manchester around 1970 as discussed in the article

---

[190] Andrew Walker and James Atherton, 'An Easter Pentecostal Convention: The Successful Management of "A Time of Blessing"', *Sociological Review*, Vol. 19, 1971, pp. 367-87.

[191] Walker and Atherton, 'An Easter Pentecostal Convention', pp. 382, 383.

[192] Walker and Atherton, 'An Easter Pentecostal Convention', pp. 374, 377.

[193] Walker and Atherton, 'An Easter Pentecostal Convention', pp. 383-4.

by Walker and Atherton?[194] For one, there were the same large numbers drawn from the different centres where Band members had been active—Armagh, Bangor, Ballymena, Lisburn, Lurgan, Monaghan and Portadown. There was the same frequency of meetings, three on Easter Monday, two on Easter Tuesday and an evening service on the Wednesday and Thursday with at least two speakers at each of the meetings which were led by Jeffreys. Leech and Hackett featured prominently as preachers and Pastor Potma from Holland supplied the 'exotic' element.[195] A report of the convention in the *Belfast News-Letter* spoke of the meetings being 'imbued with a sense of the Divine Presence. The outpouring of the Holy Spirit was not an ancient belief to any of the speakers or worshippers, but a present reality... In this atmosphere of faith, the work of the Convention proceeded and hence the earnestness and expectancy'.[196]

There was the same emphasis on 'blessing'. Mrs Leech in a letter to Boddy informing readers of *Confidence* of the Convention wrote that she was sending 'a little report of the ***blessing*** received and of His gracious working in our midst [and she was thankful to] be in the midst of a ***happy*** Pentecostal Convention in which souls were saved and ***baptized into the Holy Spirit*** and His people ***blessed*** and filled with his ***praises*** and the ***joy of the Holy Ghost'***.[197]

It is clear that a visitor visiting the conventions in Belfast and Manchester, even though separated by a gap of over fifty years, would have readily picked up the similarities and spotted some differences. The differences would have reflected to some extent the temperaments of the two leaders. Parr was a spry and exuberant extrovert, the type of revivalist easily lampooned as the quintessential Pentecostal preacher of popular imagination.[198] Jeffreys was of a different stamp and *Picture Post* captured the essence of Jeffreys, the preacher, in an article written some years later: 'If you go to a Jeffreys' meeting expecting the Bible-thumping and the capers of the conventional hot-gospeller, you will be

---

[194] The convention meetings were held in the Kinghan Hall, Botanic Avenue, to accommodate the larger numbers. The Kinghan Hall, endowed to serve as a ministry of the Presbyterian Church to the deaf and dumb, had the advantage of being a neutral venue as well as being more accessible and attractive to the casual visitor than the back-street Elim hall in the same district.

[195] Cornelis Potma (1861-1929) stayed in Belfast for another week to conduct a mission in the Hunter Street assembly.

[196] Quoted in *Confidence,* May 1916, pp. 80-1.

[197] *Confidence,* May 1916, p. 81, emphasis added.

[198] At the Manchester Convention, Parr demonstrated his joy in the Lord and his eighty-year-old youthfulness 'by leaping around the platform, kicking his heels, and waving his Bible at those below'. (Walker and Atherton, 'An Easter Pentecostal Convention', p. 380.)

disappointed... Without a lift of the voice he can rock the [congregation] more surely than any other evangelist of our time... It can shake congregations'.[199]

While the tenor and thrust of both conventions comes through as broadly similar, yet there was a difference of tone. The Belfast correspondent commented on the 'one thing that impressed throughout the whole proceedings was the spirit of seriousness'.[200] In Manchester, the researchers found 'most curious...the intermingling of jokes with serious ideological content. In our initial looking through their data we did try to separate and contrast the seriousness of the sermons (or serious parts of sermons) with the comic turns. We were at first embarrassed by what seemed to be a constant emotional *volte-face* from seriousness to raucous laughter, or vice versa'.[201] The academic and professional training of Leech and Hackett as well as the emotionally restrained temperament of Jeffreys, all three with formidable rhetorical skills, go some way to explaining the contrast.[202] The broader socio-cultural shift between the two periods must also be taken into account. The changes were profound, furthered as they were by the advent of mass entertainment, the decline of social deference, the rejection of puritanical restraint and the declining hold of moral and religious earnestness.

However, the Easter Convention of 1916, for quite different reasons, was to prove a momentous one for the Leechs. That particular week was the occasion of the historic Easter Rising which began on Easter Monday, 24 April 1916. In human terms, the cost of the Rising was 500 deaths (426 in Dublin, of which 250 were civilians) with over 2,500 injured. The Leechs left Dublin on the Easter Saturday and arrived in Belfast in time to take part in an open-air meeting in Shaftesbury Square. Mrs Leech saw the hand of God in the timing, 'bringing us here to a place of safety, whilst rioting, rebellion and bloodshed was going on' in Dublin.[203] Their home was situated in Herbert Street just over a mile south of the General Post Office from the steps of which the insurgents declared the establishment of the Provisional Government of the Irish Republic. She added:

> Owing to the trouble in Dublin many of the Christians who came to [Belfast] for the holiday could not return, so we had some of them at our gatherings... One dear

[199] *Picture Post*, 11 May 1946.

[200] *Confidence,* May 1916, p. 80.

[201] Walker and Atherton, 'An Easter Pentecostal Convention', p. 375.

[202] Leech was equally composed and the article described him as 'a very clear and logical speaker, with any amount of power to impress, as well as ability to instruct'. (*Confidence*, May 1916, p. 81.)

[203] *Confidence,* May 1916, p. 81.

> servant of God, Colonel —, gave us a helpful message at the Tuesday Convention meeting...
>
> It is probable we may be able to return to our home (if it still exists) to-morrow or Wednesday (DV).[204]

From this it is possible to glean something of the social standing of the Leechs. Herbert Street was part of Dublin's rich Georgian architectural heritage and, in all probability, the Colonel was part of their circle, facilitated possibly by the fact that Mrs Leech's father had been an officer in the British Army. Acting as he did as Senior Counsel for the county of Longford and holding other legal appointments, John Leech's involvement with the British judicial presence was unsustainable in the new Ireland that was coming to birth in that portentous Easter week. The family was forced to move to the North where Leech quickly established himself in high legal circles. That the Leechs were able to speak with such effect at the time says much for them both. John Leech usually enjoyed his visits to Belfast and the opportunity for a break from his judicial responsibilities. With that touch of the humour for which he was noted, he would break out singing the words of the gospel hymn, 'Free from the law /Oh, happy condition!'.[205]

Hackett attended the Christmas Convention in Hunter Street in 1917 and described it as 'a Berachah'—the valley/place of blessing.[206] One woman from the Armagh assembly 'was for hours under a trance-power of God, drawn close as she testified all the time to the very heart of Christ'.[207] A young Jewish woman, born in Poland and brought up in a girls' home in Edinburgh, testified to her having received healing. She had been converted through contact with the Christian warden of the home. After joining the Salvation Army, she broke under the strain, 'with eyesight gone, and to all appearances a hopeless imbecile as the result, apparently, of an operation for the eyes'. She was befriended by two women belonging to a Mission who 'took hold of God and prayed her back then and there out of insanity into the full use of her reason, and later into recovered eye-sight, so that she now reads the smallest print'.[208] It was through the dramatic orality of such a testimony that Pentecostals

---

[204] *Confidence,* May 1916, p. 81. The 'to-morrow' reference would suggest that at the time of writing the report the Leechs had remained in the North at least a week or more. The train service between Belfast and Dublin was cancelled for part of Easter Monday week.

[205] Edsor, *'Set Your House In Order',* pp. 31-2.

[206] *Confidence,* May 1916, p. 81. 'Berachah' was the name given to A.B. Simpson's Healing Home opened in 1884.

[207] *Confidence*, April-June 1918, p. 21.

[208] *Confidence*, April-June 1918, p. 21.

hammered out a practical, rather than a speculative, theology grounded as it was in the experience of a God who acts in the here and now.

In conclusion, the three-year period 1915-18 saw the Elim movement make its first toehold in Ireland. Restricted as it was by the modest number of personnel and meagre finances, it managed to win for itself a small place in the variegated religious life of the province. George Jeffreys was its greatest human asset. A young man of an undoubted charisma that reflected the message he bore, he was beginning to attract sizeable crowds wherever he preached. He evoked from colleagues an intense loyalty and the next few years were to see a large increase in their number working in the province. The beginnings of an administrative and legal framework were put in place and the movement had attracted into its ranks some people from the comfortable middle class whose experience of the Spirit defied the barriers of class and status. The future seemed to hold a promise that the vision of 1915 was more than a pipe dream.

CHAPTER 7

The Years of Expansion in Elim (1918-c.1923)

7.1 Membership of the Elim Evangelistic Band

At the end of 1915 the Elim Evangelistic Band consisted of three members—George Jeffreys, Margaret Streight and R.E. Darragh. In 1916, Henderson and Farlow joined the Band while Hackett and Leech were enlisted as its advisory members. In the succeeding two years, T. J. Logan and Robert Mercer were added, bringing the total to seven by the end of 1918. The year 1919 saw a sharp rise in the number of recruits to sixteen and by the end of 1920 the total membership of the Band had reached twenty-one. By any standard, this trebling in numbers over the two-year period was a considerable achievement. Of the twenty-one, three were women, not counting two wives, the Mrs Fletcher and Every, who were described as deaconesses. Thirteen of the Band came from Ulster, five had a Welsh background and the remaining four were from England (Photograph D). With the exception of Stephen Jeffreys, most spent a good proportion of their time during the years 1918-23 working in Ireland. One reason for the rapid expansion of numbers was the ending of conscription in 1918 which freed young men from Britain to engage in the ministry of the Band. Another was the willingness of the Band members to live on faith lines with the consequent acceptance of an insecure financial future. Miss Dougherty who joined the Band around September 1921 recollected forty-four years later that 'for eight years I served in the ministry without salary, and every need was supplied and not one hour's care had I for finance'.[1] The Band members, as Hudson points out, 'looked to [Jeffreys] for their cause, their place in society and their finance'.[2]

Even so, funds were precarious and financial forward planning was scarcely achievable without a reliable support base. In fact, when E.J. Phillips first arrived in Belfast in 1919 he was aghast to find an administrative shambles: 'Nothing. No accounts, no list of properties,

---

[1] *EE,* 20 November 1965, p. 756.

[2] Hudson, 'A Schism and its Aftermath', p. 131

hopeless'.[3] Sometimes good financial intentions were thwarted by circumstance. On one occasion, the Elim Pentecostal Alliance Council (EPAC)[4] agreed that a special missionary fund should be set up 'to facilitate any intending missionary in going to the Foreign Field' and to this end 'half of the proceeds of all the boxes be given to this special...Fund, after the usual percentage had been deducted for the PMU'.[5] This arrangement did not last a year because at the October 1920 meeting the Council acknowledged that the 'low state of finances' made it impossible to continue the scheme.[6]

What type of young person was attracted to join the Band? Robert Tweed, in pronouncing that Jeffreys weilded considerable influence in engaging young men in the ministry, added that 'university men were no exception'.[7] He had in mind E. Woodroffe Hare and Cyril Taylor. Hare, from Cheltenham, had been president of the Cambridge University Christian Union in his undergraduate days. He was seen as the ideal person to act as the editor of the *Elim Evangel*, first published in Belfast in December 1919. His main ministerial responsibility was to lead the Elim work in Bangor. Taylor joined the Band as a final year medical student and was ordained in April 1920 for service in the Belgian Congo. There is no clear evidence that Taylor ever qualified or practised as a doctor. He paid a visit to Ireland in 1920 before setting off for Africa and, while in the province, attended a mission conducted by Tweed at Tullynahinnion, County Tyrone. While there, he joined a number of the young men who were in the habit of holding 'heather prayer meetings' on the upper moorland slopes of the adjacent hillside. At one of these meetings they had an experience of numinous intensity and, for Taylor, one of confirmatory significance. Tweed was an eyewitness of the incident:

> It was if a great and strong wind swept the hillside and those of us present were blown in different directions. In the midst, Dr Taylor stood up and with upstretched arms started speaking [in] a very loud voice what seemed to be a variety of different languages. I asked him afterwards what he saw of the valley below where we were and what he was doing. He said the whole valley was filled with black people and he was preaching to them. It was not long before he joined W. Burton, the founder of the Congo Evangelistic Mission.[8]

---

[3] Hudson, 'A Schism and its Aftermath', Appendix 1.

[4] This was the title given to the executive committee of the recognised body in law. It was established early in 1918 and set up initially for the purpose of holding property.

[5] *EEBM*, 31 December 1919.

[6] *EEBM*, 31 December 1919.

[7] *Tweed Memoir*, p. 18.

[8] *Tweed Memoir*, p. 18.

George Fletcher, with his background as a Salvation Army officer, was more representative of the Band members than the previous two men were. In March 1915, while conducting a gospel campaign in a Baptist mission hall in Plymouth, he found his meetings overlapped with those of George Jeffreys in a nearby Baptist church. Free to attend the Jeffreys' Sunday evening service, he received his Spirit-baptism while sitting behind the preacher on the platform of the crowded church. Within a few months he was working full-time in a Pentecostal work in Lewisham, London. He joined the Band and crossed to Ireland in October 1919. Within a few weeks of arrival he wrote that 'I am now stationed in Portadown and have here a work after my own heart—an aggressive Evangelistic work'.[9] Nine months later he reported that fifteen had received their Spirit-baptism including an eighty-three old man who had witnessed the 1859 Revival and 'recognised and testified to the same Power operating in both revivals'.[10]

Among those who joined the Band in 1919-20 period were men who would go on to become leading figures in the wider Pentecostal movement, T.J. Jones (c.1895-1970), E.J. Phillips (1893-1973) and John Carter (1893-1981). Jones was a member of a Brethren assembly in Birmingham when he first came in contact with Pentecostalism through attending the mission hall where the Carter brothers, Howard and John, were leaders. When he told his Brethren assembly where he had been, they warned him against attending any more Pentecostal meetings. His reply to them was 'Brethren, if I go wrong, I will go wrong on God's Word'.[11] Suffering from a heart murmur, Jones avoided conscription on medical grounds. He was persuaded by John Carter to join him as a member of the Band. The two worked closely together in the province for fifteen months before their return to England. Jones soon moved to California and became a noted Bible teacher, starting with the Assemblies of God Bible and Missionary Training School at San Francisco. An outstanding preacher, he was much in demand at many camp meetings throughout America.

Phillips and Carter were born in the same year, and their prominent careers within the Pentecostal movement ran parallel. As Carter put it, 'their destinies and ministries [were] singularly intertwined'.[12] Phillips first met the Carter brothers on the boat crossing to Belfast when all three found themselves occupying the same cabin. Howard Carter was crossing, at the invitation of Jeffreys, to speak at the 1919 Christmas Convention,

---

[9] *EEBM*, 31 December 1919.

[10] *EE,* September 1920, p. 55.

[11] John Carter, *Howard Carter: Man of the Spirit*, (Nottingham: AOG Publishing, 1971), p. 32.

[12] John Carter, *E.J. Phillips—Architect of Elim*, (typescript 1973, *Mattersey Archives*).

while John, like Phillips, was on his way to join the Band. Phillips was to become the administrative head of the Elim Church from 1923 till 1957 and John Carter the General Secretary of the Assemblies of God in Great Britain and Ireland from 1936 till 1963. Thus their terms of office overlapped by twenty-one years. Each acted for periods as an editor of their respective denominational magazines. When the British Pentecostal Fellowship was formed in 1948 Phillips was its first Secretary-Treasurer and Carter became his successor. They were both on the committee responsible for *Redemption Hymnal*, a publication that came to be used extensively throughout the British Pentecostal movement.[13] Their shared experience in the EEB in Ireland anticipated the mutual regard they held for each other.

Phillips first came into contact with the Pentecostal movement in Bedford where Cecil Polhill had established an assembly in Costain Street which Phillips and his two brothers attended. In 1912 he most likely became a student at the PMU missionary college at Preston where he would have encountered Jeffreys for the first time. When he arrived in Ireland he had a fund of administrative experience behind him. On leaving school he first worked in an estate agency and was later was employed by Lord Lichfield, probably in some administrative role on the estate: Tweed referred to him simply as 'an estate agent'.[14] He, together with his brother Hubert, had been leading a small assembly in Tamworth for about three years when Jeffreys approached him. It may have been the desire to raise the level of quality in his team that brought Jeffreys during his visits to England to exert pressure on people of proven worth to consider coming to Ireland. Phillips distinctly recalled the occasion of their meeting: 'Mr. Jeffreys earnestly requested me to become a full-time pastor in his work'.[15] Besides not quite seeing eye to eye with Jeffreys on matters of church government, Phillips also had to consider the impact of a move on the Tamworth assembly. In his quandary he sought divine guidance:

---

[13] They also had some similarities of temperament. Phillips was reserved and undemonstrative and, though a formidable debater, was not a naturally gifted public speaker, so his voice was rarely heard at the Conventions during his time in Ireland. Carter mentioned that the members of the Band saw little of Phillips. The youthful Carter had, according to Missen, 'a reserved and diffident disposition [that] proved an embarrassment and a hindrance to him when afterwards facing a congregation'. (Missen, *The Sound of a Going*, p. 41.) On the other hand, their *forte*, or 'gift' in Pentecostal understanding, lay more in administration (see 1 Cor 12:28). Carter had the experience of having been a bank official behind him and Phillips worked in an administrative role.

[14] *Tweed Memoir*, p. 49

[15] *EE*, Vol. 50.46, November 1969, p. 765.

> It so happened that a severe throat infection had me in its grip just then, and in simple faith I asked the Lord would He please instantaneously clear up this throat trouble as a sign. Never have I had so immediate a healing! When I rose from my knees all was well and I knew that God had graciously heard my prayers for His leading.[16]

Here, as in many other cases, healing was taken as a confirmatory sign for one to shoulder Pentecostal leadership.

Phillips' first responsibility in Ireland was to pastor the small assembly formed early in 1920 in the linen village of Milford, near Armagh. He remained there for the next three and a half years, becoming for a time joint-editor with Hare of the *Elim Evangel* in 1922. With the resignation of Hare from Elim in 1923, Phillips became sole editor of the *Elim Evangel* for a short time, and subsequently for a longer period from 1923 till 1930. His proven administrative abilities were recognised in his taking over the administration of the Elim movement in August 1923, a move that coincided with the relocation of the headquarters from 3 University Avenue, Belfast, to Clapham, London. He became, in John Carter's words, 'the human architect of Elim'.[17] Carter added that Phillips was 'always calm and composed, meticulous, unruffled, unflappable. As a man, E.J. was always courteous, well mannered, dignified. He was quiet, never raising his voice, very precise in speech. He was strong-willed but not stubborn. Where principle was involved, he was adamant. Some thought him unapproachable, but this was because time was precious to him and he had no time for idle talk'.[18] After the potentially ruinous split in 1940, arguably, Phillips became the guardian of Elim by playing a key role in sustaining institutional coherence within the denomination. If Jeffreys gave Elim its heart and ethos, Phillips lent it shape and structure.

Before coming to Ireland at the age of twenty-six, John Carter with his brother had pioneered two Pentecostal assemblies in Birmingham. He joined the Band in 1919 with six years of leadership responsibility behind him. He remained a member of the Band 'for a happy period of fifteen months'.[19] With a policy of sending out workers two-by-two, Jeffreys was enabled to mix and match his experienced and inexperienced workers, such as the combination of Carter and the comparatively untried Miss Adams in running the mission at Moneyslane, near Rathfriland, County Down (Figure III). Jeffreys and Darragh had visited the area in 1918 and Miss Adams took charge of the work for a short while to be succeeded by the Everys. A sizeable congregation, many of them young converts,

---

[16] *EE,* Vol. 50.46, November 1969, p. 765.

[17] Carter, *E.J. Phillips,* p. 1.

[18] Carter, *E.J. Phillips,* p. 1.

[19] John Carter, *British Pentecostal History*, [typescript (n.d.), *Mattersey Archives*), p. 15.

became established in the Orange Hall. The *Evangel* reported that among them 'quite a number of the children here have experienced the Baptism in the Holy Ghost in true scriptural fashion'.[20] It was a phenomenon that Pentecostals seem to have taken in their stride, apparently neither encouraging nor discouraging it. It was a matter that never seems to have been queried at the time though it was often enough reported. An article in the *Daily Chronicle* in October 1907 reported that Boddy spoke, apparently approvingly, of a recent visit to a very bare low mission-room in Oslo where there were 'boys and girls around me, from say, seven to twelve years of age, seeing visions and speaking in tongues as well as older people'.[21] With a youthful congregation, the stationing at Moneyslane of a married couple, the Everys, may well have been a judicious move on Jeffreys' part. Carter, in all liklihood, had to deal with a vibrant, unsophisticated congregation in full flow.

Carter, when lodging at the home of an elder of a church where he was conducting a mission, came across a phenomenon in Ireland that he had never met before—the practice of 'charming'.[22] He was introduced to it when a caller at the house asked to see the householder as he had brought a boy with a broken wrist to see him. The elder was not at home and Carter enquired from his wife about the purpose of the unexpected visit. The wife explained the nature of charming, adding that her husband had the specific charm for broken wrists though she added that he no longer practised it. This led Carter to remonstrate, 'That is not sufficient; he must let people know it is of the devil, that he has completely renounced it since becoming a Christian'.[23] When the elder returned he reiterated his plea to him and directed his attention to the scripture passage in Deuteronomy where the charmer is described as 'an abomination unto the Lord'.[24] Carter later discovered that others had testified to being healed through the practice, including a Pentecostal young woman who had lodged in the same house. He wrote: 'I have forgotten what her trouble was but she was quite emphatic that the exercize (sic) of the charm had immediately and completely healed her... She could now see that the whole practice is unscriptural and devilish in its origin'.[25] The

---

[20] *EE*, December 1919, p. 3.

[21] T.B. Barratt, *When the Fire Fell and an Outline of my Life*, (Oslo: Alfons Hansen & Soner, 1927), p. 155.

[22] Carter was acting precisely the same as the Bishop of Derry in the seventeenth century when he warned against the diabolical powers behind 'traditional...charms and incantations'. (Raymond Gillespie, *Devoted People: Belief and Religion in Early Modern Ireland*, [Manchester: Manchester University Press, 1997], p. 65.)

[23] John Carter, *A Full Life:The Autobiography of a Pentecostal Pioneer,* (London: Evangel Press, 1979), p. 48.

[24] Carter, *A Full Life,* p. 48.

[25] Carter, *A Full Life,* p. 49.

one lesson he drew from the whole episode was to claim an insight into the charism of 'Gifts of Healings [1 Cor. 12:9]. If the counterfeit of this gift operates in this way, then it appeared feasible that in the Gifts of Healing (sic) the Holy Spirit uses one person for the healing of one kind of disease and another for a different complaint'.[26] He provided no indication to suggest that such a conjecture carried any discernible guidance for the practice of divine healing.

While ministering in Ulster, Carter recorded that he received 'the spiritual Gift of Interpretation of Tongues' at the Bangor Elim assembly where he had been invited by Hare to speak.[27] After a message in tongues had been uttered, he waited expectantly for an interpretation: 'no one appeared to be doing so, when I found myself speaking aloud and realised I had received the gift'.[28] Carter went on to relate an incident when Margaret Streight exercised a different gift, 'the discerning of spirits'.[29] He probably heard it directly from her when they worked together for a short period in leading the sizeable assembly at Lurgan. During the Christmas Convention, either 1917 or 1918, Streight refused point-blank to preach when Jeffreys invited her to minister along with a Band colleague:

> She informed Mr. Jeffreys that she could not sit on the platform with the other speaker as she declared he was morally unclean... When [Jeffreys] learned she had no evidence to support her statement beyond a strong intuition he chided her, putting it down to feminine illogicalness (sic). However, subsequent events proved it...when the young man was dismissed from the work for immorality.[30]

The 'young man' in question was T.J. Logan from Limavady. He was one of the earliest recruits to the Band, joining as its fifth member in January 1917. Tweed, who first heard Logan preach at the Rasharkin mission in 1918, found himself 'much attracted to the preaching of Mr. Logan, who was a very eloquent and powerful evangelical preacher'.[31] Logan was known to have held 'some very successful missions' in other centres in the province.[32]

A whole sorry episode began in December 1917 when Logan made a full confession to Jeffreys of having engaged in a sexual affair. Jeffreys kept the matter private and it was not revealed by him until May 1919, eighteen months later, when Logan admitted to a similar lapse with a

---

26 Carter, *A Full Life,* p. 48.
27 Carter, *A Full Life,* p. 48.
28 Carter, *A Full Life,* p. 49.
29 Carter, *A Full Life,* p. 49.
30 Carter, *A Full Life,* p. 50.
31 *Tweed Memoir*, p. 7.
32 *Tweed Memoir*, p. 16.

different woman. Logan, for his part, had agreed after the first disclosure to write a confession 'that he fell and repented'.[33] When Margaret Streight refused to share the platform with Logan, she must have jolted Jeffreys considerably, privy as he may have been to the substance of her charge. In his handling of Margaret Streight, Jeffreys was faced with the dilemma of needing to keep a promised confidence to Logan in the long-time interest of a young and promising evangelist and, at the same time, the obligation to face squarely the validity of the charism of the 'word of knowledge' or discernment given by a valued colleague.[34] It was a predicament peculiar to a Pentecostal leader. He was greatly aided by having the participation of John Leech who on two occasions had cause to question Logan in a tough juridical manner that left Logan's protestations of innocence sounding hollow and his dismissal from the Band inevitable. The whole process modifies without undermining Wilson's characterisation of the early Elim congregation as 'unstructured, inarticulate, probably quite unknowing in [technical, legal and administrative] matters', a comment he applied specifically to the typical revival-recruited congregation.[35]

What were the consequences of this whole case for Elim and how did Jeffreys come out of it? For Jeffreys personally, it must have been a great strain. Margaret Streight's noted moral rigorism would have led to tension between her and Jeffreys and, before the matter came to light, a feeling of discomfiture in all likelihood permeated the Band.[36] Logan was not an easy person to deal with when put on the spot. He was given to lash out with unsubstantiated accusations and blustered denials. At the final meeting, he alleged that 'Mr. Jeffreys is a very bossy man and a hard man to work with'.[37] At one point Leech had to stop him when he introduced charges against Mr Jeffreys on the grounds that they were irrelevant to the matter under discussion. In reply to a question put to him by Leech, Logan admitted that at the time of the second confession he had quarrelled with Jeffreys and had given him 'cheek'.[38] It is barely conceivable that anyone had treated Jeffreys that way before—certainly not in Elim.

---

[33] *Minutes of the special meeting for the purpose of going fully into the matter of charges against Mr. T.J. Logan,* held on 13 February 1920, p. 3.

[34] The appropriateness of Jeffreys' 'chiding' of Margaret Streight is difficult to judge from the documentation available, particularly on the exact timing of events.

[35] Wilson, *Sects and Society*, p. 44.

[36] Before the matter became public, Logan wrote to Norah Adams, a member of the EEB: 'I suppose you know I am no longer a member of the Elim Evangelistic Band. I suppose you wonder why. Well, I may tell you it was all my own fault'. (*Logan Enquiry*, p. 8.)

[37] *Logan Enquiry*, p. 4.

[38] *Logan Enquiry*, p. 7.

Organisationally, the whole episode revealed the importance of retaining the advisory members in the EPAC. It also revealed a need to set up more formal structures for the initiation and supervision of new Band members. The use of Leech to chair disciplinary proceedings demonstrated just how invaluable it was to have people of his reputation on the Council. Standing somewhat apart from those most acutely involved, Leech could bring a certain steely dispassionateness to the proceedings. The minutes of the meeting, when Logan's 'own contradictions' finally sank him, recorded that at the end, 'Mr. Leech then as an act of grace allowed Mr. Logan to read out his charges against Pastor Jeffreys which were denied by the Pastor. In no charge which Mr. Logan brought against the Pastor had he two witnesses according to his own confession'.[39] Leech then asked Logan if he was satisfied with the hearing he had been given, to which Logan replied in the affirmative. He went further and, somewhat obsequiously, said that he knew that if Leech were in charge 'he would get a fair hearing and that justice would be done'.[40] However, the matter was not left to rest there. Logan subsequently threatened to take Jeffreys to court for defamation of character. A special prayer meeting was called to face this threat. Tweed later reflected that 'this satanic attempt to discredit the great work...was defeated'.[41] The support and mastery of Leech had alleviated the messiness of the whole episode. Throughout the whole sorry episode, Jeffreys kept his poise and sought to apply the scriptural principles of using only substantiated evidence and seeking the restoration, upon repentance, of the offender. Some of the lessons learned must have informed his thinking when he was drawing up a new constitution for Elim in the latter half of 1922.[42]

7.2 Impact of Constitutional Changes

The new constitution that was introduced in 1922 replaced the previous one that had been approved in 1916 which, *strictu senso*, applied only to Elim Christ Church, Hunter Street. With the rapid growth of the movement and its personnel, it was clearly necessary to formalise procedures, the overall impact of which was to tighten control over

[39] *Logan Enquiry*, p. 10.

[40] *Logan Enquiry*, p. 10.

[41] *Logan Enquiry*, p. 16.

[42] A similar case is presented in early Methodism. (See C.E. Vulliamy, *John Wesley*, [New Jersey: Barbour, ed.1985], pp. 264-6.) In 1751, faced with evidence of immoral conduct, Wesley expelled James Wheatley from the Methodist Connexion. The scandal was almost the only one of its kind in the early history of Methodism and 'induced Wesley to examine more closely the doctrine, behaviour and reputation of his preachers'. In 1753, the Leeds Conference issued the *Rules of a Helper*.

ministers. The 1916 constitution was little more than a rehearsal, with short commentary, of the 'fundamental truths' written by Jeffreys and agreed by the oversight.[43] The new constitution was designed for the denomination as a whole and was largely given to formalising procedures within the Band. It was approved by the members of the Band at the 1922 Christmas Convention in Belfast, the proposals being accepted, with some amendments, over the course of two days after 'a most helpful and prolonged discussion, each item being separately dealt with'.[44] In the Introduction, Jeffreys wrote: 'Some of the following arrangements have always been recognised as unwritten rules by all members in the past, and it is amazing to think of how smoothly the work has proceeded without any definite tie to bind them to a rule'.[45]

A cursory reading of the document would give the impression that Band members were assigned to specific assemblies. That, however, does not accord with the listings recorded in the *Elim Evangel.* For instance, the January 1923 issue assigned only six pastors to a specific assembly while the other eighteen members of the Band were peripatetic. The latter group, besides conducting different missions, were often placed in charge of assemblies for short periods, enough to see them established before moving on to another posting. The frequent switching of Band personnel to meet the changing demands of the movement in its period of rapid expansion gave them little sense of stability and depended to great measure on their willingness to live with constant reshuffling.

The constitution was not set in stone and the meeting agreed that it should run for a trial period of a minimum of six months. Aspects of it were more blueprint than reality. The division of the country into districts each with its Superintendent became fully operational only towards the end of the 1920s.[46] With the growth of the movement throwing up new problems, the rules and regulations were frequently updated to forestall unacceptable practices and cover new eventualities. The 1923 Constitution was amended in the 1920s at least three times before the most far-reaching revision of all took place in 1934 with the introduction of the Deed Poll which effectively put an end to Jeffreys' personal

---

[43] At the meeting of the EEB that approved the constitution the motion was accepted that 'a member before teaching anything contrary to the *fundamental truths* contained in the constitution in private or in public must acquaint the sec. of his intention at least two weeks before it is done'. *(EEBM,* 27-28 December 1922). Of the eighteen numbered articles, twelve present the theological stance and doctrinal bases of Elim Christ Church, two relate to the ordinances of baptism and the Lord's Supper, and four to church discipline.

[44] *EEBM*, 27-28 December 1922.

[45] *The Constitution of the Elim Pentecostal Alliance: Introduction*, by Pastor George Jeffreys, 1922. (Henceforth *1922 Constitution.*)

[46] Hathaway, 'The Elim Pentecostal Church', pp. 18-19.

control of Elim. The fact that many of the pastors were young and inexperienced and were sometimes placed in charge of sizeable, revival-garnered congregations furthered the need to make explicit the regulatory framework within which they worked.

Under the 1923 Constitution, candidates seeking to join the Band had to serve six months probation and to be willing to work in the place and with the person 'arranged by the Principal Overseer' [Jeffreys].[47] There were three levels of accountability, that of the local church leader, the district overseer and the principal overseer. The last of the three positions was to be held by Jeffreys 'as long as he is willing to act in the capacity of Principal Overseer'.[48] At the lowest level, the leader in charge was to be responsible with the elders 'to God and the Overseers for [the church's] good government'.[49] The section headed *The Duties of All Band Members* is the most extensive section in the document and sets out in detail nineteen rules. Requirements laid down included: the need 'to keep a list of the hymns and their numbers that are well-known in that particular assembly';[50] workers to hand over to their successor 'a book of various instructions regarding the working arrangements of the assembly', with the book regarded as the property of the Band; [51] wherever circumstances permitted, two workers should be stationed at any one centre; whoever was the younger or less experienced of two workers stationed at the same centre was to act as the assistant to the other. The intent behind the rules was to make the transition between changes of workers as smooth as possible in a situation where fluidity rather than stability was the norm. They were devised for a church on the move.

Each Overseer, later known as Divisional Superintendent, was expected to convene periodically 'a meeting with all the workers under his supervision' and aim to visit each assembly 'at least once in six months'.[52] The Divisional Superintendent was to be held, in turn, 'responsible to the Principal Overseer for the whole work in that District'.[53] A striking feature of the constitution is the minimal part played by the EPAC, mention of which is confined to the Introduction. Though by origin established as a property holding body, the EPAC was generally accepted as having a wider remit to act as 'a representative body of control with plenary powers'.[54] It had all the makings of a

---

[47] *1922 Constitution*, p. 13.

[48] *Revised 1923 Constitution,* p. 10, rule 3.

[49] *1922 Constitution*, p. 7

[50] *1922 Constitution*, p. 10.

[51] *1922 Constitution*, pp. 10-11.

[52] *1922 Constitution*, p. 12. In the *1922 Constitution* they were referred to as District Superintendents. Divisional Superintendents operated in the period 1929-34.

[53] *1922 Constitution*, p. 12.

[54] *BEM*, 8 October 1918.

Council of Reference that could have been given reserve powers to act independently of Jeffreys in situations where he was placed as a disputant, as in the Logan case. In the system of checks and balances, the only person who was not answerable to another was Jeffreys himself, who as 'Founder and Principal Overseer'[55] had the sole responsibility for choosing the Overseers from within the Band. Throughout much of the 1920s the overseers rarely, if ever, met as a body so that any attempt to put a curb on the power of the Principal Overseer would have been difficult to the point of impossibility.[56] By such means Jeffreys remained the pivotal figure within Elim.

Logan was the one failure in the early days of the Band, a contingency that was counterbalanced by the single-minded dedication of its other members. Jeffreys was, in general, a good judge of ability and character, but in the case of Logan where talent transcended character an understandable mistake was made. Tweed was keen to point out that 'application for membership of the Band was not so easy as some might imagine'.[57] When he first intimated to Jeffreys his desire to join the Band, he was told 'to go home and study the Bible and wait for guidance'.[58] He seems then to have launched out as a freelance worker with an ill-defined association with Elim in stating that 'I had stepped out on the lines of Matthew 10:10 as all the other evangelists had done'.[59] When he was engaged by Jeffreys to speak at the 1918 Christmas Convention in Hunter Street, he surmised 'that Pastor Jeffreys was testing me to see if I would be suitable for the ministry'.[60] Tweed recollected that Logan spoke before him and gave 'a wonderful address'[61] and that when he, himself, was speaking, 'Pastor Jeffreys had seated himself on a "high seat" covering a gas meter at the back of the church where he sat with his legs dangling. He had a good view of the mannerisms of his new recruit'.[62]

---

[55] *Revised 1923 Constitution,* p. 7.

[56] This is confirmed in a reply to a query from Walter Hollenweger by H.W. Greenway, secretary-general of Elim at the time: 'It is true that he [George Jeffreys] appointed overseers about five years after the work was founded, but they had no power whatever, and in fact as far as the only surviving overseer can remember, they never met to discuss anything. Mr. Jeffreys formulated strict rules for both ministers and churches'. (Letter dated 4 April 1963, *Mattersey Archives.*) It was, as Malcolm Hathaway comments, all 'somewhat paternalistic... The style of leadership was reminiscent of the Salvation Army, with Jeffreys in command and the work divided into districts under superintendents from 1929. Ministers had little say in their affairs, a factor that caused increasing unrest as the denomination matured'. (Hathaway, 'The Elim Pentecostal Church', p. 18-19.)

[57] *Tweed Memoir*, p. 13.

[58] *Tweed Memoir*, p. 14.

[59] *Tweed Memoir*, p. 7.

[60] *Tweed Memoir*, p. 8.

[61] *Tweed Memoir*, p. 8.

[62] *Tweed Memoir*, p. 8.

His sermon was well received by the people with 'ejaculations of praise',[63] but it was fully another year before he was confirmed as a member of the Band at the 1919 Christmas Convention. In effect, he had served, by an informal arrangement, over a year as a probationer. In a similar way, Joseph Smith assisted members of the Band before becoming a member himself. In August 1920, he helped Darragh and Norah Adams in their tent mission in Lurgan before his acceptance a few months later, possibly with their recommendation.[64]

A heavy weight of financial responsibility hung upon the youthful shoulders of the evangelists and pastors. The personal income of each pastor and evangelist was determined by the income derived from collections, private gifts and gifts in kind. From the sum total of these sources was deducted the general expenses whether of the assembly, evangelistic mission or convention. Of the balance remaining, ten per cent. was to be deducted as each Band member's contribution to the denominational General Fund. The general expenses included such items as heating, lighting, rent, advertising and ministry gifts to others. Evangelists were responsible for the expenses incurred during their missions; similarly, convenors were responsible for the conventions they organized, and pastors for the assemblies they led. Put crudely, there was an element of 'payment by results' in the system: the bigger and better the assembly or mission, the more sizeable the worker's income. The fact that missions could last for a month or more allowed for the possibility that numbers might build up and income grow in step. For the Band members, falling attendances were not only a source of spiritual and emotional dejection but also an occasion of financial hardship. With neither fixity of tenure nor security of income, there was no joy to be obtained in the financial arrangements of Elim for the lifeless preacher who failed to stir an expectant congregation—not that many could accuse Pentecostals of being dry turn-offs.

The General Fund provided a rationale for the strong central control that came to characterise Elim. The Fund provided the financial backing for the expansion of the whole denomination. Payments were made from it for the purchase of buildings, pioneering work and the running of the General Secretary's office. Apart from the tithes of the workers, the main contributions towards the General Fund were received from the Elim Home and Foreign Mission boxes distributed to assemblies where there was a settled pastor. The first call on the box income was the tithe for foreign mission work. If the rent and fixed charges on the premises was not covered at the end of a quarter from the balance of the box income, then the pastor could be made liable to meet the deficit out of his own

---

[63] *Tweed Memoir*, p. 8.

[64] *EE*, December 1920, p. 2.

financial resources, though resort to a special offering was always an option. Pastors needed little encouragement, as the 1923 amended Constitution ruled, 'to aim at sufficient interest being aroused in the boxes in each assembly to secure a substantial surplus each quarter...to go to the General Fund for pioneering and general work'.[65]

The Elim enterprise was clearly very dependent on ceaseless activity if it was to thrive. Growth was predicated on growth, on a virtuous circle of swelling attendance providing increased income; numerical growth was inextricably tied to income swelling. It was a scenario suggestive of the capitalist enterprise. As capitalism has to face periodic crises associated with the vagaries of the trade cycle, in an analogous way so did Elim. At the meeting of the deacons of the Elim Tabernacle held in June 1922, a letter from George Jeffreys was read, that stated:

> He was away from the city at this distressing time, but that owing to the heavy burden of paying interest on the debt on the Irish work, he was compelled to accept engagements in England to earn the money and that the legacy was a great disappointment & that he had no doubt that the elders [would] do their best to help him in shouldering the burden which was very heavily pressing upon him at present.[66]

It was a difficult enough time for the elders having to cope with the civil strife that flared up in the aftermath of partition, without having to cope with a burden of debt. With lowered attendance, offerings plummeted and the Rees legacy that promised much yielded little. To drive the analogy to breaking point, the time-honoured answer to stagnant markets at home was overseas expansion to promote more lucrative pickings: so it was in this case. It formed the prelude to the removal of Elim's core interests to England, a process that Boulton in his chapter headed, suggestively in this context, 'Invading England'.[67]

7.3 The Initiation and Training of Band Members

Holding a team together, developing among them an *esprit de corps* and giving a sense of direction, these all present a formidable challenge to any leader. A number of measures were in place to encourage such team spirit. Once a member was accepted into the Band, ordination followed. Boulton, generally close to Jeffreys' thinking, gave the background to Jeffreys' ordination in Belfast:

---

[65] *Revised 1923 Constitution,* p. 9.

[66] *BEM*, 6 June 1922.

[67] Boulton, *Ministry of the Miraculous*, title of Ch. 7. Control of territory to gain access to new resources has been a potent factor in the spread of colonialism.

> The number of preachers joining the work was rapidly increasing, and the burden of leadership was beginning to be realised by the one who was himself directly responsible for the direction of the work. That some authoritative ordination of the leader was necessary was becoming apparent in view of the fact that he himself would soon be called upon to officiate at the ordination of those of his followers who were called into the regular ministry.[68]

The deacons of Elim Christ Church invited the Rev. Moelfryn Morgan, minister of the Welsh Congregational Church at Ammanford, to be responsible for the ordination of George Jeffreys. The ordination took place when Morgan and Stephen Jeffreys were in Belfast conducting a tent mission held in the large Ormeau Park in Belfast during July and August 1917. For Boulton, Jeffreys' ordination was of one 'who, in the Divine plan, was destined to ordain many others to the work of God'.[69] Strangely, Hackett, in a report in *Confidence* that gave an account of the Ormeau Park mission, made no mention of it.[70] Is there a hint in this lapse that Hackett, with his Anglican background, was not particularly comfortable with the status and regularity of such a ceremony, carrying as it did denomination-forming undertones? Boulton, on the other hand, would appear to give an almost sacramental connotation to the ordination ceremony. The formal nature of the event was for the ordinands the defining moment in their call to the ministry.

Like most Pentecostals at the time, Jeffreys would appear not to have agonised greatly over the theological implications of multiple ordination. He clearly was none too questioning of his ordination in 1912 in Maesteg,[71] and he was happy to receive an ordination certificate from the Pentecostal Assemblies of Canada when he visited that country.[72] However, it would be a very partial view of the 1917 ordination to think that Jeffreys treated it in a cavalier fashion. Boulton's use of the term 'authoritative ordination' suggests that, for Jeffreys, it was a supreme moment. That it was performed by a fellow Welshman and Congregational minister, Moelfryn Morgan, is a measure of the strong

---

[68] Boulton, *Ministry of the Miraculous*, p. 40.

[69] Boulton, *Ministry of the Miraculous*, pp. 40-41.

[70] *Confidence,* April-June 1918, p. 20.

[71] See pp. 96-97.

[72] The relationship between revivalism and ministerial orders has often been contentious. George Whitefield, when asked his view on a matter of bitter dispute over church polity in Scotland, replied scathingly that he had no view at all, 'being too busy about matters of...greater importance'. (Harry S. Stout, *The Divine Dramatist: George Whitefield and the Rise of Modern Evangelicalism*, [Grand Rapids, MI: Eerdmans, 1991], p. 138.) One suspects that Jeffreys would have been less cavalier about the rite and would have been more in accord with the practice of Wesley who conducted his first ordinations in Scotland in 1788. Unlike Whitefield, both men were key players in the formation of new denominations.

emotional ties he retained with his homeland as well as with the church of his upbringing and the standing of its ministers. That it saw it as necessary, in turn, to ordain new members of the team is suggestive of a successional and, to that extent, a 'high' element in his understanding of the rite. The reception and ordination of new members of the Band normally took place at the Christmas conventions in Belfast. In a tribute to the memory of Darragh, a correspondent vividly recalled one particular convention some forty years earlier: 'It was an ordination service, and truly waves of glory swept over the place, and it became hallowed ground. On that particular occasion Mr Darragh gave a message in tongues, the thrill of which I still catch. It seemed to me just like a voice from heaven, and we knew God was in that place'.[73] Services of such intensity must have made an immense impression on the ordinands, sending them, assured of their calling and their Lord, into the sometimes unpropitious backwaters of rural Ireland.

In Hackett's estimation, Moelfryn Morgan was 'one of the most gifted Bible preachers of our time'.[74] Hackett saw in him qualities that made him 'an illustration of this wondrous power of Pentecost'. He told something of Morgan's spiritual journey: 'For twenty-seven years in the ministry and not converted, yet souls were saved under his preaching, so great was the power of the Spirit and the Word in the Welsh churches during the Revival. Brought to Christ in July 1915, he received the Baptism in the Spirit some five months later'. Addressing the congregation in the tent, Morgan confessed that he had never before spoken at a public meeting in English and had carefully prepared a dozen sermons in correct English, both in grammar and pronunciation. Shortly after making this statement, his delivery became laboured and he flung his manuscript to the ground. He then 'launched out in the power of the mighty Spirit and found himself upborne and carried forward with astonishing ease and liberty', till, as his English deteriorated, he was forced to close.

Hudson believes that in this incident Morgan experienced the use of *xenolalia*.[75] Such a conclusion, based as it is on Hackett's account, is hard to sustain. Morgan was not so unfamiliar with English that he had to be coached to deliver his addresses parrot-fashion in English. He had probably drilled himself to the point that he had virtually memorised the address. It was likely that, in the heightened atmosphere of the meeting and with growing confidence, he felt an inner release that enabled him to preach with freedom. It was, and is, a not uncommon experience. A feature of the Welsh Revival, publicised at the time by *The Yorkshire Post*,

---

[73] Edsor, *'Set Your House In Order'*, p. 178.

[74] All quotes in this paragraph are from *Confidence*, April-June 1918, p. 20

[75] Hudson, 'A Schism and its Aftermath', p. 163.

was the young people who lived in Anglicised areas of the Principality and who had no facility in their parents' Welsh tongue, found themselves speaking Welsh with great fluency in the meetings. Williams disputes that such utterances were either *glossolalia* or *xenolalia*. He concludes that the young people 'had probably retained far more impressions from childhood, more than they realised, and that *cryptomnesia* may be the clue to the events described'. He defines cryptomnesia as 'an unusual fortification of memory in an altered state of consciousness'.[76]

Not all the new members of the Band joined it with the preaching and pastoral experience of people like John Carter and E.J. Phillips. As a generalisation, those who came from England and Wales were more experienced in ministry than the raw recruits from Ulster. Tweed made the point that with the movement growing rapidly, young men and women 'began to desire a call to the ministry, but were deterred from making their desires known on the grounds that they might not have the necessary qualifications'.[77] It became more straightforward to enter the Elim ministry once the Bible School was opened at Clapham in January 1925 in that the initial step towards the ministry became more formalised. The Elim Tabernacle nurtured a number of young men who were to become prominent figures in the denomination, such as Samuel Gorman, James McAvoy and William Nolan, the latter two becoming students at the Elim Bible College. These three may well have been among those who supported the Elim work in Lisburn which for lengthy periods was without the services of Band members and depended on the young men from Melbourne Street in the period 1918-22 to keep the services going in the Good Templar Hall.[78] Before the opening of the Bible School, other means of equipping the youthful recruits for the work and giving them a sense of identity were provided. Three can be identified and are discussed next.

7.3.1. Informal Induction

Tweed's memoir makes passing reference to those who had some expertise as teachers within the Band. John Long, the former Cooneyite

---

[76] Cyril G. Williams, *Tongues of the Spirit,* (Cardiff: University of Wales Press, 1981), pp. 54, 187. On the broader issue of *xenolalia*, Wacker maintains that 'by the beginning of the second generation the concept of missionary tongues had receded into the hazy realm of Pentecostal mythology'. (Grant Wacker, *Heaven Below: Early Pentecostals and American Culture*, [Cambridge: Harvard University Press, 2001], p. 51.)

[77] *Tweed Memoir*, p. 32.

[78] Such service provided good training and had something of the flavour of the 'seminaries in the streets' in Chile where learning on the hoof is the means of initiating new recruits to the Pentecostal ministry. (See C. Peter Wagner, *Spiritual Power and Church Growth*, [London: Hodder and Stoughton, 1986].)

preacher,[79] was a member of the Band for about a year. His resignation was accepted at the meeting of the EEB held at the end of December 1919.[80] To the artless Tweed, he was 'a scholar'[81] because of his knowledge of Greek and Hebrew, languages in which Long must have been largely self-taught. Before Tweed joined the Band, he assisted Long in a mission in Randalstown. This would have enabled him to gain new insights into Scripture from Long's interest in the biblical languages. Tweed added to the list of influences on his ministry in a passage that reveals his jejune assessment of scholarly prowess: 'We could not boast of a "Bible College" but we had Pastor R. Mercer who was a great theologian, as such, and we had a number of very learned men who were also good Bible teachers... One of the new members of 1919 was a B.A. [Hare]'.[82] As for Jeffreys, 'he was not behind in gifts and learning' though his influence was wider than the bookish:[83] 'He taught us regular visitations of the "flock" was of vital importance'.[84]

When Tweed came to pastor the Elim Tabernacle after the departure of Jeffreys and Henderson to England he found that in Jeffrey's time 'the membership had become used to regular visitation, like the Presbyterian ministry' and this practice he sought to maintain.[85] When he acted as assistant pastor to Henderson in Melbourne Street before the latter's departure to England, he found him a 'a good pastor and teacher, but not as an evangelist. He was also a great personal soul winner. I learned much from him on his "doorstep missions"'.[86] Jack Tetchner impressed Tweed by his facility to quote Scripture: 'His knowledge of it and frequent quotations influenced me to memorising those chapters of the Bible, which I would repeat even today'.[87] He also had special cause to be grateful to William Campbell, a young fellow Ulsterman who had joined the Band six months before him. In the course of their conducting the

---

[79] See p. 36.

[80] In his letter of resignation Long stated that 'he preferred to be free from a membership in the Band, believing he was acting in accordance with the leading of God'. (*EEBM*, 31 December 1919.) Living a life of stark simplicity, he resumed an independent itinerant ministry modelled on the style of his 'Go-preacher' days, only this time pursued with Pentecostal sympathies.

[81] *Tweed Memoir*, p. 25.

[82] *Tweed Memoir*, p. 19.

[83] *Tweed Memoir*, p. 19.

[84] *Tweed Memoir*, p. 33.

[85] *Tweed Memoir*, p. 36.

[86] *Tweed Memoir*, p. 33. Elsewhere, he described Henderson as 'a gracious, intelligent, capable Christian gentleman' (p. 31).

[87] *Tweed Memoir*, p. 35. Tetchner was in all likelihood the son of a Salvation Army officer in Sunderland. If so, his father was associated with Reader Harris' Pentecostal League in that town which provided the League with its largest support.

Eskylane barn mission in 1919, Tweed had reached low point in his first-time ministry:

> For the first few nights I had preached with great freedom, but one night...I had no freedom... My thoughts got muddled that at the end of the meeting I told Mr. Campbell in the bedroom that I would never attempt to preach again, all I could do was to give out tracts and do personal work. But he so encouraged me that I did preach again, and with greater freedom, depending much more on the help and power of the Holy Spirit.[88]

This experience led him to understand better 'why the Lord sent his workers "two by two"' and, when circumstances permitted, why it was the practice adopted by Jeffreys for Elim.[89] New pairings of Band members were frequently arranged which allowed closer fellowship throughout the Band and enabled the older and/or more experienced partner to take on the role of mentor.[90] In ways like these the tyro Tweed and fellow initiates became better versed in the comprehensive nature of the Christian ministry.[91]

7.3.2 More Formal Induction

The most structured occasions for fellowship and discussion were the summer camp season and the convention periods, though they were not necessarily limited to these two. Tweed mentioned that 'frequent meetings of the Band were held when convenient, when the development of the work was discussed and difficulties were shared and prayed over'.[92] The summer camp, held at Bangor during the 'Twelfth Fortnight' in July, was 'something very special' for the Band members.[93] Two tents were used, one outside the town at the campsite and the other near the town centre for evening services. At the camp, 'Bible studies were arranged at

---

[88] *Tweed Memoir*, p. 26.

[89] *Tweed Memoir*, p. 26.

[90] In that situation, the rule was that the 'the younger [was] to act as an assistant'. (*Revised 1923 Constitution*, p. 12.)

[91] The article by Allan Anderson, 'The "Fury and Wonder"? Pentecostal-Charismatic Spirituality in Theological Education', *Pneuma*, Vol 23.2, Fall 2001, pp. 287-302, takes up the topic of the theological training best suited to advance Pentecostal spirituality at the beginning of the twenty-first century. Lessons drawn from Chilean Pentecostalism show the effectiveness for growth through training 'by the street' and serving a 'practical apprenticeship [thereby following] the biblical model', the method adopted by Jesus and Paul. This section shows how significant this form of induction was for the pioneer Pentecostal leaders in the Irish context.

[92] *Tweed Memoir*, p. 25.

[93] *Tweed Memoir*, p. 21.

certain hours, conducted by men of great ability', with Jeffreys, Mercer and Long specifically named, 'all qualified men as our teachers'.[94]

The best documented of the camps was the second, held in July 1921, when there 'were something like forty brothers living in happy fellowship under canvas'.[95] At this camp there was a potentially damaging issue raised. It centred on the second part of Article 10 of the 'Statement of Fundamental Truths' set out in the 1922 Constitution: 'We believe...in the eternal conscious punishment of all Christ rejecters'.[96] Tweed commented that there was 'considerable discussion on some of the Fundamentals, some having been influenced by the teaching of A.E. Saxby on the doctrine "the ultimate reconciliation of all things"'.[97]

This doctrine may not have been the only debatable point at the Bangor camp—'not all who attended the lectures or Bible studies agreed on the Fundamentals or certain *points* of doctrine'[98]—though it was the most serious. Though none of the proponents of ultimate reconciliation were named, it is likely that E.W. Hare leaned that way without being as vocal as some others. Hare's report on the camp for the September 1921 issue of the *Elim Evangel*, which he then edited, was bland on the matters of controversy. He indicated that the diverse opinions expressed 'on the deeper truths...might have given place to the enemy, who did make a bold bid to trade on these differences, but we are glad to say that the general result was otherwise'.[99] It was a critical moment for a fundamentalist body like Elim, enough to make Jeffreys take decisive action. After he read out the Fundamentals and 'explained them, copies were given out, and it was made clear that those who did not accept them could not be in membership of Elim'.[100] Hare might have felt some estrangement as a result of this edict that only came to resolution after he left the Band. In a letter he wrote to the *Elim Evangel* in 1924, he stated that the period since he left Ireland had 'not been unfruitful in my experience' and added: 'Very soon after leaving Ireland I came into direct contact with the teaching of Universalism, or, as it is often styled, the Ultimate Reconciliation of All Things. The arguments put forward from Scripture seemed so plausible, and the testimony of the supernatural, alas!, so strong, that there was little wonder that I began to lean in that direction'.[101]

---

94 *Tweed Memoir*, p. 21.

95 *EE,* September 1921, p. 66.

96 *1922 Constitution,* p. 6.

97 *Tweed Memoir*, p. 22.

98 *EEBM*, 31 December 1919.

99 *EE,* September 1921, p. 67

100 *Tweed Memoir*, p. 23.

101 *EE,* May 1924, p. 106. The 'testimony of the supernatural' was most likely prophetic utterance.

By writing of 'direct' contact, Hare rather implied that he had engaged himself in the issue before leaving Ireland, and this preoccupation had led to his making direct contact with circles where the universalist position was taken. It is more than likely that Saxby would have been one of his contacts. Hare was particularly thankful that he, personally, had 'never publicly taught this doctrine' but, nevertheless, it did take its toll: 'What I went through at that time I can never fully describe but it was one of the severest conflicts with Satanic powers that I ever expect to engage in' before he emerged into 'the sunshine' of received orthodoxy, though not again into the Elim movement.[102]

Albert Saxby's high standing with Pentecostals made his teaching on ultimate reconciliation one of the most serious the movement had to face. It was especially hard for a body that prided itself on its biblical orthodoxy. Prior to 1915, Saxby was the minister of a Baptist church in Haringey, north London. To have accepted his teaching would have been a step, the first and possibly not the last, towards doctrinal latitude. He began to articulate his views in a serious way at the Pentecostal leaders' conference at Swanwick, Derbyshire, in 1921, of which Gee wrote 'unhappy doctrinal issues clouded the spiritual sky'.[103] In 1923 he started his own magazine, *Things New and Old*, in which he promulgated more widely his views on final destiny. Gee expressed his disquiet at the effect of the whole controversy in a letter to a colleague in London:

> We are having a big fight here against Brother Saxby's doctrines... The east of Scotland seems to be their stronghold. They have held a big Convention at Leith this weekend! Thank God, the assembly at Leith are standing firm with me for the truth, and more and more are expressing their gratitude for the stand we are taking. We are standing alone but the Lord is with us.[104]

He saw in the whole situation 'the subtle tendency of this age of "higher criticism" to whittle down and undermine all the fundamentals of evangelical belief'.[105] Jeffreys' most forceful critique of Saxby's teaching appeared in the *Elim Evangel* in 1924. He and Gee were at one on this issue. One likely side effect of this controversy was the giving of almost sacrosanct status to the *Fundamental Truths* of Elim. The Deed Poll and Constitution of 1934 maintained the proviso that the *Fundamentals* were something to which 'every Minister of the Alliance

---

[102] *EE,* May 1924, p. 106.

[103] Richard Massey, *Another Springtime: Donald Gee: Pentecostal Pioneer*, (Guildford: Highland, 1992), p. 70. Saxby was Gee's former pastor and a person for whom he had utmost respect.

[104] Massey, *Another Springtime,* p. 71.

[105] Massey, *Another Springtime,* p. 72.

shall subscribe and contrary to which no teaching shall be permitted...and shall for ever be'.[106]

Hare also provided a little of the setting and atmosphere of the dormitory tent where they all slept: 'One brother had actually brought with him, as part of the camp outfit, a ponderous theological work, and our readers can perhaps picture a circle of young men, some on beds and others on the ground, listening to our theological brother reading from the large tome'.[107] Who the 'brother' was can only be guessed. It was most likely Hackett, even Leech, both, doubtless, having access to large theological tomes. It might be of some significance that in Boulton's biography of Jeffreys the two photographs of the crowds attending sea-front baptismal services in Bangor are on the same page as one of Hackett.[108] The blurb attached to the Hackett photograph states that 'many a happy hour has been spent in his company. The "boys", as he called them, loved to gather around him for teaching and instruction'—a picture entirely consonant with Hare's cameo.

Robert Mercer cannot to be dismissed as a possibility as he was a studious, earnest type, enthused enough to revel in sharing newly discovered exegetical insights. He made it his task to foster biblical understanding among suitable young converts in the Ballymena area. Among them were William Spence and his brother, both recently converted at a Faith Mission outreach, who then associated themselves with the Elim church in Cullybackey. William showed an aptitude for preaching and many opportunities to engage in it were presented to him in the growing Elim circle in mid-Antrim. He began to attend training classes held by Mercer. From these, 'he received much benefit...and the knowledge gained became very useful in the ongoing work of the small assembly in Pottinger Street'.[109]

Conventions were another source of extended teaching for Band members. Little did those who attended the Ballymena Convention in the summer of 1920 realise that they were hearing the first thunder rumbles of the controversial teaching, introduced to them by Gerrit Polman and his wife, that would disturb the International Pentecostal Conference in Amsterdam in January 1921. That Conference, hosted by Polman, ex-Dowieite and the founder of the Dutch Pentecostal movement, brought British and Continental leaders together for the first time since the ending of the war that, as it turned out, proved to be the last.[110] The message of

---

[106] *Deed Poll of the Elim Foursquare Gospel Alliance*, April 1934, p. 3.

[107] *EE*, September 1921, p. 67.

[108] Boulton, *Ministry of the Miraculous*, p. 76.

[109] Spence: *Elim in Cullybacky*, p. 3

[110] C. van der Laan, *Sectarian Against His Will*, p. 117. Polman had attended the German Mülheim Conference in 1918 and had embraced this teaching. The September

'death to the self-life' was one that the Polmans brought to Britain and Ireland. In Ballymena, Polman shared the platform with Saxby and his old friend Arthur Booth-Clibborn. An English visitor at the conference observed:

> It is very difficult to give a general impression of the messages without going into detail, but the dominant note seemed to be—Surrender of all to the Lord, death to the self life, and an absolutely unconditional yielding to the Lord that he might have *all* the glory... The Lord was calling us...to face greater separation and depths of death we had not known yet.[111]

It is probable that Mrs Polman addressed the conference because the next issue of the *Evangel* published a report of hers on *What God is doing in Holland.* She spoke of some of her compatriots attending a conference in Mülheim-Ruhr the previous year where 'the Lord spoke to us through the conscience, through prophecy, through visions. Nothing remained for us but to go down before the Lord in brokenness of spirit, with a contrite heart'.[112]

To Gee, this was all a bit too much: 'The avidity with which they were seeking to "die" was rather embarrassing... Unconsciously to themselves they were suffering from depression consequent upon their defeat in the war, and wanted to impose their own emotional condition upon us all under the guise of a spiritual experience'.[113] This was Gee's first excursion abroad and he was able to report on the issue troubling the leaders: 'The German preachers seemed determined to monopolise the Convention with a new teaching they were very much stressing at that time, of a deeper death to self that all must pass through, and their doctrine was reinforced by frequent visions of an extremely personal nature for those present, and by prophecies'.[114] Even the less astute reporter on the Ballymena Conference was aware of an unsettling undercurrent in the meetings which he termed 'an apparent contradiction' between 'the joy of the Lord' and the 'tense feeling' aroused by the call to 'greater separation and depths of death'—despite which the Convention ended in a 'wonderful harmony [that] was remarkable'.[115] Gee came to a similar verdict on the Amsterdam Conference which in its conclusion 'provided a shining example of the

---

1919 issue of *Spade Regen*, the periodical he edited, was dominated by the call to the readers to come under the judgement of God and to crucify the human spirit.

[111] *EE*, September 1920, p. 68.

[112] *EE*, December 1920, p. 19.

[113] Brian R. Ross, 'Donald Gee: In Search of a Church; Sectarian in Transition', (ThD thesis, Knox College, Toronto School of Theology, 1974), p. 23.

[114] Van der Laan, *Sectarian Against His Will*, p. 117.

[115] *EE*, September 1920, p. 68.

victory of Christian love...after which all separated in unbroken love and fellowship in Christ'.[116] It was an outcome he hoped for most: 'God's shepherds need the fruit of the Spirit every bit as much as the gifts of the Spirit—perhaps more'.[117]

The type of piety that the Polmans enunciated in their visit to Ulster in 1921 was alien to the Higher Life tradition that shaped much of British Pentecostalism. That tradition, in the form of Keswick teaching, Packer judged as aspiring to 'a quiet, sunny, tidy life without agony, free from distress at the quality of one's walk with God and one's work for others'.[118] Given the prominence of Keswick teaching within British evangelicalism at the time, it was hardly likely that neither it nor its Pentecostal offshoot would lapse into the spiral of spiritual *angst* that afflicted the post-war German Pentecostal movement. There were, however, some in Britain, such as Arthur Booth-Clibborn and Jessie Penn-Lewis, who revealed a quietist strain. They often felt an affinity with the works of Madame Guyon, who through her retreat into a life of private contemplation found consummation in a mystical espousal to Christ. Penn-Lewis wrote of an experience where 'I wanted only to be left alone to retire within for communion with my Beloved... I gladly chose the path of the cross and consented to walk in the night of faith to that goal where God would be All in All'.[119] At the 1920 July Convention in Belfast, Booth-Clibborn spoke of 'a fuller measure of abandonment to God...and the absolute necessity of being wholly lost in order to be wholly saved'.[120] Such sentiments were not readily assimilated by Ulster audiences who felt more in tune with a theme of the Bangor Convention during its second week. The emphasis then was on 'the Advocacy of our Glorified Lord Jesus Christ, Who died that we might live and Who lives that we might have life more abundant'.[121]

7.3.3 The Contribution of the Elim Evangel

The third means of stimulating an Elim mindset among the Band and a sense of identity within the denomination at large was advanced by the publication of the *Elim Evangel*.[122] An analysis of a sample of the first

[116] Van der Laan, *Sectarian Against His Will*, p. 117

[117] D. Gee, *Fruitful or Barren?: Studies in the Fruit of the Spirit*, [Springfield, MO: Gospel Publishing House, 1961], p. 19.

[118] J.I. Packer, *Keep in Step in the Spirit*, (Leicester, IVP, 1984), p. 153.

[119] J.C. Metcalf, *Molded by the Cross: The Biography of Jessie Penn Lewis*, (Fort Washington, PA: Christian Literature Crusade, 1997), p. 41.

[120] *EE*, September 1920, p. 66.

[121] *EE*, September 1920, p. 67.

[122] Tweed observed that 'the members of the Evangelistic Band were delighted with the introduction of this quarterly periodical, and regarded it as another great step forward'.

four volumes of the *Evangel* (1919-23) shows the extent to which great weight was placed on Pentecostal subject matter.[123] Gee described it as 'altogether...a thoroughly Pentecostal little publication, and immediately achieved popularity as such'.[124] Of the twenty-six articles in the sample, many of them written-up convention addresses, twelve relate specifically to Pentecostal themes. Of these, five were devoted to Spirit-baptism and spiritual gifts, two to the Second Coming and the remaining five to divine healing. At least three of the remaining fourteen articles could have been written only by authors with Pentecostal sympathies. Relatively few of the articles dealt with concerns that would have resonated within the wider evangelical constituency. W.F.P. Burton's three articles dealing with *Foreknowledge and Predestination*, *How to Know the Will of God* and *Feasting and Feeding* [*on the Bible*], as well as an article on *Tithing*, would have carried a wider appeal. The second and third of the Burton articles were transcripts of addresses given at Convention meetings in Belfast. Hare commented on Burton's contribution at the 1921 Christmas Convention that he took 'difficult subjects' and for each subject 'thrashed it out in a way that was lucid and interesting and, at the same time, inspiring'.[125] It was his desire to see some of these 'good things' reach a wider audience that he decided to publish them in the *Evangel*.[126] Some editions carried short extracts from the writings of contemporary or recent evangelical writers. A.B. Simpson featured the most with three extracts, two of which dealt with divine healing, while D.M. Panton and the American attorney, Phillip Mauro, provided others.[127] Almost all editions carried Bible study material. E.C.W. Boulton wrote *Studies in the Life of Faith*; A.E. Saxby provided *Notes on First Corinthians*; Thomas Myerscough contributed a series on *Romans* and Archdeacon W.R.G. Phair on *Genesis*.

(*Tweed Memoir*, p. 31.) The first edition was published in December 1919 and for the next two years it appeared as a quarterly. With Vol. 3.1 (January 1922) it became a monthly publication and from January 1925 it was issued fortnightly in a new, enlarged format and sales were encouraging.

[123] The thirteen (out of twenty-six) issues of *EE* that made up the sample were taken from years 1919 till 1923. They were: 1919-20—Vol. 1.1; Vol. 1.3; 1921—Vol. 2.2; Vol. 2.4, 1922—Vol. 3.1; Vol. 3.3; Vol. 3.6; Vol. 3.9; Vol. 3.11; 1923—Vol. 4.2; Vol. 4.5; Vol. 4.9; Vol. 4.12. The sample was based on the need to reflect the different periods of the year and to pick up any longitudinal trend occurring during this period.

[124] Gee, *Wind and Flame*, pp. 97-8.

[125] *EE*, February 1922, p. 21.

[126] *EE*, February 1922, p. 21.

[127] Panton was the former, minister of the independent Surrey Chapel, Norwich, and a leading partial rapturist. He was strongly anti-Pentecostal to the extent that he was instrumental, in part, for the withdrawal of an invitation to George and Stephen Jeffreys to address a London Prophetic Conference in 1922. (Randall, *Evangelical Experiences*, p. 229.)

Robert Phair (1837-1931) was a naturalised Canadian with an Ulster background. He was born in County Tyrone and was converted during the 1859 Revival. Moving to Canada, he spent most of his active ministry among the Native American people of northern Ontario. He received his Spirit-baptism in Winnipeg in 1907 and without compromising his position in the Anglican Church became a father figure in Canadian Pentecostalism. To what extent his conversion experience in the tumultuous 1859 Revival predisposed him towards Pentecostalism is as intriguing as it is unanswerable. On his retirement, he travelled extensively bearing witness to the Pentecostal message and experience.[128]

The magazine was not confined to didactic material but aimed at the same time to be advisory and inspirational. It is germane to note that in its first two years (1920-21) the *Evangel*, carried a total of twenty-three items, either in snippet or full report form, that gave news of current activities in Ireland as against fourteen for the rest of Britain. In 1923, the equivalent figures were twenty-five for Ireland and thirty for the rest of the United Kingdom. The figures indicate that the shift of the centre of gravity of the Elim work from Ireland to Britain was gathering pace.

In these ways, the members of the Band developed their ministry, though some more successfully than others. Boulton rather implies in his characteristically flowery prose that not all the recruits were equally acceptable to the people:

> If some of these preachers lacked the polish of the more professional ministry, and in the estimation of their critics did not always appear to advantage in the pulpits, yet the fruit which they bore in transformed lives and homes and the splendid spiritual absorption which possessed them, formed an excellent apology for any scholastic or social deficiency from which they might appear to suffer.[129]

He acknowledged that though some at times might proclaim their message 'with faltering tongue', it was always 'with flowing hearts'.[130] It must have proved difficult at times for the less accomplished Band members to avoid invidious distinctions being made between them and Jeffreys and his more experienced colleagues. This would have been particularly true of the growing number of young men from Ulster who had less experience of leadership compared to those of their colleagues who had pioneered Pentecostal assemblies in England, notably Carter and Phillips.

Another promising young Englishman to join the Band was Charles Kingston from Leigh-on-Sea, Essex, who arrived in Ireland around

---

[128] See the article on Phair in *NIDPCM,* pp. 987-8.

[129] Boulton, *Ministry of the Miraculous*, p. 49.

[130] Boulton, *Ministry of the Miraculous*, p. 49.

March 1921.[131] Kingston first encountered Jeffreys at a pre-arranged meeting at Victoria Station, London, in 1920 to see if there was an opening for him as an evangelist in the Band.[132] He had been singularly unimpressed by a Pentecostal convention he had recently attended in London; 'the congregation was middle-aged; the meetings seemed listless, the speakers boring'.[133] Jeffreys invited him to attend the 1920 Christmas Convention in Belfast to get a feel for the work and he was immediately taken by what he saw: 'What a difference I found in the Pentecostal work in Ireland. There was a spiritual verve in the meetings, a vitality in the messages that plucked at one's heart strings, and sent one singing for joy, that proved God was real and working in His power. This was the real thing in religion! These people were my people! Their God was my God!' [134]

Kingston, unbeknown to himself, was witnessing and at the same time contributing to a turning point in the British movement, signalled by the efforts of Jeffreys in Ireland. The Polhill era was fading, yet, as Gee finely expressed it, 'not before he had helped with the foundations of a spiritual movement that contained dynamic qualities that I think he only dimly understood'.[135] Ulster was thus in the vanguard of this shift within British Pentecostalism, showing the way whether in the back streets of Belfast or the market towns and villages of eastern Ulster.

7.4 The Spatial Distribution of Elim Work

The question has to be raised as to the extent the Elim work in Ireland was subject to a degree of strategic planning. Since no documentation exists to give a clear-cut answer, the approach adopted here aims to provide an analysis that may elucidate those factors that operated in the diffusion of the early movement in the province. The first step will be to examine the distribution of locations outside Belfast where missions were held and churches established in the period 1915-23 and the factors that played a part in their origin. To do this, particular attention will be focused on the central area of the Lower Bann valley for which source

---

[131] His father, George, the owner of a prosperous butchery business in Leigh-on-Sea, Essex, had the distinction of leading the first Elim church in England after its opening in 1921.

[132] *EE*, Vol. 43.7, February 1962, p. 106.

[133] *EE*, Vol. 43.7, February 1962, p. 106. It was all very reminiscent of the atmosphere that so depressed Donald Gee at the meetings convened by Polhill in the 1920s when the latter 'inflicted on the [audience] his little homilies from the chair [and] his continual repetition of 'Beloved Friends' became a byword and a joke'. (Gee, *These Men I Knew*, p. 75.)

[134] *EE*, Vol. 43.7, February 1962, p. 106.

[135] Gee, *These Men I Knew*, p. 76.

material is available. The *Tweed Memoir*, limited and fitful as it is, and reports in the *Elim Evangel* provide much of the detail for the area with Ballymena at its hub. The focus will then shift to a study of the situation in Belfast.

7.4.1 Outside Belfast

Map A reveals that the distribution of the locations of Elim assemblies and places where protracted missions were held was confined largely to the eastern half of the province. The main centres are found within three broad tracts, viz. the Bann-Braid Corridor, the Lisburn-Monaghan Axis cutting across the Linen Triangle, and the Belfast Lough Arc as shown on Map B. The corridors are both physiographical features and transportation arteries. Map B, which shows *inter alia* the rail network in 1922, underscores the point.

Railways were the most efficient way for Band members to travel around the province and it was not entirely adventitious that all the main centres of Elim in Ulster were on or near the railway network—Ballymena, Ballymoney, Lisburn, Portadown, Lurgan, Armagh, Monaghan and Bangor, with Belfast at the hub. The 1921 Christmas Convention season lasted a fortnight with no less than three centres (Belfast, Ballymena and Lurgan) to be serviced by members of the Band. Hare and a companion arrived on the Wednesday of the second week at the Great Northern terminus at Belfast to travel to Lurgan only to find 'something like twenty people, nearly all members of the Evangelistic Band, off by the same train to take Lurgan by storm in the Name of the Lord'.[136] The Band members were not people to miss an opportunity to witness. They spoke to three strangers in their compartments 'about eternal things' and as they neared Lurgan they began to break into chorus singing. It was little wonder that 'people pass the windows and gaze in with a curious expression on their faces of mingled interest and pity!'[137] It was noted that at the 1922-23 New Year Convention held in the Protestant Hall in Ballymena that 'some of the Elim Evangelists were to be seen as in former years coming off the afternoon train, and the early arrival of some of the saints from the country districts was quite noticeable', in all probability through having to fit in with train times.[138]

When compared with Map C, which shows the core areas of the three largest Protestant denominations, it can be observed that the centres of Elim work lie almost entirely within the Protestant heartland. The only exception is the area lying towards the south-western end of the Lisburn-

136 *EE*, February 1922, p. 23.
137 *EE*, February 1922. p. 23.
138 *EE*, February 1923. p. 22.

Monaghan Axis between Armagh and Monaghan. It was in this last area that undercurrents of sectarianism can be detected when an assembly was started in Milford which lay on the interface between Protestant-Catholic majority areas. Progress in the village was made difficult reportedly 'by the Adversary (who) was also busy, seeking to stop the work'.[139] The hindrance was not specified but when Milford was first mentioned in the *Elim Evangel* it was to indicate that it was near Armagh, 'a stronghold of Roman Catholicism'[140] and this may have had some bearing on the threat of closure hanging over the assembly, troubled as they were with the threat of civil disorder that was gathering force in the period leading up to the partition of the island. Milford was one of the first places to organise a band of civilian Specials, a locally recruited group of volunteer vigilantes organised to protect life and property. The Milford Platoon was organised at the end of March 1920 and grew from twenty men to one hundred. This was taking place at the same time as the Milford Elim was becoming established. It was a time when neither community could breathe easily.[141]

The Elim work at Milford was transferred northwards to Armagh city in the early autumn of 1920 when the offer of a room in which to hold services was accepted. The group soon outgrew this restricted accommodation and was able to rent a vacant church in the town centre. Gee, as part of a tour round the Elim assemblies in Ulster in 1923, visited the work in Armagh and 'would have fain stayed longer, but before leaving we had a glimpse of the situation that makes work very difficult there when a hurried visit was paid both to the ornate Roman Catholic Cathedral and also the Protestant Cathedral, situated in striking proximity'.[142] While not entirely explicit, the remark hints of sectarian tension within the Primate City. Armagh was indeed a focus of communal tension at the time. Catherine Booth-Clibborn (the Maréchale) conducted a mission there in the early 1920s. The night before she and her party arrived in the city, the bodies of seven men, brutally murdered, were laid on the steps leading up to the door of the church where she was preaching. As people were beginning to arrive, there were people still on their knees trying to scrub the bloodstains off the stone.[143]

---

[139] *EE*, June 1920, p. 39.

[140] *EE*, December 1919, p. 3.

[141] See John Redmond, *Church, State, Industry 1827-1929 in East Belfast*, [privately published, 1960], p. 23. It was only with the collapse in 1925 of the Boundary Commission, set up to delineate the boundary between the new Irish Republic and Northern Ireland, a constituent part of the United Kingdom, that partition became an entrenched, though deeply contentious, reality.

[142] *EE*, May 1923, pp. 81-82.

[143] See Scott, *Heavenly Witch*, p. 223.

Map C shows that the Bann-Braid Corridor defines a large part of the area of Scottish settlement which took place largely in the seventeenth century. To this day Presbyterians continue to be the dominant religious group. It was in this area that the 1859 Revival had its origin and probably its most marked impact. By contrast, the 'Linen Triangle'[144] is not so dominantly Presbyterian and the greater influence of the Church of Ireland, and its correlate Methodism, reflects the Anglicanism of the original English settlers in the seventeenth-century Ulster Plantation. Elim concentrated its efforts in the three core areas identified and little attempt was made in the early years to penetrate the three western counties of Londonderry, Tyrone and Fermanagh. These counties had sizeable areas where Catholicism was dominant. In the western counties, it was only in the lowland corridors attached to the eastern counties by good communication links that Protestants were in a majority.

What is striking about the geographical distribution of the Elim work in Ulster is its essential rurality. Many of the missions and succeeding assemblies were situated in little known villages and townlands. Reports in the *Evangel* could wax quite lyrical about some of the settings. Of the mission conducted by Farlow and Kingston in the spring of 1923 at Hamilton's Bawn, four miles east of Armagh, the correspondent (probably Kingston) wrote:

> Hamilton's Bawn! What memories that name awakens!... A picture in which the foreground consists of a village with little white-washed houses, and the background of undulating countryside, stretching for miles, of ploughed fields and grassland, of white farmhouses and green trees—until in the distance can be seen the Mountains of Mourne showing up hazily in the sunshine.[145]

When Florence Vipan, a visiting Pentecostal missionary, journeyed to Moneyslane (Figure III), near Rathfriland, County Down, it was through 'a district where farm-houses are situated at intervals in the midst of lovely scenery, with the beautiful Mourne Mountains at no great distance' (Photograph E).[146] With locations in such bucolic settings, transport was something of a problem, but eased by the ubiquitous bicycle. She knew that some attending the meetings 'drove, cycled or walked for miles to be

---

[144] The 'Linen Triangle' was a major centre of the Irish linen manufacturing industry. The industry began its expansion in the latter part of the eighteenth century. It was in this area that early Methodism witnessed some of its greatest growth, much of it in pulses of religious revivalism throughout the period 1780-1845.

[145] *EE,* May 1923, p. 96.

[146] *EE,* December 1919, p. 12. In *Confidence* September 1916, p. 154, mention is made of 'Miss Vipan (Dublin)' as a speaker at the August convention at Heathfield, Sussex. As an experienced 'lady worker', Florence Vipan would have been a capable speaker.

present'.[147] Many, equally, were content to walk. At the mission conducted by Jeffreys, 'away in the heart of the country',[148] at Annaghanoon, near Waringstown, County Down, walking home from the mission was lightened considerably for the young people by their comportment: 'Far away on the clear midnight air could be heard the songs of bands of these young people as they wended their way home, singing the songs of the redeemed'.[149] Even as late as 1955, a news report still commented on its seclusion: 'Ask the bus conductor for Annaghanoon, and he will give you a blank stare, for Annaghanoon as a place is not on the map! There is no town or village, only green fields. Alighting at the lonely cross roads, the visiting preacher will wonder what sort of congregation these hedgerows and fields can produce, a wonder not diminished when he comes upon the Elim Hall, nestling among its surrounding conifers. It is well named "the church in the fields"'.[150]

In the period under discussion, Elim probably put more effort into its campaigns in the Irish Free State than into the western counties of Northern Ireland. Times were not propitious for work in the South until the IRA called a cease-fire in the Irish Civil War (1921-23) at the end of April 1923. Hostilities quickly ceased and this allowed a degree of normality to return to the state after seven convulsive years (1916-23) in which the new state was born. In July 1923 a mission conducted by two Band members, Fletcher and a probationer Stronge, was held in Ballyjamesduff, County Cavan. The meetings were held in a large granary owned by a local supporter. The following month the two evangelists conducted another campaign in the same county at Graddum. Between these two missions they travelled from the border county of Cavan, with its 18% Protestant minority and then deeper into the Free State to conduct meetings in Carlow. A report in the *Elim Evangel* stated that the writer who lived in the town 'had prayed for over twelve months for Pentecostal preachers to be sent'.[151] On the first Sunday morning Fletcher preached in the Methodist Church and on the final Saturday a baptismal service was held beside the River Barrow. In the following year, Fletcher continued to hold missions in County Cavan. Like many northern-based denominations, Elim sought to have a southern extension to give it an all-Ireland dimension. It was at the heart of the vision that energised the young men who came together in Monaghan in 1915. It was an ideal made possible by the fact that in most southern counties there was often a sufficient number of enlivened Protestants, though few disenchanted Catholics, to allow an evangelical nucleus to form. Any great expectation

---

147 *EE,* December 1919, p. 12.

148 *EE,* March 1924, p. 69.

149 *EE,* March 1924, p. 69.

150 *EE*, 9 July 1955, p. 302.

151 *EE,* September 1923, p. 192.

of growth in the long-run had to take consideration of the demographic changes induced by the sizeable emigration of Protestants from the South following the partition and by the acquiescence of the rest to the prevailing religio-cultural ethos of the new state.

Throughout the island it was the ubiquitous bicycle that did much to bring town and country together, particularly so for the less well-heeled and the younger people. When Florence Vipan conducted meetings in Portadown, she commented on the 'number of cycles put up which told of interest by those at a distance from the town'.[152] They were used not only by the congregation but also the evangelists who at times had no other alternative in the more rural areas. Miss Dougherty recalled some of the difficulties she had to cope with in her assignments:

> Some of the churches were and still are in country places. I well remember walking through storm and sunshine along country roads and lanes to visit the people. Some of the town churches had branch churches in the village and one had to cycle six or seven miles on winter nights as well as summer nights to minister. And how eerie it seemed sometimes cycling late at night in the darkness with no light but that of the bicycle lamp, and perhaps not meeting a single person for miles.[153]

John Long was another evangelist who relied on the bicycle. With his Cooneyite background, in which the bicycle was almost *de rigueur* for the Go-preachers, he persisted in its use into old age covering a mileage in the British Isles of Wesleyan proportions. What the horse was to the Methodist circuit rider, the bicycle was to the impecunious itinerant evangelist, Elim or otherwise.

Travel was made even more arduous for the evangelists in the early 1920s by the political situation within the province.[154] Miss Dougherty was left wondering 'if the experiences in those early days could not in some small way compare with the experiences we read of missionaries having in other fields, when to be out after the 11 p.m. curfew was to risk being arrested, fined, or even shot'.[155] These hazards could have been at the hands of the 'B Specials', a wing of the Special Constabulary

---

[152] *EE,* December 1919, p. 12. The role of the modern bicycle, perfected in the last two decades of the nineteenth century, cannot be underestimated in that it increased the distance within which it was feasible for the interested and merely curious to attend the mission meetings, many of them young people who cycled to the meetings from surrounding small farms.

[153] *EE,* Vol. 46.47, November 1965, p. 756.

[154] Following the final transfer of security powers to Belfast in May 1922, the new Northern Ireland Government proscribed the IRA and the police were given the authority to close any road, lane or bridge at a moment's notice to restrict Republican snipers. From 1 June 1922 a curfew was extended to rural areas for the hours between 11 pm and 5 am. (Hennessey, *A History of Northern Ireland,* p. 32.)

[155] *EE,* November 1965, p. 756.

recruited on a part-time basis to operate in their local area and thus well equipped to use their local knowledge of its people and byways.[156]

On the face of it, the concentration of evangelistic effort on the more rural areas, as opposed to the densely populated Belfast area would appear to be misplaced and indicative of a failure to observe a fundamental principle of strategic thinking, namely the need to prioritise, in this case to focus more on sizeable settlements. Before such a judgement can be reached, it is necessary to know something of the nature of rural life in the province because in a number of significant ways Northern Ireland in the inter-war years was quite different from most other parts of the United Kingdom. Agriculture was the single largest industry around the time of partition, accounting for 26% of the workforce compared to 6.2% in the rest of the United Kingdom.[157] Small farms dominated the province's rural economy, with only 4.4% exceeding 100 acres compared to 20.9% in England and Wales and 8.8% in Scotland; a census in 1937 showed that 82.7% of farms were below fifty acres and almost all the farms were owner-occupied, necessitating family assistance at times in the farming cycle. As a result, there was a high density of rural population, especially in the fertile eastern lowlands.

The many mill villages that dotted the rural landscape were another feature that contributed to the making of a busy landscape.[158] Cullybackey, Milford, near Armagh, and Balnamore, near Ballymoney, were three of the mill villages where Elim had a presence. Milford lies along the south-western edge of the area Hempton defined as the 'Linen Triangle of Ulster' (Map B). The early mill villages were dependent on waterpower, which in the case of Milford was supplied by the River Callan, with Darkley lying south of it and situated on the same river.[159]

---

[156] Their effectiveness was acknowledged by an IRA commanding officer who admitted that his 3rd Northern Division had been forced to abandon its flying pickets in Antrim and Down in the summer of 1923. (Hennessey, *A History of Northern Ireland,* p. 39.)

[157] Bardon, *A History of Ulster*, p. 520. Other statistical material in the paragraph comes from the same source.

[158] A feature of the Industrial Revolution, the mill village developed out of the eighteenth-century domestic linen industry which preceded the factory era. As the linen industry became increasingly factory based, manufacturers built housing for their workers and created communities over which they exercised varying forms of paternalistic influence and, in some cases, social experimentation. Bessbrook is a perfect exemplar of such a village and it was there that Arthur Booth-Clibborn had his earliest work experience in management in the large linen mill owned by his Quaker relatives.

[159] Darkley was the scene of one of the most infamous incidents in the recent Troubles. On the 20 November 1983, three church elders were shot dead and seven members wounded in an attack by the INLA (Irish National Liberation Army) on the Elim Church in the village. The village is only a few miles from the border in a dominantly Catholic area. Dominic McGlinchy, a leading figure in INLA, denied personal involvement in the incident and stated; 'They were entirely innocent hill-billy folk who

The Triangle enclosed almost all the early Elim centres in the southern part of the province, notably the largest towns of Lisburn, Lurgan, Portadown and Armagh. The significance of the Triangle lies in its being one of the two core areas, the other being the 'Lough Erne Rectangle', where the Methodist Revival won many of its adherents from among its farmer-weavers in recurrent revivals between 1780 and 1821. In both areas, especially Fermanagh, 'a well-established rural revivalistic tradition' was laid.[160]

If the Methodist revival created a radical evangelical tradition in the more Anglican part of the Linen Triangle, the Presbyterian revival tradition that owed much to the Six Mile Water Revival in the seventeenth century and the 1859 Revival shaped the revival tradition in the Bann Corridor.[161] Certainly, if reports in the *Elim Evangel* are anything to go by, it was within this area that folk memories of the 1859 Revival were jogged most and expectations of a similar move of the Spirit were at their highest.[162] Within the Corridor lay Balnamore, a typical mill village of about thirty families. John M. Barkley, minister of its Presbyterian Church in the 1930s, provided a description of conditions then prevailing:

> It was quite common to see the women and girls in bare feet wearing a flimsy frock...walking across (the roadway to the mill) on a winter's evening with the sweat of their work lashing off them. No wonder the place was rife with tuberculosis... All the houses had electric light, DC run off the dynamo of the mill, but earthen floors. You can guess what it was like on a winter's night with snow on the ground.[163]

It was from this village during the period of the first Ballymoney mission held by Elim Band evangelists that 'many of [the workforce] attended the

---

had done no harm to anyone'. The doctor who attended the scene said he had never seen a place for such an atrocity to happen that the people were so calm. (David McKittrick *et al*, *Lost Lives: The Stories of the Men, Women and Children Who Died as a Result of the Northern Ireland Troubles*, [Edinburgh, Mainstream Publishing, 1999], pp. 963-4.)

[160] D. Hempton and M. Hill, *Evangelical Protestantism in Ulster Society 1740-1890*, (London: Routledge, 1992), p. 31. Methodism was quite strong in the southern border counties because it penetrated largely from the south where majority Protestant affiliation was Anglican.

[161] Darragh is of the opinion that the striking physical manifestations that characterised the 1859 Revival 'would appear to be partly in the process of historical continuity with the 1615 Six Mile Water Revival and the [American] Frontier Revival providing models to be emulated'. (Paul Darragh, 'Epidemiological Observations on Episodes of Communicable Psychogenic Illness', [PhD thesis, Queens University Belfast, 1988], p. 545.)

[162] See pp. 139 and 163-64.

[163] J.M. Barkley, *Blackmouth and Dissenter*, (Belfast: White Row Press, 1991), p. 53.

mission and were saved and baptised in the Holy Spirit'.[164] Barkley's reaction to the socio-economic problems of the village was, 'I saw something must be done about it' and set about establishing a club for boys and men six nights a week—a response quite alien to the thinking of the Band.[165] Hunt has summarised the reasons for the apolitical stance of the early Pentecostals, with their fighting shy of social activism, as 'primarily linked to aspects of sectarianism, above all retreatism, spiritual elitism, millenarianism and boundary maintenance with the outside world'.[166]

Thanks to the *Tweed Memoir* and snippets of information in the early editions of the *Elim Evangel*, a picture can be built of the arrival of Elim in the Bann Corridor. A study of the advance of Elim in the Braid Corridor reveals some of the dynamics involved in the growth of the new movement. Figure IV is an attempt to show the network of relationships between people and assemblies that developed in the Corridor in the early years. It aims to summarise some of the interactions of people and groups within the Bann Corridor.

The focal point of the corridor is Ballymena, described once as 'the most devoutly Presbyterian town in the North'.[167] When W.P. Nicholson conducted a mission in the town in 1923, over 2,500 people professed conversion, more than a quarter of its total Protestant population.[168] The

---

[164] *Tweed Memoir,* p. 9.

[165] Barkley, *Blackmouth and Dissenter* pp. 53-4. In this oft-quoted book, Liston Pope examined a workers' strike in a cotton mill town in North Carolina held in 1929 and the contrasting reactions of churches and new sects, particularly the Pentecostal Holiness Church to the strike. His conclusion—'Preachers of the newer sects, who are closer to those most disadvantaged under existing arrangements and presumably are in better position to see need for changes in economic affairs, display even less interest in the social sphere than ministers of older denominations'—is entirely consonant with the situation in Ulster in the inter-war period. (Liston Pope: *Millhands and Preachers: A Study of Gastonia,* [New Haven, CT: Yale University Press, 1942], p. 164.)

[166] Stephen J. Hunt, 'Deprivation and Western Pentecostalism Revisited: Neo-Pentecostalism', *Online Journal for the Interdisciplinary Study of Pentecostalism and Charismatic Movements, Pentecostal Studies*, Vol. 1.2, 2002, p. 4. A quote from his lengthy treatment of the topic gives something of the tenor of his analysis: 'The first Pentecostals...had little or no organizational expertise: they did not possess the means to effect changes in the political systems even if they so desired. The leaders of the movement had a somewhat limited social and professional experience (being drawn from the rank and file) and thus had to formulate alternative interpretations of social events. Defined as a unique religious experience given by God to those he deemed worthy, it gave the Pentecostals a reason to feel that they had a greater degree of spirituality than other religious groups'. (Hunt, 'Deprivation and Western Pentecostalism Revisited', pp. 11-12.)

[167] Ed Moloney and Andy Pollak, *Paisley*, (Dublin: Poolbeg, 1986), p. 14.

[168] Moloney and Pollak, *Paisley*, p. 14.

early history of Ballymena Elim was recounted in the previous chapter, so the main thrust here is to draw attention to some of the links with its hinterland. The five-week summer mission in the summer of 1916 drew people from the surrounding countryside and, in particular, four farmers, three named and one unnamed, who were to play a link role in advancing the Elim cause in their own districts. Edward Harris and William John McKeown from Tullynahinion and James Gault from Eskylane became prominent laymen in the movement especially in the southern sector of the Corridor while the fourth, unnamed and from Rasharkin, played a significant part in the development of the work in the northern sector.

William John McKeown was the first in the district to come in contact with the Pentecostal experience.[169] McKeown, raised in a strict Presbyterian home, was converted in his teens. It was while working in Coatbridge, Scotland, that he first came into contact with Pentecostalism. The town was among the first to receive the Pentecostal message as it spread from Kilsyth and was one of the dozen centres in Scotland listed in the July 1908 issue of *Confidence*.[170] Both parents were among the first in the Coatbridge assembly to receive the Baptism in the Holy Spirit with signs following. Their son, Adam (b.1909), recalled those Saturday evenings in his mother's little shop when he saw his father 'with open Bible in his hand, expounding the word and the way more clearly to eager listeners'.[171]

When the family moved back to County Antrim in 1912, their farmhouse in the words of their sixth child, Adam McKeown, 'became a centre of Pentecostal activity. As little boys growing up in those days, we became familiar with great men of God, like George Jeffreys, and the great hero of faith, Smith Wigglesworth, and a host of others who came to our home to visit and minister'.[172] A neighbouring farmer, Edward Harris, also associated himself with the movement and it is probable that both men supported the first Jeffreys mission held in Ballymena in 1916. It was in the Harris farmhouse that William Campbell and the younger Tweed ('a blond curly hairdo boy of some 18 years') conducted their first mission in the district in 1920.[173] The eleven-year-old Adam remembered

---

[169] After his marriage in 1896, McKeown and his young wife moved to Scotland to take up labouring jobs, first at a brickworks and then at the ironworks at Coatbridge. The first seven of their nine children were born in Coatbridge in the period 1898-1910 before they returned to purchase a farm in the family townland of Tullynahinion.

[170] *Confidence*, July 1908, p. 2.

[171] Adam McKeown, *A Man Called Adam*, (privately printed, 1984), p. 13.

[172] McKeown, *A Man Called Adam*, p. 13.

[173] McKeown, *A Man Called Adam*, p. 13.

> watching these two men, day by day, going into the Harris barn. I learned that they spent hours there, fasting and praying. In the evenings they conducted meetings in the Harris home, which had become a gathering point for neighbours and friends. It was quite a sight to see people with lanterns hurrying along the dark country roads, all leading to the Edward Harris home.[174]

Tweed and his colleague, sensing the mission getting off to an unpromising start, were driven in desperation to engage in intensive prayer and fasting. The breakthrough came one evening while family prayers were being conducted round the big kitchen fire. Some of the young men who had been attending the meetings entered by the back door and knelt beside the family. According to Tweed, 'A most unusual occurrence took place. A message in tongues was given, and as the interpretation was being given, one after the other, the young men were crying to God for mercy. They were all saved'.[175] In the course of the eight-week mission, over forty were converted: '[They were] mostly young farmers, whose lives had been notoriously bad... At night, when the meetings were dismissed and the people had gone, the kitchen would gradually fill again with these young men, who had returned to talk over the things of the kingdom far into the night... Conviction of sin was mighty! and we may safely say that the whole countryside was affected'.[176] Though the farmhouse was small, up to 125 people squeezed into it for the best attended meeting of the mission.[177] The congregation on this occasion spread through rooms adjacent to the kitchen and up the stairs. Of the total of forty converts, about half were young men, two of whom, Adam and his brother James, were to became leading figures in the Apostolic Church.[178]

As a result of the Tullynahinion mission there arose 'a great longing among the people for a hall in which to meet and remember the Lord's death'.[179] Their desire to come together 'to break bread', rather than an undue focus on charismatic manifestations, is suggestive of a key strand of Brethren spirituality. The policy of a table open to all believers, 'which derives from the very heart and foundation of Brethrenism', has been

---

[174] McKeown, *A Man Called Adam*, p. 13.

[175] *EE*, June 1920, p. 40.

[176] *EE*, June 1920, p. 40.

[177] Information obtained from Pastor John Harris, 5 June 2000.

[178] Another well-respected convert was Jack Kyle whose family owned Kyle's Mill, a scutch mill that in the winter months employed a small number of farmers in processing the flax fibre for making into linen yarn. The Kyles, the McKeowns, the Dempseys and the Harris's were all local extended families in good standing in the wider community, many of whom were linked by intermarriage and their involvement in the new movement.

[179] *EE*, June 1920, p. 40, article by Max Wood Moorhead.

traditionally maintained by British Pentecostals.[180] Whether in this case it was or not, Brethrenism played a part in shaping the spirituality of British Pentecostalism, especially in the high regard paid to the weekly celebration of the sacrament. For Pentecostals, as for the Brethren writer, Henry Pickering, the communion is where 'a special *realisation* of [the Lord's] presence is known and felt'.[181] An article in *Elim Evangel* saw weekly observance as part of the 'divine order'.[182] Pentecostals often adopted Brethren terminology such as 'assembly' and 'Gospel Hall', or more usually their own variant 'Full Gospel Assembly', the 'Breaking of Bread' associated with an 'open table' on Sunday morning, followed later by the evening 'Gospel service'. A description of a Pentecostal communion service in Yorkshire in the 1920s could in many respects have been that of a Brethren 'breaking of bread' except when, at a moment of worshipful intensity, 'singing in the Spirit' [glossolalaic harmonising] broke forth. The worshippers sat in a circle round the table and in was left to any member to announce or lead with a chorus or hymn from a Brethren hymnbook or read a Scripture. People acted as they felt led by the Spirit, so despite certain set features related to the act of communion, 'nobody knew what course the meeting would take'.[183]

Tweed recorded that for the next two years after the Tullynahinion mission he continued in a part-time pastoral role conducting two Sunday services as well as week-night services. With a recurrence of his former leg trouble, he was sent to Guernsey by Jeffreys to both recuperate and take charge of a Pentecostal assembly on the island. Even so, the meetings still continued in the Harris farmhouse under the supervision of Robert Mercer. He arranged a supply of preachers from within the eldership of the Ballymena assembly to conduct meetings until Alice McKinley was sent to take charge. When she left to become Tweed's assistant at Melbourne Street, Belfast, and later his wife, most of the Tullynahinion fellowship left to join the newly established Apostolic fellowship that met in the Orange Hall in Portglenone four miles away. William John McKeown was a strong influence in the withdrawal from Elim and the establishment of an Apostolic assembly in the village. He took with him his son together with members of the Kyle and Harris families. James McKeown, the eldest son of William John, was to become a Pentecostal

---

[180] Keith Warrington, 'The Ordinances: The Marginalised Aspects of Pentecostalism', in Keith Warrington (ed.), *Pentcostal Perspectives*, (Carlisle: Paternoster, 1998), p. 210.

[181] Randall, *Evangelical Experiences*, p. 157.

[182] *Elim Evangel*, 1 June 1925, p. 127. Prominent leaders of British Pentecostalism who had a Brethren background included Thomas Myerscough, T.J. Jones, John and Howard Carter, Thomas Mogridge and Nelson Parr.

[183] Kay, *Inside Story,* pp. 112-13.

missionary in the Gold Coast (Ghana). At the age of thirty-seven, he was a working as a tram driver in Glasgow when his call to Africa came.[184]

Tweed had every reason to be grateful to the Gault family who farmed in the townland of Eskylane. With the onset of a tubercular leg condition in 1919, he was placed by Jeffreys in the care of the Gault family who were with Jeffreys 'heart and soul...and kept an open house for all who were working with the Principal'.[185] The Gault parents had three grown-up children, Robert who helped on the farm, Sarah who was at college and Agnes who helped her mother with domestic duties—a fairly common division of labour in farming families. Tweed was rendered virtually immobile by his condition and was often in excruciating pain so that he had to have a room downstairs beside the large kitchen. A good night's sleep was a rarity:

> But there was a brightness in those dark hours. In the summer months, and during the harvest period, they were very early risers. At about five in the morning, the hymn books *Songs of Victory* were brought out and whoever's turn it was to select a hymn started the singing without music, but clearly and surely I would hear *What a Friend we have in Jesus* or *The Great Physician now is near.*[186]
>
> No matter how urgent the business of the day, there was no neglect of the family altar.[187]

Both Gault parents conducted meetings within the range of a pony and trap from their farmhouse. Mrs Gault was well known as 'a great visitor and soul winner in the district'.[188] It was people like the Gaults who played a large part in drawing people into the Pentecostal cause in the Ballymena area. Jean Strachan (née Dougherty) who lived four miles

---

[184] The denomination he helped to establish, the Church of Pentecost, is today the largest Protestant denomination in Ghana in terms of registered members (600,000 with one million affiliates) and number of churches (4,000), while Pentecostals account for 53% of the evangelical constituency in the country. Adam likewise became a missionary to the Gold Coast with the Apostolic Church during the period 1945-48 before taking on a pastoral and administrative role in America. His story and that of the church he founded, the Church of Pentecost, is told in Christine Leonard, *A Giant in Ghana*, (Chichester: New Wine Press, 1989). He has also merited a scholarly article by Robert W. Wyllie, 'Pioneers of Ghanaian Pentecostalism: Peter Anim and James McKeown', *Journal of Religion in Africa*, Vol. VI, 1974, pp. 109-122.

[185] *The Pattern*, May 1944, p. 5. In 1927, a few years after the setting up of the Elim Bible School in London, Jeffreys chose for himself the title of Principal, apparently to forestall Percy Parker assuming the title.

[186] *The Pattern*, May 1944, p. 5. Such Pentecostal brio was conducive to faith that he would be healed and, late in 1919, he exulted in his healing, temporary in this case as it flared up again two years later before he had complete healing in February 1923.

[187] *Tweed Memoir*, p. 24.

[188] *Tweed Memoir*, p. 25.

from the town revealed: 'We who were not privileged to attend the tent mission were made hungry by the testimony of those who recorded their experiences and told what God done in their midst. The work spread greatly by the efforts of local people and local preachers who gave their time, talents and strength to minister in homes far out in the country'.[189] When assemblies came to be formed, the first members living in such rural settings found that they could transfer those elements of familial solidarity and neighbourly cohesion that featured in much of their day-to-day life into a strongly communal ethos within their assemblies. The downside was that tensions within and between families could be carried into the life of the assembly to make them little hotbeds of dissension.

The picture that emerges from all this is that of a people who give all the appearance of having been shaped by a Presbyterian-Reformed ethos that John M. Barkley vividly depicted in his autobiography. It was marked by strong family ties, an emphasis on conversion tied to a restrictive moral code. Barkley remembered his grandfather as 'a Christian man, straight and honest, independent and stubborn—that is, he had most of the characteristics of his fellow Presbyterians'.[190] The family belonged to Trinity Presbyterian Church, Ahogill, and were regarded as 'very religious' and Glenhue was a regular centre for cottage meetings. Barkley's uncle, Andrew, had a reputation for not being 'Gospel-greedy'. Andrew rather basked, to the dismay of his sisters, in a complacent quasi-Calvinism whereby 'being a Presbyterian, he knew he had a soul, but believed it was in God's keeping so he did not worry too much about it'.[191]

The insouciant spirituality of Andrew, and his likes, in rural Ulster was subject to constant challenge from the 'hotter' forms of evangelicalism that inherited and built on the pervasive tradition of the 1859 Revival. Brethren evangelists, for one, would have been more concerned about the state of Andrew's soul than he, himself appeared to be. Cooneyites would have irritated him once he came to understand their subversive dismissal of all churches. Faith Mission pilgrims would have sought to bring him into a new dimension of spiritual experience, adding the robustness of holiness revivalism to the solid fare of his dutiful Presbyterianism. Pentecostals, coming last in this sequence, might have exasperated him most of all, by their drawing attention to parts of the Bible he hardly knew existed, and even if he did, they could be easily dismissed as only encouraging unfathomable ways among those who accepted them at face value. In the 1960s, the offspring of those showing such insouciance might conceivably have been drawn to join the Free Presbyterian Church

---

[189] *EE*, November 1965, p. 756.

[190] Barkley, *Blackmouth and Dissenter*, p. 14.

[191] Barkley, *Blackmouth and Dissenter*, p. 15.

of Ian Paisley with its brand of populist Protestant fundamentalism, ever ready to pounce at the slightest sign of 'modernism' or a 'Romeward/ecumenical trend' in other denominations.

The Ulster poet, John Hewitt (1907-87), Methodist by upbringing and atheist by conviction, conveyed something of the impact of evangelical agencies in rural Ulster. In recalling his younger days he referred to visits of 'the loud evangelist' who came 'to plead, to threaten and alarm':

> It was in corrugated mission halls
> the masters of this craft gained most success.
> In our grandparents' days such strident calls
> drew hundreds to surrender and confess,
> rise penitent, redeemed, to step transformed
> from pews where now we shifted, ill at ease.[192]

Terence Brown holds that the 1859 revival in Ulster 'remains an important, if unacknowledged, influence on the Northern psyche. Its monuments are the innumerable mission halls and tents, evangelistic crusades, and evangelical associations that make Northern Ireland an Irish extension of the Bible Belt'[193]—a reminder that though Pentecostals may have broken with fellow evangelicals in their stance on contemporary charismaticism, they recruited their adherents, in Bryan Wilson's words, not so much 'by a distinctive Pentecostal gospel, but by the traditional emphases of evangelical revivalism. The evangelical strain remained predominant in Elim, with all its Jesucentricity; the cult of the Holy Ghost was restrained'.[194]

Wilson believed it was not in the least surprising that Elim should have made significant advances in the rural areas:

> Fundamentalist creeds appear to develop best in groups to which relatively sophisticated public opinion does not penetrate. The absence of any developed critical sense, the acceptance of authority, and a background tradition of faith in the Bible, are often to be found in country areas, and these are ready-made conditions in which Pentecostalism can flourish... In market towns and country places there is often a culturally deprived population, which once aware of its own retardment, is prepared to capitalise its difference from city dwellers by exalting necessity into

---

[192] Frank Ormsby (ed.), *The Collected Poems of John Hewitt*, (Belfast: Blackstaff Press, 1991), p. 292.

[193] Terence Brown, *The Whole Protestant Community: The Making of an Historical Myth*, [Derry: Field Day, Pamphlet No. 7, 1985], pp. 17-18. Historically, there is a case for seeing Appalachia, parts of it a cultural hearthland of the Scotch-Irish, as an extension of the Ulster Bible Belt.

[194] Wilson, *Sects and Society*, p. 34. 'Restrained', possibly, rather to avoid charges of fanaticism, but certainly not hidden, otherwise the movement would not have faced the strong reproach of fellow evangelicals.

> virtue, and by giving religious value to the limitations which circumstances alone impose.[195]

Wilson concluded that in considering Northern Ireland another dimension had to be added to the equation: 'the antagonisms on political and religious issues have undoubtedly assisted [its] extreme forms of religious expression'.[196]

On first reading, Wilson would seem to play down Elim's appeal to the urban-industrial class. This flies in the face of the evidence which, especially for the period 1925-35, points to the great drawing power of Jeffreys' crusades in Britain's largest cities, all of which had extensive local press coverage, some even grabbing the headlines in the daily nationals. Landau pointed out that many who attended the great rallies in the Royal Albert Hall and the Crystal Palace travelled in full excursion trains from the depressed industrial towns of northern England. One pastor he interviewed at the Albert Hall Easter Convention told him that most of audience 'will feed on the fare given them to-day when they return to their dreary surroundings in some London slum, to their work in factories, in the black towns of the Midlands'.[197] All this is tantamount to saying that Jeffreys had mass appeal. A valid distinction can be made between the two islands in that Elim had a greater rural constituency in Ireland than it had in Britain, where its appeal reached the industrial artisan to greater measure than the small farmer. The higher proportion of people engaged in agriculture in Ulster as compared to industrial Britain goes a long way to explaining the difference. Why Belfast was not so paramount within its region as the great urban areas were in the advance of Elim in England is examined next.

7.4.2 Within Belfast

Belfast, though housing the central church and headquarters' facilities, did not play as dominant a part in the early years of Elim in the province as its status of regional capital would suggest. The most noteworthy happening in Elim circles in the city was the move from Hunter Street to Melbourne Street, a move that transferred the work from the Sandy Row district to the Shankill Road area. Both districts were and continue to be Protestant working-class heartlands. The need to find new premises was made pressing by the fact that the lease on the Hunter Street building was coming to an end, but just as important the building was becoming too small, especially when numbers swelled during the convention seasons. As the number of successful campaigns in the areas outside Belfast increased,

---

[195] Wilson, *Sects and Society*, pp. 98-99.

[196] Wilson, *Sects and Society*, p. 99.

[197] Landau, *God Is My Adventure*, p. 129.

the need to bring coherence to the movement by owning a central meeting place increased. The role of the cathedral and central hall in other denominational traditions, by helping to promote a sense of identity, was replicated in the new movement. It was a role extolled by an elder/deacon in the Melbourne Street assembly, in his report of the first convention held in the new premises: 'As usual friends came in from the country districts—some who had been before, others, who during the last year had found the Saviour, came for the first time... God is working and who can hinder? Words fail one who has seen it developing from a mere handful to a large assembly, with other country assemblies affiliated and all of one accord'.[198] The original strategy adopted four years previously in Monaghan—'establishing a church out of which evangelists would be sent into the country towns and villages'—was well on the way to realisation.[199]

The best attended conventions were not always held in Belfast but in places like Ballymena and Lurgan, where public halls holding up to a thousand people were hired. Ballymena catered primarily for the assemblies in the Bann Corridor and Lurgan for those in the Linen Triangle. By contrast, Melbourne Street held only several hundred people and it was not uncommon for people to be turned away, as happened during the 1922 Christmas Convention.[200] Melbourne Street, nevertheless, had the advantage of being more central and more accessible to the rest of the province as well as possessing a baptistery. But above all, its presence in the capital city carried the symbolic freight of presence and permanence. Put simply, it looked and felt better, more elevated and churchy, by having been a purpose-built Primitive Methodist Church[201]—a circumstance that caused Tweed, for one, much rejoicing: 'The removal...to the new building...was a delightful change, not only with reference to its change of position, but also its architecture. We could no longer be stigmatised as Pentecostals, as a "back street religion"... No one was regretful of the change to a larger building with all the architectural appearance of a place of worship equal to any other church in the district'.[202] For Tweed, the ecclesiastical connotations of the

---

198 *EE*, March 1921, p. 23.

199 *EEBM*, 7 January 1915.

200 *EE*, March 1921, p. 23.

201 At the time of purchase it was a derelict picture house. According to Boulton when enquiries were being made about the building, 'one old lady who had been resident in the district for many years volunteered the information that she remembered it in the times when it had been filled with God's people and praises'. Throughout the twentieth century the Pentecostal and the later charismatic New Churches have been players in taking over disused inner city churches.

202 *Tweed Memoir*, pp. 20 and 35. 'If you want to find the local Pentecostal church, look for the gasworks or cemetery road' is regarded as 'an adage'. (A. McEwan and E.

Melbourne Street building carried just as much weight as its location. The next move of the central church to the Ravenhill Road took place in 1926 to a completely new building, by which time early aspirations had materialised into conspicuous achievement.

In their search for a new site, the deacons of the Hunter Street assembly looked first in their own district. At their meeting on the 3 April 1919 they recorded thanks to God for the EPAC obtaining premises in Melbourne Street and a week later they agreed a name for the church—the 'Elim Pentecostal Tabernacle in Belfast', shortened by usage to the 'Elim Tabernacle'.[203] A major problem lay in raising the money to pay a deposit on the building. Belfast at the time was in one of its periodic bouts of labour unrest.[204] Elim members were not immune to the privations of the period. Considerable satisfaction was expressed at one Convention when it was announced that the offering for the work of the PMU amounted to £46, 'notwithstanding the difficulties many were placed in, owing to unemployment'.[205] Money-raising efforts in such conditions rested on the prudence of those who were committed to their Lord and the abstemious life-style that entailed. According to Tweed, it was Jeffreys' idea of asking the people to give 'promissory notes' which would signify a firm intention to contribute to the building fund when the time came.[206] Tweed was present when the redemption of the notes was called and it was found that the sum raised was sufficient to pay the deposit.

Though the Melbourne Street building was in a dilapidated state it was quickly transformed, thanks to voluntary labour working hand in hand with a local contractor. The church opened in time for the opening of the Belfast Convention, 4-11 July 1919. During the 1920 Christmas Convention seventy-five were baptised by Jeffreys and fifty-nine and

---

Robinson, *Evangelical Beliefs and Educational Standards*, [Aldershot: Avebury, 1995], p. 80.)

[203] *BEM*, 3 and10 April 1919. There was some reluctance to abandon Hunter Street entirely and it was agreed that 'a meeting on Gospel lines be held [there] on Sunday and Wednesday nights for the present'. (*BEM*, 1 September 1919.) The work continued there in a restricted way. A photograph taken in 1932 shows both its spartan interior and dingy exterior. (Vivienne Pollock and Trevor Parkhill, *Britain in Old Photographs: Belfast*, [Stroud: Sutton Publishing, 1997], p .116.)

[204] On the 14 January 1919 as part of a national campaign to create more jobs for ex-servicemen, 20,000 workers from the heavy engineering shops in Belfast went on strike to obtain the reduction of the working week to forty-four hours. The strike led in turn to a further 20,000 being laid off. The situation further exacerbated the financial stringency suffered by working class families in the city. (Paddy Devlin, *Yes, We Have No Bananas*, [Belfast: Blackstaff Press, 1981], p. 45.)

[205] *EE*, March 1921, p. 23.

[206] *Tweed Memoir*, pp. 18-19

fifty-one in the two succeeding years.[207] They provided a foretaste of the mass baptismal services in London only a few years later. If the 1928 baptismal service at the Easter Convention in the Royal Albert Hall is anyway representative, such occasions had by then become something of a spectacular. One newspaper report described the scene in London when 1,000 converts were baptised: 'The specially constructed galvanised iron tank was covered in imitation grass and surrounded with growing roses, arum lilies, palms and other plants. It was filled with water and, by means of an inflow and an outflow represented the flowing of the river Jordan'.[208] Thus the convention season provided a consummate atmosphere of exaltation and expectation for those seeking Spirit-baptism at the 'tarrying' interludes that were usually called for that purpose during the convention, though this aspect was not given specific mention in the earliest reports in the *Evangel*.

The account of the 1922 Christmas Convention recorded pleasure at the number of baptismal candidates who, in giving their testimony before the act of water baptism, 'were able to declare that they had been baptised with the Holy Spirit'.[209] This remark might suggest that in the Pentecostal *ordo salutis* Spirit-baptism preceded water baptism. However, in a discussion of the distinctive roles of the evangelist and the pastor, Jeffreys gave a more considered résumé of soteriological sequencing:

> The evangelist is to go forging ahead, firing the dynamic of the gospel message in the quarries of sin in the quest of building material for the house. Then the material is to be cleansed of disobedience in the waters of baptism, and polished off by the baptism of the Holy Spirit. We are persuaded that the evangelist should endeavour to see all these stages follow in quick and immediate succession in true Early Church manner [Acts 2:38]. The pastor is...to handle the material carefully and wisely, so that it may be put into its proper place according to the pattern.[210]

The Convention showed there was a flexibility about the proper ordering of the two baptisms that probably reflected not so much sacramental indifference as the Pentecostal imperative to claim the promised 'fullness'. No better description of such briskness could be portrayed than that recounted in the first issue of *The Apostolic Faith*: 'In about an hour and a half, a young man was converted, sanctified, and baptised with the Holy Ghost, and spoke with tongues. He was also healed from consumption... He has received many tongues, also the gift of prophecy,

---

[207] *EE*, March 1920, p. 24; March 1921 p. 23; and February 1923, p. 20.

[208] *EE*, 1 May, 1928, p. 135. The report was taken from the *Belfast Telegraph*. James McWhirter was among the earliest of 'PR men' in British evangelicalism and stage managed occasions like this.

[209] *EE*, February, 1923, p. 20.

[210] Jeffreys, *Pentecostal Rays*, p. 140.

and writing in a number of foreign languages, and has a call to a foreign field'.[211] Even by Jeffreys' standard, this was abnormally 'quick and immediate' and as a concatenation of events threatened to devalue the realities it claimed.

It was the warmth of fellowship at the conventions that stayed in the memory of those who had to face difficult circumstances, especially womenfolk: 'Sisters who have had to stand the taunts of unsympathetic members of their family are now enjoying a peaceful meal, where they can talk freely about the Lord and His work'[212]—a comment that accents how the Jesucentric nature of worship extended into everyday discourse. Pentecostals carried a self-image of themselves as a people who 'talked about the Lord' in a more uninhibited way than fellow Christians, even in informal settings. And yet, when it came to the ministry of the Word, 'a profound silence settles down upon the congregation... These people are not wild enthusiasts, incapable of appreciating anything other than loudly-voiced choruses'.[213] The speakers included Pastor F.T. Ellis, DLitt, John Leech, KC, and Howard Carter—a formidable array of talent.

The convention periods presented the best opportunity for Band members to catch up with each other. They were apparently kept busy, being expected to attend all the conventions, though not necessarily all the meetings, in any one convention season. Hare wrote a breathless account of his attending the conventions over the 1921 Christmas-New Year season. Besides duties in his own assembly on Christmas day, he participated in the Belfast, Ballymena and Lurgan conventions, at each of which he met with other members of the EEB.[214] At the 1922 Christmas Convention at the Elim Tabernacle, team solidarity was impressed on the congregation when Jeffreys led in file the speakers 'and members of the Elim Band...out of the minor hall...[who then] took their seats on and around the pulpit'.[215] When refreshments were provided, it was Band members who did the serving. They were the hosts on such occasions, returning the hospitality they had received while in the field, a practical gesture of the bond between people and worker.

While there were sporadic evangelistic forays into other parts of the city, there appears to have been no other permanent assembly established in Belfast in the period under consideration. The March 1921 *Elim Evangel* disclosed that 'a mission is in full swing in the Balmoral district...and we look forward...to a time soon coming, when the full Gospel testimony may be sounded out regularly in several other districts

---

211 *The Apostolic Faith*, September 1906, p. 1 col. 3.
212 *EE*, February 1922, p. 19.
213 *EE*, February 1923, p. 19.
214 See *EE*, February 1922, pp. 17-26.
215 *EE*, February 1923, p. 18.

in this great city'.[216] Balmoral represented the first move into a suburban district. It is not until July 1923 that news of outreach to other areas was given. It was made possible by the acquisition of a new portable structure, with its canvas roof and wooden sides, that became known as the Revival Tabernacle. It was first erected on a picturesque site beside the River Lagan at the Ormeau Park gates.

The inaugural service was held on Sunday, 30 May 1923, 'when well nigh a thousand voices made the building ring with the praises of God'.[217] The evangelist was Stephen Jeffreys who, returning for the first time in four years to the city, conducted meetings until the middle of June. Divine healing services were held in the afternoons at which Mrs John Leech, 'at the sacrifice of all engagements', played an active part 'in assisting and instructing the sisters, or in giving a word of exhortation'.[218] Some remarkable healings were claimed, including 'two cases of restoration of sight, and one of hearing. One very striking case of spinal disease was healed... A young sister testified publicly to a remarkable healing. It had been decided by earthly physicians that, owing to the condition of her leg, it was to be amputated. '"Now", she declared, "Jesus has completely healed me and my leg is not to come off"'.[219] George Jeffreys, following his brother's departure, gave a week's special lectures on the Baptism in the Holy Spirit with his own brand of compelling persuasiveness in adding a twist that was likely to stir the religio-cultural sympathies of his Ulster audience: 'Pastor Jeffreys frequently made passionate appeals to Ulstermen to hold tenaciously to the whole word of God for which their forefathers died'.[220]

The next mention of the Revival Tabernacle is of its use in the West Midlands at Tamworth. The following year it was brought out of its store at the rear of the Melbourne Street church in March 1924. This time it was erected on a spot on the Ravenhill Road near the site of where the Ulster Temple was built two years later.[221]

Once the foundation planks were laid, the sides bolted together, the roof unrolled and the planks covered with clean sawdust, attention was given to the interior: 'the decorated platform, the seats, the bright shining

---

[216] *EE*, March 1921, p. 22.

[217] *EE*, July 1923, p. 142.

[218] *EE*, July 1923, p. 143.

[219] *EE*, July 1923, p. 143

[220] *EE*, August 1923, p. 166.

[221] Evangelists Darragh and Norah Adams first conducted a mission for a fortnight, followed by Jeffreys for another two weeks and the whole brought to a conclusion by meetings led by Farlow and Kingston. In early July, the structure was re-erected in spare ground at Roden Street, off the Grosvenor Road, for another mission conducted by Farlow and Kingston. Shortly after, at the end of July, it was set up at the Lilliput Street-North Queen Street intersection, off York Road.

petrol (sic) lamps, the beautiful scrolls, all make the place as attractive as ever'.[222] While new evangelistic efforts were started by Band members in Belfast, no additional assembly was opened until 1926 when the Ulster Temple became the central church, though the work of the Melbourne Street assembly was maintained.

The tardiness to establish permanent assemblies in the capital city at the same time as Band members in the province continued to concentrate their efforts on small market towns and unheard-of rural areas calls for some explanation. In a résumé of the activities of Band members working in Ireland in the April 1924 there is mention of Ballymoney, Cullybackey, of ventures at Markethill and Bangor, and information that Margaret Streight was conducting a mission at Killyless, County Antrim, and Kingston and Hobbs were holding another at Clonmain, County Armagh.[223] The last two places, in particular, were in rural settings that would hardly feature even in the most detailed gazetteer. The same effort expended in Belfast would in all probability have touched more people with less expenditure both of time and effort. In the same issue of the *Evangel*, the Melbourne Street assembly is the only place mentioned in the city. At its annual meeting, 'it was admitted that the Elim Tabernacle was now too small for the rapidly increasing membership...and it was agreed to erect a larger building'.[224]

In seeking to answer the question as to why a low priority apparently was given to Belfast, three will be considered: (1) the problems of finance and the deployment of manpower; (2) the impact of the 'Troubles'; (3) the repercussions of the Nicholson missions.

7.4.2.1 FINANCE AND MANPOWER DEPLOYMENT

The problems of finance and manpower, endemic to most new enterprises, were a major factor in the low priority given to Belfast. It has been shown that though the deposit was raised in full for the Melbourne Street church, there was an expectation that the Rees' legacy would help to clear the full debt. When this failed to materialise in time, it affected Jeffreys' decision to accept preaching engagements in England.[225] Evangelistic advance on any scale was likely to prove expensive and this was the rationale behind the desire to own a portable facility. Such a facility had 'been laid on the hearts of the overseers of the Elim

[222] *EE*, May 1924, p. 114.

[223] *EE*, April 1924, pp. 94-95.

[224] *EE*, April 1924, p. 95.

[225] The legacy was eventually paid over to Elim in September 1925, around eight years after death of Mrs Rees. It is thought the family disputed the will. The legacy realised £901 in cash and £150 in shares. Solicitor fees were £1,034.

Alliance...for a considerable time'.[226] The problem faced was clearly presented to *Elim Evangel* readers:

> This need can only be understood by those who, having commenced a mission in expensive halls, find that after every sacrifice is called forth, the meetings have to be discontinued owing to lack of funds or the halls being engaged on different nights. Again and again, just when in the midst of a great move, we find ourselves compelled to leave a place owing to the above reasons.[227]

Readers were informed that an order had been placed for a portable structure with a contractor and the hope was expressed that the debt incurred would be cleared before the opening of a mission starting in May 1923 when it would first come into use. With the expansion of Elim into England about this time, any increase in the number of Band members, then at twenty-seven, entailed a wider deployment of them outside Ireland, a move hardly consistent with expansion of the work in Belfast.

A consideration that needs to be emphasised is that the vision that captured the imagination of the young men in Monaghan in 1915 was to start a movement that would eventually permeate *the whole island.* A movement needs wide area coverage every bit as much as local entrenchment if it is to make its presence felt. Once assemblies were established in both the countryside and market towns they then had to be nurtured if they were to be sustained. Theirs was a distinctive spirituality that needed constant and sensitive fostering, one made more ticklish by the absence of well-established precedent. They had to face the risk on one hand of collapse from emotional abandon or relapse into a stolid formalism.[228] Both conditions, the movement's distinctive Scylla and Charybdis, haunted more reflective Pentecostals. An editorial in *Elim Evangel* of May 1924 lamented: 'Amongst our readers are those who are in genuine doubt as to the real character of this present Pentecostal outpouring; honest hearts which are eager for God's best and yet who

---

[226] *EE*, April 1924, pp. 94-95.

[227] *EE*, April 1924, pp. 93-4.

[228] To maintain the delicate balance between fanaticism and stolidity made, and still makes, great demands on Pentecostal pastors. Wilson in an article subtly uncovers some of the tensions faced by Elim pastors that are 'additional to those generally experienced in the ministerial profession'. (Bryan R. Wilson, 'The Pentecostalist Minister: Role Conflicts and Contradictions of Status', in Wilson: *Patterns of Sectarianism*, pp. 138, 150.) The stresses arise from 'severe' role conflicts and 'acute' contradictions of status. An illustrative comment is: 'The ministers role in his church is diffuse and all-embracing, but in relation to headquarters it is specific and calculated; he is called upon to operate with the freedom of Spirit direction in his own church and yet to appear meticulous to headquarters'. His conclusions are decidedly germane to the period following on from this study.

hesitate to enter into the blessing because of fear [of fanaticism] which has been sown in their minds through false reports'. For such 'honest hearts' to settle for something more safe and to opt for more conventional ways would have been a tempting response. Yet, that was never a serious option as a letter from J.J. Morgan to headquarters reveals. When he was installed as pastor of the Ulster Temple, Belfast, he found a state of disturbing factionalism splitting the congregation with the result that meetings were 'as hard as flint and as dead as a cemetery... This church is no better than a Presbyterian Church, and I fear I will never be a good Presbyterian minister'. In situations like this a feeling tended to pervade that a visit from Jeffreys would make things right. So, when Jeffreys could not attend the Christmas Convention, the reaction was predictable—'the people were very disappointed'. In a movement that was still some distance from maturity and limited in seasoned leadership, there was no easy or responsible way to withdraw members of the Band from established rural assemblies and redeploy them in a reformulated strategy that prioritised outreach to the capital where almost one-third of the total population lived.

7.4.2.2 THE 'TROUBLES'

The 'Troubles' were at their height in the period 1920-24 and this fact goes some way to explaining why any marked advance in Belfast was fraught with difficulties throughout those years. The city at times lived under military curfew which required all trams to stop and all places of entertainment to close at 9.30 pm.[229] Despite this measure, the troubles reached their peak in 1922 when the death toll reached 453 in Belfast. June 1921 was a particularly bad month in the city, especially in the York Street area with violence leading to families being driven from the mixed streets between the New Lodge Road and Tiger Bay, giving rise to the further ghettoising of this working-class area of the city into Catholic and Protestant enclaves. Melbourne Street stood close by and the deacons had to cope with the problems posed by the sectarian hostilities lapping their doorstep. They met at the end of May 1921 and decided that in 'the present unsettled conditions, [they] were to encourage members to come and allay their fears'.[230] Deacons resolved to visit members of the church in their district, especially the sick, and to report to the Pastor [Henderson] or Evangelist [when the latter was absent] 'any who are not attending or whom they have cause to suspect of backsliding'.[231] With

[229] Bardon, *A History of Ulster*, pp. 194, 196-7.
[230] *BEM*, 31 May 1921.
[231] *BEM*, 31 May 1921.

such mayhem around them, it was not the most opportune time for bold advances in church planting.[232]

As the violence continued, the deacons of the Elim Tabernacle became increasingly perturbed that 'owing to the disturbances in the city and round where the Elim Tabernacle was situated a great falling off in the attendances...was occasioned thereby'.[233] The congregation would have found it difficult to display the same *sang-froid* shown by Jeffreys on the occasion when Joseph Smith hastened to tell him of a reported arson attack on the Tabernacle: 'He said, "Mr. Smith, I have committed that building to God and I am not doing anything further about it". I said, "Are you not going down to see it?" "No", he said, "I am going to my house and to my bed". I came away mystified. Yet he was right. The fire amounted to nothing. Some people...put it out before it reached the building'.[234] In the month before the next meeting of the deacons on the 6 June 1922, sixty-six people met violent deaths in Belfast and the burning of homes and business-factory premises was intensified. Snipers posed a real danger as was evidenced in an incident in the life of R.J. Kerr, pastor of the Hopeton Street assembly.[235] One solution to falling attendances that the deacons considered was the erection of a temporary wooden hall on land that had been offered them in University Street, near the Elim headquarters. That area 'was a quiet section of the city, and if a suitable buyer could be found, [then] sell the Tabernacle'.[236] The suggestion was given short shrift as the Tabernacle was 'so central' and it would be better 'to wait a little as the awful conditions then prevailing might soon be improved'.[237]

When the deacons next met informally, two years later, in February 1924, more peaceful conditions prevailed. It was at this meeting that there was agreement to look for a new site that was the first step leading eventually to the opening of the Ulster Temple two years later. This time it was not violence that changed minds, but growing numbers: 'Owing to the Lord's blessing on the work in the city, the Tabernacle was at present quite too small... At convention time people...were turned away'.[238] The Elim Tabernacle was reaping something of a peace dividend occasioned by a period of relief and expectancy following civil disturbance. If the Elim work in Belfast during the 'Troubles' was unremarkable, other

---

[232] The security situation in the province became so severe that legislation was passed to allow powers of detention and the setting up of courts of summary jurisdiction.

[233] *BEM*, 31 May 1921.

[234] *EE*, 17 February 1962, p. 105.

[235] See p. 157-8.

[236] *BEM*, 31 May 1921.

[237] *BEM*, 31 May 1921.

[238] *BEM*, 18 February 1924.

places in the province witnessed stirring revival scenes under the ministry of W.P. Nicholson.

7.4.2.3 THE NICHOLSON MISSIONS

William P. Nicholson (1876-1959) is the name that comes most readily to mind to Ulster evangelicals when memories of 'revival' in twentieth-century Belfast are recalled.[239] When Nicholson returned to his native Ulster during the years 1921-23, he was at the centre of what has been called the 'three great years of revival',[240] making him what one friendly source called 'the most loved and most hated man in Ulster'.[241] Some measure of his impact is captured in accounts of his missions held in working-class areas of Belfast, such as 2,260 people passing through the enquiry rooms of the Shankill Road Mission despite the fact that many travelling by tram had to lie on the floorboards to avoid stray bullets. There were 1,500 enquirers at St Enoch's Presbyterian Church and 1,100 at Newington Presbyterian Church. In East Belfast men from the shipyard marched *en masse* to Newtownards Road Methodist Church. On the so-called 'night of the big push', so great was the pressure of the men to get through the gate that the top of one of the pillars was pushed off.[242] Around 400 parishioners in the nearby Church of Ireland professed conversion. The shipbuilders, Harland and Wolff, were obliged to open a large storage shed, known as the 'Nicholson shed', for the return of items stolen from the workplace.[243]

To what extent the advance of Elim was stayed by the huge support given to Nicholson is impossible to gauge. For many, his interpretation of Spirit-baptism might have dampened support for the Pentecostal cause but, at the same time, he aroused a passion for a Spirit-filled experience that was capable of by-passing theological rigour. Despite Nicholson's attacking style, the doctrinal gap between him and Jeffreys was slight. At the Faith Mission Convention held at Bangor in 1925, Nicholson posed

---

[239] Nicholson was born near Bangor, County Down, into a family of well-to-do Presbyterian stock. Converted at the age of twenty-three after a life of escapades as a youth at sea and as a member of a South African railway construction gang, he studied at the Bible Training Institute in Glasgow. He then served as an evangelist with the Lanarkshire Christian Union for five years (1903-08), before accepting the invitation to join the Chapman-Alexander team in their missions in Australia and North America. He was ordained in 1914 as an evangelist in the United Presbyterian Church in the USA. and soon afterwards joined the extension staff of BIOLA (the Bible Institute of Los Angeles).

[240] Stanley Barnes, *All For Jesus*, (Belfast: Ambassador, 1996), p. 60.

[241] J.D. Douglas (ed.), *Twentieth-Century Dictionary of Christian Biography*, (Grand Rapids, MI: Baker, 1995), p. 275.

[242] S.W. Murray, *W.P. Nicholson: Flame for God in Ulster*, (Belfast: Presbyterian Fellowship, 1973), p. 23.

[243] Barnes, *All For Jesus*, pp. 76, 78.

the question: 'Let me ask you... Have you received this baptism? Are you a Spirit-baptised and fire-swept believer?... So many converted people...know Christ as their personal Saviour, but not as the "Baptiser" with the Holy Ghost and fire... They have never gone to the Jerusalem for the Pentecost which would enable them to live lives of holiness, boldness and power'.[244] He went on to state the nature of Spirit-baptism in terms, insofar as they went, that would have satisfied the most fastidious Pentecostal advocate: 'Let us remember also that this blessing is a very definite and conscious experience. This is no hazy or ambiguous, indefinite, gradual experience. It is a sudden, conscious, blessed experience'.[245]

Nicholson did not confine this holiness emphasis to conventions, but brought it to mission settings as well. In Lisburn, the first ten days were devoted to addresses to Christians in which he pressed, in the words of the minister of the local Methodist Church, 'for the baptism of the Holy Ghost as a separable and separate blessing. With true Methodist emphasis, the doctrine was enforced, and many thousand claimed the promise of the life abundant'.[246] On the day in February 1922 when ten civilians were killed and twenty wounded in Belfast, he preached to a packed Albert Hall on the Shankill Road to a congregation of over 2,500 for three-quarters of an hour on the subject of 'the Baptism of the Holy Ghost'.[247] The meeting was attended by some fourteen or fifteen ministers of various denominations. He continued with the same subject on the two following evenings.

Nicholson was no systematiser and was happy to speak at both Keswick and Southport despite their divergent theological roots in the Reformed and Wesleyan traditions. By contrast, Samuel Chadwick, principal of Cliff College, refused to speak at Keswick because it never taught the kind of crisis that would satisfy him as a leading exponent of Holiness entire sanctification. By upbringing Nicholson was of the Reformed school ('a good, well behaved, blue-stockinged Presbyterian'); by theological conviction, an admixture of Wesleyan spirituality and Keswick holiness—the first, through his early brush with the Salvation Army—'[after full surrender], I began to weep and sing and rejoice like an old-fashioned Free Methodist'—and the second through the role played in his 'second blessing' experience by J. Stuart Holden who came to dominate the Keswick scene in the 1920s and who, for Nicholson, 'made the secret of the victorious life so clear and plain'.[248]

---

[244] W.P. Nicholson, *To Win The Prize: The Spirit-filled Life*, (Belfast: Ambassador, n.d.), pp. 69-70.

[245] Nicholson, *To Win The Prize,* p. 70.

[246] Murray, *W.P. Nicholson*, p. 14.

[247] *The Northern Whig,* 15 February 1922, pp. 5, 7.

[248] Nicholson, *To Win The Prize,* pp. 82, 84, 83.

Insofar as Spirit-baptism was separable and subsequent to conversion, the views of Nicholson and Jeffreys were in harmony. The difference lay in means and evidence. For Nicholson, Spirit-baptism came when 'you surrender fully and receive by faith' and, as for evidence, 'signs never satisfied any sincere soul. They can be simulated and they don't last. Better a million times one word from the Lord, than all the fanciest feelings and ecstatic experiences one could have'.[249] For Jeffreys, Spirit-baptism for believers was not so much a surrender, more a 'birthright [received] for the glory of the Lord'.[250] He had his own distinctive views as to the evidence of Spirit-baptism which rejected both the 'by-faith, no-outward-physical-sign' of the Holiness tradition as well as the standard Pentecostal tenet of *glossolalia* as *the* evidential sign. The second position was closer to his own than the first: 'Everyone who receives should have some definite supernatural manifestation of the Spirit in the mortal body, not necessarily the sign of speaking in tongues... This view safeguards against the possibility of the seeker of the gift of the Spirit missing the blessing, and also the extravagances that might be entailed by a mere reaching out for an initial sign of speaking in tongues'.[251] The final sentence is as much a reflection of his aversion to 'extravagance' as of his exegetical acuity.

There is one documented case of a Pentecostal assembly gaining members as an outcome of a Nicholson mission. Adam McKeown wrote that though his father had identified with the Pentecostal meetings in Tullynahinion, he still kept his ties with the 3rd Portglenone Presbyterian Church , County Antrim, congregation:

> Every Sunday morning he would gather us [six boys and three girls] together for family worship in the home. Then with the Bible in hand he would walk the 2 miles to the village to attend the church service. Our pew was right up front close to the choir. There was a door on the end of the pew, and once we were in and seated, we were in for the duration.[252]

In 1924, Nicholson conducted a mission in the church. McKeown described what happened once the mission ended: 'Because of some

[249] Nicholson, *To Win The Prize,* p. 81.

[250] Jeffreys, *Pentecostal Rays*, p. 155

[251] Jeffreys, *Pentecostal Rays*, p. 35. In a somewhat similar vein, Bowdle cautions fellow Pentecostals against 'a glossocentralism [that] has come to characterize the movement, and, to its detriment... It is urgent to note that while tongues were *evidence*, witness is *essence*... Really, the paramount criterion for Pentecostal activity is the presence of the Holy Spirit in renewing power in whatever circumstance require it'. (Donald N. Bowdle, 'Informed Pentecostalism: An Alternative Paradigm' in Terry L. Cross and Emerson B. Powery, *The Spirit and the Mind*, (Lanham, MD: University Press of America, 2000), p. 17.)

[252] McKeown, *A Man Called Adam*, p. 14.

friction or misunderstanding over Rev. Nicholson being rejected in the church which we attended, my father left the Presbyterian Church, and from that day onward gave himself wholeheartedly to the Pentecostal vision and cause'.[253] There was no shortage of choice in the Ulster countryside for the religious dissentient, a situation that helped to maintain both depth and width to evangelical commitment among all classes within the province.[254]

Like Jeffreys', Nicholson's early missions were held in the smaller towns before his sponsoring committee in 1922 decided to tackle Belfast, 'where the...hope to transform Ulster would be tested'.[255] This was not, therefore, a particularly auspicious time for Elim to make a similar move. With Nicholson's dim view of Pentecostalism allied to a combative disposition, there was all the potential for recalcitrant positions being adopted.[256] There is, however, no evidence to suggest that either man publicly acknowledged or overtly criticised the other's ministry. Jeffreys could not match Nicholson's robust pulpit style that went down well with Ulster audiences because it was neither part of Jeffreys' temperament nor could he easily blend with the religio-political tradition out of which it sprang.

It was a style that surprised Henry Mogridge who, when he visited the Southport Convention specifically to hear Nicholson, was bitterly disappointed. He had been impressed by reading a sermon delivered a year before by Nicholson at Keswick and printed in the *Christian Herald*. After visiting the convention he was moved to write a letter expressing his dismay at the tone of Nicholson's sermon on the text, 'He will baptise you with the Holy Ghost and Fire' (Mark 1:8): '[Nicholson] followed on with rude remarks and scathing language, ridiculing the present Pentecostal movement with their meaningless and ridiculous babble of tongues... He urged the people to receive the Holy Ghost without that nonsense, and not look for, nor expect any signs beyond a change of life,

---

[253] McKeown, *A Man Called Adam*, p. 15.

[254] What was lost in terms of Christian unity was gained in the variety of spiritualities that were tailored to reflect the diversities within Protestantism and widen its appeal—an upshot Ulster shares with America, as the work in historical sociology of Finke and Stark would suggest. (See Roger Finke and Rodney Stark (eds), *The Churching of America 1776-1990*, [New Brunswick: Rutgers University Press, 1997], especially Ch.3.)

[255] David N. Livingstone and Ronald A. Wells, *Ulster-American Religion: Episodes in the History of a Cultural Connection*, (Indiana: University of Notre Dame Press, 1999), p. 122.

[256] While Nicholson was no particular friend of the Pentecostal movement, it was by no means his only or even main target. When asked to avoid inflammatory language about the Catholic Church, he is reported to have assented to the request: 'He would lay off the "Papishes" and instead take it out on the "Plyms [Plymouth Brethren]"'. (A.A. Fulton, *J. Ernest Davey*, [Belfast: Presbyterian Church in Ireland, 1970], p. 32.)

and power, and boldness to testify and preach the Gospel in their own tongues'.[257]

Tom Paulin has drawn attention to the exclamatory and dramatic style of those Ulster orations over the centuries that he describes as 'characteristically Presbyterian'.[258] When Paulin, poet, literary critic and Oxford academic, sampled, *inter alia,* Ulster clerical rhetoric, he found the preachers pushing

> far beyond conventional and restraining notions of decorum, propriety and 'gentlemanly civility'. Such an ethic is hostile to hierarchical codes of manners and expresses itself in a free unpolished vernacular... The Protestant imagination...sees itself dramatically as pitched against certain powerful ideas that threaten its existence and values. Feisty, restless, argumentative, never quite at home in this world, that imagination has seldom shaped itself in traditionally aesthetic form in the North of Ireland. There, its characteristic forms of cultural production are the religious sermon, the pamphlet, the political speech.

Much of Nicholson (and Ian Paisley) is captured in Paulin's assessment and goes far to explain his extraordinary hold over his audiences, particularly the men who revelled in his debunking gibes when directed against the pretentious and polished. While the evangelism of both men prospered in Belfast around the same time, Nicholson had the drawing edge over Jeffreys and arguably the greater impact on the future of evangelical Protestantism in the province.[259] The whole platform persona of the two men could hardly have been more different. In his addresses, Nicholson adopted a style that earned the sobriquet, 'the rude evangelist', from his critics.[260] For Nicholson, 'the Christ of denunciation needs to be preached... We too seldom hear in the pulpit the burning indignation, the splendid scorn, and the fiery arraignment which distinguished the old

---

[257] *RT*, February 1930, p. 7.

[258] Tom Paulin, *Writing to the Moment,* (London: Faber, 1996), pp. 88-9, 93-4.

[259] To illustrate the point, three future moderators, at least, were converted through the Nicholson missions. Two of them, the Rev. Dr James Dunlop and the Rev. John T. Carson along with the Rev. James Wisheart, a President of the Methodist Conference, took part in the funeral service of Nicholson on 2 November 1959 at Bangor, County Down.

[260] In a way, Nicholson belied his comfortable upbringing and rigorous training at the Bible Training Institute in Glasgow where among the visiting lecturers were men of scholarly distinction, names such as James Denny (New Testament), James Orr (Apologetics) and Alexander Whyte (Homiletics). Of himself, Nicholson admitted: 'It would be terrible to have two fellows like me in Ulster' (Barnes, *All For Jesus*, p. 73.)—an aside that reveals a deliberately cultivated side to his persona.

prophets'—deficiencies of which he could never be accused.[261] Adopting an outspoken manner of delivery that was laced with racy humour, he aimed to jolt his audiences out of their complacency and rivet their attention, causing W.G. Scroggie to say of him that he was 'filled with vulgarity and the Holy Ghost'.[262] Descriptions of Nicholson's preaching allude to his capacity to offend those of fastidious taste by language that had 'more of the stokehold than the university'.[263] The minister of St Enoch's Presbyterian Church remarked of him: 'He was a great evangelist, but he was very hard on his mother [the church]'.[264]

Jeffreys' style, with its 'air of quiet authority' was never belligerent.[265] The *Armagh Guardian* noted his 'deep strong voice which has no harshness in it, the trace of the clipped Welsh accent lending music'.[266] In general, women probably formed the higher proportion of his listeners. Landau noted that at the first Royal Albert Hall meeting he attended 'middle-aged women predominated'.[267] The contrast between the two men is made all the sharper by the fact that Jeffreys was born into a coal mining family and had minimal theological training, and yet was commended for his composure. A *Belfast News-Letter* reporter wrote of him: 'He eschews everything in the nature of sensationalism and avoids theatricals and vulgarity in speech or actions; neither does he attack others engaged in the many spheres of Christian activity'.[268]

---

[261] W.P. Nicholson, *The Evangelist*, (London: Marshall, Morgan and Scott, n.d), p. 10.

[262] Barnes, *All For Jesus*, p. 129.

[263] *W.P. Nicholson: A Local Perspective*, [n.d.], p. 21. The pamphlet tells the story of the Nicholson missions in south-east Antrim. Michael Ramsey, who was later to become Archbishop of Canterbury, was at Cambridge in 1926 and while there attended a Nicholson meeting. Randall writes of the outcome: 'Ramsey's antipathy towards evangelicalism was a throwback to his formative student days when W.P. Nicholson...had been one of the speakers... According to Ramsey, vulgarity and dogmatism had marked an address delivered by Nicholson. Ramsey's comment was significant: "That one evening created in me a deep and lasting dislike of the extreme evangelical style of evangelism"'. (Ian Randall, *Educating Evangelicalism: The Origins, Development and Impact of London Bible College*, [Carlisle: Paternoster, 2000], p. 99.)

[264] Murray, *W.P. Nicholson,* p. 35.

[265] Gee, *Wind and Flame*, p. 141.

[266] *Armagh Guardian*, 3 February 1931, under heading 'Principal Jeffreys' Campaign'. It might be that James McWhirter provided the copy for this item. If so, it reflects the *desiderata* embraced by the Revival Party.

[267] Landau, *God Is My Adventure,* p. 121. A report in *Picture Post*, 11 May 1946, made the same point in the caption beneath a photograph of the congregation attending a Jeffreys' meeting—'middle-aged women predominated... They come to be healed and they come to see the Healings'.

[268] *Belfast News-Letter,* 30 December 1927.

While Nicholson was absent from the province for lengthy periods after 1926, Jeffreys, who continued to pay short but regular visits to the province, came more to public attention as his standing as a national figure increased. In April 1926, Aimee Semple McPherson and her daughter, Roberta, paid a hastily arranged two-day visit to Belfast at the invitation of Jeffreys. By now internationally renowned—her photograph in the *Northern Whig* was under the heading 'the World's Greatest Woman Preacher'—she, accompanied by Jeffreys, was received by the Lord Mayor and city councillors (Photograph F).[269] A number of the councillors, accompanied by their wives, attended some of the four services she addressed at the Olympic Hall, Carew Street, off the Lower Newtownards Road, Belfast.[270] Within the province Jeffreys, as the leader of a recognised denomination, was carving a niche for himself in the hearts of a loyal constituency. By contrast, Nicholson's missions in 1925 and 1926 received little press coverage. His denunciation of churches and his naming of clergy suspected of 'modernism' grew more shrill. He began to listen less readily to the well-intentioned advice of his largely Presbyterian lay sponsors. It is of some interest to note that in J. Edwin Orr's history of twentieth-century awakenings, it is Jeffreys' name that appears in the index, while that of Orr's fellow Ulsterman in absent.[271]

Jeffreys, unlike Nicholson, did not receive the recognition handed to him by Sir James Craig, the first Prime Minister of the newly established government of Northern Ireland. If it is true that Craig admitted that the

---

[269] *The Northern Whig*, 9 April 1926.

[270] *Belfast News-Letter*, 10 April 1926, p. 9. At one meeting she referred to her previous visit to Belfast in 1910 when she was nineteen years old and accompanied by her first husband, Robert Semple, of whom she said, 'he was a saintly man, but was too good for this world'.

A measure of Jeffreys' standing with the McPherson camp was revealed in the sequel to this visit. Within a month of her visit to Belfast, sixteen years after her first stay, McPherson hit the world's headlines when she suddenly disappeared, reportedly drowned while swimming. On the 20 May 1926, Jeffreys received a cablegram from Los Angeles sent by Minnie Kennedy, Aimee's mother, which ended with the plea, 'Imperative need you here immediately this crisis hour/Cable earliest possible date you can leave'. (*EE*, 1 June 1926, p. 122.) There can be little doubt that if McPherson had been drowned and had not reappeared a few weeks later in the most bizarre circumstances of having been released from an alleged kidnapping, Jeffreys would have been under considerable pressure to become her successor at the Angelus Temple where, during his visit to California in 1924, he 'had thrilled American audiences with his powerful oratory and prayers'. (Blumhofer, *Restoring the Faith*, p. 279.)

[271] J. Edwin Orr, *The Flaming Tongue: The Impact of Twentieth Century Revivals*, (Chicago, IL: Moody Press, 1973). As a young man, Orr came under the influence of Pentecostal teaching and possibly underwent a Pentecostal experience, a fact that may account for his generally objective and balanced assessment of Pentecostalism in his many studies of revival.

Nicholson missions proved an important factor in the restoration of peace in Ulster,[272] the Prime Minister was not against bringing pressure on him when he urged Nicholson, 'in the interests of community harmony, not to preach against Catholicism'.[273] It was a request he was careful to observe. Jeffreys would have needed no such request, a measure of his more limited impact in the prevailing tense political situation and his less denunciatory preaching. The young Tweed was conscious that with Jeffreys, 'there had been no denunciations or preaching against the established churches, Catholic or Protestant'.[274] To McWhirter, an attractive feature of Jeffreys' ministry lay in the fact that 'he did not appeal to the innate selfishness of human nature to be converted in order to get rewards in heaven, nor to the lowest motive, the fear of future punishment'.[275]

One major difference between the efforts of Jeffreys and Nicholson was that the latter worked at the request of and /or with the co-operation of many of the local churches. Premises were readily made available to him and follow-up was left to the local churches. Nicholson was not seeking to start a movement that would become a denomination, so the charge of 'sheep-stealing' could not be levelled against him. His message was one that resonated with the great majority of evangelicals. By contrast, the message of the Elim evangelists carried elements that were sharply rejected by fellow evangelicals. Their Pentecostal stance provoked the 'opposition, ostracism, criticism and ridicule' that Adelaide Henderson said confronted Jeffreys 'all the time'.[276] Both men drew some advantage from the troubled conditions that prevailed in the early 1920s, providing a measure of success that in the case of Nicholson was not to be repeated in his subsequent visits, though it is not too much to postulate that his influence has continued in much of 'Paisleyism'. Ian Paisley sees himself as in the spiritual lineage of Nicholson and could lay claim to his mantle.[277] Nicholson's impact was spirited, though short-term,

---

[272] Anon., *A Local Perspective: W.P. Nicholson,* [published privately, n.d.], p. 7.

[273] Moloney and Pollak, *Paisley*, p. 13.

[274] *Tweed Memoir*, p. 9.

[275] McWhirter, *Every Barrier*, pp. 84-5. McWhirter's statement is rather too sweeping. Hackett, commenting on Jeffreys' preaching on the listeners during the tent mission in Ormeau Park, Belfast, in July 1917, described that he 'presented calmly but with great power the fearful position some, possibly many of those present, might very shortly find themselves in, if by rejecting such messages they had to face the terrible great tribulation time under the coming Antichrist'. (*Confidence*, April-June, 1918, p. 20.)

[276] *EE*, 17 February 1962, p. 105.

[277] Paisley tells the story that, when he was aged twenty, Nicholson paid a visit to his church. At the end of the service, Nicholson approached him and said: 'I have one prayer I want to offer to this young man. I pray that God will give him a tongue like an old cow.

and buttressed the more fundamentalist wing of evangelicalism in the province. Jeffreys' influence was more long-term and diffusive in that he brought a newer, Pentecostal, spirituality to a wider audience than any other person or body had hitherto succeeded in doing and, to a measure, that has rarely been emulated since.

7.5 Conclusion: Vision and Achievement

The young men who met in Monaghan in January 1915 were fired by a vision that was backed by a rudimentary strategy. It was a vision for the whole island, a natural enough assumption in pre-partition times. The core thrust of the strategy was the establishment of *a centre* from which evangelists would reach out into the *country towns and villages.*[278] No intention to form a denomination was expressed, only *a permanent evangelistic work,* an objective that is suggestive more of a Pentecostal version of the Faith Mission or Reader Harris' Pentecostal League of Prayer. The strategy was advanced most clearly with the lease of the Hunter Street building and by the sharp increase in Band numbers in the period 1918-21. The need of a *tent* for summer missions was minuted at the Monaghan meeting and its purchase was soon justified in that the five-week tent mission conducted by Jeffreys in Ballymena in 1916 saw the first major expansion into a *country town.* In turn, Ballymena became the focus of the work in the Bann Corridor. Outreach into the surrounding countryside and *villages* either stemmed from Ballymena or looked to it for support, much of it placed on the shoulders of Robert Mercer. He was both pastor of the assembly there throughout the period of study and, in all but name, overseer of the work in the Bann Corridor.

On the face of it, then, the evidence suggests that the strategy envisioned at the first Monaghan meeting had come to effective realisation in that 'a centre', 'evangelists' working in 'country towns and villages' and a 'tent' ministry were all operative on the ground.[279] Well could an elder of the Melbourne Street assembly exclaim in 1921: 'When we view in retrospect the progress of the work in Ireland since its inception in 1915 we can only exclaim—"Wonderful"'.[280] In effect, the first steps in the formation of a movement were being taken.

Go in, young man, to a butcher's shop and ask to see a cow's tongue. You will find it sharper than a file. God give you such a tongue. Make this church a converting shop and make the preacher a disturber of Hell and the Devil!' (Clifford Smyth, *Ian Paisley: Voice of Protestant Ulster*, [Edinburgh: Scottish Academic Press, 1987], p. 3.)

[278] *EEBM*, 7 January 1915. All the words in italics in this paragraph appeared in the first minutes.

[279] *EEBM*, 7 January 1915.

[280] *EE*, March 1921, p. 23. Report by elder McCullough under the heading *Christmas at Belfast Tabernacle.*

In conclusion, it can be seen that the period 1918-23 was one of promise for the Elim movement. In December 1919, the EEB consisted of fifteen members; four years later, there were thirty-one members in the regular work of the ministry, two missionaries in the field, two probationers and three associate members. The percentage of the workers who had an Ulster background was 53% and 45% in 1919 and 1923 respectively, a marker of the shift of Elim from Ulster towards mainland Britain. In the April 1922 edition of the *Elim Evangel*, twenty-one centres of Elim work are listed centres in Ulster, five of which are identified as having a pastor with the rest either in the charge of members of the EEB or laymen where the local situation required it. At the very least, it could be said that a firm toehold had been established in the crowded market place of Ulster Protestantism and a tentative beginning made in the rest of the island.

The future of the Elim, up to 1920 the only organised Pentecostal body in the province, was one of modest anticipation, but the discerning observer would have spotted some darkening clouds on the horizon. Jeffreys was the human linchpin of Elim in the province and, with the headquarters moving to London, his involvement with the province declined, raising in some souls a fear of abandonment. Boulton found it hard to disguise the apprehension of the 'dear Irish saints [who] felt the priority of claim upon the founder'. However, realising it was part of the price of progress that they were called upon to pay, they gladly suffered the sacrifice, knowing full well their loss would mean gain to the Alliance work in general.[281] Other concerns intruded: dismay that the discrepancy between the large number who professed conversion at the campaigns and the number of permanent converts who became members of established assemblies; anxiety that assemblies were growing in number faster than they could be serviced by mature leadership; uneasiness over the quality of ministerial candidates; concern that too many fellowships might be left for lengthy periods in the hands of local untried and unlearned leadership; apprehension that some fellowships were too small making them vulnerable to internal division and external pressure.

Many of these concerns come across in an anonymous letter written by a member of the Lurgan Elim assembly to headquarters expressing concern over the state of the work in the town. It is recorded here verbatim, though spacing has been adjusted to assist readability, as a gauge of the standard of literacy that probably prevailed among the membership.

> We the old members of the Lurgan assembly beg to inform you about the assembly as we want to know what is going to be done as the old members are all leaving

[281] Boulton, *Ministry of the Miraculous*, p. 48.

> there is scarcely a member there that was there when the last workers was here and we think it would be better for the Pastor [Jeffreys?] to send another worker along for to build up the assembly (sic) as it is very sad to see the way things are going an their (sic) is nothing in the place now only trouble and disorder and the work is going down and the people of Lurgan are beginning to talk and the members will not come back till their (sic) is a change of workers and the sooner their (sic) is a change of workers the better please forward this letter to the Pastor.
>
> From a few of the old members Yours in the Lord.[282]

While internal division was one problem, no less problematic were the issues raised by the arrival of the Apostolic Church in the province, a topic to which attention will now be turned.

[282] Letter dated 9 May 1924 in *Mattersey Archives..*

CHAPTER 8

The Apostolic Church in Ireland

8.1 Apostolic Distinctives

A sharp rift between the Apostolic Church and much of the rest of the movement marked the early development of the Pentecostal movement in the British Isles. Andrew Walker goes as far as to say that 'the rest of the movement has never really accepted them [the Apostolics]'.[1] The flavour of the strained relationships at the time is revealed in the memoirs written by Robert Tweed and W. Robert Mercer. Tweed from his experience of pastoring the Elim assembly in Portglenone described the Apostolics as 'real sheep stealers' and added that their belief that '*the voice of the prophet is the voice of God* has led to marriages being made through prophecy'.[2] Mercer was aware of people who would not take personal or business decisions until they had received some direction from the local prophet. Writing at a time when relationships were not quite so strained, he was still aware of tensions: 'When conducting united Pentecostal conventions in which Apostolics were involved, we had some difficulty in restraining some of them from promoting their own point of view. When they insisted on absolute platform freedom some uncomfortable situations arose'.[3]

Donald Gee experienced considerable grief in his first pastorate at Leith in his tussles to counteract Apostolic advance in east-central Scotland. Massey saw Gee's fleeing to London in 1923 for a fortnight as the symptom of a personal crisis, verging on a nervous breakdown; Gee

---

[1] Walker, *Restoring the Kingdom,* p. 251. At the same time, he sees the Apostolic Church as scene setters for post-war British Restorationism (House Church movement) with a theological bond to the nineteenth-century Irvingite movement.

The period covered by this study is one when relationships between the Apostolic Church and the other bodies were at their most strained. To read present relationships in terms of the past would not reflect the degree of convergence, starting in the 1940s, that has taken place within classical Pentecostalism. What this study indicates is the strength of feeling raised by the contentious issues separating the parties in the 1920s and what the two sides took as at stake in the controversy that made it so embittered.

[2] *Tweed Memoir,* p. 29, original emphasis.

[3] Mercer, *Memoir,* p. 8.

said of himself, 'I felt my nerves could stand no more'.[4] He attributed his anxieties to an accumulation of factors, among them the 'ill-disciplined behaviour and aggressive proselytism from various Pentecostal factions in Scotland such as the Apostolic Churches'.[5] In a thinly veiled reference to the Apostolic Church, he wrote of this painful time: 'In one sad case practically all our members were personally canvassed in an attempt to undermine loyalty both to pastor and assembly. Following that I received nothing short of a downright ultimatum from an aggressive sect that if I did not bring the Assembly into their organisation, they would open up a work in direct opposition. Finally they did so'.[6]

Restored to mental equilibrium, Gee was strengthened in his resolve to become a Bible teacher, declaring, 'I found myself compelled as a shepherd to defend the flock by voice and pen'.[7] He was to remain a trenchant critic of outré teachings and superficial experience from whatever quarter in the Pentecostal movement, sensing the need to halt it from becoming its own worst enemy.[8]

The Pentecostal movement from its beginning was forced to wrestle with the issue of prophecy. The International Pentecostal Council, an informal gathering of European leaders that met only four times during the period of its short existence (1912-14), repeatedly discussed the dangers inherent in establishing a cultus of prophetic guidance, as much out of pastoral concern as doctrinal orthodoxy. Mrs Polman was of the opinion that 'if we had accepted every prophecy that had been sent to us, we should all have been dead, but such are all put in the waste-paper basket'.[9] British leaders, notably Jeffreys and Gee, drew lessons from Irvingism as to what can happen when the prophetic gift is misused. For Jeffreys the Irvingite concept of rule through 'set prophets' was 'a most pernicious system of church government'.[10] Jeffreys considered 'the absurdity of this title is very pronounced. If the liberty is given to convert verbs in the New Testament into adjectives for the purpose of providing handles to the nouns they govern then we shall be in a chaotic state indeed. We would have [following 1 Cor. 12:28] set apostles, set teachers, set miracles, set healings, set helps, set governments, set tongues. Yet this absurd proposition is put forth by men who claim to be leaders of the church'.[11] Gee, acknowledging the benefit of hindsight, recognised that

---

[4] D. Gee, *Bonnington Toll—And After*, (London: Victory Press, 1943), p. 22.

[5] Massey: *Another Springtime*, pp. 40-41.

[6] Gee, *Bonnington Toll*, pp. 22-23.

[7] Gee, *Bonnington Toll*, p. 23.

[8] His teaching prowess earned him the sobriquet 'Apostle of Balance'.

[9] C. van der Laan, 'Proceedings of the Leaders' Meetings (1908-1911) and of the International Pentecostal Council (1912-1914)', *JEPTA*, vol. VI, 1987, pp. 78-79.

[10] Jeffreys, *Pentecostal Rays*, p. 112.

[11] Jeffreys, *Pentecostal Rays*, p. 112.

'the so-called "Irvingite" Movement [had] missed the way... The prophesying was *the crux of the matter*'.[12] He was amazed that the Catholic Apostolic Church did not see 'how utterly false to the whole spirit of the New Testament was their slavish imitation of the titles given to the brethren in the early church, and then the clothing of that mimicry with pomp borrowed from the temple ritual of a former Dispensation. How desperately they needed sound teachers. But they surrendered themselves completely to their prophets'.[13] With such strong feelings, it was only to be expected that stout resistance would be put up against any advance of the Apostolic Church, both for its aggressive proselytising and the disturbing effects of directive prophecy on individuals and groups.[14]

The Apostolic Church, in emphasising the role of apostles and prophets, claimed a 'fuller/higher vision' of church order and government. It was an assertion guaranteed not to endear it to fellow Pentecostals who were 'determined to stake out ground which was [more] identifiably within central conservative evangelical spirituality'.[15] In essence, the Apostolic Church holds to a theocratic model of church government, designating the five offices mentioned in Ephesians 5:11—apostle, prophet, evangelist, pastor and teacher—'Gifts of Christ in the Ascension Ministries'.[16] These offices were understood as having been positioned both permanently and irrevocably in the church. It was the standing and function of apostle and prophet in Apostolic Church understanding that lay at the heart of the controversy; the character of the other three offices accorded broadly with those of the wider movement. The Apostolic Church considered the callings of apostle and prophet as governmental, and for that reason 'the ministry gifts were never withdrawn by the Lord [since] they are necessary functions for the entire Church Age'.[17] This was the gloss put on the word 'set' as translated in 1 Corinthains 12:28 (KJV), 'God has *set* some in the church, first apostles, second prophets, third teachers'.

---

[12] *RT*, 24 April 1942, pp. 4-5.

[13] *RT*, 24 April 1942, pp. 4-5.

[14] Apostolics similarly critiqued other forms of church government on a number of grounds: the *congregational*, because it produces 'no general unity of faith and activity'; the Presbyterian, because 'the Apostolic office...is divinely used to appoint and ordain elders or presbyters (Titus 1:5). No government could be complete without the higher office'; the Episcopal, because it 'would appear to magnify the office of eldership into the authority of that of the apostleship but in the name of a bishopric'. (W.A.C. Rowe: *One Faith, One Lord,* [Penygroes: Apostolic Publications, 1988], pp. 239-40.)

[15] Randall, *Evangelical Experiences*, p. 211.

[16] *Introducing The Apostolic Church: A Manual of Belief, Practice and History* (Penygroes: The Apostolic Church, 1988), p. 23, henceforth referred to as *The Manual.*

[17] *The Manual*, p. 11.

Pastor T. Evans, in 1921, in response to the question what is the difference between the Apostolic Church and other Pentecostal churches summarised the essential distinction thus:

> Pentecostals believe in the nine gifts mentioned in 1 Cor. 12:8-10 but the Word of the Lord, what we term 'the Spoken Word' is not allowed to lead and guide the members of the Pentecostal Church... Unfortunately, nothing more is heard of the Spoken Word in the majority of the Pentecostal Assemblies once the message is given, and it is treated as though God would not bring His Word again to remembrance.
>
> Again, when electing officers...in the Pentecostal body, they are put in office by a system common in the world, the 'vote by ballot'. [Our office-bearers] are elected by the Holy Ghost through the mouth of the Prophet called of God in the Body to acquaint His People of God's election and choice.[18]

Weeks is of the view that while other Pentecostals are vehement in their criticism of the Apostolics' understanding of the role of prophecy in the church, they are less than forthcoming in giving positive teaching on its function in matters of church government.[19]

Prophecy in Apostolic understanding can be exercised at two levels—first, by any member for edification, exhortation and comfort (1 Cor. 14:3) and then for the government and direction of the church. Prophetic utterances used for the latter are exclusively 'within...the sphere of the Office and function of the Prophet'[20]—in other words, the set prophet. Prophetic direction from the lips of such a person can be given on such matters as the appointment and stationing of pastors and the settling of doctrinal issues. Apostles in the earliest days of the denomination, almost without exception, were chosen by the word of prophecy and were ordained to the office for life.[21] The most contentious function of the set prophet was the giving of personal guidance on personal, social and business affairs. It was referred to as 'enquiring of the Lord through the prophet'.[22] Directive prophecy accordingly remains a distinctive practice in the life of the Apostolic Church though its application in the area of the private life of individuals has since become considerably constrained.

In the Apostolic Church the roles of the apostle and prophet are intertwined. For Rowe, when functioning properly they 'operate as a

---

[18] *Weeks MS*, II, pp.28-29, with some internal rearrangement.

[19] Personal communication.

[20] *The Manual*, pp. 157-8.

[21] 'Men cannot make apostles or any other ministry; they are gifts of Christ... A man cannot nominate himself an apostle, it is a ministry eternally predestined by God. The Church can only recognise apostleship as it is given by Christ'. (*The Manual*, p. 178.)

[22] The phrase is of Old Testament provenance as used, for example, in 1 Kgs 22:7.

single gift much in the same way as two are one in the ideal partnership of marriage'.[23] In current practice, an apostle comes to be recognised through a revelation disclosed by the Spirit to the 'set prophet' or by 'a direct revelation to the Apostleship at a General Council'.[24] A prophet is recognised as such by one of the following—the Council of Apostles, an individual apostle or a number of apostles serving in a region, area or district.[25] The prophet is considered to have 'a distinct gift for the purpose of bringing the Word of the Lord into the spiritual government of the church', but it is the apostles alone who are responsible for weighing and, if agreed, implementing any revelation given.[26] This covering by apostolic authority obviates the danger of giving the prophet unbounded authority. The process is illustrative of what Apostolics maintain is an 'active theocracy' in operation.[27]

The present Apostolic Church without claiming any direct historic link with the Catholic Apostolic Church, nevertheless, feels a special affinity with it as its most immediate precursor. Worsfold wrote that an upshot of the Welsh Revival was 'the scriptures which referred to the function of apostles and prophets were again carefully studied, the outcome being the establishment of the Apostolic Faith Church with its headquarters in Winton, Bournemouth... The inheritance from Catholic Apostolic theology enriched considerably the foundation teaching of the Apostolic Church in regard to its ecclesiastical polity'.[28] Worsfold recalled with some emotion visiting with three other Apostolic colleagues the Apostles' Chapel and Board Room at Albury in the former grounds of Henry Drummond's estate: 'During a time of prayer and praise around the altar,

---

[23] Rowe, *One Lord, One Faith*, p. 243

[24] Quoted by Williams, *Tongues of the Spirit*, p. 65. 'The General Council is composed of all the Apostles in the United Kingdom, together with representatives of the other Ascension Ministries as appointed by the General Executive... Up to eight prophets chosen...from among the prophets in the United Kingdom attend to bring revelation of the mind of the Lord'. (*The Manual*, p. 80.)

[25] The Apostleship exercises its powers in the following areas: 1. Clarification of doctrinal matters. 2. The sole power to call, ordain and locate ministers. 3. Control of the administrative affairs at General Council, Regional, Area, District and Local levels. 4. The right to apply discipline. 5. The right to chair any business meeting or church service within their sphere of jurisdiction.

[26] *The Manual*, p. 57.

[27] The terminology is that of Rowe: 'Apostolic Church Government is a sincere response to a desperate present-day need of fuller submission to divine headship in the corporate life of the church... We find *no* call or appointment in the New Testament except by Apostolic or Prophetic revelation or direction'. (Rowe, *One Lord, One Faith*, pp. 240-41, 246.)

[28] James E. Worsfold, *A History of the Charismatic Movements in New Zealand, with a Breviate of the Catholic Apostolic Church in Great Britain*, (Bradford: Julian Literature Trust, 1974), p. 63.

prophetic utterance was pronounced to the effect that Apostolic ministries 'would be accepted in a greater way throughout the Church of God in the United Kingdom'.[29]

The visit had something of the nature of a pilgrimage and it is difficult to conceive of other Pentecostal leaders making such a journey. Strachan takes a similar view of the link between the two churches: 'In the Apostolic Church the number of the apostles was not limited to twelve and the ritual and vestments were absent, but the office and function of the fourfold ministry [Eph. 4:11] was derived from the same Scripture passages and was the same in authority and rule as in the Catholic Apostolic Church'.[30] For Andrew Walker, the Williams brothers had no idea that the new Apostolic Church was interpreting Ephesians 4 on the same lines as the Irvingite movement: 'Their discovery of this fact increased their sense of awe and conviction that this time God would call out a New Testament church in all her glory'.[31] The founder of the Apostolic Church, Daniel Powell Williams (1882-1947), spoke of his debt to the early Irvingite movement in declaring that he had 'been confirmed by and had found lessons in the history of [Irving's] labour that are of great benefit'.[32]

The Apostolic Church saw a deficiency in the other branches of the Pentecostal movement in their failure to exercise scriptural control functions by not recognising the Apostolic ministries, which in their view were divinely decreed for this very purpose: 'Nothing proves the goodness of God more than the impartation of Divine wisdom through the Apostolic Order, as it brings out of all confusion, occasioned by ignorance and wilfulness, order and beauty in the House of God, which He seeks to establish among His baptised Holy Ghost people, lest the work remains on the lines that different movements have done in the past'.[33]

---

[29] Worsfold, *A History of the Charismatic Movements in New Zealand,* p. 58. It could be argued that to some extent the realisation of this prophecy was to found in the 'house church' phase of the post-war Charismatic Renewal Movement. (See David Matthews (ed.), *Apostles Today*, [Bradford: Harvestime, 1988], a compilation of articles from *Restoration* magazine.)

[30] Gordon Strachan, *The Pentecostal Theology of Edward Irving*, [Peabody, MA: Hendrickson, ed. 1988), p. 20. 'Fourfold' is obtained by combining the roles of pastor and teacher.

[31] Andrew Walker, *Restoring the Kingdom*, p. 251.

[32] The booklet referred to is *The Prophetical Ministry (or the Voice Gifts) in the Church*, (Penygroes: The Apostolic Church, ed.1931), p. 97. When the work was reprinted in 1956, the section on Irving and the Catholic Apostolic Church was omitted. The booklet was a reprint of editorials Williams wrote in 1930 for *Riches of Grace*.

[33] Williams, *The Prophetical Ministry*, p. 82.

Gee, for one, gave short shrift to such fine sentiments. For him, the New Testament never makes distinctions between prophets to the extent that some are endued with greater authority or lesser fallibility than others are. Prophecy has a role to play in the church:

> Yet there is absolutely no basis for making this into a *system* of church government and appointment to office... The practice of 'enquiring of the Lord' through prophets is out of accord with the New Testament, where such a practice is *not once mentioned.* This is a method of finding out the mind of the Lord strictly confined to the *Old* Testament, before the general outpouring of the Holy Spirit on the day of Pentecost.[34]

The Apostolic Church came in time to modify some of its practices but it has never given way on its core belief. Williams expressed it thus: 'If we are called as an Apostolic Church to witness for some thing above another, we witness to the unassailable truth that we are a standing Body that is an evidence of the existence and value of the prophetic ministry'.[35] The early history of the Apostolic Church and its beginnings in Ireland provide evidence of how the prophetic element operated within its church life as the movement spread from South Wales to other parts of the British Isles. This part of the story will now be considered.

8.2 The Origin of the Apostolic Church

The Apostolic Church was established in South Wales in 1916 with the brothers Daniel P. Williams and William Jones Williams (1891-1945) as its founder members. They were respectively the second and seventh siblings in a family of twelve children. Their father, William Williams, worked a smallholding about a mile to the south of Penygroes. When

---

[34] Gee, *The 'Apostolic Church' Error*, p. 7, original emphases. That directive prophecy can play a significant role in the church is suggested in the story of the Christian Renewal Centre at Rostrevor, County Down. In 1971, Cecil Kerr, the then Anglican chaplain at Queen's University, Belfast, met three Americans on the campus. Coming from the charismatic Anglican Church of the Redeemer in Houston, Texas, they told Kerr that they had been sent to Belfast by the Holy Spirit. They stated that they had no prior knowledge of the city other than that through 'a word of prophecy' which presented them with a directive to go there. Kerr subsequently paid a visit to Houston that left him open to a positive vision of what might happen in Ulster, then in the middle of experiencing its worst communal conflict, if the whole church were open to the Spirit. This led in 1974 to the opening of the Rostrevor Centre, distinguished by an ethos that is both charismatic and ecumenical. It is dedicated to the ministry of reconciliation within Ulster and, as such, it continues to play a modest part in the on-going peace process. (Ronald A. Wells, *People behind the Peace; Community and Reconciliation in Northern Ireland,* [Grand Rapids, MI: Eerdmans, 1999]: pp. 85-86.)

[35] Williams, *The Prophetical Ministry*, p. 100.

Daniel was aged ten his father became blind and to help support the family he was sent to work in the local colliery. Both parents were churchgoers and the children were reared in a religious atmosphere backed by the strict regime of chapel attendance. The young Daniel Williams had a wild, tempestuous streak in his nature that left him often unruly and intractable.[36] He worked out some of his frustrations through contesting in local Welsh cultural festivals. Home and chapel combined to give him a love of public speaking and he won many awards with his recitation of Welsh classical and modern poetry. His trained voice and platform skills proved their great value when he held large congregations in rapt attention. Such training helped to outweigh his lack of formal education.

Dan Williams dated his conversion to Christmas Day 1904 in response to an evangelistic sermon preached by Evan Roberts. Fired by the Revival, he became officially recognised by the Welsh Congregational Church as a lay preacher and for a period of six years, while still working in the mine, he had the opportunity to minister in eighty different chapels. He first encountered Pentecostalism in 1909 while on holiday at Aberaeron, Cardiganshire, where, in the company of a group of like-minded Christians, he received his Spirit-baptism. At the convocation of Apostles and Prophets held at Bradford in 1932, he related how he had 'holy laughter' before receiving the gift of tongues.[37] For a time he associated with Yr Eglwys Efengylaidd (the Evangelistic Church) in Penygroes which had been established in 1907 to meet the needs of the Children of the Revival who acted as the ginger-group who sought to perpetuate the passion of the 1904-05 Revival.

Early in 1910, Williams' determination to become an ordained minister in the Congregational Church was shattered by a prophetic message directed at him through a friend whom he held in high regard. It included such sentiments as, 'Chosen art thou by the Lord thy God to gather My sheep, for, verily, scattered they are on the mountains of Israel... But I will gather them, and thou shalt shepherd them'.[38] For

[36] In a sermon he preached in later life, he stated, 'No man could manage me as a boy. I was hysterical in fits of rage. Father and mother could not control me, and I could not control myself'. He rejoiced in another sermon that after his conversion 'by the grace of God, it is a long time since I lost my temper'. (Quoted in T.N. Turnbull, *Brothers in Arms* [Bradford: Puritan Press, 1963], pp.15-16.)

[37] Randall, *Evangelical Experiences*, p. 218.

[38] Quoted in Worsfold, *The Origins of the Apostolic Church,* p. 20. Most prophecies are invariably expressed in sentences redolent of Old Testament prophecy. To its hearers, such a speech form, heightened by an emotionally charged atmosphere, gave added import to the prophecy. Writing of Old Testament prophecy, John Barton suggests that the use of the messenger formula and the divine call motif may be no more than 'a ploy to

Williams, 'the overwhelming influence of this word was so drastic that all my future plans were broken, my prospects, seemingly, hampered'.[39] Later in the same year he made contact with the newly established Swansea Apostolic Faith Church, an outpost of the Bournemouth-based work founded by William Oliver Hutchinson.[40] This link led subsequently to a visit to Penygroes by Hutchinson and his pastoral assistant, James Dennis, in response to a prophetic word given through a recognised prophetess living in London.[41]

The prophecy directed them 'to go to Penygroes and to anoint His servant in a farm before a number of people'.[42] The ordination of Williams by Hutchinson followed at Tynewydd farm over the 1910 Christmas period in the presence of some of the leaders of the Evangelistic Church. Hutchinson envisaged Williams becoming established as leader of the Evangelistic Church, but not all members were happy either with the growing Pentecostal emphasis or with the thought of a pastor replacing the existing governance by elders. Tensions between the two factions in the Church came to a head in March 1913 when Williams and his supporters were locked out of the premises before morning service. The displaced group worshipped in a number of different venues in Penygroes before erecting a sectional building for its use known as the 'Babell' or 'Tabernacle'. The congregation continued to meet there until 1933, when the congregation moved to a nearby site where the new Apostolic Temple was erected. When it later came to be extended it was among the larger auditoriums in Wales with a seating capacity for 3,000 people.

By the middle of 1911 there were in South Wales fourteen Pentecostal assemblies associated with the Apostolic Faith Church. Williams soon came to be recognised as the overseer of the Welsh assemblies.[43] With the Welsh language as the dominant means of communication in many of the AFC assemblies, it was inevitable that a strong Welsh cultural identity was impressed on the denomination in Wales, making it all the more inevitable that a local person would be recognised leader of the work in the Principality.[44] Williams, after the split within the Evangelistic Mission,

---

command a hearing'. (W. Brueggemann, *Theology of the Old Testament*, [Minneapolis, MN: Fortress Press, 1997], p. 631.)

39 Worsfold, *The Origins of the Apostolic Church,* p. 20.

40 See p. 94.

41 James Dennis was Hutchinson's son-in law and later adopted the name Hutchinson-Dennis.

42 Turnbull, *What God hath Wrought,* p. 19.

43 The AFC at the time had six assemblies in Scotland and eleven in England, four of which were in London.

44 English readers of *Showers of Blessing* sometimes complained about the standard of the written English found in articles written by the Welsh pastors. Hutchinson reminded

became the pastor of the flock that met in the Tabernacle in Penygroes and, at the same time, played a major role in establishing the AFC in Wales.[45] It was while attending a convention held in Swansea in 1913 that Williams heard the directive prophecy calling him to the apostolate. When he attended a convention in London the following year, his call was formally recognised by his ordination to apostleship by Hutchinson.

Jones Williams, Dan's brother, emerged about the same time as a prophet. Jones had been converted during the Welsh Revival, then had backslidden but was restored through a word of prophecy. He was present at a convention in Swansea when it was prophesied that he too would be a prophet. He had gone straight to the convention from his shift in the pit at Penygroes in his miner's working clothes. In the course of the service, Hutchinson, acting with apostolic authority, extended formal recognition to Jones. As a set prophet, Jones Williams was to exercise the prophetic office for the remaining forty years of his life. It was he who gave the prophetic word that led to the choice and acquisition of the site for the Tabernacle in Penygroes. To Worsfold, 'he was a true church prophet in that, when prophesying, his personality appeared to recede entirely into the background and congregations and council alike felt that, in those moments, he was the mouthpiece of the Almighty'.[46] Not that the words of the prophets were always readily assimilable as Hutchinson, rather inelegantly, was the first to concede: 'These are sometimes so strange as to go very near pulling the life out of you in the filling them up, but nevertheless it has been the word of the Lord and we have waited for a little while and seen the whole thing filled up that God has spoken of'.[47]

The two brothers exercised their authority in the AFC in Wales until the 8 January 1916, when the Welsh assemblies in the AFC network severed their link with Hutchinson and the Bournemouth headquarters. The causal factors behind the secession has occasioned considerable debate, one that had to await the published work of Worsfold in which he identified three main elements, all of them having a bearing on each other.[48] Kent White summed up the pained feelings of Bournemouth on the secession when he wrote of the Welsh leaders:

---

them, 'Please remember our Welsh brethren are not speaking English every day'. (Worsfold, *The Origins of the Apostolic Church,* p. 63.)

[45] Speaking at a Convention held at Kilsyth in 1915, Williams stated of his call to be overseer of the Penygroes assembly that 'God pushed me into this' and, further, he was now overseer of twenty others that had been built upon his ministry. (Worsfold, *The Origins of the Apostolic Church,* pp. 116-7.)

[46] Worsfold, *The Origins of the Apostolic Church,* p. 314.

[47] Worsfold, *The Origins of the Apostolic Church,* p. 126.

[48] Worsfold, *The Origins of the Apostolic Church,* pp. 152-6. The *first* was disagreement over the direction and tenor of Hutchinson's authority, especially in regard to finance. The centralising of finance and property control in Bournemouth was perhaps

> [They] went out desiring to be independent; they did it in the face of strong words of exhortation, formerly spoken through the gifts in use among themselves, declaring that in no wise should they separate from the movement at Bournemouth: that it was in the plan and order of God for them... The prophecies on the apostleship and plan, given through those who have gone out, being the spoken word of God, will remain in the records of the Church—a memorial to God of the truth of His spoken word, and as a witness against those who departed.[49]

In this passage something of the 'sinister element' when prophecies are of the 'threatening nature'—something that Gee so reacted against in Apostolic circles—comes through. White also came perilously close to equating the 'spoken word' of prophecy with that of Scripture, a position the rest of the Pentecostal movement could only but decry.[50]

The break of the Welsh assemblies with the AFC was both 'calculated and decisive'.[51] The new group was composed of nineteen assemblies, all of which had been linked to the AFC. Any spiritual debt they owed to Hutchinson and the Bournemouth headquarters was rarely acknowledged and most accounts of the history of the Apostolic Church written before Worsfold's work largely played down this episode in the denomination's past. The fact that the apostles and prophets transferred across without reordination is a measure of the continuity of the secessionist body with the AFC.[52] The new body adopted as its title the Apostolic Church in Wales (ACW) for the first six years of its existence. The removal of the

---

the single most important factor. Weeks holds that the aspiration of Hutchinson to the 'unscriptural office of Chief Apostle' was a factor. (*Weeks MS,* p. 82.) *Second,* the strong sense of Welsh national identity tied to the Welsh language played a significant part. Williams went as far as to admit, 'I have had a temptation many a time, and the whispering of a demon, "What have I to do with English people?"' (Worsfold, *The Origins of the Apostolic Church,* p. 330.) *Third,* when the AFC published its first Constitution in 1916, it was known that the Welsh harboured a fear of the institutionalisation of their movement that could only end in its becoming yet another conventional denomination.

[49] Kent White, *The Word of God Coming Again*, (Winton: Apostolic Faith Mission, 1919), p. 70.

[50] Hutchinson-Dennis went as far as stating that 'the spoken word of God ...is infallible', in the same terms as the 'written Word of God'—a comment he acknowledged as being 'very strong meat and no doubt will be [too?] strong for some'. (Worsfold, *The Origins of the Apostolic Church,* p. 121.) Worsfold (p.183) was prepared to admit that 'the tendency did exist to elevate the prophetic word at times to the level of infallibility'.

[51] Worsfold, *The Origins of the Apostolic Church,* p. 164.

[52] Worsfold finds the turning of a blind eye by Apostolic Church commentators of their church's early links with the AFC 'quite remarkable' and could find no single reason for it. We have seen that George Jeffreys also was anxious to hide his early links with Hutchinson. It is likely that with increasing doctrinal aberration in Bournemouth, mention of previous links might well have proved a source of acute embarrassment in both cases.

'Wales' tag in the early 1920s was a recognition of the fact that assemblies in Scotland and the English districts around Hereford and Bradford had come into fellowship with the Welsh body. It was not until 1920 that the ACW made a positive move to expand beyond its core region of the Welsh mining valleys. That foray was to Ulster and was facilitated by the province's traditional links with Scotland.

In Worsfold's view, 'the addition "in Wales" provided all the evidence needed that the secessionists saw themselves and their movement identifying now even more fully with their beloved Welsh nation. Their vision was Wales and most of the leadership...was content not to think or look beyond Wales'.[53] Much of the content in the early editions of the magazine *Riches of Grace*, as well as other material emanating from Penygroes, was printed in Welsh.[54] While the Welsh ethos remained predominant in Apostolic circles for many years, on occasions it was reproved in prophetic utterance.[55] At one Penygroes International Convention, prophetic ministry through Omri Jones challenged 'the national spirit' among Welsh Apostolics.[56] This eased the way for the ACW to extend itself beyond the Principality, a step that was facilitated by some Pentecostal independent groups in other parts of Britain finding themselves sympathetic to its doctrinal stance on church government. Often this grew from earlier contact with the AFC. This was true for Scotland where, under the leadership of Andrew Turnbull, an autonomous branch of the Apostolic Church had been established. Scotland was to play a key role in forging closer links with Ulster.

The autonomy of the 'Scottish section' lasted in practice until 1933 when the seven sections that then constituted the Apostolic Church in the British Isles were united into a national centralised body, though its constitution was not agreed until 1937. Before reaching that stage, it was at a conference held over Easter 1922 at Bradford that the leadership of four regional centres agreed to affiliate and become the one Apostolic

---

53 Worsfold, *The Origins of the Apostolic Church,* p. 174.

54 The first issue of *Riches of Grace* was published in 1916 and included a prophetic word through Jones Williams in Welsh but with an English translation. D.P. Williams was its first editor and was to remain so for life.

55 Walker, *Restoring the Kingdom,* p. 253. Walker states it has not ceased: 'There is something essentially Welsh chapel about the Apostolic Church that you cannot find in Elim and the Assemblies of God'.

56 Worsfold, *The Origins of the Apostolic Church,* p. 324. Presumably this is a plea against an exclusivist narrow nationalism. Even so, national temperamental differences continued to intrude. At the Penygroes Convention in 1937, Cecil Cousen, who was later to play a key role in the Charismatic Renewal Movement in the 1960s, remarked, 'you Welsh friends chaff us from Yorkshire that we do not like the noise and the shout'. (Worsfold, *The Origins of the Apostolic Church*, p. 305.)

Church.[57] Unlike the 1933 settlement which was strongly centralist, the 1922 agreement constituted more of a federation, one in doctrine and ethos, but with each section responsible for its region and handling its own finances. Responsibility and authority were delegated. The General Headquarters was located at Penygroes while the Headquarters of what was to become the dynamic Apostolic Church Missionary Movement was sited at Bradford. A twenty-eight-man Missionary Council was called into being and began to take on some of the role of a General Council. Williams was President of the Council and each region was represented on it. There was no question of a 'Chief Apostle' being appointed *à la débâcle* of 1916.

8.3 Establishing the Apostolic Church in Ireland

It was suggested in an earlier chapter that a work associated with the Apostolic Faith Church might have been established in Belfast around 1914 under the leadership of Pastor Hardie.[58] That there might have been more than one assembly is hinted at by an unattributed reference in Worsfold's history of the Apostolic Church. He pointed out that 'the Welsh and Scottish presbyteries and, for that matter, the Irish presbytery, had full liberty to act without consulting Hutchinson in all spiritual matters'.[59] It would be stretching words to conceive of a presbytery of one but, with no statement to elucidate the 'Irish presbytery' reference, it is impossible to ascertain the situation. Hardie, as a Seaforth Highlander in the 1914-18 War, was in all likelihood a Scot and may have been influenced by the advance of the AFC in Scotland. Be that as it may, the first definite steps to establish an Apostolic work in Ireland began to take effect in the course of 1919. Andrew Turnbull had established by some unknown means contact with Benjamin Fisher (1863-1948) in Belfast. Fisher was a leader of a small group of Pentecostals who met in the Independent Orange Hall in Great Victoria Street near the heart of the city. As was suggested in a previous chapter, it is almost certain that he had been baptised by J.A. Dowie in 1905.[60] Fisher had played a part in organising meetings for Robert Semple and his new bride Aimee on her first visit to Ireland in 1910.[61] Probably as a result of his contact with

[57] The centres and leading figures were—Wales (D.P. Williams), Scotland (A. Turnbull), Bradford (H.V. Chanter) and Hereford (F. Hodges).

[58] See p. 97.

[59] Worsfold, *The Origins of the Apostolic Church,* p. 153.

[60] See p. 47.

[61] Information provided by Fisher's grandson, another Benjamin, in conversation, 7 October 2000. The venue is said to have taken place in the 'wee upper room' in/near Ravenscroft Avenue in East Belfast. Semple's wife was, of course, to become Aimee Semple McPherson.

Turnbull, Fisher had written to Dan Williams inviting him to minister in Ireland. It was agreed that a visit would be made in January 1920 and Fisher's brother, Elisha, travelled to the first New Year Convention of the Apostolic Church in Glasgow to bring a party back from there to Belfast.[62] Among them was Andrew Turnbull.

Whether or not Fisher had associated himself with the AFC in Ulster remains unknown. What is clear from a letter he wrote, published in *Riches of Grace* in 1920, is that he was the leader of a small Pentecostal group that met in the Independent Orange Hall in Great Victoria Street, not far from the recently vacated Hunter Street Elim assembly which had moved to Melbourne Street in 1919. The decision to write to Williams was a shared one: 'After prayerful consideration of the word of the Lord to us [presumably through prophecy], we decided, as a church, to write to pastor D.P. Williams to see if we could induce him to come across to Ireland at his earliest open date'.[63] The letter also referred to 'our dear friend, Pastor Turnbull, of Glasgow',[64] which confirms a close relationship with Turnbull and the work in Glasgow. In mother church terms, the Glasgow assembly stood in relation to Great Victoria Street assembly as the Kilsyth assembly stood to Hopeton Street.[65] Such bonds are illustrative of the close historical links between the two regions. In addition, George Jeffreys and the Williams' brothers provide a reminder of the Welsh contribution to the Pentecostal work in the province and with it the lingering influence of the Welsh Revival.

The party that accompanied Elisha Fisher from the New Year conference in Glasgow was made up of seven Welshmen and Andrew Turnbull. Besides the Williams brothers there was J. Omri Jones, Alfred Lewis, William James, Evan Jones and William Phillips.[66] The last two were soon to play a significant role in establishing the earliest Apostolic work in Ireland. The party arrived in Belfast early in the morning of Saturday, 10 January 1920. The same evening they were conducting an open-air meeting at Shaftesbury Square, pulling in 'a delighted and eager-

---

[62] *Weeks MS*, p. 1 (part II).

[63] *Riches of Grace*, April 1920, p. 24. The headline was 'A Letter from Pastor B. Fisher, of Belfast'.

[64] *Riches of Grace*, April 1920, p. 24.

[65] See pp. 68-70.

[66] Omri Jones' father, Thomas, had been an apostle in the AFC and he was a prophet in his own right. Jones never placed on record his past association with the AFC. Father and son retained their respective offices when they became part of the Apostolic Church in Wales. Alfred Lewis was overseer of the Apostolic Church at Skewen on the outskirts of Neath. William James was a long-standing friend of Dan Williams who became overseer of the Pontardawe assembly. Both he and Alfred Lewis were to become founder members in 1922 of the International Missionary Council of the church.

listening audience'[67] attracted by the Welsh singing. The party then conducted a mission in the Orange Hall for a fortnight. Fisher wrote that after a slow start, at the final meeting 'it stirred us to our innermost being to see thirty souls on their knees crying out to God, some in tears, others exulting in the joy of finding a Saviour, and others again glorifying God for the wider vision that had been given to them'.[68] At the end of the mission eighty-seven were received into membership of the assembly.

It was Fisher's opinion that if the visiting party had been able to extend its stay, then 'the Orange Halls would have been at their disposal everywhere to hold their meetings. I know personally that great blessing has followed the Apostle's addresses to the three large gatherings of Independent Orangemen'.[69] This comment would hint at some association of Fisher and/or his associates having some close ties with the Independent Orange Order.[70] Worsfold was sufficiently informed of the Ulster situation to note:

> It must be conceded that the foundation preaching in the Apostolic preaching in Belfast was strongly and rigidly Protestant as well as anti-Catholic. This continued to be typical of the movement and in 1927, at the Penygroes International Convention, the prophetic word through the prophet Omri Jones declared, 'Some of you are wearing the Cross on your garments. It is an abomination in My sight'.[71]

---

[67] *Riches of Grace*, April 1920, p. 24.

[68] *Riches of Grace*, April 1920, p. 24. The 'wider vision', in Apostolic parlance, generally means the vision for the church cast in terms of the fivefold Ascension ministries of Eph. 4:11. Atter opines that the growth of the Apostolic Church in Australia since 1927 was 'mainly because of their insistence on their form of government being a 'higher vision' which they stressed as the 'Apostolic vision'. (Gordon F. Atter, *The Third Force*, [Peterborough: College Press, 1962], p. 115.) It seems there was already a predilection in the Great Victoria Street assembly towards Apostolic ways of thinking, possibly picked up from Hardie's links with the AFC and reinforced through contact with Turnbull. Fisher rejoiced that his assembly 'is intent on going forward on the path and in the Order we have been shown'. (*Riches of Grace*, Vol. 1.9, p. 25.) In Elim circles, by contrast, 'vision' would have taken on a more in missionary/evangelistic connotation. Without driving the distinction too hard, some of the differences in ethos between the two denominations are summed up in this distinction.

[69] *Riches of Grace*, April 1920, pp. 24-5.

[70] The Independent Orange Order, founded in 1903, was a breakaway movement from the mainstream Orange Order. It represented a radical working-class revolt against the dominance of the monied classes within early Edwardian Unionism which it saw as in collusion with the 'Romanising' policies pursued by the then Conservative government.

[71] Worsfold, *The Origins of the Apostolic Church,* p. 204. Worsfold speaks here as one who belongs to the era of greater liberality in evangelical thinking about such an issue. He was one of the fifteen dialogue partners who came together at the very first meeting of the Roman Catholic-Pentecostal Dialogue held in Rome in October 1977. (See

D.P. Williams often expanded on words of prophecy, a practice accepted as an apostolic gifting for which he was acclaimed in Apostolic circles. In his gloss on this prophecy, he said of the wearing of the cross, 'That is a practice of Roman Catholicism—some of you are wearing the cross on your garments and are not willing for the Cross to cross things out in your affections and in the inner man. Let the outward abomination be abolished, especially if you are not prepared to be crucified with Him'.[72]

When the visiting delegation were about to leave Belfast in January 1920, Williams was pressed to leave at least one of the Welshmen behind 'to feed the flock',[73] but a prophetic message spoken in the course of a meeting indicated otherwise: 'Fear not, my servants, but trust in Me. Leave the building set now; let the weather beat on the walls, for a while. Be not fearful, trust my word! For I see another twelve on the water coming over to help you'.[74] Early in May, the leaders in Belfast appealed for a Conference to be convened in the city during the 'Twelfth Fortnight', the traditional holiday period in July, to which assemblies throughout Britain would be invited.[75] Subsequently, a prophetic word was given that the date of the Conference was to be in June and not July—a date at which the Ulster members voiced some displeasure. Williams replied by exhorting them to accept the situation, 'as the Lord had arranged the Conference and not man'.[76] A circular letter was sent to all assemblies in Britain inviting them to the Conference in Belfast during the second week in June. Fifty-two responded positively but with the news of 'the Troubles' besetting Belfast the numbers dropped to four. On the Thursday before the scheduled sailing, three others withdrew, leaving the organiser, William Phillips, as the only definite visitor. When he was on the steamer to Belfast, he found that there were eleven other Apostolics on board, travelling from at least three different centres in Britain, none of whom had made any prior arrangement. Taking this as confirmation of the 'twelve-on-the-water' prophecy, Phillips wrote:

> Beholding the reality of God's word, we were strengthened to land in Belfast, which was anything but pleasant. The first thing we had to do was to open our cases for

Jerry L. Sandige, *Roman Catholic/ Pentecostal Dialogue, 1977-1982: A Study in Developing Ecumenism, Vol. II*, [Frankfurt: Peter Lang, 1987], p. 1.)

72 Worsfold, *The Origins of the Apostolic Church*, p. 204.

73 *Souvenir Exhibiting the Movements of God in the Apostolic Church*, p. 40. This was a booklet issued to commemorate the opening of the Apostolic Temple, Penygroes, 6 August, 1933.

74 *Souvenir*, p. 40.

75 The date of 12 July is the main celebratory day of the Orange Order in which the defeat of Catholic James II by Protestant William of Orange in 1690 is commemorated by colourful parades throughout the historic nine counties of Ulster.

76 *Souvenir*, p. 40.

> examination. Had we any firearms or ammunition? Every eye was upon us as suspicious characters. So we held a week's Conference [whilst men were mowed down by guns...in the open streets.] The saints were glad to see us, and God gave us a great time... Here we would add, that if the Conference was held in July, maybe not one would dare to come near, for the fray grew worse instead of better.[77]

Such an incident, perceived as the fulfilment of prophecy, lent credence to the Apostolic enterprise and, when retailed in various settings, added to the sense of divine direction and was seized upon as an affirmation of the whole movement.

One query arises from Phillips' account. It is clear that the twelve all travelled on the one vessel from Liverpool. A separate account written by another of the Welsh visitors, David Jones, at the same Conference endorses this figure. He noted that 'we were twelve in number', but then added, 'many of the saints in Belfast gathered together to hear the good news from the lips of their Welsh and Scottish brethren'.[78] It is clear that the talk of 'twelve from over the water' did not apply, in a strict sense, to all of those who had travelled from Britain to support the new work in Belfast, but only to the Welsh party; the 'Scottish brethren' did not feature. William Phillips identified the party as follows: 'On arrival at the Liverpool Docks I saw two young men with a banner… At the boat I found W.T. Evans at the quay. On crossing the gangway there was pastor Congo Jones, his wife, and Miriam Jones, Pontypridd... As we sang in Welsh another three from Skewen [near Neath] joined us. Later another two came making our party twelve… God had said I see another twelve on the water coming over. I wept for joy'.[79] Pastor David Matthews, while in South Wales, heard accounts of the story that carried the understanding that it referred only to a contingent from Wales.[80] The story became imbued with deep symbolic meaning, providing providential legitimisation for the work in Ireland. Those involved at the time drew their own lessons from the episode. For David Jones, the number twelve spoke of 'the Apostles of old'.[81] For Phillips, it carried more of an experiential resonance: 'We knew nothing of each other, but when we counted the delegates, we found that 12 exactly were on board according to the Word of the Lord in January, at Belfast... We felt like Peter when he said "Depart from me; for I am a sinful man"'.[82]

David Jones, the pastor of the Apostolic Church in Pontypridd, was among the twelve who travelled to Belfast. He remarked that the party

---

[77] *Souvenir*, p. 41.
[78] *Riches of Grace*, July 1920, p. 10.
[79] *Apostolic Herald,* May 1970, p. 88.
[80] Personal interview, 6 November 2000.
[81] *Riches of Grace*, July 1920, p. 10.
[82] *Souvenir*, p. 41.

'found the people very congenial, kind-hearted, and very religious. Even the inebriates that gathered round the [open-air] ring were respectful... We found a great similarity between the Irish people and the Welsh people even by nature'.[83] Jones commented on the importance of 'cottage meetings' in the promotion of the Apostolic cause:

> Some of the saints in the different parts of the City throw open their door, for afternoon or evening meetings, when many of the next door neighbours would attend and hear the gospel story... They reminded us often of the disciples at the time of the Pentecost breaking of bread together in their own homes... The little church in Belfast is only just beginning to carry on their work on apostolic lines. Quite a few have been baptised with the Holy Ghost and speaking with tongues; others are anxious to obtain the blessing.[84]

The one piece of disturbing news he sent was the departure of Benjamin Fisher to Canada, for reasons that were not stated. Fisher's abrupt farewell led to a Macedonian 'cry across the waters, calling upon the Welsh brethren to come over and help them'.[85]

Wales responded to the call and sent two men to the province. The work in Ireland was treated at first as a missionary branch of the ACW and as such was the first 'overseas' outreach of the movement. With the establishment of the Missionary Council in 1922, Ireland then came under the jurisdiction of the Bradford office, though in 1924 the Irish work was accorded a measure of autonomy. The two newly designated leaders, Pastor William Phillips and Evangelist Evan Jones, arrived in Belfast in October 1920 shortly after a valedictory service was held for them on 16 October 1920 at the Congregational Church at Dafen, a northern suburb of Llanelli. A report of the meeting announced that the two 'were leaving a place of peace and contentment for an untried and turbulent country, so that those who were sitting in darkness might see a

---

83 *Riches of Grace*, July 1920, p. 11. Welsh sensitivity to the question of national identity is again suggested.

84 *Riches of Grace*, July 1920, p. 11.

85 *Riches of Grace*, July 1920, p. 11. A reference to 'Bro. Fisher' is made in a meeting of the elders four years later. It is not clear if it refers to Benjamin or his brother Elisha. In either case its suggests a cool relationship between him and the ruling body. The minute reads, 'Pastor Phillips stated it was the word of the Lord concerning Bro. Fisher that he take his place as a member until the apostles come and set things in order... Pray much that he may come My way'. (*Apostolic Church Minutes,* 1 February, 1924—henceforth referred to as *ACM.*) The most likely interpretation would seem to be that the reference is to Benjamin, who on returning from Canada, may have expected to take up again a leadership role in the church, but this did not prove acceptable to the new regime. His earlier departure may have left a residual resentment. The name 'Fisher' does not appear in subsequent minutes of the Apostolic Church for the period of this study.

great light'.[86] Both men had been in Belfast earlier in the year when they attended the 1920 January Conference and Phillips seems to have spent some time in the province over the summer months.[87] His responsibility as the superintendent of the Apostolic work in Ireland was to last in Ireland from 1920 till 1934.

William Phillips, who came from a family of twelve, was born near Swansea.[88] He started work in the mine but then migrated to America where he found work for the next five years in the steel works at Cleveland, Ohio. A tall, fair-haired athletic type, he was as hard a drinker as he was a worker. At the time of the Welsh Revival, one particular letter from his anxious mother made him take the earliest boat home. After his conversion, he opened a small mission hall in Aberaeron, working in a full-time capacity and living by faith. He came to accept water baptism and then Pentecostal Spirit-baptism. He attached himself to the AFC under the ministry of James Brooke in Swansea where Hutchinson ordained him to its apostolate. In 1916, he joined the newly constituted Apostolic Church and was ordained by Williams who, surprisingly, issued him an AFC ordination certificate though he was not ordained to the apostolate of the ACW until later.[89] It was during the 1920 Penygroes Conference in August that the prophetic word through Jones Williams revealed that Phillips was to be the leader and superintendent of the work in Ireland and Evan Jones was to assist him.[90]

Evan Jones (b.1888) was aged thirty-two when he arrived in the province. An imposing, handsome figure, he had a magnificent trained baritone voice that was used to great effect at open-air services, accompanying himself on his piano accordion. The Apostolics had a stand at the Customs House steps, Belfast's Hyde Park Corner, where thousands congregated on Sunday afternoons to hear and often bait the

---

[86] *Riches of Grace*, December 1920, p. 24.

[87] Phillips wrote of the time: 'In the month of August we recrossed the sea with the first fruits of Ireland. (*Apostolic Herald,* May 1970, p. 88.) Among the twenty-five 'first-fruits' travelling to the Penygroes Convention was the caretaker of the Great Victoria Street Church, Robert Matchett, who had been 'a big, ham-fisted Irishman, one time heavy whiskey drinker and a man to be reckoned with in a fight'. Converted under Phillips' ministry, 'he now radiated a Christian gentleness that is most attractive'. (Idris J. Vaughan, *Pilgrim with a Lamp: This is my Story*, [printed privately, c.1980], p. 31. Henceforth referred to as the *Vaughan Memoir*.

[88] More detail on Phillips is given in the *Vaughan Memoir*, pp. 27-29.

[89] Worsfold, *The Origins of the Apostolic Church,* p. 64. At the time of the split in 1916, Phillips had an article printed in the January-February issue of *Showers of Blessing* that was supportive of the AFC teaching on the Divine order in the church. There was no hint of his imminent secession. (Worsfold, *The Origins of the Apostolic Church,* p. 143.) In the first issue of *Riches of Grace,* in 1916, he was called 'Assistant Overseer' along with Jones Williams and E.C.W. Boulton.

[90] Worsfold, *The Origins of the Apostolic Church,* p. 203.

street orators. Idris Vaughan commented that 'it only needed Evan Jones to be at one of his solos for a meagre audience to be immediately augmented by many hundreds... The thing about my friend was that he sang with his whole personality and with the unction of the Holy Spirit; so much so that, on one occasion, a lady in the crowd remarked, "He has the face of an angel!"'[91]

Recalling their arrival in the city in October 1920, Jones mentioned that they were met by 'Brother Matchett who escorted us to his home above the Independent Orange Hall at the Blythe Street end of Sandy Row. Shots were being fired in the distance but we were listened to by a large crowd'.[92] They were soon engaged in vigorous outreach. Saturday evenings were devoted to open-air work in the area of Shaftesbury Square. They reported:

> We spend an hour with God on our knees before we go to the open-air meeting. We leave the Hall in time to meet them coming out of various houses of amusement, and they come thronging to listen to the singing. Brother Evan Jones draws the Irish hearts, they being so fond of music. They listen attentively and with respect in every meeting. We feel happy in giving our testimonies because the Irish have a receptive disposition.[93]

They had a particular memory of an open-air meeting held on 31 May 1921, when they went together as a church to a small village: 'The little organ was put down in the square, and Evan sang, "He [Christ] died of a broken heart"! No sooner did the words reach the ears of the listeners than all suspicion was washed away... Later on many came down to the water-side to witness the most glorious Baptism I was ever at... Twenty-eight were baptised in water'.[94] Other opportunities for ministry were made available to them. After a Baptist minister heard Evan Jones sing,

---

[91] *Vaughan Memoir,* p. 30. Vaughan came from Wales to Ireland in 1920 as prophet and evangelist. He then spent many years in Nigeria as an Apostolic missionary. He finished his active ministry in the Welsh Congregational Church

[92] *Apostolic Herald,* May 1970, p. 88. This was the recollection of an eighty-two-year old.

[93] *Riches of Grace*, December 1920, p. 25, with some reordering of sentences. The receptivity of the Belfast listeners impressed the Welshmen possibly because they were used to more robust treatment back home. Welsh evangelical fervour declined rapidly, especially after the Great War, and the 1905 Revival had become by the 1920s more a matter of lore than life. (See Brynmor P. Jones, *Voices from the Welsh Revival,* [Bridgend: Evangelical Press of Wales, 1995], especially Ch. 18, 'Quenching the Spirit'.)

[94] *Riches of Grace*, July 1921, p. 18. The name given in the account to the village was 'Conier'—a name not found in any accessible source of reference. It might be Comber which has a well-proportioned square and is not far from the shallow, though muddy, shores of Strangford Lough

they were asked to take part in a service in his church. They were also invited to speak at a number of Orange services. Speaking of the two cottage meetings they held each week they stated the 'that God hath chosen the poor to be rich in grace'—a remark that distinguishes the social class to which they appealed.[95]

On their arrival they found a membership in Great Victoria Street of between fifty and sixty, with numbers swelling for the Gospel meetings. Vaughan, who arrived a year later, spoke of his first impression of the church:

> Here, instead of meeting with miners, tinplate workers and farmers, the congregation consisted largely of factory workers, shipyard men, together with a sprinkling of businessmen. For the most part they came from the Sandy Row district and similar streets in that area. A hard-working, humble folk having a real sense of sweat for their meagre wage, these found wonderful relief and inspiration for their coming together to, what for them, was the Lord's House—a rented Orange hall at their disposal for Sundays and on Tuesday and Thursday nights until 1966 when the premises became theirs by purchase.[96]

By the middle of 1921 numbers had increased sufficiently for the assembly to move into a bigger hall inside the three-story building. Phillips added at the time that 'it means much more rent, but we firmly believe that the Lord will supply our need'.[97] The extra space was needed by the time of the 1921 July Convention at which Andrew Turnbull and one of his sons preached 'in the power of the Holy Ghost'.[98] The prophetic gift was by then well established in the assembly. Vaughan recalled that his first personal assay in prophetic ministry in Belfast was made easier by the presence of two women members who were noted for their exercise of spiritual gifts, 'with Mrs. Horner, as I recall, a gifted

---

[95] *A Letter from Ireland* in *Riches of Grace*, December 1920, p. 26.

[96] 113 Great Victoria Street has an interesting history. It was built in 1871 as the first Jewish synagogue in the province. The new Independent Orange Order then purchased it and rented parts of it to the independent Pentecostal group that joined itself to the Apostolic Church in 1920. The building was damaged by a nearby bomb in 1992 and had to be demolished in 1993. (See Marcus Patton, *Central Belfast*, [Belfast: Ulster Architectural Heritage Society, 1993], p. 168.) Few, if any, Apostolics would have been aware that the Orange Hall was only about 550 metres from the Catholic Apostolic Church in Cromwell Street, off Botanic Avenue—a denomination that in its early days was closer to them theologically, though not socially or culturally, than any other denomination.

[97] *Riches of Grace*, July 1921, p. 18.

[98] *Riches of Grace*, July 1921, p. 19.

prophetess and with Mrs. Bloomer having the gift of interpretation of tongues'.[99]

The Apostolic Church was more male-dominated in leadership than Elim at the time. No women held a recognised pastoral or teaching ministry in the Church. Mrs Horner may have had the gift of prophecy but was not a 'set prophet' in the assembly. Vaughan alone, as a man, could hold that particular Ascension Ministry. Nevertheless, women had a bigger role in the public worship of the Church in this the most male-hierarchical of the Pentecostal denominations than in the generality of Protestant churches. There was biblical warrant for women exercising the prophetic gift in public (cf. Acts 21:9). When the Missionary Council was initiated at Bradford in 1922, it was recorded that 'Mrs F. Bairstow and Mrs G. Perfect had given prophetic words of edification and comfort during the Easter public services of worship and preaching'.[100] Andrew Turnbull's work in Glasgow was served at one time by twelve 'bonneted deaconesses', some of whom had a preaching ministry. In Belfast, the role of the deaconess was outlined in a prophetic message: 'Well have ye spoken concerning my Handmaidens, not on the governmental side, but as messengers of mercy'.[101]

Mrs Bloomer was known for enacting a ritual act described as 'sprinkling the blood' whereby she moved up and down the aisles with arms outstretched and shaking her dangling fingers.[102] This practice can be considered as an to adaptation and legacy from the 'blood' emphasis that featured strongly in some early Pentecostal circles, notably the Kilsyth assembly and in the AFC network from where it passed into Apostolic assemblies. As exercised in Belfast, there was attached to it an element of 'charismatic improvisation'.[103] The act possibly symbolised

---

[99] *Vaughan Memoir*, p. 9. Mrs Horner's son, James, was to play a prominent part in the Pentecostal movement in the province, working largely as an independent evangelist, heading up a number of Pentecostal initiatives, notably in the field of radio evangelism.

[100] Worsfold, *The Origins of the Apostolic Church,* p. 216.

[101] *ACM,* 20 September 1924.

[102] David Matthews remembers this practice from his boyhood in the days about twenty years later than the period under discussion. Whether or not it had been practised throughout the intervening years is not known. Even so, it shows the persistence of a ritual act in this setting that in general was well past its continuance elsewhere.

[103] A term coined by Daniel E. Albrecht, *Rites in the Spirit: A Ritual Approach to Pentecostal/Charismatic Spirituality*, [Sheffield: Sheffield Academic Press, 1999], p. 173. Albrecht's title is a reminder that Pentecostals have meaningful and diverse liturgical practices: 'Pentecostals experience and enact their beliefs in the liturgy... [Indeed], the transmission of the tradition is more dependent on liturgical action than on an external structured verbal catechises'. (Albrecht, *Rites in the Spirit*, p. 205). In ritual studies' terms, Mrs Bloomer's action might be described as 'dramatic performance' and, as such, was akin in its formalisation to the ritual of the swinging of a censer during the

divine purifying and protection on lines cognate to an explication developed earlier by Hutchinson. In his exposition on 'the pleading of the Blood', Hutchinson pronounced that in contending 'with wicked spirits in heavenly places who hinder us receiving the fullness of blessing, if a person with a true heart pleads the blood against these unseen forces, victory would soon come. There are three that bear witness on earth—the Spirit, the Water and the Blood (1 John 5)'.[104]

With a steady, though unspectacular, growth in numbers and the need to maintain the momentum of outreach, a decision to send another full-time worker to Ireland was taken. Another factor in taking this step, one peculiar to the Apostolic Church, was the desirability of having a set prophet to complement the ministries of the superintendent (Phillips) and the evangelist (Jones) in what was regarded as a missionary situation. Vaughan said of his appointment that it was 'no arbitrary imposition as such, but one that coincided with the need there at the time for a worker able to provide the dual prophet/evangelist type of ministry I had been deemed capable of supplying'.[105] His call had come through a prophetic message delivered by Jones Williams at Penygroes: 'It was spoken in good, grammatical Welsh, parts of which I was not able to follow... It was a call that I prepare myself to leave secular work for the full-time ministry; this in the capacity of evangelist/prophet, and the location Northern Ireland'.[106] His prophetic ministry was, in Worsfold's evaluation, 'invaluable to the leadership as it gave overall guidance for the development of the congregations in their region'.[107]

Idris Vaughan (b.1900) was converted at the age of twelve under the ministry of Stephen Jeffreys, who became for him a powerful role model: 'As I saw it in those days, if I were to become a preacher it must be after the style and power of Stephen Jeffreys. It never quite worked out like that, of course; it never does!'[108] Three years later he received his Spirit-baptism after the laying-on of hands by Stephen Jeffreys and Mrs Crisp.[109] Between 1916 and 1919, he began to preach at mission halls and churches during the weekends when he was not required to work in the

---

incensation in Catholic and Orthodox worship. In one case the symbolism was of prayer-worship, in the other divine protection/redemptive deliverance.

[104] Worsfold, *The Origins of the Apostolic Church,* p. 47.

[105] *Vaughan Memoir*, p. 23.

[106] *Vaughan Memoir*, p. 22.

[107] Worsfold, *The Origins of the Apostolic Church,* p. 204.

[108] *Vaughan Memoir*, p. 35.

[109] Idris J. Vaughan, *Nigeria: The Origins of the Apostolic Church Pentecostalism, 1931-52*, (published privately, 1991). Mrs Crisp was the Principal of the Women's Training Home of the PMU in London. Gee said of her that 'She seemed to radiate competency... One felt there would be no nonsense if she could prevent it'. (Gee, *These Men I Knew,* p. 34.)

mine. He then enlisted in the Royal Navy at the age of eighteen as a stoker for a twelve-year period, but after a year he came to the realisation that his calling was to be an evangelist and not a mariner. On his discharge from the Navy, he promised God that he would return to West Africa to serve Him there, a pledge he was to fulfil for over thirty years mainly in the Calabar region of south-east Nigeria.

While he was serving his year in the navy, his home assembly joined the Apostolic Church. At the time of his prophetic call to work in Ireland, he was employed in his old job and earning the top wage rate at the colliery, a situation that presented him with the dilemma of staying put or engaging in Christian work with no guarantee of immediate financial support. He was released from working his notice by the mine manager, whose farewell words were, 'Off you go; they need your sort over there', a reference to the state of prevailing civil unrest in the province at the time.[110] Before departure, he was ordained to the full-time ministry on the 20 December 1921 in D.P. Williams' sitting room.

Jones Williams and T.V. Lewis, who was later to become President of the Apostolic Church, accompanied Vaughan to Ireland.[111] En route, they attended the Scottish Annual Convention over the New Year period and, with Joseph Larkins, Andrew and Tom Turnbull in tow, they finally reached Belfast to conduct a series of meetings.[112] At first, Vaughan had difficulty finding suitable accommodation. The Church was able to support financially only Phillips and Evan Jones, but one of the members of the Belfast assembly, Andrew Jackson, had previously offered free board and lodging to any volunteer willing to work in Ireland. Though Jackson, a railway signalman, was a genial host, his wife, a Christian Polish Jewess, was out of sympathy with her husband's Apostolic views and was not averse to dropping hints about the additional expense that Vaughan's stay involved. He found that it was her 'general attitude that was an embarrassment to one of my rather marked shyness'.[113] The Matchetts came to the rescue and before long he was placed on the salaried staff—£2 a week with just over half of it going on digs—and was able to join his other two Welsh colleagues as their third boarder.

Vaughan, along with his Apostolic colleagues, found himself on a steep learning curve when it came to engaging in prophetic ministry. He later said of that time, 'I was in *school* as were my fellow-workers in their

110 *Vaughan Memoir*, p. 23.

111 Lewis joined the Apostolic Church in Wales in 1920, having previously been connected with the Apostolic Church of God in Bradford.

112 T.N. Turnbull, son of Andrew, was ordained a prophet at the 1923 New Year Convention at Glasgow by the laying on of hands of the apostles. In the same year, Larkins was called to be an apostle at the Edinburgh Convention in October.

113 *Vaughan Memoir*, p. 36.

respective capacities'.[114] His own prophetic ministry for the five years he was in Ireland was, in his own words, 'in a minor capacity, limited in authority to the Irish work on certain levels only as, indeed, was the case with my superintendent who had at not at that time been elevated to the apostleship'.[115] It was a period when 'enlightenment [enquiring of the Lord through the prophet] was sought and given regarding personal matters to the servants of God'.[116] He confessed that on his arrival in Ireland, he felt a need for directive guidance for himself and 'had received a word implying that mine was a matter I would have to work out for myself'.[117] It was in this area of prophecy that the first signs of tension can be detected between Phillips and Vaughan which the latter put down to 'growing pains':

> There was much we had to learn and some things, from hard experience, that we had to unlearn. Many of my own problems arose out of the *personal inquiry* business in which a word of the Lord was sought for individuals, something my superintendent was pretty keen on, so unbounded was his enthusiasm for the 'spoken' word. There were times when my doubts about particular prophecies were only the more intensified by the way...in which my colleagues tried to explain them away.[118]

On another occasion when he was conducting a tent mission at Gilford, County Down, an area he described as 'strongly held Plymouth Brethren territory that had meant hard work for me by way of house-to-house visitation to create sufficient interest to fill the tent to capacity', he encountered another upset.[119] He conducted the meetings, 'preaching on sound Evangelical lines', with no marked Pentecostal emphasis. However, when Phillips, with a busload of supporters from Belfast, addressed a

---

[114] *Vaughan Memoir*, p. 36.

[115] *Vaughan Memoir*, p. 36. In the Apostolic Church there was a limitation placed on the range of a prophet's authority. It was to be expected of Vaughan at this stage that his prophecies would be confined to the local area. On the other hand, Jones Williams had the authority to make prophetic utterances that would have application to the wider Church.

[116] *Vaughan Memoir*, p. 36. The quotation is from Turnbull, *Brothers in Arms*, pp. 112-3. Vaughan dates this period to the years 1915-late 1920s.

[117] *Vaughan Memoir*, p. 36

[118] *Vaughan Memoir*, p. 44. See T.C. Darrand and A. Shupe, *Metaphors of Social Control in a Pentecostal Sect*, (New York: Edwin Mellen Press, 1983), p. 188. Darrand, in writing of his painful defection from a Latter Rain church in America, puts forward a taxonomy of the disaffiliation process. Of the six stages, the first is distinguished by 'a build-up of increasingly recognised anomalous events and the church authorities' subsequent attempts to dispel doubts and correct actions on an *ad hoc* basis'. In the case of Vaughan it was over four decades before the last stage [defection] was reached. One suspects that this and the Gilford incident are illustrative of the first stage in the process of disaffiliation.

[119] *Vaughan Memoir*, p. 44.

Sunday afternoon service, 'he spoke with some eloquence on the *Apostolic Vision*, after which he was moved to exercise a gift of the Spirit which in turn was interpreted by a Spirit-gifted sister Bloomer. Time was then taken by the Pastor [now in his element] to evaluate and/or explain to the mystified hearers the, to them, strange goings on'.[120] The numbers fell away rapidly in succeeding meetings, with Vaughan left ruefully to reflect on the appropriateness of 1 Cor. 14:19 where Paul indicated 'a time when five words spoken with understanding are to be preferred to ten thousand words in an "unknown tongue"'.[121]

For evangelists lacking the particular charisma of the Jeffreys brothers, there were to be no easy gains in the Irish countryside. In general, growth was slow, much of it coming through small-scale ventures—individual contact, cottage meetings, tent and open-air meetings—besides growth by the amalgamation of small independent fellowships coming under the umbrella of the Apostolic Church. It was a *modus operandi* that differed from that of the large rally that was the hallmark of the strategy adopted by George Jeffreys and one built round his own ministry. By the end of 1920 there were around eighty-five members in the Great Victoria Street assembly. After three years, four other assemblies had been added and by 1927 a further five were added, followed by three more by the end of 1929.

8.4 The Earliest Apostolic Assemblies

In terms of their origin, the assemblies can be divided into three groups: A. Those originating in cottage meetings—*Memel Street*, Henry Street, Ava Street. B. Those developing through informal personal contact—*Waringstown,* Drumbo and Larne, C. Independent groups that joined the Apostolic Church—*Battlehill,* Great Victoria Street and Portglenone. Those places named in italics in each group are treated more fully in succeeding paragraphs while the others named in Groups A and B are considered in the Appendix.

8.4.1 Assemblies Originating in Cottage Meetings

One of the earliest cottage meetings was held in the home of an elderly couple, Mr and Mrs James Henry Matthews in Memel Street in an east Belfast working-class district. Their son, James, was converted at the very first Apostolic meetings in Great Victoria Street in January 1920. A shipyard worker, he was to become an elder first in the Great Victoria Street and then in the Ava Street assemblies. He taught himself both

120 *Vaughan Memoir*, p. 36.

121 *Vaughan Memoir*, p. 36.

shorthand and bookkeeping. The first enabled him to record the prophetic word and the second equipped him for church administration His son, David, grandson of James Henry, was to become a minister in the Apostolic Church and in the period 1978-88 was superintendent of the Irish churches. Having ministered throughout Britain, he has been able to bring his wide experience as an apostle to the work of the denomination's highest court, the General Council.[122] Endogamous marriage, a feature of smaller and more exclusive groups, has promoted a strong family feeling and generational continuity within the Apostolic Church, probably more so than within the other Pentecostal bodies.

The Memel Street meeting had a short-lived existence and seems to have fulfilled its essential purpose within a few months. The possibility of renting a hall in the street was first discussed at a general Elders' Meeting in April when it was announced that 'Memel Street Mission Hall can be had at six shillings [30p] weekly'.[123] At the next Elders' Meeting, it was reported that there was 'a good attendance and Hall lovely... Decided that the rent be paid to the Dart Club for three months'.[124] A few weeks later, a prophecy elucidated the purpose of the meetings: 'The object of such gatherings as these to give interest in the Vision and they will find their way to come to the central places'.[125] With Memel Street within walking distance of Great Victoria Street it is more than likely that the meetings did not last even three months as no further minuted reference is made to them within the next year.

Memel Street lay within the parish of St Patrick's, Ballymacarrett, the Anglican Church that under its evangelical vicar, John Redmond, gained greatly from the Nicholson mission. On one occasion after the diocesan Bishop spoke to the converts of the mission, seventy-seven of them volunteered for Sunday school work, fifty-one for open-air work, twenty-two for running a cottage meeting, and 123 promised to attend the Bible Class. Another outcome was the opening of the New Day School and Mission Hall in Memel Street in 1923. It is uncertain as to whether or not the Apostolic group used a part of the building or even if the Dart Club had its own premises. The argument for the first is that the hall was described as 'lovely', as would be fitting for new premises, in which case some form of 'sub-letting' was a possibility. If so, it was open-handed of the Anglican Church to rent its premises to a 'suspect' religious group

---

[122] One son is at present the assistant pastor of the Great Victoria Street assembly and another, a schoolmaster, is a member of the same church.

[123] *ACM*, 2 April 1925.

[124] *ACM*, 9 May 1925.

[125] *ACM*, 30 May 1925.

and a 'worldly' Dart Club. It is likely that some of the Nicholson converts attended the Apostolic meetings.[126]

8.4.2 Assemblies Developing through Personal Contact

John Cardwell and his wife played a major part in establishing an Apostolic assembly in Ava Street, Belfast.[127] But, significantly for this section, they also set in train a series of events that led to the establishment of assemblies in the village of Waringstown and the neighbouring town of Lurgan. It is a story that again reveals the importance of personal and family links in the growth of the Apostolic Church and the weight given to prophetic guidance in Apostolic decision-making. John Cardwell's parents lived in Waringstown and while his mother was attending the Royal Infirmary in Belfast as an outpatient she was persuaded by her daughter-in-law to attend the meetings at Great Victoria Street. While attending the meetings there she was converted and received her healing. On her return home she found that, while her friends rejoiced in her healing, they had difficulty with her conversion.[128] She soon showed the sincerity of her convictions when she invited the Welsh leaders to visit the village to hold a mission.

In mid-1924, a decision was taken at the Elders' Meeting in Belfast to purchase a tent for evangelistic outreach.[129] Vaughan wrote that, having acquired the tent, 'we were on the move outwards from the city. Waringstown [was] indicated by prophecy through myself'.[130] The prophecy was more a confirmation of prior leadings rather than a *de nouveau* prophecy. Phillips and John Cardwell were delegated to reconnoitre for a suitable site in the Waringstown area. Because a curfew was then in operation, their taxi driver had to drop them about two miles from the village. The next morning they hit on what seemed an ideal site. However, when they returned to Belfast, a word of prophecy was given to the effect that 'this was not the chosen spot; the pastor [Phillips] must return again. This was something that delighted William Phillips so

---

[126] The Henry Street and Ava Street assemblies are also in this group. See Appendix for details.

[127] See Appendix for the Caldwells and the Ava Street church.

[128] It is not clear why her neighbours were so questioning of her conversion. Phillips stated it was 'because she did not get saved according to their order!' Vaughan's *Memoir* would lend credence to the idea that they might have been Brethren. He conducted meetings in the area for three months and described it as 'of strong Church of Ireland and Plymouth Brethren persuasion'. (*Vaughan Memoir*, p. 42.)

[129] Another similar tent was purchased for £20 and donated to the Church in Wales 'because of the Welsh saints kindness in the past. Money to be taken from the Church Building Fund'. (*ACM*, 13 July 1924.)

[130] *Vaughan Memoir*, p. 41.

implicit was his faith in the prophetic word; so off he went [accompanied by] Evan Jones. The result was that after much searching the only available land was in a field right at the point where the taxi driver had previously dropped the men'.[131] The tent mission attracted modest numbers but was well enough attended as to require the borrowing of more seats and hymnbooks. Sodden ground conditions proved a problem, the solution to which was the spread of sawdust.[132] At the August 1924 Elders' Meeting, Evan Jones reported that 'there was evidence of a warm feeling for the continuance of the meetings and for the establishment of a meeting place'.[133]

Among the converts at the twelve week long mission conducted by Vaughan were Mr and Mrs Samuel Cheyne, along with Harry Gregson and his mother, the son and wife of Thomas Gregson on whose land the tent was erected. Eighteen people in all were baptised by immersion in the nearby River Lagan in the course of two baptismal services, the first on Sunday, 5 October 1924 and the second a fortnight later. Thomas Gregson was later to give the plot of land on which the tent had stood as freehold gift to the church. The site was at Moore's Hill about a mile and a half to the north-east of Waringstown village. Until the church was completed in 1927, cottage meetings were held during the winter months in the large bedroom of Margaret and Samuel Cheyne's modest weaver's cottage adjacent to the site of the tent.[134] Through Margaret Cheyne's influence, her brother and sister-in-law, Joseph and Lily Patterson who ran a credit drapery business in nearby Lurgan, joined the fellowship at Moore's Hill. The Pattersons seem to have played no part in the establishing of the Apostolic assembly in Lurgan in 1928, though Vaughan states that it was a 'development from the Moore's Hill work'.[135]

To help with the building of the Moore's Hill assembly, Phillips made the suggestion at an Elders' Meeting 'of risking £80 out of the Building Fund...and exhorted the elders to be open-hearted on the matter and allow the saints at Waringstown to repay the money out of offerings. At

---

[131] *Vaughan Memoir*, pp. 41-2.

[132] About this time the expression 'hitting the sawdust trail' was becoming familiar from the Billy Sunday tent missions in America. The expression referred to those who responded to the gospel appeal by moving to the front of the tent along the sawdust aisles.

[133] *ACM*, 22 August 1924.

[134] Samuel Cheyne was converted during the mission. It is quite possible that he was a domestic handloom weaver, though factory production was overtaking the domestic industry. A bleach works and a linen mill were in operation at Milltown about a mile along the road leading south from his cottage.

[135] *Vaughan Memoir*, p. 44.

present they were able to pay 15 shillings [75p] a week'.[136] The prophetic word that bore on this suggestion was that they 'present the matter in unity before the four members of the Missionary Council that are coming over to our Convention'.[137] Minutes are not available to show how the matter proceeded but the fact that the church was built would indicate that an arrangement on these lines was forthcoming.

The arrival of Pentecostal preachers in the district and the establishment of the assembly unleashed some youthful devilment and calculated adult opposition.[138] The tent was liable to vandalism and youths subjected the Cheyne house to a highly dangerous 'sport' in which they tied together the front and back doors and blocked the chimney with sods, exposing the inhabitants to the threat of asphyxiation. Two of the local shops refused to serve the members with the result that shoppers had to walk to Waringstown. Nothing daunted, the young converts who sought water baptism faced the rigours of an outdoor October ceremony in the nearby River Lagan before a large number of gawking bystanders. The regular versifier of the *Lurgan Mail* was there and captured some of the buzz surrounding the occasion:

> It was no doubt a solemn time, but there
> were urchins there
> Who for the solemn side of things had
> not a thought to spare,
> And sods and twigs across the stream in
> mimic strife were thrown,
> Which made the day seem one of sport
> and not the Lord's alone.[139]

Not only were the seasonal temperatures low but the Lagan was in full spate from the autumnal rains. Evan Jones who officiated had a rope around his waist that was held by William Phillips. The rope not only held Jones securely but also acted as a handrail for the converts entering and leaving the cold swirling waters.

> The Lagan in October is a colder stream

---

[136] *ACM*, 31 October 1925.

[137] *ACM*, 31 October 1925.

[138] Mr Joseph Cheyne, son of Samuel and Margaret Cheyne, provided some of the information in this paragraph in manuscript form. He also provided the newspaper cutting referred to in the next note.

[139] *The Lurgan Mail*, 15 January 1987, p. 22. This page was given over to the celebration of the diamond anniversary of the Moore's Hill Church. The poem was written by John Malcomson and entitled *Geighon's Bridge*, the bridge across the Lagan near the baptismal site.

by far
Than that beside which long ago the
eunuch stopped his car;
But when the heart is 'strangely warmed'
—as Wesley's was of old—
Who cares for mud, or cloudy skies, or
waters dark and cold? [140]

The Moore's Hill assembly is one of the few assemblies built in a completely rural setting that has continued to survive unmodified and in its original location.[141]

8.4.3 Independent Groups that Joined the Apostolic Church

It was shown in the previous chapter that the Portglenone Apostolic Church developed from a split in the Elim work at Tullynahinion and will not be discussed further here.[142] About the same time as Tullynahinion was applying to come under the Apostolic umbrella, an independent group of Pentecostal believers at Battlehill, about four miles to the west of Portadown, was doing likewise. It began with a visit of an American deputation from Pennsylvania led by Dobson Hunniford who was accompanied by two others. Hunniford, visiting his birthplace at Battlehill after an absence of thirty-six years, brought with him the Pentecostal message in its Apostolic version.[143] He was part of a delegation from the Ferndale assembly, near Williamsport, Pennsylvania. This assembly developed a link with the Apostolic Church through a visit of Anna Doak to the Apostolic Convention at Glasgow over the New Year period in 1922. At the time she was a member of what was then an independent Pentecostal assembly at Ferndale. Impressed by what she observed at the Conference, she invited the Apostolic Church to send a leader to the United States. It was to prove another year before the Williams brothers, Andrew Turnbull and Frank Hodges travelled together to America during

[140] *The Lurgan Mail*, 15 January 1987, p. 22. A photograph of one of the two baptismal services shows two officiating in the river—possibly Phillips or Jones and the smaller Vaughan—and without a sign of a rope even though the two ministers and the convert are standing up to their knees in the centre of the river. The 'eunuch...car' [chariot] reference is to the incident recorded in Acts 8:26-40.

[141] The other two assemblies in this group were at Drumbo and Larne. See Appendix for details.

[142] See p. 208.

[143] The visitors came to Ireland after visiting all the other Apostolic churches in Britain.

August 1923 and it was through this contact that the Ferndale assembly became the first Apostolic Church to be established in North America.[144]

The three American visitors arrived in Ireland in the autumn of 1923.[145] When Hunniford arrived at the family home, an Irish evangelist, George Gibson, was holding a mission in the small Methodist Church at Battlehill.[146] Gibson, hearing that Hunniford was at home, invited him 'to say a word'.[147] Hunniford took the opportunity to speak not only of his conversion in America but also of his Pentecostal Spirit-baptism. While this caused a certain unease, some were interested enough to cluster round Hunniford at the end and ask him to show them from the Bible the evidence that tongues were a sign of Spirit-baptism. About sixteen proceeded to the home of Joshua Johnson and tarried all night, in the course of which twelve claimed their Spirit-baptism.

The breakaway group decided to build a fine sectional hall, but soon disagreement arose over the *charismata*, causing a further split. Some separated to a farmhouse at Clonroot while the others who remained in the hall at Battlehill refrained from exercising the gifts. It was at this point that the two groups invited the Apostolic leadership in Belfast to help heal the rift and restore unity. Their visit proved successful enough for Johnston Kane, one of the leaders at Battlehill, to state at an Elders' Meeting that 'he was willing for the vision to be preached in the Hall' and 'Brother Hunniford said he was willing to follow the Lord and go by His guidance'.[148] It is not stated which Hunniford this was as there were a number of brothers in the family but it was almost certainly Joseph E. Hunniford who was to become prominent in Apostolic circles. It was he who wrote the letter in the middle of 1925 to Phillips 'asking that their little church be set in order and recognised as part of the Apostolic Church'.[149] It is fairly certain that Dobson Hunniford returned with the 'American Delegation' to America but during his visit two years earlier he would, doubtless, have pressed his Apostolic views on his brother. The next mention of the Battlehill assembly in the minutes indicated that Evan

---

[144] Worsfold, *The Origins of the Apostolic Church,* pp. 221-2.

[145] *ACM*, 3 November 1923.

[146] Battlehill lies in the heart of mid-Ulster Methodism, inside the Linen Triangle (Maps B and C). Mid-Ulster Methodism had 20% of all Methodists in the province in the 1970 census. (Paul A. Compton: *Northern Ireland: A Census Atlas*, [Dublin: Gill and Macmillan,1978] p. 86-7.) Writing of the area in the 1840s, Crookshank, the nineteenth-century historian of Irish Methodism, wrote of Robert Croan's household that they 'were "head-and-hand" Methodists in whose granary quarterly love-feasts were held'—a reminder of a long tradition of informal meeting places where fervent religious expression was commonplace. (Crookshank, *History of Methodism,* p. 218.)

[147] *Souvenir*, p. 41.

[148] *ACM*, 26 December 1925.

[149] *ACM*, 19 July 1925.

Jones was deputed to conduct a baptismal service on Sunday, 23 May 1926.[150] The Apostolic Church in Portadown was a spin-off from the Battlehill work, opening the same year as the Lurgan assembly in 1928.[151]

Vaughan recalled hearing Dobson Hunniford preach and wrote also of his own visits to the Battlefield assembly. He remembered Hunniford as a fiery and fast talker, much of whose Ulster mindset, despite his Americanised ways, had proved resistant to the subtle processes of transatlantic acculturation: '[Hunniford] preached in our central hall in Belfast, but all I can remember of his addresses was...that he thought of Britain as being one of the lost ten tribes of Israel and that he made reference to the British *Union Jack* as the "Union Jacob"'.[152] When Vaughan came to visit the Battlehill assembly, he found 'a fine body of men and women worshipping in their own fine building and knowing the liberty of the Spirit. The men I found to be hard-working tough types, physically speaking: keen Bible students, eager for new truth. This I must say though: *They were the worst singers in the world!*'[153] He enjoyed the hospitality of Johnston Kane and his young wife at their farm at Tullamore and remembered the former for his 'sturdy godliness' and his wife for 'her kind, gentle hospitality'.[154] Their eldest son, James Kane, was to become an Apostolic minister and vice-president of the General Council of the denomination.

8.5 Factors Influencing the Development of the Apostolic Church

Worsfold admitted that the Apostolic work in Ireland 'despite the enthusiastic beginnings and the faithful ministry of the Welsh ministers (and later some very gifted Irish ministers and elders) progress in Ireland has been slow and difficult'.[155] The reasons for the more limited

---

[150] *ACM*, 15 May 1926. The Hunniford name appeared for the first time in the list of Elders who attended this meeting.

[151] *Vaughan Memoir*, p. 43.

[152] *Vaughan Memoir*, p. 43. The Battlehill area is only a few miles south of the Diamond, considered as the birthplace of the Orange Order in 1795. Mid-Ulster has traditionally been a stronghold of British-Israel belief, commonly associated with some of the more religious elements within Orangeism.

[153] *Vaughan Memoir*, p. 43.

[154] *Vaughan Memoir*, p. 44. Mrs Kane was a former member of the Church of Ireland at Kilmore. The Battlehill assembly was closed in the 1980s and the members transferred to the Portadown assembly—a common pattern of change for the more rurally located assemblies. The Elim Annaghanoon assembly, similarly, was replaced by the church in the sizeable village of Donaghcloney, County Down, three miles away. Declining and ageing membership as well as greater transport mobility account for much of this downsizing.

[155] Worsfold, *The Origins of the Apostolic Church,* p. 204. A prophecy given at an Elders' Meeting upbraided the hearers, 'There is a tendency in your hearts when ye see the

influence of the Apostolic Church as compared to that of Elim in the province will be examined under four headings.

8.5.1 The Separatist Nature of the Apostolic Church

A pattern of enthusiastic beginnings and slow consolidation is a not unfamiliar one in the dynamics of movements. It is as if for every new movement there lies a pool of people of an expectant disposition who find an almost immediate affinity with it and become readily absorbed—hence the early spurt—but once mopped up further advance is more painstaking. The arrival of Elim some five years earlier gave it a head start in attracting those finding spiritual fulfilment in the Pentecostal experience. Those seeking for something 'extra' from charismatic spirituality would have been open to the appeal of the 'Apostolic Vision' with its breathtaking claim to unmediated divine direction and a greater liberty for emotional expression in Apostolic worship as against the trademark measure of control in Elim meetings.[156] Ben Fisher and J.N. Arnold were cases in point. As was shown earlier, Arnold became identified with Pentecostalism at Sunderland in 1907, hosted Boddy in his visit to Belfast and was a link between the Dover Street assembly and the young men who invited George Jeffreys to Monaghan.[157] With the arrival of the Apostolic Church, he was among those ordained an elder in the Great Victoria Street assembly and soon to be numbered among the leading figures in the Apostolic Church in Ireland. By the prophetic word, both he and Phillips were called to membership of the newly constituted Missionary Council of the denomination.[158]

The previous paragraph, if correct in its analysis, provides one consideration informing Worsfold's sober assessment of slow growth, but the relatively greater success of Elim needs to be teased out further. Jeffreys' overall message was of broad acceptance because, promulgated as it was in a revivalist atmosphere, it was seen by many to be biblically grounded, demonstrable in visible healings and persuasively presented by a young evangelist coming to the height of his powers—a preacher of undoubted charisma. His message did not seek to promote an ecclesiology such as that wrapped up in 'the Apostolic Vision', a

---

work not progressing to search out for the hindrance. Ye have no time and looking here and there when the fault lies with yourselves'. (*ACM*, 30 July 1925.)

[156] Writing of a visit to Wales, Andrew Walker observed that 'the Apostolic Churches...were the most emotionally intense that I have experienced in Pentecostalism outside Black Churches. I recall wonderful *hwyl* preaching and elegant prophecies'. Such intensity may well have been the impression gained by a sympathetic observer in the early days. (Walker, *Restoring the Kingdom*, p. 253.)

[157] See Ch. 4.4.

[158] *ACM*, 11 November 1923.

teaching that was quite alien to the evangelical tradition in Ulster, even more so to other denominational traditions.

Worsfold said of Williams: 'He knew that in teaching the doctrine of the church there was the element of mystery—not philosophy, but theology. The mystery of prophecy made...them more constantly aware that the Divine purpose was to be further unfolded and fulfilled'.[159] The first issues of *Riches of Grace,* when compared with its AFC predecessor, *Showers of Blessing*, were, to Worsfold's mind, 'more ecclesial in content and style', suggesting that it was even less populist in tone than its predecessor.[160]

The Apostolic understanding of church order, distinguished by its theocratic ecclesiology, was so different that it required a high degree of acculturation to its more rarefied doctrinal positions. The Apostolic way of thinking had a particular appeal to the more reflective who had had a previous encounter with Pentecostalism and were accepting of the 'fuller vision' promulgated by the Apostolic Church. For such, the acceptability of a less individualist, more corporatist view of the Body of Christ, seemed but part and parcel of a natural progression from the *gift* of prophecy, with which they would have been familiar, to that of the *office* of both prophet and apostle, together with the other Ascension Ministries of Eph. 4:11.[161] In sum, as Andrew Walker asserts, 'sectarianism and separatism were built in to the Apostolic Church'[162]—or, at least, to a greater extent than was the case with Elim, the only other Pentecostal denomination of any size in the period leading up to 1924. In stating this, Walker speaks from some experience. At the age of fourteen at Neath Apostolic Church, he had an experience that Pentecostals would have taken as Spirit-baptism but for which, with hindsight, he makes no direct claim. When he arrived back at the home of the Elim pastor where he was staying, the latter 'poured cold water on my baptism of fire (it was, remember, from the hands of the less than favoured Apostolics) and I went to bed dispirited'.[163]

Whereas Jeffreys had no serious problem of engaging with fellow evangelicals and was prepared to accept invitations to preach in mainstream church pulpits on the few occasions when he was he was invited, Apostolics were markedly inhibited in engaging with other

---

[159] Worsfold, *The Origins of the Apostolic Church,* p. 168.

[160] Worsfold, *The Origins of the Apostolic Church,* p. 169.

[161] Worsfold makes the point that, 'from the beginning the Apostolic Church has sought to develop a corporate strength'. (Worsfold, *The Origins of the Apostolic Church,* p. 176.)

[162] Walker, *Restoring the Kingdom*, pp. 249-50.

[163] Tom Smail, Andrew Walker and Nigel Wright, *Charismatic Renewal: The Search for a Theology*, [London: SPCK, 1995], p. 37.

bodies.[164] The issue of openness to other 'camps', a term applied to other Christian bodies, was raised on a number of occasions at the Elders' Meetings in Befast. William Lauder (d. 1946) was the first full-time minister of Irish background to be appointed by the Apostolic Church. Formerly a Methodist lay preacher, he associated himself with the Apostolics in 1923 after he experienced healing at one of their meetings. Later in the same year the question was raised at an Elders' meeting as to whether or not he should attend the Methodist Lay Preachers' Society. Jones Williams was at the meeting and his directive prophecy was clearly dismissive of the idea: 'Concerning Lauder's call to visit. When I called thee, I said "Yoke not thyself with these. Go not with these. I have plenty for thee to do; this applies to all. Say in your hearts we will see to our calling and we will look after those under our charge and care"'.[165] This chariness seems to have been born of as much of a desire to conserve energy and resources as of doctrinal loftiness. In the same prophecy it was declared: 'Your attitude towards your brethren, whatever they be in any corner—Love them; not to fight! not to cause strife!... Let them see you are not interfering with any other person's work. Enough to mind your own work... When something takes place in other Camps, rejoice not at the downfall of any one'.[166] Lauder's ministry continued in the Apostolic Church and he was a leading speaker at the open-air meetings at the Custom House steps as well as at indoor meetings in the Grosvenor Hall, the Methodist Central Hall in the middle of Belfast, the use of which was probably eased by his Methodist contacts.

A similar issue arose three years later when 'Bro. Andrews asked if he did wrong in identifying himself with the Salvation Army in the open air'.[167] The answer this time grew out of general discussion rather than prophecy but came to a similar conclusion—'we should keep clear'.[168] Another elder, Crawford, wanted to know 'if an elder was at liberty to go and preach to any sect if invited'. This time the response came through prophecy:

> The Lord answered the question by saying that if those that invite you know what ye preach and believe and give ye permission to preach it, by all means go but I will not come to meet the opinions of men...

---

[164] Examples of Jeffreys' 'openness' in Ireland include the following: the membership of Hackett and Leech, both firm Anglicans, of the EPAC, and his addressing a Church of Ireland congregation in Ballymena in 1917.

[165] *ACM*, 19 November 1923.

[166] *ACM*, 19 November 1923.

[167] *ACM*, 13 July 1926.

[168] *ACM*, 13 July 1926.

> There are other rivers but they are not powerful enough and they [have] become stagnant. If ye would know the secret of victory, keep independence and let them alone. Let them retain their integrity [and] do not attack them, but go on doing my will.[169]

It was the defensiveness of the Apostolic position as revealed in details such as these that tended to chafe their fellow Pentecostals and presented a further hurdle to acceptance by the interested outsider. Lacking the dynamic thrust that Jeffreys and his team gave Elim in Ireland, the Apostolics tended to consolidate their position through familial allegiance and informal contact, rather than by the larger revivalist pulses associated with Jeffreys' crusades.[170]

Was the distancing of Elim and the Apostolics confined solely to the ideological or did the competitiveness that so disturbed Gee in Edinburgh with its attendant acerbity spread to Ulster? Such records as exist that relate to the province would suggest that the two bodies seem to have been careful not to upset each other, avoiding provocation and going their separate ways without any overt but, at the same time, little well-disposed contact. This can be seen in the informal working out of ground rules in the Waringstown area when the Apostolics first came to the village to seek a site for their new tent. Phillips and John Cardwell discovered what seemed a suitable site until the farmer who owned it informed them that the hall on the other side of the road belonged to Elim. In Phillips' words, 'we thanked him for his goodwill, but refused to put the tent there, for if we wanted to rival our Elim friends we could have done so in Wales, without coming 300 miles to do so! Neither did we wish to build on others' foundation'.[171]

This policy seems to have prevailed in Ulster on both sides though a superficial view of Figure V might suggest otherwise. The diagram shows the geographical distribution of the Apostolic assemblies outside Belfast in relation to those of Elim. A number of points can be drawn from it. Outside Belfast, Elim had a stronger presence, having twenty-three as against eleven Apostolic centres. Within the city the ratio was around 4:1 in favour of Apostolic assemblies though active membership numbers would have been in closer balance as most of the Apostolic assemblies were small and struggling. Elim had a greater spatial spread from Belfast—from Monaghan in the south to Ballymoney in the north as

---

[169] *ACM*, 13 July 1926.

[170] The chapter so far has given examples of family linkages and the ministerial-leadership continuity through successive generations as with the Matthews, Cheyne, Kane, Cardwell and Horner families. The same, of course, is true of Elim but with its recurring evangelistic thrusts, usually associated with Jeffreys' periodic visits to the province throughout the 1920s and 1930s, it did not become as ingrown.

[171] *Souvenir*, p. 41.

compared to that from Gilford to Portglenone. The overall distribution of the eleven Apostolic assemblies and mission centres outside Belfast shows that 64% of the Apostolic locations were broadly aligned along the Lisburn-Monaghan axis and 27% in the Bann Corridor, whereas the balance was more even in the case of Elim, 53% and 47% respectively. But the point most pertinent to this discussion is that of the eleven Apostolic locations, eight (73%) were within five miles, as the crow flies, of an Elim a centre and the remainder were separated by between five to ten miles. Phillips' statement about not building on others' foundation makes it difficult to conceive that such proximity as measured was the result of considered policy. Rather, it is better to look to those features within the revivalist, religio-cultural predisposition of the two areas that made them responsive to the overtures of almost any broadly evangelical movement.

Other, more specific, factors were operative at the local and personal level. In at least one case, the Apostolic developed out of an earlier Elim work, as at Portglenone. In other cases individuals, such as J.N. Arnold, were drawn from Pentecostals who were convinced of the truth of the 'Apostolic Vision'. Probably more were won over through links of friendship and family, not limited to any particular theological position. One such was John B. Hamilton who joined the Apostolic Church shortly after he and his wife resigned from the EEB in 1925. He was attracted to the Apostolics by friendship and then came to accept their doctrinal position, albeit for a short time only. Between leaving the EEB and joining the Apostolic Church, he had short spells with a mainstream church and then, 'with an old friend', set up an independent Pentecostal assembly. Of the former he wrote that he accepted for a short time 'an Assistantship in a Presbyterian Church, officiating principally at the Mission Church'—a reference, possibly, to helping at a Belfast City Mission. When the second work failed and a buyer sought for the seating and furniture, he came in contact with the Apostolics through William Phillips. Of the contact, he wrote that 'in spite of the fact that I was greatly opposed to the teaching and government of the Apostolic Church (which I honestly believed to be in error), I was bound to acknowledge that their disposition towards me was the kindest'.[172]

He decided to integrate his small work with a local Apostolic Church, despite the fact that at the beginning he was 'in antagonism to the Apostolic Church work'. He and his wife came to accept the Apostolic distinctives. He stated his reason for accepting the controversial practice of 'enquiring of the Lord' by reflecting on John 16:7:

> The Lord revealed to me that by this the Comforter was to be to us all that Jesus would be if he were here actually in the flesh. If He were here actually and bodily, I

[172] *Riches of Grace*, Vol. 4.3, January 1929, p. 104.

> would ask Him any questions, and He would answer me, clear up my difficulties, solve my problems, become Lord of my life, and plan my way. Well then, since this is not so, the wisest means have been devised in the presence of the Comforter, the Holy Ghost, Gifts of the Spirit and Offices in the Church to reveal His Mind and Will. I saw the revelation and vision of the Apostolic Church of the New Testament: saw, and believed, and accepted the truth.[173]

Such convictions were short-lived and the Hamiltons, for some undeclared reason, did not to remain long in the Apostolic Church.

8.5.2 The Mix of Welsh Ethos and Bradford Control

Another factor to be taken into account in explaining the slower advance in the province of the Apostolic witness as compared to Elim is captured in Walker's remark that 'there is something essentially Welsh about the Apostolic Church', an awareness that he attributed to the Apostolics having 'encapsulated the old Welsh revivalism in an institutional form'.[174] Ireland was treated in the early days as the first mission field of the ACW and the first three missionaries were Welshmen, with Penygroes their spiritual home. In a letter to H.V. Chanter, D.P. Williams wrote, 'I may say that the work in Ireland is more directly under our control than the work in England, because in Ireland we have our own God-appointed men at work'.[175] A few months later at the Easter Conference, as part of the Bradford agreement, responsibility for the three missionaries in Ireland was transferred from Penygroes to Bradford. Phillips, as superintendent of the Irish work, was required to send a monthly report on the work in Ireland to Bradford, with a copy directed to Penygroes. By contrast, Elim in the early 1920s had established itself in Ireland with headquarters in Belfast. Jeffreys, though Welsh, was of more cosmopolitan instincts than the Williams brothers and, indeed, had very little contact in ministerial terms with his native land: Wales was considered Apostolic territory. Most of the early members of the Elim Evangelistic Band had an Ulster background and his closest colleagues, Henderson and Darragh, were Ulstermen, though the 'Ulster feel' about Elim began to dissipate once the headquarters removed to London in 1923.

William Kay, in his *Pentecostals in Britain*, makes the point that because the Apostolic Church was based in Wales, 'it was to an extent, insulated from the main cultural currents that flowed through the United Kingdom'.[176] That Penygroes, a mining village in South Wales, was both the location of the headquarters and the annual convention of the Church,

---

[173] *Riches of Grace*, Vol. 4.3, January 1929, p. 104.

[174] Walker, *Restoring the Kingdom*, p. 253.

[175] Letter of D.P. Williams to H.V. Chanter (Bradford), dated 22 January 1922.

[176] Kay, *Pentecostals in Britain*, p. 177.

only helped to accentuate its inherent provincialism. Such provincialism was not necessarily a drawback in relations between Penygroes and Ulster. The province, likewise, was a place apart, made all the more so in the early 1920s by its preoccupation with the outworking of its newfound constitutional status. Also, it was more like those large parts of Wales that were 'rural and more family-based than was the case in the great urban sprawls of...England [and central Scotland]'.[177] The three Welshmen remained in Ireland long enough, Phillips for fourteen years, to become attuned to Ulster ways to the extent of calling on well-worn Protestant sympathies. At the baptismal service at Moore's Hill, previously alluded to, a verse in the poem published in the local newspaper contained this slant in the preaching of one of the Welshmen:

> He spoke of William and the Boyne and
> how our fathers bled
> In order that the Book of books might be
> with safety read.[178]

As was shown earlier there was an anti-Catholicism strain in the Apostolic Church in its earlier days, an attitude that accorded well with the religio-cultural complexion of much within Ulster Protestanism.[179]

The local Apostolics adopted the Welsh custom of giving their assemblies a name with a biblical connotation. Examples include Moore's Hill ('Eden'), Portglenone ('Hephzibah'), Battlehill ('Carmel') and Ava Street ('Jerusalem').[180] There is no doubting the high regard in which

---

[177] Kay, *Pentecostals in Britain*, p. 177.

[178] *The Lurgan Mail*, 15 January 1987, p. 22. The battle of the Boyne, fought in July 1690, marked a decisive defeat for the forces supporting the Catholic King James II at the hands of the army of William III [of Orange]. Despite the wider European dimension of the war, in ultra-Protestant circles it has been crudely portrayed as a victory for Protestant Ireland over Catholic Ireland and, as such, the victory continues to be celebrated every 12 July by the Orange Order throughout Ulster.

[179] As late as the 1943 Penygroes Convention, D.P. Williams referred to 'the priests and the Pope's Gestapo...working in our country. This calls for much alertness so that our Protestant principles may not be undermined'. (Worsfold, *The Origins of the Apostolic Church*, p. 228, n. 2.) It was, doubtless, a view coloured by such events as the discrimination against Pentecostals in Italy which led to the closure of the Apostolic Church in Rome by government interdict in 1936 and the exigencies of World War II. A detailed study of anti-Catholicism in Ulster Protestantism is found in John D. Brewer and Gareth I. Higgins, *Anti-Catholicism in Northern Ireland 1600-1998: The Mote and the Beam*, (Basingstoke: Macmillan 1998)..

[180] The appellation 'Eden' for the Moore's Hill assembly was most likely derived from the name of the townland in which it stands, viz., *Eden*ballycoghill. 'Jerusalem' (Ava Street) was possibly suggested by its nearness to that part of Belfast known as 'the Holy Land' because of the many streets named after places in the then Palestine.

D.P. Williams was held among the Apostolic people in Ulster. At an Elder's Meeting, it was suggested that a letter should be written to 'ask Pastor Dan to come to the Convention as he has a warm spot in all of our hearts which was agreed to do so by all'.[181] By that stage, the elders had to deal as much, if not more, with Bradford since the work in Ireland had become the responsibility in 1922 of the Missionary Council with its headquarters in that city.[182]

The Bradford connection led to Herbert Chanter visiting the province quite frequently. In his role of apostle, he had the authority to chair the Elders' Meetings and any service he attended, except when Dan Williams was present. Chanter probably did not gel as easily with the Ulster Apostolics as Williams. The Bradford leadership had a harder business edge to it and Worsfold was of the opinion that 'it is both interesting and significant that the ideology of a fully inclusive administrative centralism began in Bradford'.[183] The end result of this internal pressure was the new Constitution of 1937 that brought the Apostolic Church for the first time in its twenty-year history into a centralised administrative framework under a General Council of apostles and prophets.[184]

Chanter did not always bring good news to Belfast. In November 1923, he informed the Elders' Meeting that, with £200 having been spent from the central Missionary Fund on the Drumbo Hall, finances were very low:

---

[181] *ACM*, 31 October 1925. Gee described Williams as 'the beloved leader'. (Gee, *Wind and Flame*, p. 68.) Even the maverick, former Apostolic pastor, Robert Jardine, who had hardly a good word to say for Jones Williams, could say of his brother, 'Against Pastor Dan I have nothing to say. I love him and esteem him as a Saint of God'. (Letter to H.V. Chanter, 30 December 1921.)

[182] At the 1922 Easter Convention at Bradford the hitherto independent Apostolic Church of God led by H.V. Chanter (1872-1949) joined forces with the Apostolic Church. It was formed from a group that left the Bowland Street Mission in 1917. The Mission was closely associated with Smith Wigglesworth whose stern opposition to directive prophecy was the cause of the split that caused the Chanter group to move to a hall in Albert Street. By 1922 Albert Street was part of a wider fellowship of eight assemblies which then became part of the Apostolic Church. Chanter was the chairman of the groundbreaking Bradford Conference, held over the 1922 Easter period, and first editor of the *Apostolic Church Missionary Herald.*

[183] Worsfold, *The Origins of the Apostolic Church,* p. 212.

[184] Worsfold, *The Origins of the Apostolic Church,* pp. 305-7, maintains that the greater bureaucratisation of the denomination heralded by the new Constitution stored up problems when the Latter Rain issue reached the British Isles from Canada in the 1950s. The Latter Rain Movement originated as a counterblast to the growing institutionalism within the Pentecostal movement in general. Its impact was greatest on the Apostolic Church of all the Pentecostal denominations within the British Isles. In Ulster, the issue split the Portglenone Apostolic Church and gave rise to a new assembly, Bethel Temple, that stands at the opposite end of the main street of the village from that of the original Apostolic church.

'The income from Ireland is 50% short of the expenses... Expenditure for Ireland last year amounted to £700. [He] went on to say, "We want to create a feeling that you are one with us in the work"'.[185] Things do not appear to have been going well at the time and Jones Williams' prophecy at the meeting hints of low morale allied to some disquiet among the elders over matters of Welsh leadership, both local and national: 'Some ask the question, "What doeth these few?" That was the opinion of the public... They say nothing will come of this, it will come to the ground. Their words shall not come to pass... Try not to disenthrone those whom I have sent, for ye will disenthrone yourself. Honour those I have sent and ye will honour Me.'[186]

Unlike other regional sections in Britain, the work in Ireland was not autonomous in the early years of the Church. Prophetic utterances were often the means of bringing the local eldership to heel and reminding its members where authority lay. Before the opening of the Henry Street work, Jones Williams' 'spoken word' called on the leaders to 'separate two nights for the furnishing of the new place and appeal [for funds] to my people and do according to that I have revealed from H.Q.'.[187] At the January 1924 Elders' Meeting, Phillips reported on the Missionary Council's decisions over the New Year period in Glasgow. One of the decisions was the constituting of a Court of Appeal, the membership of which was composed of the apostles and Jones Williams, 'the head prophet'.[188] Phillips explicated the function of the body: 'In the case of disputes, heresies, etc., this was to be the Court of Appeal, and their decision which would be God's thro' the Prophet would be final'.[189]

The following year, the elders were to experience the force of this regulation. The overseer of the Nettlefield assembly in east Belfast, Glover, had been creating some problems and had absented himself from the special meetings arranged in his own assembly which, for Phillips, was tantamount to Glover 'showing no interest in the work'.[190] Glover vented his pique by taking himself off, removing the organ and hymnbooks which he considered his own property. Phillips planned to put someone else in charge. Chanter, who was fully briefed on the background to the dispute, made a ruling that seemed to challenge the Irish superintendent's proposed action: 'If God calls a man, it is up to the man to fulfil his office. It is not an Elders' Meeting to come to a decision on any Elder. We must take these things to a Higher Court. British law says every man is innocent until proven guilty... Pastor Phillips and the Elders' powers end

185 *ACM*, 11 November 1923.

186 *ACM*, 11 November 1923.

187 *ACM*, 11 November 1923.

188 *ACM*, 11 January 1924.

189 *ACM*, 19 July 1925.

190 *ACM*, 19 July 1925.

here and the final word is the Apostles'.[191] The bark in this judgement was worse than its actual bite because Chanter proceeded to state the Apostles' decision, which was to dismiss Glover from office but with a right to appeal. He then added 'they at H.Q. had absolute confidence in those in office in the Irish work'.[192] This was followed by a show of hands to indicate that such confidence was reciprocated. It was a classic display of the iron hand of apostolic authority in the velvet glove of considered emollience.

The subordinate position of the Irish leadership was both underlined and exploited when the Elders sought to take advantage of its dependence on Bradford. A minute of the April 1925 Elders' Meeting recorded that as 'three weddings were coming off [during] Convention week...the Bradford brethren be asked to give them a wedding breakfast'.[193] At a subsequent meeting it was reported that 'H.Q. would bear half of the cost of the wedding', the upshot of which was that the elders decided to postpone their gift to the Missionary Council for the Apostolic work in Argentina.[194]

The forming of a Burial Society was another issue that the elders were keen to press on Bradford. In the hard times of the 1920s it was some form of contributory scheme set up to provide the money for a fitting burial for the poorer members. When Omri Jones prophesied at an Elders' Meeting soon after the matter was raised, its message must have brought little comfort to the hearers: 'Ye are to be on your guard in this direction. If ye open the door and let it be known, ye don't know where it would end. Ye would have to supply the need. If ye say ye are making a Fund, [then] ye must meet [it], whether ye have it or not'.[195] Without financial aid, the scheme would not be financially viable. The prophecy also carried a message that was less sanguine than many Pentecostals were accustomed to hear when facing the hardships of life: 'I am causing many to pass through trials that they may learn to live. Ye pity those who suffer?—but they are in my hands. Ye would provide clothes and food

---

[191] *ACM*, 19 July 1925.

[192] *ACM*, 19 July 1925.

[193] *ACM*, 25 April 1925.

[194] *ACM*, 17 May 1925. Argentina was the first non-English speaking country to which the Apostolic Church sent missionaries. The work started in 1922 and one of the converts was a Mr Palau whose son Luis was to become a widely recognised evangelist on the world stage. Luis Palau attended the Penygroes Convention in 1980 and expressed his spiritual debt to the Apostolic Church in sending missionaries to his homeland. (Worsfold, *The Origins of the Apostolic Church,* p. 231.)

[195] *ACM*, 24 May 1925.

for Job but I would allow dogs to lick him. His soul shone in the glory of my face. Let it suffice thee... My apostle has given you wisdom'.[196]

Any impression that this might give of Apostolics being indifferent to the needs of the poor in their midst would be quite unwarranted. The Burial Society was dropped not because it was an unworthy cause but because it was financially unsustainable. Early in the life of the ACW a Poor Fund was instituted and, through prophecy, it was directed that 1% of the tithes received should be retained locally to assist the poor.

8.5.3 Considerations of Social Class and Status

The inter-war years in Britain were marked by lengthy periods of economic austerity and Northern Ireland was one of the regions to suffer most. The cumulative decline in the economy of the province in the inter-war years is revealed by the figures for 1939 when it was calculated that the average income per head for the province was only 58% that of the United Kingdom as a whole. In 1925, the unemployment rate for the province stood at 25% compared to 11% for Britain. In the same year, shipyard workers took a wage cut of 47% for their forty-seven-hour week. Expenditure on social services in 1924, worked out annually at £4 4s (£4.20) per head, whereas it was three times higher in Britain.[197] The penury to which some of the Apostolic members was reduced can be gauged from a minute of the Elders' Meeting in November 1924: 'Mr. Hamilton (Bro. Glover's son-in-law) and Bro. Glover's own little boy being in need for help [for clothing]. Mr. Hamilton earning 24 shillings [£1.20] weekly and his four children'.[198] The prophetic word endorsed the thinking of the meeting: '[It is] well ye should help the little children, by providing boots for the boy. My handmaiden, Mrs. McConnell, should get up and make an appeal to those who could give garments to

---

[196] *ACM*, 24 May 1925. A more characteristic 'faith-victory' triumphalism can be detected in the view of Glover, the overseer of the Nettlefield assembly, that if any elders took medicine, they should not lay hands upon the sick. An elder objected to this opinion stating that this 'he believed was going beyond the limit'. A middle position was accepted by a sufferer of nine years standing in Castlerock, County Londonderry, who was anointed and prayed for by Phillips and Arnold. They reported that he 'was still a staunch believer in divine healing waiting and believing God has a purpose in his prolonged illness. [He] was waiting and believing for God's hour to come for his perfect deliverance... We left him rejoicing and believing God'. (*ACM*, 29 September 1923.)

[197] Devlin, Paddy, *Yes We Have No Bananas: Outdoor Relief in Belfast 1920-39*, (Blackstaff Press, Belfast, 1981), pp. 53-55.

[198] *ACM*, 23 November 1924. In 1925 shipyard workers had their wages cut from 87 shillings (£4.35) per week to 47 shillings (£2.35). Even at this reduced rate, Hamilton was earning a wage that was about half that of a shipyard worker. His wife had died a few months earlier.

be made suitable for them. Not my will to give money in this case'.[199] It was a responsibility of the deaconesses to visit the sick and those in need and bring their needs to the deacons who were responsible for distributing the relief.

Some of the leaders were not immune from hardship as was cited above in the case of Glover. A deaconess, Mrs Devonport, by prophetic direction was to have 'my servant Phillips to put two shillings and sixpence (12.5p) in her hand quietly'.[200] On another occasion, again through the spoken word, it was announced that elders travelling a distance to the monthly meeting 'and not in a way to pay their fare, such are to apply to the treasurer...and not be afraid to make it known as I know all your circumstances, saith the Lord'.[201] When Vaughan stayed at the Davis home at Drumbo for a fortnight to help with the building of the new hall, he offered to pay three-quarters of his salary for his upkeep. Mrs Davis turned down his offer and for Vaughan, this seemed 'an answer to prayer for a suit of clothes I was badly in need of'.[202] Nevertheless, while engaged in private prayer he was moved to give the £3 to Phillips towards the building of the Drumbo hall. In accepting it, a much relieved Phillips showed him the invoice he had received recently for the sum of £3 for a delivery of wood for the new hall, a bill he could see no way of paying until he received Vaughan's gift.[203]

The appeal of the Apostolics in the period under consideration seemed to be confined, especially in the Belfast urban area, to people at the lower end of the social spectrum. The Apostolic Church did not have the social pretensions of Elim, showing no great desire to court the influential in the way Jeffreys did. Nothing would have pleased Jeffreys more than to see Elim carry an appeal across the whole social spectrum.[204] Also, the local pastors of the Apostolic Church generally lacked the modicum of training and theological background that Elim sought to encourage in the members of the EEB. One of the first measures taken when the headquarters were established to London was the establishment of a Bible School at Clapham, London, in 1925, just ten years after the beginning of the Elim movement. The Apostolic Church took twenty

---

[199] *ACM*, 23 November 1924.

[200] *ACM*, 20 September 1924.

[201] *ACM*, 15 May 1926.

[202] *Vaughan Memoir,* p. 39. Burton, the retail tailors, were noted at the time for their 'fifty shilling suits' (£2.50)'.

[203] The wind-up of the story was that within a month he received two new suits, one from the proceeds of an unexpected gift and another purchased in Wales by his mother.

[204] It was probably this aspect of the Swedish Pentecostal movement that impressed him and drew his admiration for its leader, Lewi Pethrus.

years to open a Bible School at Penygroes in 1936[205]—a delay prompted, in Worsfold's words, by the belief that 'the spiritual power which came from the Pentecostal baptism of the Spirit was...sufficient'.[206] The part played by prophetic directive tended to curtail the exercise of more cerebral gifts in leadership and more conventional means of decision-making compared to that employed in other Pentecostal groups. One principal of the Bible School found it frustrating to work under a system which allowed Bible School students at times to be by-passed in the making of ministerial appointments in favour of those with little or no training.[207]

The prophet's voice was heard even on the intertwined issues of social class and education. Vaughan brought this message:

> The winding up of the Ages is at hand. Fishermen not educated, some would say ignorant men; who could conceive the ultimate result of that calling? The great men of today whose opinions are respected, they derive their food for thought from ignorant men, the lowly. Not to their greatness am I going to build a church in this land.
>
> Those whom I call shall not fall away, even the doctors and lawyers shall not disturb them.[208]

Like many other prophecies there is a certain opaqueness about the meaning of this passage though its central thrust is clear enough. It carries the same sentiment as 1 Corinthians 1:27, 'God has chosen the foolish things of the world to confound the wise'. The non-transparency grows in part from the problem of making a transcript of a rapidly delivered message, especially if the writer had no great expertise in shorthand and also from the fact that the immediate context in which it was delivered is not known. Prophecy usually addressed the issues of the moment. All the prophecies in the minute book were delivered by the

---

[205] The Bible School was launched in November 1933. On that occasion among the guest speakers were Professor Keri Evans, Rev. N. Williams and the Rev. F. Morgan, Moderator of the Welsh Presbyterian Church—an impressive line-up that highlighted the quintessentially Welsh nature of the Apostolic Church and its place in the religio-revivalist culture of the Principality.

[206] Worsfold, *The Origins of the Apostolic Church,* p. 205.

[207] The principal in question was Alfred Greenway who acted in that capacity in the period 1948-50. A key factor in students being bypassed was the acceptance of prophetic direction in the appointment of pastors rather than the credentialism underlying more formal procedures. The older working class bias against 'book learning' doubtless operated. A respected older pastor and former miner, Thomas Rees, maintained that the best training a man could get was 'down in the bowels of the mine'. (Worsfold, *The Origins of the Apostolic Church,* p. 207.)

[208] *ACM*, 30 May 1925.

Welsh set prophets, Jones Williams, Omri Jones and Idris Vaughan, and have a Welsh flourish about them. As well, multi-layered meaning that allows a number of interpretations is a not uncommon characteristic of the prophetic word.

In another prophecy, Vaughan brought a challenge to the deacons in terms of their calling and personal development. It is presented in a series of disjointed images:

> When a man goeth into a strange land...he will seek to civilise them... There are degrees of progress in the vegetable realm. The seed if ye keep it in the house it is not profitable... I have called you as deacons, but ye are as seed yet. [It is] well to cultivate that which is given to you in the *natural* as well as the *spiritual.* Ye that serve should be *manly* and *clean* in their appearance and willing to be servants of all. There was chaos at the beginning and the earth was darkness and I had a plan. I spake the word and the land became into sight.[209]

This prophecy as written, like many others, fits in with the explication Forbes makes of the Delphic utterances, the obscurity of which he sees as 'not a matter of *linguistic* unintelligibility at all. It is simply that such oracles were formulated, at the level of literary allusion [here biblical] and metaphor, in obscure, cryptic and enigmatic terms. They were, in a word, oracular'.[210] The equation of Delphic utterance and prophecy here is, of course, one of genre and not content or source.

The theme of the second extract—with its ideas of unlocking potential, promoting civility and creating order—places the making of a deacon within the arena of the wider created order and thus brings a sweep of grandeur to the office. The deacons were assured, 'Your office is not a small one, not a minor but a Great Office'.[211] Such lofty sentiments were at complete odds with the economic privation suffered by many of the Apostolic leaders and their families. What Apostolic office bearers may have lacked in formal education was counterpoised by the sense of divine affirmation conveyed by the prophetic word. The Lord, indeed, had exalted those of low degree.

8.5.4 Contention over Prophecy

A theocratic ecclesiology is likely to prove the most challenging of all options. Less amenable to ratiocinative processes and the interplay of human judgement, it raises a host of questions, such as: Is theocracy *the* sole Scriptural model for church government? What are the criteria to

---

[209] *ACM*, 20 September 1924.

[210] Christopher Forbes, *Prophecy and Inspired Speech: In Early Christianity and its Hellenistic Environment*, (Peabody, MA: Hendrickson, 1997), p. 109.

[211] *ACM*, 20 September 1924.

judge whether or not a church that claims to be theocratic is what it claims to be? If theocracy is the model, then what aspects of divine intention are reserved for rational decision-making and which for unmediated intervention? More basic even, Is there such a thing as a 'pure' revelation untarnished by intermediation between the giver and the hearer? To what extent can the claim for prophetic direction act as a cover for human manipulation? These are but a few of the questions that could be posed and it is not the intention here to address them, other than incidentally, but rather to reveal some of the complexity and seriousness of the issues raised and to account for the vehemence of the debate within Pentecostal circles at the time—enough certainly to alarm potential adherents.

Waiting on the revelation of the Lord's will through prophecy made constitution-making and forward strategic planning less penetrable in the Apostolic Church. It was not until 1937 that the publication of a Constitution and Guiding Principles was finally agreed. Doctrinal tenets, derived essentially from AFC days, were a formal basis for fellowship but were not the cement that held the denomination together. That lay in the 'fuller vision' of the restored Ascension Ministries of Ephesians 4:11. This meant that much of the decision-making on the ground was on an *ad hoc* basis, addressed directly through prophecy to the needs of the moment. Longer term planning such as featured in the early days of Elim, however embryonic, was virtually ruled out. Informal guidelines can be picked out here and there throughout the minutes but there was nothing to match the rules and procedures introduced into Elim by the Constitution of 1922. A sample of the guidelines adopted include the following: 'no local elders' meeting to be held apart from the knowledge of the superintendent;[212] 'no accusation to be brought to the superintendent apart the pastor's knowledge';[213] pastors or elders visiting another assembly were not to 'use the Gifts of God in [that] assembly';[214] 'no elder has the right to get the mind of the Lord in dealing with any matter in the assembly apart from the knowledge of the other elders'.[215] These guidelines arose, most likely, out of tension-induced incidents within local church settings. They were all predicated more on stability than on growth.

Sufficient examples have been quoted to indicate the major role that directive, governmental prophecy played in the life of the Apostolic Church. Its place was central to the concept of a theocratic ecclesiology. Worsfold was prepared to admit that the 'tendency did exist to elevate the prophetic word at times to the level of infallibility' but, with time and under the authority of the apostleship, the ministry of the prophet

212 *ACM*, 23 November 1924.

213 *ACM*, 27 December 1924

214 *ACM*, 27 December 1924.

215 *ACM*, 23 November 1923.

matured without it becoming overly institutionalized.[216] As prophecy came in time under stricter apostolic and elder control, it was confined increasingly to governmental matters and less to individual direction. In Walker's opinion, 'the Apostolic Church faced with a conflict between the prophets and the apostles (which the Catholic Apostolic Church faced before them) settled in favour of a dominating apostolate'.[217] That such conflict was inevitable was challenged on those occasions when the ministries of the apostle and prophet blended. A singular intertwining of the two was a feature of those meetings where the Williams brothers exercised their respective ministries. On such occasions the prophecies of Jones Williams made the listeners feel that 'he was the mouthpiece of the Almighty'.[218] Worsfold commented that some of Jones' prophecies 'had a profundity that can only be described as awesome'.[219] When Dan explicated and developed his brother's prophecies, placing his own distinctive apostolic gloss upon them, it was to his hearers the very gate of heaven.

Weeks concedes that there were cases of abuse in 'enquiring of the Lord', but their incidence has been over-estimated and they could never outweigh the blessings that had come through the ministry of the prophets. He presents the case for the prophetic office in the Apostolic Church:

> It is very obvious that those who write and speak [critically] have never taken the trouble to research our archives and read quietly and prayerfully the reams of proven prophecies in our headquarters. They are awe-inspiring... The many prophecies in the days of the...Catholic Apostolic Church lie forgotten largely unfulfilled because of 'Apostolic' failure in that church but the prophecies we have received through many prophets are 'living words' which have blessed us many times as they have been considered by Apostleship and then implemented.[220]

More than the office of apostle, it was the understanding and practice of prophecy that set the Apostolic-type churches apart from the rest of the Pentecostal movement.[221] The distancing of the majority Pentecostal groups from the Apostolics was widely known, enough to alert those who might otherwise have considered joining the Apostolic Church. The

---

216 Worsfold, *The Origins of the Apostolic Church,* p.183.

217 Walker, *Restoring the Kingdom*, p. 254.

218 Worsfold, *The Origins of the Apostolic Church,* p. 314.

219 Worsfold, *The Origins of the Apostolic Church,* p. 183.

220 *Weeks MS*, p. 25, part II.

221 The Apostolic-type churches within classical Pentecostalism in Britain were those that looked to William Oliver Hutchinson and Winton, Bournemouth, for their foundation. They are, in order of formation, the Apostolic Faith Church, the Apostolic Church and the United Apostolic Faith Church. The Apostolic Church is still active, but the other two are on the verge of extinction in Britain.

governmental rule of apostles and prophets with its inherent element of trans-local control would have been disconcerting to the many of the independent fellowships that held dear to the congregational principle. In 1923, a sizeable number of British Pentecostal churches were so disturbed by the advance of the Apostolic Church in parts of Britain that they felt it necessary to warn Pentecostals in North America about a forthcoming visit of a British Apostolic delegation to their country.

Ahead of the visit Williams reported: 'Some brethren from England thought to do service for God by sending a circular letter which has been widely published in a Pentecostal paper, warning the American brotherhood against us'.[222] He stated that some had sent letters 'which were inserted in thousands of Pentecostal publications in America'.[223] It seems to have been the Ulster-born Dobson Hunniford who alerted Williams to the unfavourable publicity. Writing from Pennsylvania, Dobson informed the Apostolic leaders of the situation in the States: 'A few weeks ago I was reading a warning notice from England, published in the official organ of the Assemblies of God in America...warning everyone against [the Welsh Apostolic Church's] erroneous teaching and practice'.[224] The Assemblies of God in America were strong on local church autonomy so the caution had to be taken seriously. The impetus behind the letter lay partly in the fear of Apostolic proselytism within some independent Pentecostal groups in Wales that led them to approach the Assemblies of God about the possibility of their becoming affiliates of the American denomination. It was this move that added momentum to an initiative that resulted in the formation of the Assemblies of God in Great Britain and Ireland in 1924. The latter body has continued to maintain fraternal relations with its American namesake but, otherwise, is totally independent.

The letter that Hunniford referred to was printed in the August 1922 issue of *The Pentecostal Evangel*, the official organ of the American Assemblies of God. It was signed by E.C.W. Boulton on behalf of the 'General Council', writing in his capacity as secretary of the Sheffield Convention that was convened in May 1922. The Conference was called to discuss the subject of Pentecostal unity though the Apostolic Church was not invited to attend.[225] Boulton was appointed General Secretary of

---

[222] *Weeks MS*, p. 22.

[223] *Weeks MS*, p. 22. Presumably he meant thousands of copies of probably just one publication, the *Pentecostal Evangel*.

[224] *Weeks MS*, p. 23.

[225] William Burton and George Jeffreys were the main movers in calling the Conference. A recent visit of Burton to America had impressed on him the need for greater cohesion in the British movement. As well he may have expected that an administrative system to smooth out financial support for his Congo Evangelistic Mission would be one outcome of a united Pentecostal movement. Massey thinks that Jeffreys 'was half-

the Provisional General Council, a position he doubtless achieved with the full backing of George Jeffreys and Donald Gee, who both at this time had close contacts with him. [226] It was a letter, therefore, of some weight and reveals the depth of the cleavage between the Apostolic Church and the rest of the movement in the British Isles.[227] It reads as follows:

> We feel strongly as a Council here on this side that you should be warned of a proposed visit to America of several leaders of The Welsh Apostolic Church. I think you are fairly conversant with some of the their erroneous teaching and practices with which we are obliged to disassociate ourselves. I refer chiefly to their practice of 'Enquiring through the Gifts' for guidance in personal and church matters, which we regard as distinctly unscriptural. And so as we conclude that their visit will be for the purpose of propagating their views and establishing work in America on these lines, we feel constrained to warn you, in order that proper steps may be taken to protect your assemblies from danger in this direction.[228]

With such a swell of ill will so thoroughly publicised, it would not be surprising that many were chary of any dealings with the Apostolic Church.

8.6 The Operation of Prophecy in the Irish Apostolic Church

A reading of the early minutes of the Apostolic Church in Ireland cannot fail to impress on the reader the core function of prophecy in the life of the Church. The next section looks at the functioning of prophecy on the ground as recorded largely in the minutes of the Elders' Meeting. Three aspects of its operation will be considered here: 1. its significant role; 2. its range; 3. its control function. The views of those who contested the Apostolic understanding and practice of the charism will then be considered. Their reaction was sufficiently adverse to convince all but the unknowing and those sold on it to look in another direction

8.6.1 The Significant Role of Prophecy

The prominence of the prophetic element in the early days in Ireland reflected the emphasis placed on it throughout the whole Apostolic

---

consciously preparing the way for a remarkable new development of his Elim Church [especially with its move into England] and of his own part and leadership in such a development'. (Massey, 'A Sound and Scriptural Union', p. 24.)

[226] Massey, 'A Sound and Scriptural Union', pp. 24-5.

[227] At the Sheffield Conference, Jeffreys and Henderson were named as the representatives from Ireland. The Conference proved abortive but proved to be the first formal step that eventually led to the formation of the British Assemblies of God in 1924, an outcome that proved to be a nail in the coffin of wider Pentecostal unity.

[228] *The Pentecostal Evangel*, 5 August 1922, p. 9.

Church. As noted before, William Phillips 'was unbounded in his enthusiasm for it...so implicit was his faith in the prophetic word'.[229] Vaughan, on the other hand, was prepared to suspend judgement even on his own prophecies. One such occasion related to a mission when he feared a prophecy might 'be sadly remembered as "Thus saith Idris Vaughan" rather than divinely inspired'.[230] The prophecy indicated that the village of Hillsborough was to be the location for a tent mission. However, the rector proved sticky. He exercised his veto on 'so-called non-orthodox religious activities'.[231] Hillsborough was at the time a landlord controlled settlement. It was planned as a small Georgian market town, laid out in a period of enlightened patronage by the Hill family who were later to be ennobled as the Downshire line. The Downshires owned virtually all the surrounding land and their stately mansion has been the official government residence since 1924. It was, therefore, more than likely that any application for a tent site would be met with disdain. Vaughan's fear that the prophecy would prove to be entirely self-generated was, therefore, an entirely realistic one. However, his fear did not materialise. A deaconess at the Ava Street assembly, who was a native of Hillsborough, had a dream that she relayed to Phillips. In the dream she saw a childhood friend, then the village postman, and took this as a sign that Phillips should make contact with him. Phillips and Evan Jones rendezvoused with the man and he took them to a field that he owned and in which was erected the impressively tall statue of the fourth Marquis of Downshire. He told them, 'Put your tent there; that chap up there can do nothing about it!'[232] If they had not been men of some piety, this was just the outcome to prompt them to cock a snook at the towering edifice.

A concern, to a point of dread, of J.N. Arnold illustrates clearly his high view of the prophetic gift. His understanding of prophecy was stark, perceiving it as the direct, unmediated word of God and this led him to fear that, after transcribing it, he might lose or destroy the record. Vaughan directly addressed his fear through a prophecy: 'Do not be discouraged. Think not my servant Arnold by taking down my word in longhand, what if it happened to be destroyed. The word written down with pen and ink is on the heart of Jehovah. I am pleased with the labour of a truth'.[233] On another occasion, Jones Williams' prophecy carried

---

229 *Vaughan Memoir*, p. 42.

230 *Vaughan Memoir*, p. 42.

231 *Vaughan Memoir*, p. 42.

232 *Vaughan Memoir*, p. 42.

233 *ACM*, 9 May 1925. The most straightforward interpretation would seem to be that the prophetic word was sacrosanct. Arnold probably held to the 'dictation' view of Scripture—a view that has all but gone. There are enough textual variations in the source texts of the Bible—though none seriously challenging core doctrines—to have allayed Arnold's fears.

both a reproach and an affirmation of the power of the spoken word of prophecy: 'At times ye have heard these words before. Can I not repeat my words in order for ye to take hold of My words? My words are Creative Words'.[234] Once, the Elders were assured, 'My spoken word is the secret, that the Elect be not deceived'.[235] The wording by which prophecies were introduced leaves little doubt of their elevated status. Terms suggestive of unmediated immediacy spoke of the Lord who '"exhorted"/"said"/"confirmed'/"spoke"/"told"/"decided"'.[236] On similar lines, we are told, 'It was also the Word of the Lord that the next monthly meeting be in Henry Street'.[237] Dan Williams voiced, perhaps, the most startling claim: 'The principle is—God speaks definitely and finally through the "set Prophet"'.[238]

This understanding of prophecy drew a counterblast from other Pentecostal writers, among them Harold Horton in his widely used text *The Gifts of the Spirit*. He maintained it was an error that often innocent people fall into to deliver prophecy as though it were delivered straight from the Lord with no engagement of the prophet's mind or personality. He argued:

> The message is given an air of authority that is quite unscriptural by the words 'Thus saith the Lord'...or 'I, the Lord, am in the midst' or some such words. It can be easily seen that that is flinging back responsibility upon the Lord which He has already placed on the prophet... Let the prophet take responsibility in the Scriptural way for his own utterances, and let him frame them—not as speaking *in the place* of the Lord, but as speaking *about* the Lord.[239]

In Pentecostal circles outside the Apostolic Church the principle enshrined in the verse 'the spirits of the prophets are subject to the prophets' (1 Cor. 14:32), with its implication that the gift is put under the

---

[234] *ACM*, 19 November 1923.

[235] *ACM*, 15 December 1923.

[236] The reference to each is in the *ACM*, 31 October 1925 (first four), 25 April 1925 (fifth), and 3 November 1923 (sixth). The present leadership of the Apostolic Church would tone down such terminology.

[237] *ACM*, 15 December 1923.

[238] *ACM*, 23 November 1924. Context is all-important in interpreting this statement. It comes in the middle of a passage that outlines the functions of different gifts and offices. Preceding the statement is this sentence; 'The gift of prophecy is for edification. We don't take any *orders* through the Gift of Prophecy'. The contrast then is between non-governmental (gift) prophecy and that given through the words of the set prophets in their governmental capacity. It is through those words that 'God speaks definitely and finally'. It is still a strong statement and it is clear that such words are the ones that carry orders.

[239] Harold Horton, *The Gifts of the Spirit*, (Nottingham: AOG, 1934, 10th ed. 1976), pp. 173-4.

control and responsibility of the possessor, carried a salutary corrective as to the manner in which prophecy should be delivered.

Apostolics were as aware of the verse quoted as anyone and were no less concerned than others about the misuse of prophecy. D.P. Williams wrote: 'All the Gifts are under the charge of the Elders of the assemblies to which they belong, and are to be used only under their supervision. Once they use the Gifts at their own disposal, or for personal messages, they open the door to disorder, and to by-ways that lead to confusion and disaster. The gifts are the property of the church'.[240] In practice, there was probably not as wide a difference over the issue as the heat of the controversy would suggest. It was the privileged role of the 'set prophet' that fuelled much of the heat. For Gee, 'The New Testament never makes any distinctions, so that some are clothed with a greater degree of official authority or infallibility than others'.[241]

The record of the prophecies in the Irish minutes leaves a strong impression that, in any weighing of prophetic revelation against apostle-elder authority, it came down rather heavily on the side of the prophetic. This may well reflect the partiality that Phillips, as the Irish superintendent, had for the prophetic word. Arnold probably wrote the minutes, and, with his background as one of the longest-standing Pentecostals in the province, it is reasonable to assume that his decision to join the Apostolic Church must have been one of serious deliberation. It is likely that his commitment to prophecy would have been as strong as that of Phillips. The prophetic text, on a crude estimate, takes up a good half of the content of the minutes, reflecting the view that the presumptive locus of much of the decision-making was heaven.

8.6.2 The Range of Prophecy

Nothing seems to have been too small or trivial to be subjected to prophetic direction. A few examples will suffice. At the Elders' Meeting in August 1923 the following topics were raised: 1. the possibility of holding an evening meeting in Henry Street; 2. the church excursion; 3. the children's picnic arrangements; 4. an issue over tithes; 5. a baptismal service at Whitehead; 6. the handling of money; 7. the frequent absences of elder Allen. Decisions on the first three items seem to have been reached without recourse to prophetic intervention. The rest were subject to direction by the spoken word. On the question of tithes, 'the Lord spake through the prophet saying, "I know the human heart. Ye are not

---

240 Williams, *And They Shall Prophesy*, pp. 28-29.

241 Gee, *'Apostolic Church' Error*, p. 6. The divide may have been bridged if the contending parties had come together in dialogue, but there never was a serious meeting of minds. Aggressive proselytism by Apostolics in some areas and the inflexible stand they took on their claim to have 'a fuller vision' made resolution difficult.

willing to give. It is true there is need for money. I value the principle more than the money. Those who have little, fail me not, saith the Lord. I would have obedience"'.[242] On the topic of Allen's absence, 'the Lord spake and said, "He is coming back. I will use some of ye to bring him back"'.[243] On a different occasion, Phillips, who was keen to purchase a typewriter, was directed to wait and the Lord 'would supply that which was needed in the work'.[244] At another meeting the question of how to handle disruptive boys attending the youth meeting at Great Victoria Street was raised. The guidance was given at the next meeting; 'When [the boys] going too far, be careful; be not too narrow. Well that they come. My word shall have its effect. Let them not see your temper. If leaders are out of sort, what of the meetings?'[245] It is difficult to discern any pattern in those items that were subject to prophetic direction as opposed to those were not. It could be surmised that those matters that might prove embarrassing or require sensitive handling were more likely to be subject to prophetic guidance than less contentious ones.[246]

Other evangelicals who might have appreciated the sound sense in some of these directives questioned the appropriateness of the *systematic* use of prophecy in matters of this kind and feared its habitual use would lead ultimately to its trivialization. When he attended an annual Penygroes Convention, G.H. Lang, the influential Bible teacher, who was in some ways more open to the charismatic dimension than most Brethren, was not particularly impressed by the quality of the prophecy on which such store was placed:

> There were no 'tongues' but there was a lengthy 'prophecy'. It differed nothing from any ordinary exhortation to Christian living except that it purported to be spoken by God Himself. I have read many such 'prophetic' utterances and can only be amazed that godly people should so often presume to put platitudes into the mouth of Almighty God. In many small gatherings, where no claim is made to a special enduement of the Spirit, I have felt more His presence and unction.[247]

Gee was insistent that

---

[242] *ACM*, 25 August 1923.

[243] *ACM*, 25 August 1923.

[244] *ACM*, 31 October 1925.

[245] *ACM*, 27 December 1924.

[246] A possibility that has to be kept in mind is that the wording of minutes may, in the main, give only the sense of the prophecy and not its precise wording. There are inevitably gaps in what was transmitted and a feel for the manner or tone in which it was delivered is impossible to recapture.

[247] G.H. Lang, *The Earlier Years of the Modern Tongues Movement*, (Miami Springs, FL: Conley & Schoettle, 1958), p. 70.

> in most cases [the early Christians] made their decisions by the use of which we often call 'sanctified common sense'... Many of our errors where spiritual gifts are concerned arise when we want the extraordinary and exceptional to be made the frequent and the habitual. Let all who develop excessive desire for 'messages' through the gifts take warning from the wreckage of past generations as well as of contemporaries.[248]

On past evidence, Gee's targets in his last sentence would have included Montanists and Irvingites from the past and Apostolics in the present.

He made the point that in making major decisions even the early church did not necessarily resort to prophecy. He cites the major dispute that arose over circumcision in Acts 15. Again, in handling the prophetic warning of Agabus, Paul decided his own course of action (Acts 21:13). It is an interesting reflection that Vaughan should, at an Elders' Meeting, pronounce through prophecy, 'Do not rely on my Spirit at all times, when ye could have been meditating upon my Word. Ye might say "We have not the time as those called out". How much time do you spend on idle conversation?'.[249]

8.6.3 The Control Function of Prophecy

There are abundant examples in the minutes to demonstrate the governmental function of prophecy in the life of the Apostolic Churches in Ireland. One prophecy laid down that 'Pastor Phillips will supervise over the other assemblies moving in and around. Pastor Arnold will be responsible for Great Victoria Street assembly in conjunction with the Elders'.[250] The position of superintendent of Henry Street assembly was filled through prophecy: 'My servant Ferguson to be superintendent'.[251] Not all prophecy was so pin-pointedly directive. Accommodation to more practised ways of decision-making was not ruled out: 'It is not always my plan to give thee that word that shall be definite as if to see one that has the pitcher'.[252] Direction through prophecy in the Elders' Meeting could just as easily carry a prohibitive as an affirmative message. When the opening of a new work was under consideration at Skipton Street in east Belfast, the message was, 'It is not My will to move in this direction. Move

---

[248] D. Gee, *Spiritual Gifts in the Ministry of the Church Today*, (Springfield, MO: Gospel Publishing House, 1963), pp. 51-2. Dean Inge coined the term 'theopath' for those who seem to put excessive weight on direct illumination and have a weakened regard for rational self-direction.

[249] *ACM*, 25 April 1925,

[250] *ACM*, 18 November 1923.

[251] *ACM*, 30 May 1925.

[252] *ACM*, 30 May 1925. This awkward instruction appears to be a reference to Luke 22:10, where the disciples were given an unambiguous instruction to follow a man carrying a pitcher of water into the house where Last Supper was to be prepared.

as doors open. In getting cottage meetings, take no definite steps in this direction'.[253] 'Seek not to run out of the city [Belfast] at present'[254] was the directive in the early minutes, whereas a year later when consideration was given to the purchase of two tents, there was prophetic encouragement: 'There is yet land to be possessed. I would have ye go forth acknowledging H.Q.'.[255] Indeed, the different strategies for geographical expansion adopted by the Apostolics and Elim owe much to prophetic direction.

As previously shown, Elim in its expansive early days, spread with some rapidity into the market towns and rural byways of Ireland and it was some time before there was an increase in the number of assemblies established in Belfast. By contrast, the Apostolic Church had its strongest base in Belfast with five assemblies, though mostly small, as against Elim's one. The Apostolics were slower to move beyond the city and prophetic direction was on the side of caution on the question of physical expansion. It was not until May 1925 that a prophetic command was given to pray that 'a door be opened into the South of Ireland'.[256] Elim faced the constant danger of extending itself beyond its physical and human resources. Apostolics, confirmed in their caution through the prophetic word, were disposed more to conserve and consolidate their gains before pursuing their more limited advance. One prophecy sounded a guarded note: 'I am not going to move on the Revival System of the past. I am not going to give a flood'.[257] Revival, for Jeffreys, was the permanent norm of the Church insofar as it operated in Pentecostal mode.

The prophetic word could be piercing and uncomfortable in the burden of its message. It was in the area of rebuke that its control function was most distinctively operable. Through prophecy things could be said that would either be left unsaid or else toned down in other settings. Depending on one's perception of the prophetic gift, it was in this area that its potential either for manipulation or salutary guidance was at its highest.[258] There is little record in the Irish minutes of reprimand being directed towards named individuals, though there is an enigmatic

---

[253] *ACM*, 22 August 1924.

[254] *ACM*, 11 November 1923.

[255] *ACM*, 4 June 1924.

[256] *ACM*, 30 May 1925.

[257] *ACM*, 30 May 1925.

[258] An example from a quite different setting illustrates the point. T.C. Darrand wrote of his painful disaffiliation from a Latter Rain church in California in the 1970s. One of his problems was the way the doubts that he confided to elders were recycled in a manipulative way in prophecy addressed to him despite the teaching of the church that prophecy 'was solely the inspiration of God'. (T.C. Darrand and A. Shupe, *Metaphors of Social Control*, p. 183.)

reference to a situation where the leader was warned to 'hold thy peace. Not well with those with foolish talk, [they] hinder My work... If My word is not kept secret, I will bring down my hand upon this work'. The prophecy conveys a degree of warning that becomes heightened by bearing the aura of divine sanction. It is the latter that marks out admonitory prophecy and intensifies the element of threat. Other communions had more formal ways of handling internal disputes that were quite consonant with biblical practice and principle without a weight of impending threat hanging over the outcome.

In most other situations where the rebuke was administered, the target is not specified. At one Elders' Meeting those present were informed by prophecy: 'I am fulfilling my word but some of ye are not fully believing it. I have the thunder at my disposal but I do not desire to frighten ye, therefore I am leading ye by my voice' [259] At another meeting, the prophetic statement that ' Not one of you can say, "I have not failed. I am perfect"' is set in a context that is suggestive of some unease between Bradford and Belfast.[260] Tension is suggested by such utterances as, 'The light from the H.Q. is shining. You, my servant, don't work apart, but take a pattern. Reckon this Central Place [Bradford] to decide', or again, ' There is but one Channel in this land for guidance and wisdom. Despise not that Channel. I have my eye upon you', and finally ' If from the Mount [Penygroes] ye get your directions, your face will shine'. The prophecy could be read as a rap across the knuckles of the elders who were told, 'I am getting ye slowly to become subject'.[261] Was it statements of this nature that roused Gee to assert, 'Indeed, one of the usual results of an abuse of the "prophetic" gift and office is that believers are held under a system of spiritual bondage that has all the elements in it of the despotic rule of the Church of Rome'.[262]

On another occasion, the elders were informed: 'Where there is no principle, each one seeks his own benefit and builds his own house and thinks not about others... There is a crisis'.[263] The context appears to be the reluctance of some leaders to accept responsibilities in assemblies assigned to them by the superintendent. The prophecy spoke of action to be taken and warning of the consequences if it was not taken. The action advised was, 'Be willing to sacrifice to labour to go where I send you. "My disposition", ye say, "is not to be able to go"... It is no light thing that ye are on a Council like this'.[264] In this situation, 'the grindstone is turning [and] you will feel your body against it... Someone's work shall

---

[259] *ACM*, 12 December 1926.

[260] *ACM*, 11 January 1924.

[261] *ACM*, 11 January 1924.

[262] Gee, '*Apostolic Church*' *Error*, pp. 9-10

[263] *ACM*, 3 May 1924.

[264] *ACM*, 3 May 1924.

fall to the ground. It shall crumble. The wagon is going for the stones'.[265] In this particular situation the superintendent—whose responsibility it was to make up the monthly stationing list and who was answerable to Bradford—possibly felt thwarted by a mood of recalcitrance. The solution was crisply expressed: 'To the extent ye are obedient to this Council body, ye shall prosper'.[266]

The prophetic word was not always readily accepted, suggesting that either the hearers or the prophecies, possibly both, were at fault. Egos will out in any situation, prophetic ministry or not. For some, merest slights had to be massaged as in the case 'of Bro. Jones having to apologise to Bro. Kelly for not asking him to take his usual place on the platform [of the tent in Waringstown] when coming in late to one of the meetings'.[267] There were constant calls through prophecy to the leaders to be more self-effacing: 'Ye claim that all fullness is yours but how insufficient you are. Many of you shall have to be led to see your utter failure... Some of ye have rebelled against my ordinations'.[268] The context in this example is obscure but from the final sentence it can be postulated there may have been murmuring against the choice of leaders through prophecy. With little control in the hands of local leaders there was always the potential for an 'us and them' attitude to develop. That some unease caused by the conflation of nationality and leadership is suggested in the remaining words of the prophecy: 'If national be a hindrance, then I can remove them... One nation have I come to call, not holy nations! Everyone has his citizenship, not in the land he was born, but in heaven'.[269]

Some may have been aggrieved at being by-passed, feeling that their gifts and abilities had not been recognised. That this was so is more than hinted at in another prophecy: 'If a man is not satisfied with his calling, I will speak to him... Think not that ye can speak and sow discord behind another's back... If any one soweth discord, ye shall fall away as a branch withereth. Truly the office hath been left vacant. I have removed him'.[270]

---

[265] *ACM*, 3 May 1924.

The minutes record occasional pithy *obiter dicta*, part of what Andrew Walker called 'elegant prophecies'. They include: 'Dip the sword in honey first'; 'What kind of sea is always calm'; 'True joy is the offspring of suffering'; 'Where there is a church without trouble, there is no church'; 'Be willing to be still on the operating table'; 'It is not by great commotion or stamping of the foot but by the foreordained power of the cross [is the way] to true victory'.

[266] *ACM*, 3 May 1924. Underlining in the original.

[267] *ACM*, 13 July 1924.

[268] *ACM*, 24 May 1925.

[269] *ACM*, 24 May 1925. This prophecy was delivered by Omri Jones.

[270] *ACM*, 23 November 1924. The 'him' is not named. The prophecy was given by Herbert Cousen from Bradford who two years earlier had been appointed treasurer of the first Missionary Council. The prophecy would indicate that headquarters had its fingers

In ruling the church, prophecy then could be wielded as a sharp sword. It was made all the more unnerving by the sweeping nature of its targets. Used in the ways discussed here, it could and did act as a powerful means of directive control. Whether or not in any one situation it served the divine purpose or muddied human interests remains imponderable to the detached outsider.

The rest of the Pentecostal movement was uncomfortable with the Apostolic understanding of the role of prophecy in the governance of the church. None denied that God at times could use prophecy in a directive way but that was an insufficient basis for turning it into a system. In Gee's exegesis of 1 Timothy 3, he held that 'it is not prophetic utterances, but plain fitness for office that is the Divine basis of selection [to office]'.[271] Horton was adamant that

> In the New Testament, correction and rebuke come not this way [by prophecy/interpretation of tongues] but through the application of the Word in teaching and doctrine. Concerning all the improprieties and excesses that needed correction and rebuke in Corinth, Paul ministers not as a prophet but as a teacher and pastor... He wrote pastoral advice, applying the Written Word of God to every problem...[272]

> The Lord has not left His people at the mercy either of office-hunters or even genuine holders of spiritual gifts misusing them through ignorance or prejudice or selfishness.[273]

To Gee the acceptance of the principle of systematic prophetic guidance 'will *always* mean that sooner or later there will come a bitter disillusionment when the supposed infallibility and presumed Divine

---

on the pulse of the situation in Ireland, and that most assuredly through the superintendent.

[271] Gee,'*Apostolic Church*' *Error*, p. 7.

[272] Horton, *The Gifts of the Spirit*, p. 169. Horton's proposition as expressed here is not well considered. For one, it could be deemed anachronistic. Paul's pastoral ministry began before there was 'the Written Word of God'. Andrie du Toit points out in an article on the NT canon, 'Initially the gospel message was transmitted orally. In this period the young church was guided in addition to the Old Testament, first by the apostolic witness, which developed into the apostolic tradition, and second by early Christian prophecy ...The authors of the early Christian documents did not visualise their writings as part of a future canon'. (See Bruce M. Metzger and Michael D. Coogan, *The Oxford Companion to the Bible*, [New York: O.U.P, 1993, p. 102).

I Cor. 14: 3 would suggest that prophecy extended to the pastoral as well as the didactic needs of the early Christians: Paul writes of it being 'for their strengthening, encouragement and comfort'. Malherbe, for example, identifies 'the term ('comfort') closely with the attitude and activity of *pastoral care*'. (Anthony C. Thistleton, *The First Epistle to the Corinthians*, [Grand Rapids: Eerdmans, 2000], p. 1089.)

[273] Horton, *The Gifts of the Spirit*, p. 173.

source of the inspiration is sometimes plainly at fault'.[274] He also drew attention to 'a sinister element in all such systems' whereby, on occasions when members show signs of restlessness and dissatisfaction, an attempt is made to coerce others by 'prophecies' of a threatening nature, creating a spirit of fear'.[275] People then were placed in the invidious position of being cowed into submission because for them to question the prophet was to question God. To be critical, therefore, was tantamount to showing a lack of faith and being unspiritual. The outcome, as Gee had 'sometimes seen by experience', was that one of three paths could be taken: '(a) To coerce one's conscience into accepting a system which the heart knows to be wrong; or (b) the temptation to throw the whole thing up altogether and relapse into utter worldliness; or (c) by the grace of God be delivered from this error'.[276]

8.7 The Apostolic Option within Pentecostalism

In conclusion, it can be seen that the Apostolic Church in Ireland brought a variant of Pentecostalism that did not sit easily with the dominant Elim movement or the minority independents. Arriving later than Elim it never achieved the same hold in the province for reasons which have been suggested. The Apostolic Church, drawing much of its inspiration from Hutchinson's bold experimentation, presented to the rest of the movement a challenge on the adequacy of its ecclesiology and the sincerity of its desire to reclaim the panoply of the primitive church. Gee acknowledged as much and stated it was 'a challenge which needs thorough examining. No believer who is seriously anxious to go all the way with God will lightly turn away from what *may* be a fuller revelation of the Divine Mind'.[277] He also presented a rationale for its early growth period: 'It was largely due to the fact that their vision of church

---

[274] Gee,'*Apostolic Church' Error*, p. 9

[275] Gee,'*Apostolic Church' Error*, p. 10.

Nigel Scotland cites the fairly recent example of Chris Brain, the leader of the Sheffield Nine O'clock Service, who 'began prophesying as a means of controlling his leadership team who he felt were undermining him'. (Scotland, *Charismatics and the New Millennium*, p. 168.)

[276] Gee,'*Apostolic Church' Error*, p. 9. Though he spoke at the Apostolic Convention at Penygroes in 1939, Gee, despite his ecumenical heart, never found it easy to apply his generosity of spirit to the Apostolic Church, even as late as 1947. When the first meeting of the World Pentecostal Conference at Zurich was at the planning stage, he led the opposition to the Apostolic Church being invited to send delegates, though he did not hold out at the end for their exclusion. (Peter Hocken, *Donald Gee- Pentecostal Ecumenist?*, p. 13; paper delivered at the joint meeting of The Society for Pentecostal Studies and The European Pentecostal and Charismatic Research Association, 1995.)

[277] Gee, '*Apostolic Church' Error*, p. 3.

government came at a time when the need for something of that sort was desperately realised among many Pentecostal people'.[278] He should know because he was one of such people but saw the answer lying within a structured fellowship of independent assemblies operating on different principles from Elim's centralised and the Apostolics' theocratic polity.

The theocratic ideal within Christianity is probably one of the most difficult to sustain in a fallen world. There are few models on offer in recent church history. In the early days of the Apostolic Faith Church at Bournemouth, W.O. Hutchinson found that those called to the prophetic office had to cope with doubt and despondency. In an editorial he wrote in 1915, he admitted that 'the experience of the earlier Catholic Apostolic Church ministry was extremely helpful to him in the dilemma he was facing. He saw a parallel between the recantation of Robert Baxter [then] and one of his own prophets, E.C.W. Boulton'.[279] The Irvingite experiment was hardly a conspicuous success and those sections of the 'House Church' movement in the 1960s that adopted a similar polity were soon to find they were running into similar problems to those encountered in this chapter. The Apostolic Church adapted to changing conditions in modifying much of its prophetic practice, most notably in bridling the practice of 'enquiring of the Lord through the prophet' when it came to dealing with personal and private matters. Prophecy came more assuredly under the covering of the apostles and elders. Within the Pentecostal movement as a whole the old wounds over the contentious issues of the past have all but healed with the first purposeful start made through the Unity Conferences of 1939 and 1940. The whole movement has come to terms with the more painful side of its internal quarrels. Marching with the greater spirit of openness that developed between all denominations in the second half of the twentieth century, the Pentecostal movement has accommodated itself increasingly to the spirit of the times where dialogue and convergence have replaced cold-shouldering and divergence. On the other hand, that this has happened without seriously compromising the imprinted core beliefs, values and practices of the different parties, means that organic unity between all the classical Pentecostal denominations can scarcely be contemplated.[280]

The period studied in this chapter is of wider interest to the church historian who has few readily available examples of an ecclesial polity that challenges all others by claiming a biblically warranted privilege of direct access to the Divine Mind in the government of the church, a position that other traditions, both Pentecostal and mainstream, perceived as disturbingly flawed. Yet, a surprisingly favourable reaction, springing

---

[278] Gee, *Wind and Flame*, p. 106.

[279] Worsfold, *The Origins of the Apostolic Church,* p. 136.

[280] The relationship between Elim and the AOG has grown increasingly harmonious in recent years.

from a purely adventitious contact with an Apostolic assembly, was expressed by B.H. Streeter (1874-1937), the distinguished Oxford New Testament scholar, when, as Canon-in-Residence at Hereford Cathedral, he visited a back street Apostolic Church under the impression it was some American sect of dubious orthodoxy. From what he saw and heard, he came to the conclusion that 'if history was to have the last word and a choice had to be made between the Church of England and the Hereford sect,..the latter was quite clearly nearer the apostolic pattern'.[281] As to the question which type of church would have the greater appeal, then 'for the majority of men in these days, there was...a real danger of the Church of England being strangled by archaeology'—a surmise that has proved to be not without substance. This remark of Streeter, based as it was on a fleeting visit, was not a typical reaction which at the time was one more of sharp opposition to the Apostolic Church in the British Isles from its fellow Pentecostals. However, time brings change and new adaptations and at present the whole 'apostolic' concept has witnessed a remarkable renascence among influential networks of charismatic churches operating largely from America but extending to global scale.

Two representative figures of this development are Bill Hamon, founder of Christian International, an ecclesial network over which he exercises the office of apostle, and Peter Wagner, retired professor at Fuller Seminary and a specialist in Church Growth and leader of the New Apostolic Reformation network. This body is but part of a wider movement of essentially autonomous churches that, while avoiding conventional denominational structures, recognise the apostolic authority of a prophetically called leadership.[282] Wagner was informed in 1996 by David Barrett, editor of the *World Christian Encyclopaedia,* that he had 1,000 apostolic networks on his data-base and he estimated that at that point there was more than 100 million new apostolic adherents world-wide.[283] He added that in virtually every region of the world, these new apostolic churches constitute the fastest growing segment of Christianity.

---

[281] Stuart Mews: 'The revival of spiritual healing in the Church of England', in W. J. Shiels (ed.), *The Church and Healing*, (Oxford: Blackwell, 1982), p. 321.

[282] Titles of books by the two men catch the burden of their vision for the church of the future: Bill Hamon, *Apostles, Prophets and the Coming Moves of God: God's End-time Plans for his Church and Planet Earth*, (Shippenburg, PA: Destiny Image Publishers, 1997), and C. Peter Wagner, *Apostles and Prophets: The Foundation of the Church*, (Ventura, CA: Regal, 2000). The author on a visit to New Zealand in 2001 passed such a church going under the name 'New Apostolic Reformation Church'.

[283] C. Peter Wagner, *Churchquake: How the New Apostolic Reformation is Shaking Up the Church As We Know It,* (Ventura: Regal, 1999), p. 47. For recent trends see *Annual Statistical Table on Global Mission: 2001* in the *International Bulletin of Missionary Research*, Vol. 25, January 2001, pp. 24-5.

Conclusion

The growth of Pentecostalism on the global scale is little short of spectacular, though it is not evenly spread. By 2010, it is estimated that Europe will have only 3% of the world's Pentecostals, a figure places it near the bottom of the league table. In comparison, the two American continents will account for around 65%.[1] The 1998 figure for Sunday attendance at church in England show that around 6% are Pentecostal and if the New Churches, which are mainly charismatic, are added then the figure increases to near 12%.[2] A roughly comparable figure for Northern Ireland at the last census in the year 2001 is around 1% of all church members, or 2% of the Protestant population.[3] In the province about 4% of congregations and 5% of ministers are Pentecostal.[4] On the assumption that these figures give a reasonably accurate snapshot of Pentecostalism at the end of the twentieth century in Ulster, then these figures hardly portray a movement that has enjoyed unremitting success, even when the statistics are teased out.[5]

---

[1] Peter Brierley, *Future Church: A Global Analysis of the Christian Community to the Year 2000*, (Crowborough: Monarch Book), p. 124. It is estimated that North America will account for 27% and South America for 38% of world Pentecostals.

[2] Peter Brierley, *The Tide is Running Out: What the English Church Attendance Survey Reveals,* (London: Christian Research, 2000), pp. 34; 37.

[3] Peter Brierley (ed.), *Irish Christian Handbook 1995/6,* (London: Christian Research, 1994), p. 29. The figures for England referred to Sunday attenders, a more limited group than church membership numbers. It is likely that measured by the English criterion the percentage of Pentecostals would be higher, though hardly more than the figures (4-5%) quoted in the next sentence in the text.

[4] The figures would indicate that the average size of Pentecostal church buildings and congregations is appreciably smaller than those of mainstream churches.

[5] Some of the statistical information provided in the *Irish Christian Handbook 1995/6* has been treated with some scepticism in denominational headquarters. The 2001 Northern Ireland Census gave the figure of 5,448 (5,847 if Whitewell Metropolitan Tabernacle is added) for the Elim Church, whereas the *Handbook* estimated 6,500 for 1995 and the internally collated Elim figure based on Sunday attendance was 10,000. Comparable figures for the Presbyterian Church (PCI) were a Census total of 348,742, a *Handbook* estimate of 194,718 and an internal audit based on actual attendance gave 288,000. The Elim audit showed it was considerably under-represented in the national Census while that for the PCI would indicate a sizeable nominal membership. (Norman Richardson (ed.), *A Tapestry of Beliefs: Christian Traditions in Northern Ireland,* [Belfast: Blackstaff Press, 1998], p. 6.) The 2001 census figures for the smaller Pentecostal groups were: Church of God (990), Apostolic Church (237), AOG (216), Bible-Pattern Church (10). Other figures lack denominational precision: Pentecostal (5,533), Charismatic (93). The grand total of all these groups, including Elim, is 13,026.

There are good extrinsic reasons, irrespective of any intrinsic deficiencies, why it was never going to be easy to establish Pentecostal denominations in the already crowded market place of Ulster Protestantism. The historic 'settler' Churches, essentially the Anglican and Presbyterian, still account for around 80% of those claiming membership of the Protestant churches. These Churches have traditionally reflected the ethno-political attitudes of their membership. The sometimes bitter struggle between the Anglican Established Church and Presbyterian Nonconformity of the seventeenth and eighteenth centuries evoked an intense loyalty to their own tradition in the members of the two denominations. Intra-Protestant rivalry only began to abate in the first half of the nineteenth century with the rising perceived threat of Catholic domination of the political and religious life of the island. It was during this period that evangelicalism began to take on the mantle of guardian of the soul of Ulster Protestantism in its resistance to Catholic and nationalist claims. Bruce goes as far as to argue that, for the majority Protestant community, 'beyond evangelical Protestantism, no secure identity is available'.[6] This identification has unleashed powerful forces of conservatism inside the settler churches and has continued to evoke a strong loyalty to them.

That loyalty to the church of one's forefathers remains strong is demonstrated in the fortunes of the Free Presbyterian Church of Ulster, which, except for one year, has recognised Ian Paisley as its Moderator since its foundation in 1951. While his Democratic Unionist Party in 2004 became for the first time the largest Unionist Party, his Free Presbyterian Church has never constituted a serious threat to the older churches. In the 2001 Census, the Free Presbyterians numbered 11,902 adherents, a figure that places the Church within sight of the total of Pentecostals. Clearly, Paisleyism as an identity marker is much stronger politically than ecclesially.

The argument presented here is that if the Free Presbyterian Church, carrying as it does some of the powerful resonance of political Paisleyism

---

The figures do not give a clear picture of the strength of the New Churches which constitute part of the wider charismatic movement and owe little to direct contact with classical Pentecostalism. Of the latter, Peter Smith wrote that 'help and advice were offered in many cases, but generally speaking, these were rejected, the implication being that the classical Pentecostal churches had run their course and had nothing to contribute to the current debate'. Smith is pastor of the Ballymena Elim Church and contributed Chapter 9, 'The Elim Pentecostal Church', to Richardson, *A Tapestry of Beliefs*. See p. 149.

[6] Steve Bruce, *God Save Ulster: The Religion and Politics of Paisleyism,* (Oxford: Clarendon Press, 1986), p. 258. The popular support for Paisley's brand of unionism, for Bruce (p. 264), 'defies any explanation other than the obvious one; evangelicalism provides the core beliefs, values, and symbols of what it means to be a Protestant'.

and established in conditions that could scarcely have been more favourable to it, could only bite at the edge of the support of the mainline churches, then that is a measure of the uphill task faced by any new movement, of whatever provenance, to make its presence felt in the province. The same point can be illustrated from the Christian Brethren. This nineteenth-century renewal movement that has been operative in Ireland for well over a century had, according to the most recent Census, 8,595 adherents, a figure that that represents a 30% decline from the previous census, when its membership was about the same as the Free Presbyterians. Pentecostalism began to establish itself approximately midway in time between these two movements and finds itself in a similar numerical league as the other two. Map D illustrates the point that the main concentrations of Free Presbyterians and Brethren, outside Belfast, are to be found in or contiguous to the Bann-Braid corridor and the Linen Triangle similar, in other words, to that of the Pentecostals. Thus, all three bodies, at different times, have found themselves fishing in the same pool, enough to generate a certain wariness among themselves. These three together with others of kindred zeal and outlook, such as the Faith Mission, also had their own tussles with the mainline churches.[7]

Despite their numerical strength, the impression must not be conveyed that the settler Churches were or remain monolithic blocs. At times they were subject to severe internal tensions and minor schisms, but it was not until the challenge of Methodist revivalism and the aftermath of the 1859 Revival that their dominant position was seriously tested. It was that event, more than any other, that opened up the countryside in particular to new, dynamic movements. Hempton asserts that the Revival 'was prompted chiefly by the laity, not the clergy, and transcended traditional boundaries of authority, taste and religious respectability'.[8] Popular evangelicalism continued to be drip-fed by numerous evangelistic bodies and proselytising sects, enough to keep the larger bodies on their toes if they were ever tempted to decry conversionist zeal.[9] If they were suspected of slipping in this regard, then others were not slow to move in.[10] The Presbyterian historian, W.L. Latimer, saw, among the undesirable outcomes of the 1859 Revival, the strengthening of 'almost all the smaller

---

[7] See p. 32 for the spat between the Ballymena Presbytery and a supporter of the Faith Mission.

[8] S.J. Connolly (ed.), *The Oxford Companion to Irish History*, (Oxford: Oxford University Press, 1998), p. 485.

[9] Three such that arose in the latter part of the century were the Irish Evangelisation Society, for which Robert Mercer's father was a lay preacher, the Faith Mission and the Irish Christian and Missionary Workers' Union, founded in 1898. None of these bodies sought to take denominational form.

[10] W.T. Latimer, *A History of the Irish Presbyterians,* (Belfast: James Cleeland, 1902), p. 496.

sects of religious enthusiasts' with a concomitant increase in 'a desire for modes of worship which excite the feelings'.[11] Stewart Brown contends that the Revival 'rather than restore the ideal of the covenanted community, under the leadership of an educated and ordained Presbyterian clergy, instead contributed to the spread of a personal and subjective faith, deeply concerned with personal salvation and open to charismatic influences'.[12] It was for the group of young men who invited George Jeffreys to Ireland to test just how ready the religiously inclined people of Ireland could advance in the charismatic dimension.

When Jeffreys arrived in the province in 1913, it was a place apart where its countryside and towns were generously provided with gospel outlets and the itinerant evangelist was no stranger. The gospel halls were, and to a lesser extent still are, in Hempton's words, 'theatres of popular religious conflict as well as centres of genuine religious devotion... At the peak of their influence they sustained a peripatetic ministry of lay preachers which sometimes acted as a springboard for all kinds of leadership in working-class neighbourhoods'.[13] It was not unusual for members of the mainline churches to support and engage in the work of the mission hall and at the same time retain their membership of a larger denominational body. The denomination represented family, community, *pietas*, while the mission hall appealed to the heart, a place of intimate fellowship where a more vital religion could be sustained.

The 1859 Revival facilitated denominational pluralism that downplayed denominational differences and theological distinctions. Such pluralism, while it could encourage sizeable gatherings, could not always guarantee a membership committed to a new denomination, as leaders of Elim at times found to their chagrin. The anonymous letter dealing with the problems of the Elim assembly in Lurgan quoted previously was written some four years after the first stirring events in the town.[14] Jeffreys held a two-week long mission in August 1920 in the Town Hall that was filled to its capacity of 1,000 seats. Many nights people had to be turned away and soon an assembly was formed and a new hall erected on the site where the tent had been set up and used before the move to the Town Hall. Around 200 conversions were recorded during the mission and the *Evangel* reported that 'some have been baptised in the Holy Ghost. Others have testified to having been

---

[11] Latimer, *A History of the Irish Presbyterians*, p. 494.

[12] Stewart Brown, 'Presbyterian Communities, Transatlantic Visions and the Ulster Revival of 1859', in J.P. Mackey (ed.), *The Cultures of Europe: The Irish Contribution*, (Belfast: Institute of Irish Studies, 1992), p. 103.

[13] D. Hempton, 'Gospel Halls', in Connolly, *Oxford Companion to Irish History*, p. 223.

[14] See pp. 231-32.

healed of bodily infirmities'.[15] Yet, a few years later the assembly gave every impression of going into a tailspin.

Having examined some factors external to the Pentecostal movement that have impinged upon its impact in the province, it is possible to come to a tentative conclusion. If the movement has not seen great numerical growth, then it is no more or less successful than other denominations that might, on the face of it, have a bigger claim to expect it. Such elevated expectation could apply to the Free Presbyterians whose leader has swept all before him in electoral success, yet his church has never seriously challenged the dominance of the settler churches. In terms of numerical strength, Elim and the Free Presbyterians are in the second league of the churches in Ulster.[16] However, it would be facile to equate influence with numerical strength because a growing awareness, even appreciation, of Pentecostal/Charismatic spirituality is not limited to the classical Pentecostal bodies. Other agents of diffusion continue to be operative, creating a more tolerant and accepting attitude towards the charismatic dimension in the life of the church. Such agencies include: Irish participants in the Spring Harvest festivals; the architectural impressiveness of the Whitewell Metropolitan Tabernacle, Belfast, and the weekly services on a TV channel transmitted from it; the growing number of independent 'new churches' most of them born from the 1960s' Charismatic Movement; the Christian Renewal Centre at Rostrevor, County Down; the Charismatic Renewal Prayer Meetings found in Catholic congregations throughout Ireland and the ecumenical fellowships that have grown out of a mutually recognised 'oneness in the Spirit'.[17] Some churches now sponsor courses to help the participants 'discover one's gifting'—a direction that owes much to the mild charismaticism that has entered many 'lively' churches. Pentecostals find

---

[15] *EE*, December 1920, p. 3.

[16] In the *first category* are the Roman Catholic, Presbyterian, Church of Ireland, and Methodist Churches. Baptists and Brethren join the Free Presbyterians and Elim in the *second category* (defined here as lying in the range of 5,000-20,000 members, and based on the figures as estimated in Brierley [ed.], *Irish Christian Handbook*, p. 6). Included in the *third category* are Congregationalists, Non-Subscribing, Reformed and Evangelical Presbyterians, Holiness Groups (Salvation Army, Church of the Nazarene and Free Methodists), Quakers and the smaller Pentecostal groups (Apostolic Church and the Assemblies of God).

[17] *NIPCDM*, p. 132, gives the following statistics for Ireland: Pentecostals 3,056; Charismatics 466,998; Neocharismatics 19,946; Total Renewal 490,000. The 2001 edition of Johnstone, *Operation World,* p.359, modifies these figures considerably—Pentecostals 9,000; Charismatics 246,000. The population of the Republic of Ireland is c.3.8 million. For a summary survey of evangelicalism in Ireland see Patrick Mitchel, 'Living with Difference: Evangelical Diversity', in Robert Dunlop (ed.), *Evangelicals in Ireland: An Introduction*, (Dublin: Columba Press, 2004), pp. 140-69.

many of these sessions rather pallid in that the gifting usually 'discovered' tends to undervalue the more 'supernatural' gifts detailed in 1 Corinthians 12, a chapter that provides much of the biblical backing for the whole enterprise. Probably the most potent source of diffusion will prove to be the *Alpha Course*. The course has been promoted in many of the mainline churches throughout the island. Much store is laid by the devisers of the *Alpha* material on groups convening week-end conferences, roughly mid-course, when the topics of Spirit-baptism and *glossolalia* are discussed, not just to raise awareness among the participants of the charismatic dimension but also to encourage them to move in that realm.

A theme of this work has been to examine some of the ways the Pentecostal movement has conformed to the religio-cultural environment of Ulster during its early years. Cultural context always carries the potential to have a weighty effect on any movement, enough to lend it a distinctive regional form. The strength of popular Protestantism as a cultural force in Ulster is unmatched in few other places, except possibly some parts of the southern states of the USA. In the province newly arrived movements face something of a bear's hug: they have either to accept an embrace to sniff out their orthodoxy or, failing in that regard, be squeezed to death. Neither avoidance of theological liberalism nor doctrinal heterodoxy is enough for acceptability; there must also be no hint of socio-political radicalism. On both scores, early Pentecostalism passed, certainly enough to satisfy the management of Orange Halls of the movement's *bona fides*. Pentecostals never questioned the verbal inspiration and authority of Scripture and biblical warrant was always their prime recourse in debate. The movement's eschatological acceptance of premillennial dispensationalism disposed it towards quiescence on social and political matters.[18] At the end of the twentieth century, there was no substantive evidence that the movement as a whole sought to escape its cultural accommodation to the socio-political conservatism embedded in Ulster Protestantism.

The movement as a whole has not moved greatly from its early stance of pietistic wariness towards 'the things of the world'. Any involvement in tackling wider politico-societal concerns tends to focus on defending the 'Protestant heritage' rather than contributing to a wider Christian search for reconciliation in a notoriously divided society. It is in this area that a major theological divide between 'conservative' and 'liberal-conservative' evangelical traditions is at its most stark. Brewer is of the opinion that the measure of its intensity is reflected today in the struggle

[18] There is a fairly well-established link between premillennialism and otherworldly spirituality. Once Christabel Pankhurst accepted premillennial teaching, she abandoned her commitment to the cause of the electoral enfranchisement of women. (Randall, *Evangelical Experiences*, p. 162.)

to represent the soul of evangelicalism between the more fundamentalist Caleb Foundation and the 'neo-evangelical' ECONI (Evangelical Contribution on Northern Ireland).[19] A representative voice of the former holds that 'what Ulster needs today is not the neo-evangelism (*sic*) of ...ECONI, but a revival of the sound Biblical evangelicalism of the apostles, reformers, puritans and leaders of the evangelical awakening. This could transform the whole political and spiritual climate of our Province to the glory of God and for the good of all'.[20] The Director of ECONI sees the situation differently: 'For religious Protestants, raised on the myths of protest, defiance and martyrdom, compromise is a dirty word. To have an unyielding mind is a compliment, a sign of faithfulness to the biblical gospel... The reality is that for a significant number of Protestants, particularly Evangelicals, to negotiate the political future is, at least subconsciously, an act of religious compromise'.[21] An archetypal publication of ECONI is one with the title *The Future with Hope: Biblical Frameworks for Peace and Reconciliation.*

The Caleb Foundation is representative of those evangelicals profoundly disturbed by the recent political and constitutional changes that have taken place in the province, particularly since the signing of the Anglo-Irish Agreement in 1985 which for the first time gave the Republic a significant consultative role in the affairs of Northern Ireland. In general, 'liberal-conservative' evangelicals have been more prepared than more fundamentalist evangelicals to accept the degree of accommodation to nationalist opinion that events subsequent to 1985 have necessitated. Besides people drawn from the smaller conservative denominations, including Elim, the Foundation also has supporters from the Lord's Day Observance Society, the Evangelical Protestant Society, the Independent Fundamentalist Mission and the European Institute of Protestant Studies based at Dr Paisley's Martyrs Memorial Church.[22] At the time of writing, the secretary of the Foundation is the pastor of an Elim church. When, in 2000, a DUP member of the Assembly urged the Community Relations Council to review its core funding to ECONI, he stated that his call had the support, *inter alia,* 'of the Elim and Pentecostal churches, and anti-ecumenist organisations such as the Caleb Foundation'.[23] He added that

---

[19] See John D. Brewer, 'Continuity and Change in Contemporary Ulster Protestantism', *The Sociological Review*, Vol. 52.2, May 2004, pp. 265-83.

[20] Wallace Thompson, 'An Exercise in Propaganda', *Lion & Lamb*, (Belfast: ECONI, 2000), Vol. 27, p. 17.

[21] David Porter, 'Negotiating the Future', in *Lion & Lamb*, (Belfast: ECONI, 1996), Vol. 9, p. 3.

[22] *Belfast Telegraph*, 10 October 1998.

[23] Dr Ian Paisley leads the Democratic Unionist Party (DUP). It became the largest Unionist party for the first time in its history in the election to the Northern Ireland

'ECONI had persistently attacked aspects of Protestant culture and did not have the confidence of the evangelical community'.[24] At the time of asking, only one Pentecostal adherent was known to have some contact with ECONI.

At least two points for debate can be raised by the general alignment of classic Pentecostalism in Ulster with theological fundamentalism. First, historically the theological differences between the two have rendered them anything but easy partners. In 1928, the World's Christian Fundamentals Association in America formally ousted Pentecostalism, passing a resolution that spoke of the movement as 'a menace in many churches and a real injury to the sane testimony of Fundamental Christians' and declared itself 'unreservedly opposed to modern Pentecostalism, including the speaking in unknown tongues, and the fanatical healing known as general healing in the atonement'.[25] The tempestuous Carl McIntire wrote of tongues as 'one of the great signs of the apostasy'.[26] Synan takes the view that the break with Fundamentalism in America in 1928 and compounded later in 1943 'turned out to be a blessing that freed the rising Pentecostals from the dead cultural and theological baggage of a discredited movement and opened up the way for unparalleled influence and growth and influence in the last half of the twentieth century'.[27] One of the contributors to *The Fundamentals*, the series of pamphlets published in 1910 from which the term fundamentalism is derived, was the noted British preacher and biblical expositor, G. Campbell Morgan. He is reputed to have stated that Pentecostalism was 'the last vomit of Satan'. This remark as stated and attributed to Morgan has never been traced to any reliable source. However, similar sentiments demonising Pentecostalism abounded at the time from a variety of sources. In a personal letter to Mrs Jessie Penn-Lewis, A.A. Boddy called on her not to tell the newly Spirit-baptised that 'they are possessed by the Devil or any but by the Holy Spirit Himself'.[28]

Assembly in 2004. The Assembly was suspended at the time and, at the time of writing, its future is subject to on-going negotiation and agreement.

[24] *Belfast Telegraph*, 19 February 2000.

[25] H.V. Synan, 'Fundamentalism', in *NIDPCM*, pp. 657-8.

[26] Quoted in Hollenweger, *Pentecostalism: Origins and Developments,* p. 193.

[27] Synan, 'Fundamentalism', p. 658. There is some validity in the view that American and British fundamentalism are sufficiently different not to allow easy comparison. Nevertheless, some leading fundamentalists in America have long-standing ties and sympathies with Ulster fundamentalism, notably the link between Bob Jones University and Dr Ian Paisley who was awarded an honorary doctorate from the university in 1966 in recognition of his services to fundamentalism. The American Scopes 'Monkey Trial' in 1925 and Caleb's current protestations, both dealing with the issue of teaching evolution in schools, are markers of a shared theological mindset.

[28] Letter dated 1 June 1907, *Mattersey Archives.*

Boddy could speak feelingly on this issue in that his brother-in-law, the Rev. James Pollock came to renounce his Pentecostal experience as of the Devil.

The growing influence that Synan alluded to can find no better illustration than the swing to accommodate Pentecostal spirituality at Fuller Theological Seminary, California, a highly regarded institution that sees itself itself as conforming to a 'classic evangelical ethos'.[29] In 1958 the Seminary established the David J. du Plessis Centre for Christian Spirituality, du Plessis being a leading figure in the charismatic renewal in the 1960s. The centre was headed by Russell P. Spittler, an Assemblies of God minister who by the time of his retirement was Provost and Vice President of Academic Affairs. In the *Festschrift* presented to Spittler, Hollenweger said of him that though Spittler grew up in a climate that thought the best bulwark against unbelief was a rigorous doctrine of the inerrancy of Scripture, he also 'found out that this fundamentalism proved as ineffective as a lifeless liberalism. It did not prevent Pentecostalism and Evangelicalism from developing vastly differing spiritualities, theologies and political loyalties, all of them claiming that they stood for nothing less than the truth of the biblical message'.[30] The Pentecostal critique of other traditions dwelt more on their wilted spiritualities than either their watered down or cessationist theologies.

Pentecostalism needs neither to take its identity from others nor lose it in others. With its growing maturity it can be less defensive and more prepared at its thinking edge to engage intellectually and spiritually with other traditions. Harvey Cox, speaking largely of America, recognises that the movement has developed its own critical tradition: 'Young Pentecostal pastors and theologians are studying social ethics and liberation theology... Many are co-operating in ecumenical organisations and working with other churches in social action programmes'.[31] Similarly, moves to engage with academia have taken place in Britain. For example, postgraduate courses in Pentecostal and Charismatic Studies are presently provided at the Universities of Birmingham and Bangor (University of Wales). Dr William Kay, an Assemblies of God minister, is Director of the Centre for Pentecostal and Charismatic Studies, Bangor. In addition to holding his position in Bangor, he is Senior Lecturer in Religious and Theological Education, King's College, London. Elim's residential Regents Theological College at Nantwich provides courses accredited by

---

[29] Quoted in George M. Marsden, *Reforming Fundamentalism: Fuller Seminary and the New Evangelicalism*, (Grand Rapids, MI: Eerdmans, 1987), p. 295

[30] Walter J. Hollenweger, 'Critical Loyalty', in Wonsuk Ma and Robert P. Menzies (eds), *The Spirit and Spirituality: Essays in Honour of Russell P. Spittler*, (London: T&T Clark International, 2004), p. 6.

[31] Harvey Cox, 'Into the Age of Miracles: Culture, Religion and the Market Revolution', *World Policy Journal*, Vol. 14 (Spring, 1997), p. 95.

Manchester University for both undergraduates and the postgraduate MA in Pentecostal and Charismatic Studies. It is by such advances that 'poor hermeneutics and unreflective theology'[32] may be stemmed in their undermining of a movement of its potential to appeal to a wider constituency than at present.

A second area of debate goes to the very heart of Pentecostal teaching, namely the nature and range of Spirit-baptism. Is Spirit-baptism no more than a top layer to fundamentalism or, as sometimes put, a sort of fundamentalism plus? Or is it a spirituality that gives rise to a different way of being a Christian, one that moves into a new dimension with its 'own mission, its own hermeneutic and its own agenda'[33]—not, wastefully, to boost its own identity but, more radically, to bear witness to its insights to the whole people of God in all their different hues? Dempster points out that after the mid-century Charismatic Renewal, 'Pentecostals surprisingly found themselves sharing their *distinctive* experience of Holy Spirit baptism with Roman Catholic and Orthodox Christians. And equally surprising, the Third Wave of the Holy Spirit has more recently brought evangelical Christians into the supernatural experience of the Spirit's empowerment for Christian mission. These liberating movements provide a more inclusive community for

[32] See paper given at the Annual Conference of the Society for Pentecostal Studies 20001 by Derek Vreeland, 'Reconstructing Word of Raith Theology', published in *Refleks* 1-2 (Oslo: 2002), pp. 51-68. Vreeland makes the point that 'Pentecostal history has taught the lesson that charismatic movements begin in a flurry of spiritual intensity that produce a raw and somewhat primitive theology... It requires humility to admit areas of excess and biblical weakness... An attempt must be made to join the Pentecostal struggle to synthesize experience and scholarship in the pursuit to understand the truth of God's Word and proclaim it to the world' (p. 68) . In Percy's view, such a synthesis 'may prove illusive for a movement that essentially works by abrogating rationality [and] is mainly configured through feeling'. (Martyn Percy, 'Is there a Modern Charismatic Theology?', www.farmington.ac.uk/documents/ol_docs/mt6.html.)

[33] D. William Faupel, 'Whither Pentecostalism?', *Pneuma*, 15.1 (1993), p. 26. In terms of historical dating, Pentecostalism preceded modern fundamentalism. Faupel, from his studies, concluded that Pentecostalism 'arose, in large part, as a critique directed at an emerging fundamentalism which was attaching itself to the [nineteenth-century] Old Princeton Theology'. (Hollenweger, *Pentecostalism: Origins and Developments,* p. 191.) Indeed, as Cox points out, 'not long after the Pentecostals appeared on the scene, one stern Princeton Presbyterian naysayer declared that because they believed in contemporary miracles they were as bad as Catholics'. (Harvey Cox, 'Age of Miracles' *World Policy Journal*, Vol. 14 (Spring, 1997), pp. 87-95, on the website http://www.dickinson.edu/~rose/coxrevpqdweb.html. The writings of Princetonians, notably Warfield, Machen, the Hodges, father and son, remain favoured by the many well read evangelicals in the older Reformed/Calvinist tradition in Ulster.

theological reflection on Pentecostal identity'.[34] Robeck believes that Pentecostals, if true to their roots, are ecumenical but 'just don't know it', and multi-cultural but have yet to learn 'how to act like it'.[35] Mary Boddy said of her father that he 'had always been ecumenically minded and indeed was much in advance of his day in his ideas of unity'.[36] Boddy was in a position to commend his friend Cecil Polhill for convening a 'remarkable gathering...of Christian workers to consider "the deplorable need of London"'.[37] Proceedings were opened by the Bishop of Southwark and addresses were given a variety of speakers, including a Moravian Bishop, the chairman of the Keswick Convention, Albert Head, the Scottish Presbyterian gentleman-evangelist, Lord Kinnaird, together with Pastor Gerrit Polman from Amsterdam. Boddy wrote of his friend: 'The Lord having given "Pentecost" to our dear brother, Mr Cecil Polhill, has moved him to use his influence and position for God's glory, for...the bringing together of Christians of very diverse modes of thought and worship'.[38]

No one represents this shift in thinking within British Pentecostalism better than Donald Gee. In a keynote sermon, 'Another Springtime', at the AOG Annual Conference on 1960, he remarked: 'Strangely enough, some of the so-called "liberal" theologians are more open to receive both the Pentecostal witness and the Pentecostal blessing in its fullness than those of our esteemed brethren in the fundamentalist camp. There is such a deep and widespread hunger to know the fullness of the Spirit, and such a recognition that it is the church's greatest need'.[39] In the last six years of his life when he was Principal of the AOG Bible School at Kenley, Surrey, Gee developed a friendship with a Benedictine monk, Dom Benedict Heron. Correspondence between the two came to light after his death. In a letter to Heron, he wrote:

> I am more convinced than ever of the essential unity of those truly in Christ Jesus, even when members of communions as utterly diverse as Roman Catholic and Pentecostal. This is really an amazing thing, perhaps more of a 'miracle' than some of the things we mutually call 'miracles'... In the Pentecostal Movement I am trying to inculcate a bigger vision in many ways, and I am sure that the atmosphere

---

[34] Murray W. Dempster, 'The Search for Pentecostal Identity', *Pneuma*, 15.1 (1993), p. 3.

[35] Dempster, 'The Search for Pentecostal Identity', p. 6.

[36] 'Alexander Alfred Boddy (1854-1930)', typescript tribute to her father. (*Mattersey Archive*.) Mary received Spirit-baptism at the age of fourteen when T.B. Barratt laid hands on her in the dining room of the vicarage where she had been doing school homework. She later joined the Anglo-Catholic Community of the Resurrection and as Mother Joann Mary, C.R. engaged in its mission work in South Africa.

[37] *Confidence*, February 1909, p. 47.

[38] *Confidence*, February 1909, pp. 48-9.

[39] Massey, *Another Springtime*, p. 189.

> is changing in that direction... I would like you to attend a really good Pentecostal meeting, but I fear there are many that I hesitate to commend because of their weaknesses. And yet the Holy Spirit is greater than Pentecostal meetings when the manifestations of the Holy Spirit are in evidence.[40]

Miroslav Volf, who grew up in the Pentecostal tradition in his native Croatia, writes from firsthand experience of Croatia, a Balkan country that has been the scene of ethnic conflict more fierce and for centuries longer and than Ulster has had to face. Drawing from his religio-ethnic background, Volf, is in a strong position to challenge Pentecostals when he asks in the light of Luke 4:19:

> Is it legitimate to speak only of deliverance from captivity to demonic forces and oppression by sickness?... Are Pentecostals so fascinated with the personal and miraculous that they do not see the economic dimensions of Christ's ministry? A 'full Gospel'—to use a favourite Pentecostal phrase—can consist only in the unity of personal-spiritual, individual-physical, socio-economic and ecological aspects of soteriology. A soteriology that does justice to Jesus' programmatic sermon must begin with the righteousness of the 'heart' but must also encompass justice and the integrity of the whole creation.[41]

Michael Harper contends that 'the Holy Spirit in the Acts of the Apostles was constantly destroying racial barriers, and reconciling deeply entrenched prejudices. It is important to notice that in 1 Cor. 12:13 the baptism in the Spirit is seen in this context... But if we are to speak and act in order with authority in the sphere of social concern, then we not only need an accurate knowledge of the facts, but also prophetic insight and power which only God can supply'.[42]

Insofar as the Pentecostal movement has followed the exclusivist agenda of popular Ulster Protestantism then it has taken a direction that, on the witness of those cited, is not inherent in its spirituality. By contrast, in the markedly different cultural world of modern Brazil, an entirely different brand of Pentecostalism is in the making. Vasquez makes the point: 'As life conditions deteriorate further for poor people who have joined Pentecostal churches, there is a strong possibility for the emergence of a popular Pentecostalism that could take a more historicised [as opposed to a demonological?] vision of evil in the world. [One study] suggests that this type of Pentecostalism might create a

---

[40] Massey, *Another Springtime*, pp. 173-4.

[41] Miroslav Volf, 'Materiality of Salvation: An Investigation in the Soteriologies of Liberation and Pentecostal Theologies', *Journal of Ecumenical Studies*, 26.3 (Summer, 1989), pp. 447-67. See also his book, Miroslav Volf, *Exclusion and Embrace: A Theological Exploration of Identity, Otherness and Reconciliation*, (Nashville, TN: Abingdon Press, 1996).

[42] Michael Harper, *Walk in the Spirit*, (London: Hodder & Stoughton, 1968), p. 60.

predisposition towards radical, critical citizenship'.[43] Freston attests that he and fellow sociologists are coming to recognise in Pentecostalism 'a source of effective changes because it creates communities of discontinuity and transformation, confronts machismo more effectively than feminism, deals convincingly with matters of money, sickness, moral crises, and family problems, and is able to offer the principal alternative to the drug culture by giving people a new identity and values'.[44]

These different sequels are a sharp reminder that Pentecostalism cannot be treated as some religious monolith: Pentecost has always been larger than Pentecostalism. It is best seen as a generative spirituality, freely accommodative to the diverse cultural *milieux* of the world's peoples, leaving it open to being shaped by the spiritual and life-enhancing aspirations particularly of less literate and articulate members of oppressed communities.[45] But, like all religious reform movements, it continuously faces the threat of succumbing to cultural entrapment and the distortion of its core values in the process.[46] One Catholic observer, Killian McDonnell, is realistic, even pessimistic, enough to realise that personal and societal change to a wider and more inclusivist stance will always be difficult. He writes: 'The Pentecostal experience does seem to elicit a new openness and generosity towards others, [but] it does not seem to endow people with a new passion for political and social justice. If socio-political awareness were present before one became involved in

---

[43] Manuel A. Vasquez, The *Brazilian Church and the Crisis of Modernity*, (Cambridge: Cambridge University Press, 1998), pp. 95-6.

[44] Richard Shaull and Waldo Cesar, *Pentecostalism and the Future of the Christian Churches*, (Grand Rapids, MI: Eerdmans, 2000), p. 228.

[45] Cheryl Johns has engaged with the published work of Paulo Friere, the Brazilian pioneer in adult education whose 'pedagogy of the oppressed' seeks political empowerment through literacy and conscientization. By 'conscientization' Friere means 'a coming to an awareness of one's place in society and its power structure, pathways to transforming one's existence by becoming an active subject rather than a passive victim'. (Chris Rohmann, *The Dictionary of Important Ideas and Thinkers*, [London: Hutchinson, 2000] p. 148.) She sees Pentecostal theologising as essentially oral-narrative, an experiential, praxis-oriented hermeneutic. Such a theology 'allows for theology to become a part of the life of the community of faith. Hence, belief is forged in the context of community with everyone having a voice in the on-going dialectic of the kingdom of God'. (Cheryl Bridges Johns, *Pentecostal Formation: A Pedagogy among the Oppressed*, [Sheffield: Sheffield Academic Press, 1993], p. 87.) Johns speaks as an academic whose travels have taken her to massive street services in Chile, to prayer vigils in Korea and to church gatherings in Guatemala.

[46] To cite an example, the so-called 'prosperity gospel' is a reflection more of the values of western consumer society than those of the Kingdom of God. 'For the rising middle class of newly prosperous Pentecostals and charismatics, the teaching held an irresistible attraction'. (Vinson Synan, *The Century of the Holy Spirit: 100 Years of Pentecostal and Charismatic Renewal*, [Nashville, TN: Thomas Nelson, 2001], p. 358.)

Pentecostalism, the experience supports and reinforces it. But the experience will not, by and of itself, supply one with socio-political awareness'.[47] If this is generalisation is correct, then such change as comes will most likely be dictated more by arbitrary circumstance than considered response.

Pentecostalism must now be seen as one of the major forces in church history which have democratised the deep-seated quest for experiencing the reality of the living God as captured succinctly in Wesley's line, 'My God, I know, I *feel* Thee mine'. From the second century to the late medieval period, deeper spirituality was more or less confined to a spiritual elite, following ascetic and mystical models; true miracles were normatively associated with sainthood. It was such spiritual paragons alone who could expect to see visions and perform miracles. There were popular 'spirit-movements' like the Cathari and the Brethren of the Free Spirit, but their brand of radical dualism allied to illuminism supports the dictum of J.S. Whale that the inner light is often the shortest way to the outer darkness. Sandwiched between the claims of the Catholic Church and the Anabaptists, the magisterial reformers adopted the same stance as Augustine took to second-century Montanism in excluding the Spirit's 'extraordinary works' from the Church's armoury.[48] It was as a result of the Great Awakenings, modelled in ways in the Six Mile Water Revival in seventeenth-century Ulster, and the outworking of the Pietist and Methodist revivals, that humble lay people in sizeable numbers could

---

[47] Quoted in Richard Quebedeaux, *The New Charismatics II; How a Christian Renewal Movement became Part of the American Religious Mainstream*, (San Francisco, CA: Harper and Row, 1983), p. 166. McDonald is the primary interpreter of Roman Catholic charismatic renewal and co-chaired, with David du Plessis, the Roman Catholic-Pentecostal Dialogue that on the Pentecostal side was predominantly American in composition. (See Jerry L. Sandridge, *The Roman Catholic-Pentecostal Dialogue (1977-82): A Study in Developing Ecumenism*, [Peter Lang, Frankfurt, 1987].) In an evaluation of the five rounds of Dialogue, the last in 1998-2002, Robeck and Sandridge (*NIDPCM*, p. 580) conclude, *inter alia*, that it is essential that Pentecostals approach such Dialogue with an understanding of the Roman Catholic Church 'from a post-Vatican II perspective and not from the stereotypes of Rome that are rooted in the 16th century'. They admit that only a few Pentecostal groups in America embraced the Dialogue while others 'worked tirelessly to put an end to it by calling for the discipline of its participants or suppressing news of its work among their constituents'.

[48] The Anabaptists re-established believer's baptism and, in general, allowed more play for the Holy Spirit than the leading reformers. One of its leaders, Thomas Müntzer, in the *Prague Manifesto* (1521), claimed for himself direct instruction 'from the Holy Spirit in the form of visions, dreams, ecstatic utterances and inspired exegesis'. (Stanley M. Burgess, *The Holy Spirit: Medieval, Roman Catholic and Reformation Traditions*, [Peabody, MA: Hendrickson, 1997], p. 208.)

cultivate a much more direct relationship with God.[49] Something of the richness and diversity of spiritual experience and achievement, such as was known only to the greatest saints of the past, whether by supererogatory travail or ascetic privation, became the prerogative to all seeking and expectant souls. It has fallen to Pentecostalism and the later Charismatic Renewal Movement to be cast in the role of a major carrier of this intense and dynamic spirituality at this point in the history of the Christian Church. Alister McGrath sees the strength of Pentecostalism lying in its message 'that it is possible to encounter God directly and personally through the power of the Holy Spirit. God is to be known immediately and directly, not indirectly through the text. Whereas traditional Protestantism is wary of allowing any such experience of God, Pentecostalism celebrates it and makes it a hall-mark of Christian living'.[50] In his discussions with leading Pentecostals, especially in the great urban sprawls of Asia, he found their response gave force to his contention that atheism is becoming increasingly insupportable. The leaders reaction was to point to the reality of God in their lives: 'How can God's relevance be doubted, when God inspires us to care for the poor, heal the sick and work for the dispossessed?'[51]

Such deep heart-searching was particularly marked among the first generation of Pentecostals who often came from a background informed by Holiness spirituality. In the spiritual journeys of such ordinary believers, it is this pursuit that was to find its fulfilment in biblically informed, experiential ways that is overlooked in most scholarly studies of Pentecostalism, especially in the social sciences. But, for the seekers, there runs through the narrative of their lives a common thread of a yearning for a fresh spiritual reality that up to the moment of their Spirit-baptism had become increasingly elusive. For such, Gee maintained that 'the moment of one's baptism in the Spirit may well be the supreme moment of spiritual, and even physical consciousness in the whole life...

---

[49] The Six Mile Water Revival (1625) has been described as 'the first example of a phenomenon which has become a key mechanism of Protestantism worldwide: the revivalist meeting'. (Diarmaid MacCulloch, *Reformation: Europe's House Divided 1490-1700*, [London: Penguin, 2003], p.603.)

[50] Alister McGrath, *The Twilight of Atheism: The Rise and Fall of Disbelief in the Modern World*, (New York: Doubleday, 2004) p. 215. McGrath argues that Protestantism in much of the early Reformed tradition saw 'no possibility of a direct encounter with the sacred or an experience of the divine other than that mediated indirectly through reading the Bible and the public exposition of its message'. A dry and dusty spirituality came to characterise much of Protestant spirituality by the end of the seventeenth century. It was challenged first by the Pietist and Methodist movements in the eighteenth century, the great Awakenings and Revivals of the nineteenth century, and the Pentecostal-Charismatic movements in the twentieth century.

[51] McGrath, *The Twilight of Atheism,* p. 216.

To those who stood firm their personal experience became more precious than any words can tell'.[52]

The historical and psycho-sociological dimensions of Pentecostalism do not exhaust it. In Christian understanding, it is either a datum expressive of the will of God for His church or else it is only of limited significance, dangerously flawed by its overblown self-regard. Gee, reflecting on the first great Royal Albert Hall meeting in 1926, saw deeper than the externals of that particular event. Of George Jeffreys he wrote that 'in this comparatively unschooled man who a few short years ago had been an obscure young evangelist in Ulster, we gladly recognise there was manifested a spiritual gift for ministry from the Ascended Christ (Eph. 4:8-11) similar in character to the endowments given to the Primitive Church'.[53] Jeffreys in his gifting was but one among many otherwise unremarkable men and women who have been so enlivened by the Spirit that they could be said to embody, in small part, the answer to the yearning of the New England, Puritan divine, Cotton Mather (1663-1728) that God would be pleased to fulfil the 'ancient prophecy, of *pouring out the Spirit on all Flesh*, and revive the extraordinary and supernatural Operations with which He planted His Religion in the primitive Times of Christianity'.[54]

The President of a leading American University of Pentecostal foundation outlined his vision for Pentecostalism in the future of the institution he led. He presented a longing worthy of any part of the movement for today and beyond:

> It is Pentecostalism without anger, Pentecostalism without cheap sensationalism, Pentecostalism without obsessive denominationalism. Pentecostalism without self-righteous impulse to exclude those of a slightly different hue or stripe. It is Pentecostalism without 'oneupmanship', without need to identify itself as the highest rung on the ecclesiastical ladder. It is Pentecostalism that centres on Jesus Christ, which understands the Upper Room not as an ecclesiastical museum, but as a staging area for those who would take the love of Christ to the world. It is Pentecostalism with the humility to acknowledge that we have much to learn from others. It is informed Pentecostalism, which does not call attention to itself but to Jesus Christ.[55]

---

[52] Gee, *Wind and Flame*, p. 45.

[53] Gee, *Wind and Flame*, p. 141.

[54] Quoted in Richard F. Lovelace, *Revival as a Way of Life*, (Exeter: Paternoster Press, 1985), p. 109. The original is found in Cotton Mather: *Diary, II,* (New York: Unger, 1957), pp. 365-6.

[55] Paul Conn, 'A Letter to the Reader', in Cross and Powery (eds), *Spirit and the Mind,* p. xvii. Conn is the President of Lee University, Cleveland, TN, the leading academic institution of the Church of God. The Church dates its origin to 1896 when revival broke out in a schoolhouse in the heart of Appalachian North Carolina. About 130 spoke in

It is an aspiration to which the more reflective leaders met with in these pages would have lent their *Amen*.

---

tongues, an experience which they identified as Spirit-baptism. The Church sees itself as the oldest Pentecostal body of all. The denomination in 1986 numbered 1.6 million members.

APPENDIX

Other Early Apostolic Assemblies

A. Those Originating in Cottage Meetings: Henry Street and Ava Street

The Henry Street assembly had its beginnings in a cottage meeting at the home of Mr and Mrs Andrews of St George's Street in the Belfast dockland area. By 1924 the membership had reached forty, when the work moved to a hall on the upper floor of existing premises. In not having complete possession of the whole building the assembly was denied the legal right to have a license for solemnising marriage ceremonies.[1] Other premises were considered but the prophetic word came that 'the Lord desired not to take Dover Street Hall but could secure the seats, etc., for Henry St. Hall. There were six old seats in Henry St. and we put feet on them'.—all of which gives an indication of the size of the regular congregation and its dependence on prophecy for direction.[2] The formal opening of the Hall was favoured by a visit of apostles D.P. Williams and A.V. Chanter, together with prophet Jones Williams and the small group referred to as the 'American delegation'. Pastor Dobson Hunniford, of Philadelphia, who was paying a visit to his homeland after thirty-seven years absence, headed this delegation.

With post-war redevelopment, the church transferred to the northern edge of the city. The assembly was the spiritual home of Pastor A. Ferran who in later years was to become the first Principal of the Apostolic Bible College in the Calabar district of Nigeria. By the early 1990s, the autonomous Apostolic Church in Nigeria was its eighth largest denomination with c.1.2 million members and affiliates.[3]

The Ava Street assembly was another to develop from a cottage meeting. Situated in south Belfast, off the Ormeau Road in the Ballynefeigh district, it was the first purpose-built Apostolic Church in the province. It grew from meetings held in the home of Mrs John Cardwell in nearby Primrose Street. Mrs Cardwell had been converted at a meeting in Great Victoria Street in 1921 and began to organise meetings without any support from her husband who, while not opposing them, always

[1] *ACM*, 9 May 1925.

[2] *ACM*, 3 November 1925.

[3] See Johnston, *Operation World*, p. 421.

managed an excuse for not attending. He came to faith in his own kitchen in 1922. The following year he was holding open-air meetings as an outreach of the house group. He first appeared in the list of elders in December 1923 and the following February he was by prophetic utterance called to be secretary of the newly established Building Fund which was set up initially to fund an alternative to the rented premises in Great Victoria Street.[4] The growth of the work in his own district led to the opening of a new church building in Ava Street in 1927.

Vaughan considered Caldwell 'not, perhaps, among the Movement's ablest preachers, yet [he] came to be among its ablest administrators'.[5] A tram-driver, he was a big man in every sense who drew this tribute from Vaughan: 'There was a gentleness about him that in no way detracted from the feeling of strength one came to associate with him morally as well as physically. Even in those early days, the conviction had grown upon me that here was...an apostle of the Lord'.[6] John Cardwell (1893-1958) was the first Ulsterman to be recognised as an apostle. He was appointed superintendent of the Irish work in the period 1937-44.

B. Those Developing through Informal Personal Contact: Drumbo and Larne

The Drumbo assembly was the first to be opened outside Belfast and it was another that grew from informal contact. The village was close enough to the city for Vaughan to speak of 'a walk of about eight miles through some fine country scenes', passing halfway through the village of Purdysburn.[7] Robert Allen, a deacon at Great Victoria Street, was virtually reared at the home of Joseph and Mary Davis at Drumbo. Allen invited Davis to the Great Victoria Street and, through this contact, the latter invited Phillips and Evan Jones to hold meetings in the village. Denied the use of the local school, he made use of a barn that hitherto had been used for dances. The first mission was held in the depth of winter and the pathway in was lighted by a newly purchased hurricane lamp hanging from a tree. Quite a number were converted and Mary Davis received the gift of prophecy. Davis, who was a carpenter, owned some land on which stood an old army hut and this building, after renovation, became the home of the new church.

On Saturday, 17 November 1923 the church was abuzz with expectancy when a large number from Belfast converged on the Drumbo church for a baptismal service during which sixteen were baptized, fourteen women and two males. Evan Jones performed the baptisms and

---

[4] *ACM*, 1 February 1924.

[5] *Vaughan Memoir*, p. 41.

[6] *Vaughan Memoir*, p. 41.

[7] *Vaughan Memoir*, p. 40.

apostles Williams and Chanter and prophet Jones Williams were present. The baptisms were more than likely performed outdoors as at Moore's Hill. Drumbo was essentially an extension work of Great Victoria Street. There seems to have been little local leadership besides Davis who, to boost numbers, was keen to promote frequent missions. On at least one occasion, a prophecy was given directing Vaughan to be the missioner and when Davis was unavoidably absent for a short period, it was decided at the central Elders' Meeting 'do our best to feed the Saints...by sending a party of three or four weekly'.[8]

The work at Larne, County Antrim, was the least planned for of all those considered here. The first outreach took place around September 1923 when it was recorded that 'meetings were held inside the Orange Hall; also outdoors and many heard the word preached'.[9] The work had its origin on the boat taking Phillips and Evan Jones to the 1924 New Year Convention in Glasgow. On board was Mrs J. Armstrong from Larne who was travelling to Glasgow to be present with her daughter who, after a difficult childbirth, was dying. Attracted by the singing of Evan Jones, who as usual started to witness publicly in song on the boat, she found herself in conversation with both men. They were able to bring her some comfort in her distress. On her return, Mrs Armstrong made contact and she and her husband opened their home for cottage meetings. Prophetic direction was given at the Elders' Meeting in June 1924 for meetings to be held in the town on 15 and 16 June. Vaughan and an elder were directed to conduct the meetings accompanied by 'a party from the Central Place, such young ones to lift up their voices and to pray'.[10]

In November 1924, plans were being made at the Elders' Meeting for the opening of a hall recently acquired in the town through Vaughan's initiative. It was arranged that Chanter and Jones Williams were to conduct meetings during the week following the opening. Larne was made the pastoral responsibility of Vaughan and it was he who saw the possibility of turning the upper floor of a disused bond store in a side street into a serviceable hall. Part of the building was rented from an enterprising cabinet maker who was only too pleased to make the suggested alterations, in particular giving a respectable appearance to the stairway and front entrance. More suitable premises were obtained later before Vaughan was recalled from Larne to engage in 'general city work, plus tent and other missions'.[11] His summation of his ministry in the town is characteristically honest: 'Insofar as my first pastorate...is concerned, the

[8] *ACM*, 31 October 1925.

[9] *ACM,* 29 September 1923.

[10] *ACM,* 4 June 1924.

[11] *Vaughan Memoir*, p. 52.

story is not one of outstanding results but rather of a small increase in membership and of holding the fort until our recall to Belfast'.[12]

[12] *Vaughan Memoir*, p. 52.

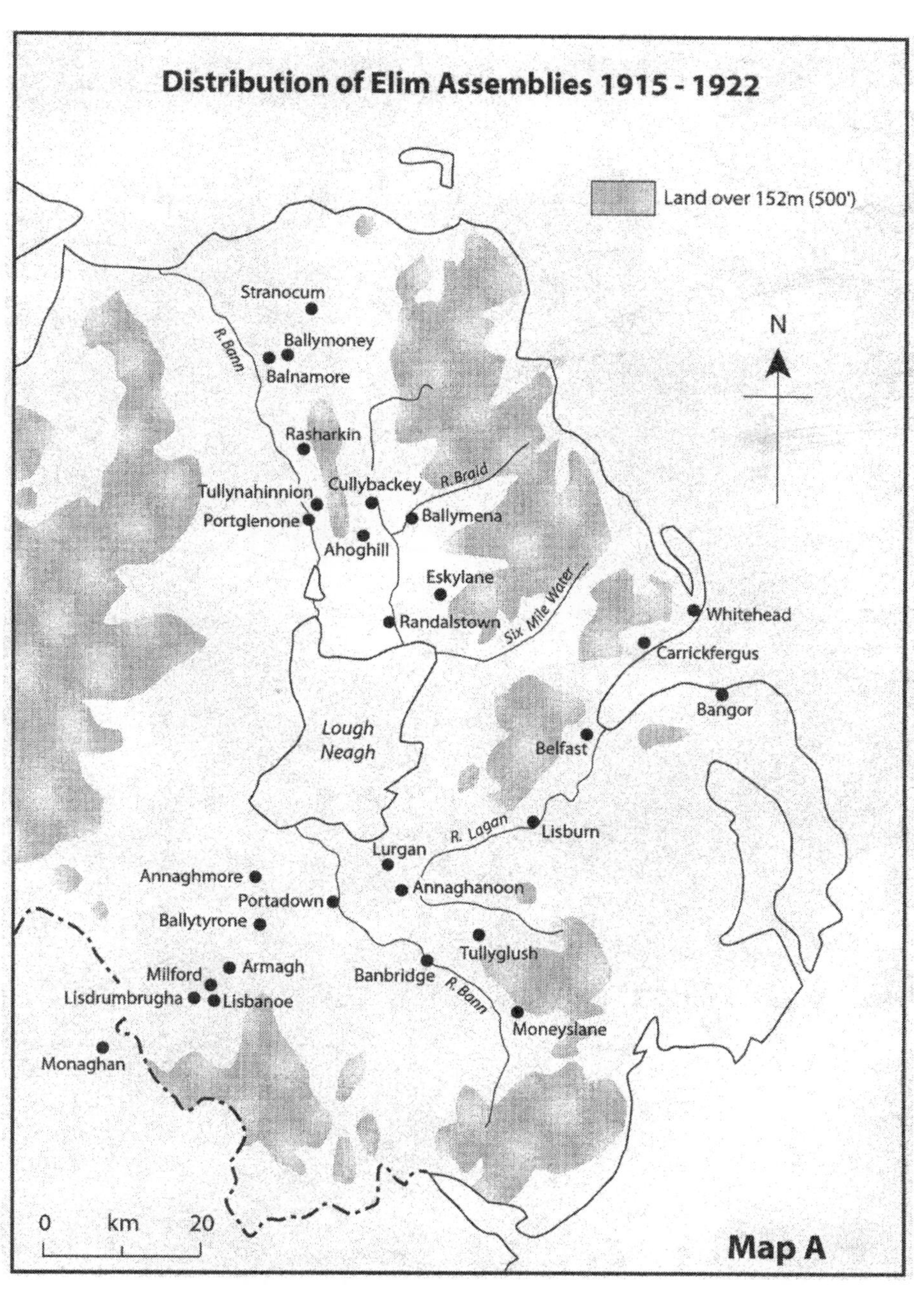
Distribution of Elim Assemblies 1915 - 1922
Land over 152m (500')
N
Stranocum
R. Bann
Ballymoney
Balnamore
Rasharkin
Tullynahinnion
Cullybackey
R. Braid
Portglenone
Ballymena
Ahoghill
Eskylane
Randalstown
Six Mile Water
Whitehead
Carrickfergus
Bangor
Lough Neagh
Belfast
R. Lagan
Lisburn
Lurgan
Annaghmore
Annaghanoon
Portadown
Ballytyrone
Tullyglush
Armagh
Milford
Banbridge
Lisdrumbrugha
Lisbanoe
R. Bann
Moneyslane
Monaghan
0 km 20
Map A

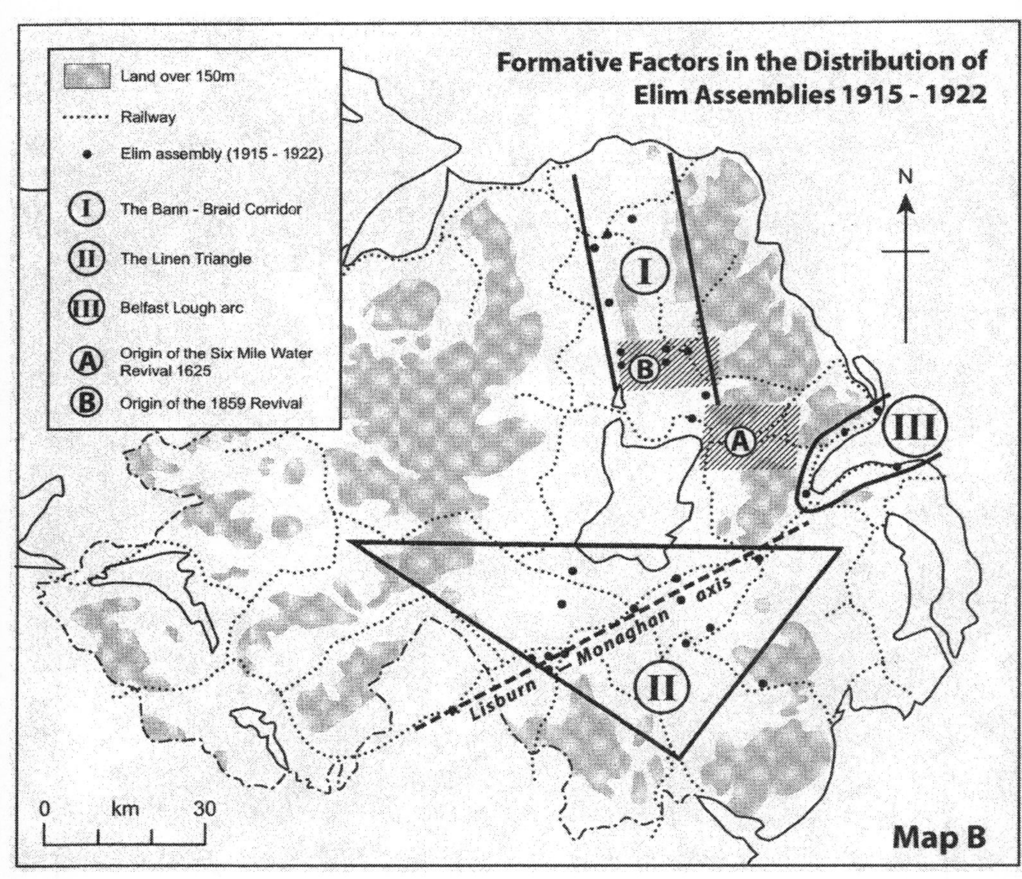

Formative Factors in the Distribution of Elim Assemblies 1915 - 1922
Land over 150m
Railway
Elim assembly (1915 - 1922)
I The Bann - Braid Corridor
II The Linen Triangle
III Belfast Lough arc
A Origin of the Six Mile Water Revival 1625
B Origin of the 1859 Revival
N
I
B
A
III
Lisburn - Monaghan axis
II
0 km 30
Map B

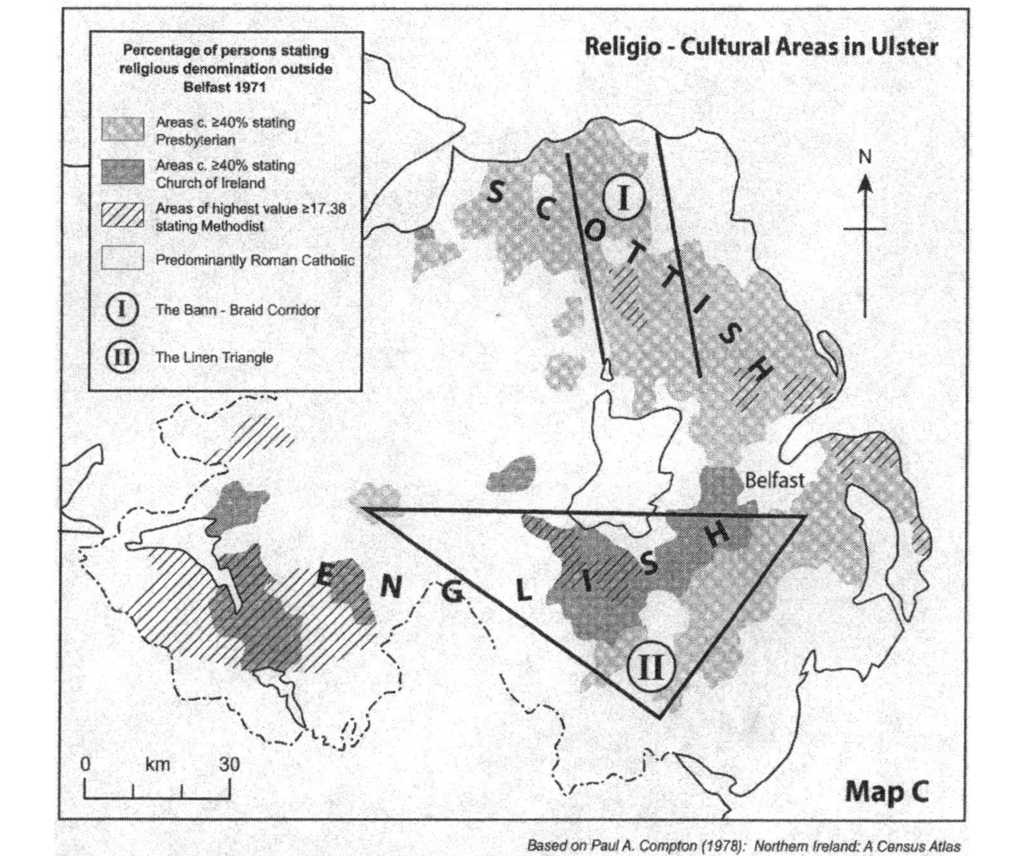

Based on Paul A. Compton (1978): *Northern Ireland: A Census Atlas*

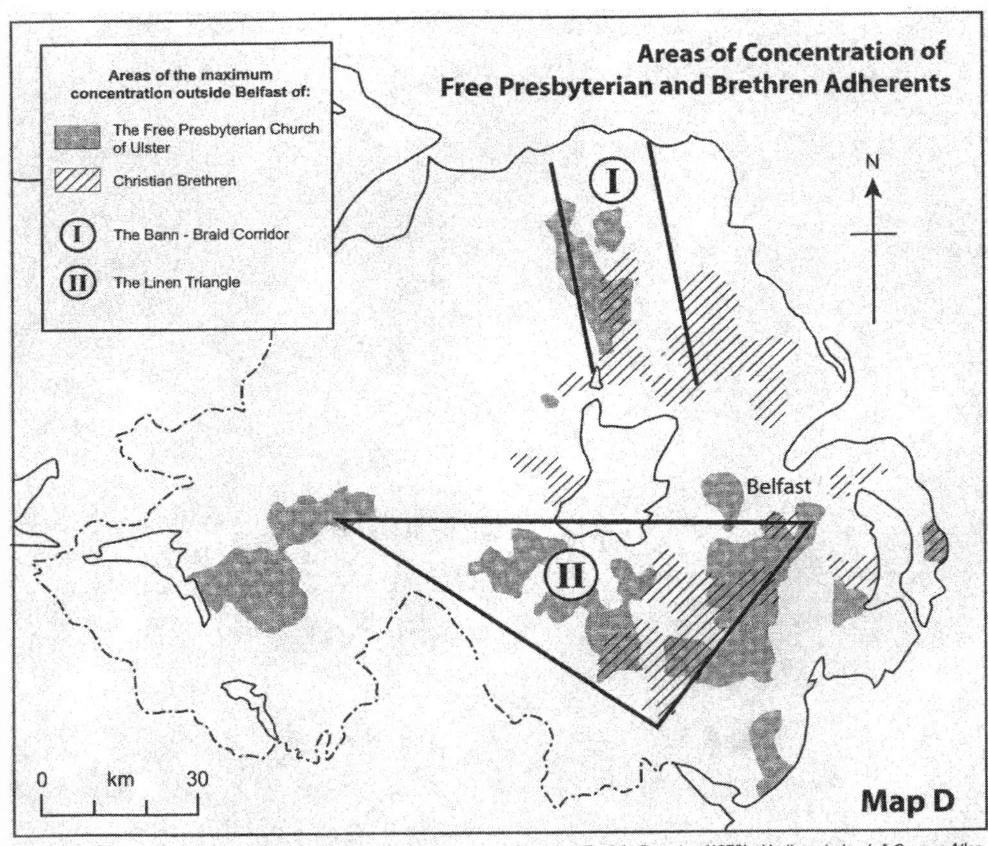

Based on Paul A. Compton (1978): Northern Ireland: A Census Atlas

FIGURE I

THE MARRIAGE CERTIFICATE OF ROBERT AND MARIE BROWN

This Certifies that

Robert A. Brown AND Marie E. Burgess

of New York of Zion City

State of N. Y. State of Illinois

WERE UNITED IN

Holy Matrimony

At Zion City

According to the Ordinance of God and the Laws of the State of Illinois

on the 14 day of October

in the year of OUR LORD One Thousand Nine Hundred and Nine

Witnesses

Clergyman

Used with the kind permission of Flower Pentecostal Heritage Center: #25486

FIGURE II

THE MARRIAGE AND ORDINATION CERTIFICATES OF ROBERT SEMPLE

No.

MARRIAGE CERTIFICATE

This is to Testify that on the Twelfth day of August 1908 were by me duly

UNITED IN MATRIMONY

Robt Jas Semple	Aimee E Kennedy
of the City of Stratford	of the Town of Ingersoll
County of Perth	County of Oxford
Province of Ontario	Province of Ontario
and Dominion of Canada.	and Dominion of Canada.

Witness my hand at Ingersoll this 12th day of August 1908

In Presence of F. E. Groh, Annie P. Kohne

John D. Sharp, Commissioned Staff Officer

Registered at Toronto, Ont.

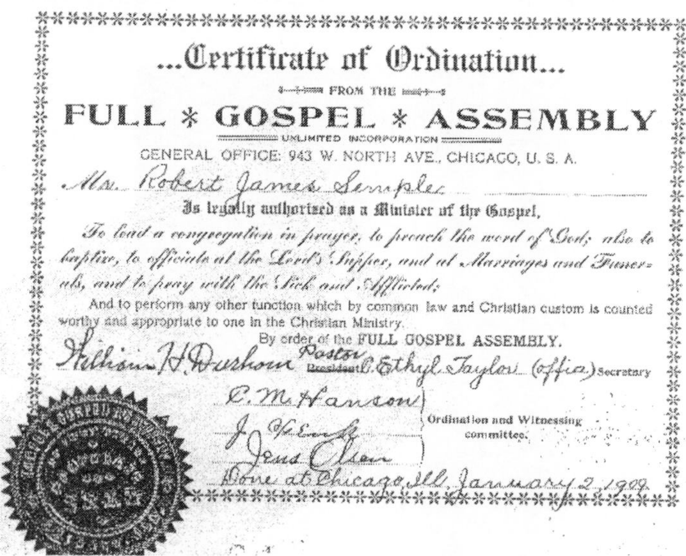

...Certificate of Ordination...

FROM THE

FULL * GOSPEL * ASSEMBLY

UNLIMITED INCORPORATION

GENERAL OFFICE: 943 W. NORTH AVE., CHICAGO, U. S. A.

Mr. Robert James Semple

Is legally authorized as a Minister of the Gospel,

To lead a congregation in prayer, to preach the word of God; also to baptize, to officiate at the Lord's Supper, and at Marriages and Funerals, and to pray with the Sick and Afflicted;

And to perform any other function which by common law and Christian custom is counted worthy and appropriate to one in the Christian Ministry.

By order of the FULL GOSPEL ASSEMBLY.

William H. Durham, Pastor, President — Ethyl Taylor (office), Secretary

C. M. Hanson
J. [illegible]
Jens Olsen
Ordination and Witnessing committee.

Done at Chicago, Ill, January 2, 1909.

Used with the kind permission of Flower Pentecostal Heritage Center: #27524 (above) #28576 (below)

FIGURE III

THE RURAL SETTING OF ELIM ASSEMBLIES

MONEYSLANE, CO. DOWN, AND ANNAGHMORE, CO. ANTRIM

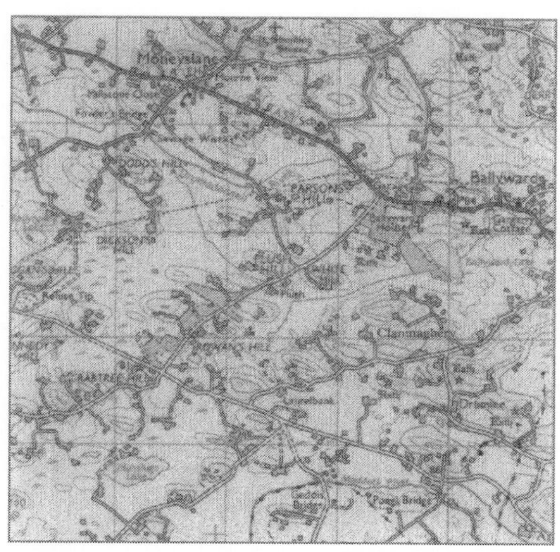

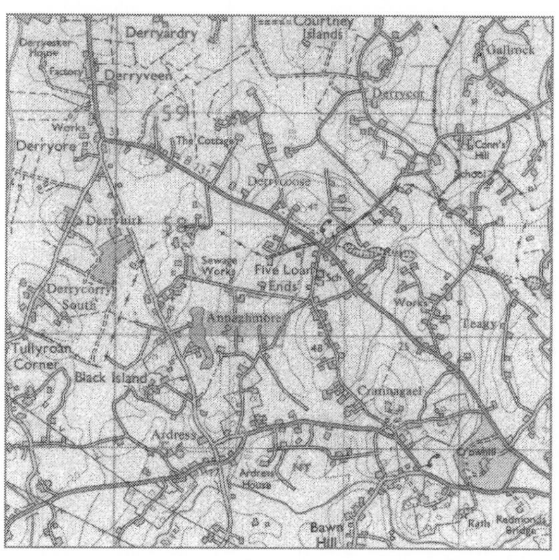

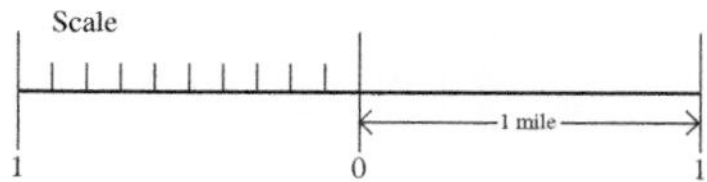

FIGURE IV

RETICULATION OF ELIM LINKS IN THE BANN-BRAID CORRIDOR

1915 - 1922

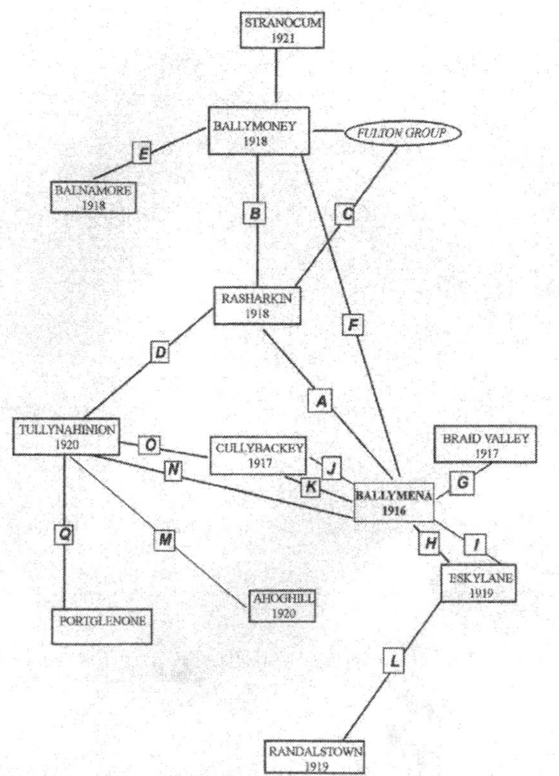

RASHARKIN
A. 1916-local farmer attends **BALLYMENA** mission. 1918-Mercer and Logan hold mission in Orange Hall. **B**-Support (financial/ personal) given to **Ballymoney** mission. **C**-Fulton group support **Rasharkin** mission. **D**-Edward Harris from **Tullynahinion** testifies to divine healing at this mission

BALLYMONEY
1918-Mercer and Logan mission in Orange Hall. **E**-Mill workers from **Balnamore** attend mission. Assembly meets in Livingstone home, then his stonemason's shed. **F**-Mercer, pastor of **BALLYMENA** Elim, gives teaching on Spirit-baptism to correct "extravagances".

BRAID VALLEY
G. 1917-Margaret Streight conducts meetings in farmhouse "under Slemish mountain" following Jeffreys' meetings in **BALLYMENA**.

ESKYLANE
H. 1916-James Gault attends **BALLYMENA** mission. 1919-Tweed and Campbell hold mission in Gault's barn. **I**-Gault ordained elder in BALLYMENA Elim Church.

CULLYBACKEY
J. 1916-Peacock and McKendry attend **BALLYMENA** meetings. 1917-Henderson conducts mission in American inventor's shed as spin-off from **BALLYMENA** missions. **K**-William and Joseph Spence attend Mercer's training classes in **BALLYMENA**. Church administered by **BALLYMENA** pastor and session

RANDALSTOWN
L. 1919 Tweed, recovering from tubercular condition at Gault farm at **Eskylane**, speaks at meetings in the "Iron Mission Hall" in the town.

AHOGHILL
1920 -Tweed and Campbell conduct mission in Orange Hall: **M**-Edward Harris from **Tullynahinion** attends these meetings.

TULLYNAHINION
1920-Tweed conducts mission in Harris farmhouse, after **Ahoghill** mission.
N-Edward Harris probably attended **BALLYMENA** mission; **0**-Edward's son, John Harris, receives Spirit-baptism on returning from meeting at **Cullybackey**. **P**. 1922-0n Tweed's departure, **BALLYMENA** accepts responsibility for oversight.

PORTGLENONE
Q-With establishment of the Apostolic Church, many from **Tullynahinion** join the new assembly.

FIGURE V

GEOGRAPHICAL DISTRIBUTION OF APOSTOLIC ASSEMBLIES IN RELATION TO NEAREST ELIM ASSEMBLIES 1920 - c. 1925

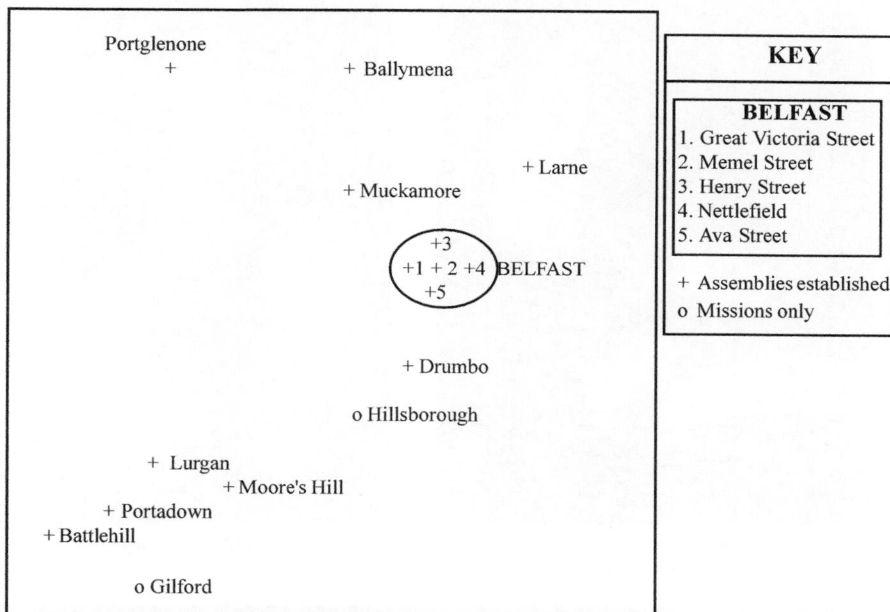

ASSEMBLIES 0-5 miles apart		**ASSEMBLIES 5-10 miles apart**	
APOSTOLIC	ELIM	APOSTOLIC	ELIM
Hillsborough	Lisburn	Larne	Whitehead
Battlehill	Annaghmore/Portadown	Drumbo	Melbourne Street, Belfast
Moore's Hill	Annaghadoon/Lurgan	Gilford	Portadown/Annaghanoon
Muckamore	Eskylane/Randalstown		
Portglenone	Portglenone		
Ballymena	Ballymena		
Lurgan	Lurgan		

PHOTOGRAPHS A

EARLY PENTECOSTAL LEADERS

Judge John Leech
© Eliot and Fry

Alexander A. Boddy

1913 Sunderland Convention
Back: Smith Wigglesworth, Pastor Edel (Silesia), Cecil Pohill
Front left: Stanley Frodsham

PHOTOGRAPHS B

CHARISMATIC CLERGYMEN and ASSOCIATED CHURCHES

Edward Irving

Catholic Apostolic Church, Cromwell Road, Belfast
(site now occupied by flats)

St. James' Church, Crinken, Bray, Co. Dublin

Rev. Thomas E. Hackett

PHOTOGRAPHS C

EARLY ELIM CHURCHES

Reopening of the Hunter Street Elim Church, April 1932 (former laundry)
Photograph reproduced with the kind permission of the Trustees of the Museums and Galleries of Northern Ireland. H10/29/202.

Elim Tabernacle, Melbourne Street (former Primitive Methodist Church)

Ballymoney Elim Church 1930

PHOTOGRAPHS D

THE ELIM EVANGELISTIC BAND 1915 AND c.1921

ELIM EVANGELISTIC BAND IN 1915

Back: F. Farlow, Margaret Streight, W. Henderson. Front: G. Jeffreys, R.E. Darragh

J. B. HAMILTON. T. J. JONES. G. EVERY. R. SMITH. E. W. HARE.
J. MCWHIRTER. J. SMITH. R. TWEED. W. CAMPBELL. MRS. EVERY. J. CARTER. G.FLETCHER. E. J. PHILLIPS
MISS. ADAMS. F. FARLOW. R. E. DARRAGH. G. JEFFREYS. W. HENDERSON. R. MERCER. MISS. STREIGHT.
MRS. FLETCHER. MISS. HENDERSON.

PHOTOGRAPHS E

MONEYSLANE ELIM CHURCH

Looking south from Moneyslane Elim Church towards the Mourne Mountains

First meetings held in the Orange Hall

Elim Church, Moneyslane

PHOTOGRAPHS F

AIMEE SEMPLE McPHERSON IN BELFAST 1926

Robert and Aimee Semple, Chicago, 1910

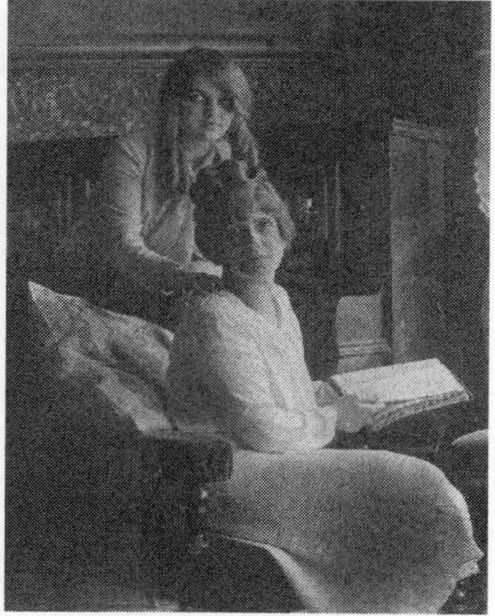

Aimee and her daughter Roberta, Belfast, April 1926

AMERICAN RADIO EVANGELIST IN BELFAST
Mrs. Semple McPherson, described as the world s greatest woman preacher, visited the City Hall, Belfast and was received by the Lord Mayor.
Front Row (l to r): Miss Roberta Semple, Mrs. Semple McPherson, The Lord Mayor and Pastor George Jeffreys.
Back Row: Councillors Clark Scott, W.J.McGowan J.P., George Stewart J.P., C.A.Hinds J.P., S.Donald Cheyne J.P., Alfred McBride J.P., and Alderman James Duff J.P.

PHOTOGRAPHS G

EARLY LEADERS OF THE APOSTOLIC CHURCH

Pastors from Wales and Scotland on their first visit to Belfast in January 1920
Front Row (from left)
The Fisher brothers, Dan Williams, Jones Williams, W. Phillips?

Welsh leaders of the Apostolic work in Ulster
From left: Idris Vaughan, William Phillips, Evan Jones

PHOTOGRAPHS H

MOORE'S HILL APOSTOLIC CHURCH

Moore's Hill Apostolic Church, near Waringstown

Site of baptisms in the River Lagan

Bibliographical Note

A dread for any researcher is to discover the hard way that primary source material of any great significance is thin on the ground. This is especially so in the case of the student of early Pentecostalism because the early Pentecostals were a people, in general, more at home communicating by mouth than pen. Theirs was more an experiential, oral religious culture than a bookish, learned or liturgical one. By way of contrast, adherents of the Oxford Movement quickly set out their stall in producing a series of powerful tracts, thus earning themselves the sobriquet 'Tractarians'. Like the converts at Corinth, not many wise, mighty or noble were found in the ranks of Pentecostals. Fortunately initial fears are quickly allayed when it becomes known that substantial British archival material is preserved at the Donald Gee Pentecostal and Charismatic Research Centre. This facility is housed at the Assemblies of God Bible College, Mattersley Hall, Mattersey, near Doncaster, Nottinghamshire. Other major archives are housed at the Flower Pentecostal Heritage Center, associated with the American Assemblies of God at Springfield, Missouri. With the financial backing of a 2.5 million strong denomination, it has the professional staff and facilities, including internet links, to match the best of all such centres in America that leave Europeans feeling like the poor relations in the area of scholarship. Against this, it has to be acknowledged that the inter-library loan system in the hands of Florence Grey of the Queens University Belfast Library service seldom failed to turn up some of the rarer books and articles requested.

The author was intrigued for many years to have in his possession an item of archival material. It was the first minute book of the Assemblies of God (Belfast and District) Presbytery and passed down from his father. Like most minute books it is short on weighty information but proved a compelling inspiration to delve more into the history of the Pentecostal movement in the province. This was heightened all the more by the author's coming from a background where some of the personalities that appear in these pages were regularly spoken of, sometimes entertained or occasionally listened to as preachers. Those other minutes drawn upon that are held at Mattersey are indicated in the Bibliography. Pastor David Matthews, who was also kind enough to be interviewed about the early days of the Apostolic Church, made the minutes of the Apostolic Church in Ulster available.

The most exhilarating serendipitous finds to come across the author's path were in the 'manuscript' category. One in particular has been extensively drawn upon in Chapters 6 and 7. The *Tweed Memoir* was compiled in its author's last years and though understandably partisan and rather bitty it is an otherwise invaluable record, lending an authentic feel to the pioneer days of Elim in the province. The *Vaughan Memoir*, though of shorter compass on Ulster, provides something similar for the Apostolic Church. Contact with David Matthews led indirectly to meeting with Mrs David McKeown who made available to the author her brother-in-law's lengthy memoir, *A Man called Adam*, which hitherto had circulated almost exclusively among the extended McKeown family and friends. All three works were written by men in later life so that accuracy in matters of minor detail cannot always be expected but that is more than compensated for by the information and insights they provide that would otherwise have been lost for ever. Pastor Gordon Weeks was kind enough to provide a draft copy of his history of the Apostolic Church which has since been published. (Gordon Weeks, *Chapter Thirty-two-part of a History of the Apostolic Church 1900-2000*, (published privately, 11 Low Laithes View, Barnsley, England, S73 8DW., 2003.) Mr Joe Cheyne provided press cuttings and other material relating to the Apostolic Church at Moore's Hill. The Rev. Sidney Barnes, minister of Hillsborough Free Presbyterian Church, has a large selection of literature relating to the 1859 Revival which he kindly loaned

Complete, or almost complete, sets of the Pentecostal periodicals are kept at Mattersey. The monthly issues of *Confidence* are almost the only source of information about the movement in the province in its pre-denominational stage until the publication of the *Elim Evangel* which started with the December 1919 issue and was published quarterly for its first two years. Thereafter for years it was issued monthly and it was only with the May 1924 edition that it ceased to be published from 3 University Avenue, Belfast. Complete sets of *Redemption Tidings* and *The Pattern*, the magazine of the Bible-Pattern Church, are held at Mattersey. Local newspapers were gleaned in either the Linenhall Library or the Newspaper Library of Belfast Central Library. Both libraries hold complete sets of the *Belfast and District Directory*, an annual publication that uncovers a surprising amount of useful information about individuals and places.

Since the original thesis was completed, the following periodicals have become available on CD-ROM: *Elim Evangel, Redemption Tidings* and Cecil Polhill's missionary magazine *Flames of Fire*. These CDs are part of the Revival Library, the brainchild of Tony Cauchi, Kings Centre, High Street, Waltham Hampshire, SO32 1AA, UK. The Flower Pentecostal Heritage Centre, Springfield, Missouri, USA, has produced a six CD set of the complete *Leaves of Healing* weekly which should bring J.A. Dowie and Zion City to a wider audience. All these CDs, with the advanced search facility, give unparalleled access to primary source material.

As for secondary sources, the end of the twentieth century saw a veritable eruption of books and journals related to Pentecostalism, though the number of theses related to Britain and Ireland still remains relatively small. This is a reflection of the low base rate of lettered Pentecostals in earlier generations and the drift from the movement of their graduate offspring. The first academic journal of Pentecostal provenance to have a wide circulation was *Pneuma*, published by the Society for Pentecostal Studies (SPS) in America. It first appeared in 1979. The papers delivered at the annual conferences of the SPS, first convened in 1971, have been made available in duplicated form. The European Pentecostal Theological Association began the production of a duplicated *Bulletin* in 1981, then in the early 1990s its *Journal of the European Pentecostal Theological Association* (*JEPTA*) was issued in a much more professional format with articles of greater coverage and depth. The *Journal of Pentecostal Theology*, originally published by Sheffield Academic Press, with American editors, was first issued in 1992. More than the other two, it draws on the pneumatological insights of non-Pentecostal scholars, many of them of international repute. On-line facilities for obtaining articles from the *Cyberjournal for Pentecostal/Charismatic Research* and the *Asian Journal of Pentecostal Studies* are currently available. Sheffield Academic Press is also responsible for publishing by the summer of 2004 twenty-five books in its *Journal of Pentecostal Theology Supplement Series*, the most specifically historical of which is William Faupel's *The Everlasting Gospel*. Its central thesis, that eschatological hope was the driving force behind Pentecostalism's rapid growth, has proved formative in the author's thinking.

For the author, the two writers who have proved the most inspirational in their approach to the writing of religious history have been David Hempton and Grant Wacker. Both brim with ideas and are masters of style. In particular, Wacker, coming from a Pentecostal background of preachers and missionaries, can hardly write a dull sentence or fail to illustrate a point without backing it by an apposite quote. His *Heaven Below* (Harvard University Press) appeared in June 2001 and, eagerly awaited, did not disappoint.

Bibliography

Primary Sources

(MA = held in the Mattersey Archives at the Donald Gee Pentecostal and Charismatic Research Centre.)

Manuscripts

'W.R. Mercer Memoir'. (Flower Pentecostal Heritage Center).
'Tweed Memoir' (1992). [MA]
Vaughan, Idris J., 'Pilgrim With a Limp: This is My Story', (mid-1980s). [Vaughan Memoir]
Vaughan, Idris J., 'Nigeria: The Origins of the Apostolic Church Pentecostalism in Nigeria, 1931-52', 1991.
'A Man Named Adam (1909-84)', Memoir of Adam McKeown.
Carter, John, 'E. J. Phillips—Architect of Elim', memorial tribute, 1973. [MA]
'Dairy of Events in the Irish Work Since 1915', a typescript probably compiled by E.J. Phillips, c.1936. [MA]
'Farlow Typescript'. [MA]
Gordon Weeks MS.
John Carter, 'British Pentecostal History'. [MA]
John Long, 'Journal'.
Alf Magowan, 'The History of an Unusual People, a play written on behalf "the Elect in Sydney in N.S.W., Australia"', (n.d.). [Cooneyites]

Minutes and Constitutions

Minutes of the Elim Evangelistic Band (*EEB Minutes*). [MA]
Belfast Elim Minutes (*BEM*). [MA]
Minutes of the Elim Foursquare Gospel Alliance; Ministerial and General Conference. [MA]
Minutes of the [Irish] Elders' Meeting or Apostolic Church Minutes. [*ACM*]
Assemblies of God Presbytery Minute Book (Belfast and District).
'Constitution of the Elim Pentecostal Alliance', revised 1923. [MA]
'Constitution of the Elim Pentecostal Alliance', 1922. [MA]
'Deed Poll of the Elim Foursquare Gospel Alliance', 1934. [MA)]
'Elim Christ Church: What We Believe', George Jeffreys, 1916. [MA]

'The Right of the Local Church', George Jeffreys. [Elim]
'Introducing The Apostolic Church: A Manual of Belief, Practice and History', Penygroes.

Secondary Sources

Books

REFERENCE BOOKS

Connolly, S.J. (ed.), *The Oxford Companion to Irish History*, (Oxford University Press, 1998).
Burgess, Stanley M. *et al.* (eds.), *Dictionary of Pentecostal and Charismatic Movements* (Grand Rapids, MI: Zondervan, 1988).
Douglas, J.D. (ed.), *The International Dictionary of the Christian Church,* (Grand Rapids, MI: Zondervan, 1978).
Cameron, Nigel M. de S. (ed.), *Dictionary of Scottish Church History and Theology,* (Edinburgh: T. & T. Clark, 1993).
Douglas, J.D. (ed.), *Twentieth-Century Dictionary of Christian Biography,* (Carlisle: Paternoster, 1995).
Elwell, Walter A. (ed.), *Evangelical Dictionary of Theology,* (Basingstoke: Marshall Pickering, 1984).
Lewis, D.M. (ed.), *Dictionary of Evangelical Biography 1730-1860,* (Oxford: Blackwell, 1995).
Livingstone, E.A. (ed.), *The Oxford Dictionary of the Christian Church,* (Oxford: Oxford University Press, 1997 ed.).
Newman, Kate (ed.), *Dictionary of Ulster Biography,* (Belfast: Institute of Irish Studies, 1993).
Reid, Daniel G. *et al,* (eds.), *Dictionary of Christianity in America,* (Downers Grove, IL: Inter-Varsity Press, 1990).
Dictionary of National Biography.
The Belfast and Ulster Directory.

GENERAL

Anon., *The Prophetical Ministry (or the Voice Gifts) in the Church,* (Penygroes: Apostolic Church, 1931 ed.)
Anon., *Record of the International Conference on Divine Healing and True Holiness, held at the Agricultural Hall, London, June 1 to 5, 1885*, (London: J. Snow, 1885).
Acheson, Alan, *A History of the Church of Ireland 1691-1996,* (Dublin: Columba Press, 1997).
Albrecht, Daniel E, *Rites in the Spirit: A Ritual Approach to Pentecostal/Charismatic Spirituality,* (Sheffield: Sheffield Academic Press, 1999).

Anderson, Allan, *An Introduction to Pentecostalism*, (Cambridge: Cambridge University Press, 2004).

Anderson, Allan, *Zion and Pentecost*, (Pretoria: University of South Africa Press, 2000).

Anderson, A.H. and Hollenweger, W.J. (eds.), *Pentecostals After A Century: Global Perspectives on a Movement in Transition*, (Sheffield: Sheffield Academic Press, 1999).

Anderson, Robert M., *Vision of the Disinherited: The Making of American Pentecostalism*, (Peabody, MA: Hendrickson, 1992).

Arthur, William, *The Tongue of Fire*, (London: Epworth Press, 1956 ed.).

Bardon, Jonathan, *Belfast: An Illustrated History*, (Belfast: Blackstaff Press, 1982).

Bardon, Jonathan, *A History of Ulster*, (Belfast: Blackstaff Press, 1992).

Barkley, J.M., *Blackmouth and Dissenter*, (Belfast: White Row Press, 1991).

Barnes, Stanley, *All For Jesus* (Belfast: Ambassador, 1996).

Barratt, T.B., *When the Fire Fell and an Outline of my Life*, (Oslo: Alfons Hansen & Soner, 1927).

Barrs, Jerram, *Freedom and Discipleship,* (Leicester: Inter-Varsity Press, 1983).

Bartleman, Frank, *Azusa Street: The Roots of Modern-day Pentecost,* (South Plainfield, NJ: Bridge Publishing, 1980 ed.).

Baxter, Robert, *Narrative of Facts, Characterizing the Supernatural Manifestationsin members of Mr. Irving's Congregation and other individuals, in England and Scotland, and formerly by the Writer himself,* (London: Nisbet, 1833).

Beaman, Jay, *Pentecostal Pacifism,* (Kansas, KS: Centre for Mennonite Studies, Hillsboro, 1989).

Bebbington, David W, *Evangelicalism in Modern Britain: A History from the 1730s to the 1980s,* (London: Unwin Hyman, 1989).

Bebbington, David W, *Holiness in Nineteenth-Century England*, (Carlisle: Paternoster, 2000).

Bendroth, Margaret, *Fundamentalism and Gender,* (New Haven, CT: Yale University Press, 1993).

Blumhofer, Edith L., *Pentecost in My Soul: Explorations in the Meaning of Pentecostal Experience in the Early Assemblies Of God,* (Springfield, MO: Gospel Publishing House, 1989).

Blumhofer, Edith L., *Aimee Semple McPherson: Everybody's Sister* (Grand Rapids, MI: Eerdmans, 1993).

Blumhofer, Edith L., *Restoring the Faith: The Assemblies of God, Pentecostalism and American Culture,* (Urbana, IL: University of Illinois Press, 1993).

Blumhofer, Edith L. and Balmer, Randall, *Modern Christian Revivals,* (Urbana, IL: University of Illinois Press, 1993).

Boulton, E.C.W., *A Ministry of the Miraculous,* (London: Elim Publishing Office, 1928).

Brewer, John and Higgins, Gareth I., *Anti-Catholicism in Northern Ireland 1600-1998: The Mote and the Beam,* (London: Macmillan, 1998).

Brierley, Peter (ed.), *Irish Christian Handbook 1995/6,* (London: Christian Research, 1994).

Brierley, Peter, *Future Church: A Global Analysis of the Christian Community to the Year 2000,* (Crowborough: Monarch, 1998).

Brierley, Peter, *The Tide Is Running Out: What the English Church Attendance Survey Reveals,* (London: Christian Research, 2000).

Brooks, Noel, *Fight for the Faith and Freedom,* (London: The Pattern Bookroom, 1948).

Brouwer, Steve et al., *Exporting the American Gospel:Global Christian Fundamentalism,* (London: Routledge, 1996).

Bruce, Steve, *God Save Ulster: The Religion and Politics of Paisleyism,* (Oxford: Clarendon Press, 1986).

Bruner, F.D., *A Theology of the Holy Spirit: The Pentecostal Experience and the New Testament Witness,* (London: Hodder & Stoughton, 1970).

Camlin, Gilbert, *The Town in Ulster,* (Belfast: Wm.Mullan & Son, 1951).

Campbell, Faith, *Stanley Frodsham: Prophet with a Pen,* (Springfield, MO: Gospel Publishing House, 1974).

Carter, John, *Howard Carter: Man of the Spirit,* (Nottingham: AOG Publishing House, 1971).

Carter, John, *A Full Life: The Autobiography of a Pentecostal Pioneer,* (Nottingham: AOG, 1979).

Cartwright, Desmond W., *The Real Smith Wigglesworth: The Man, the Myth, the Message,* (Tonbridge: Sovereign World, 2001).

Cartwright, Desmond W., *The Great Evangelists: The Lives of George and Stephen Jeffreys,* (Basingstoke: Marshall Pickering, 1986).

Carwardine, Richard, *Transatlantic Revivalism: Popular Evangelicalism in Britain and America, 1790-1865,* (Westport, CT: Greenwood Press, 1978).

Chan, Simon, *Pentecostal Theology and the Christian Spiritual Tradition,* (Sheffield: Sheffield Academic Press, 2000).

Chidester, David, *Christianity: A Global History,* (London: Penguin Press, 2000).

Coad, Roy, *A History of the Brethren Movement,* (Exeter: Paternoster Press, 1976 ed.).

Colley, Linda, *Britons: Forging The Nation 1707-1837,* (London: Pimlico, 1994 ed.).

Cook, P.L., *Zion City: Twentieth Century Utopia,* (Syracuse, NY: Syracuse University Press, 1996).

Cox, Harvey, *Fire From Heaven: The Rise of Pentecostal Spirituality and the Reshaping of Religion,* (New York: Addison-Wesley, 1995).

Crookshank, C.H., *History of Methodism in Ireland,* (Clonmel: Tentmaker Publications, 1994 ed.).

Darrand, T.C. and Shupe, A., *Metaphors of Social Control in a Pentecostal Sect, (*New York: Edwin Mellen Press, 1983).

Dayton, Donald W., *The Theological Roots of Pentecostalism,* (Peabody, MA: Hendrickson, 1987).

De Arteaga, William, *Quenching the Spirit: Examining Centuries of Opposition to the Moving of the Holy Spirit,* (Lake Mary, FL: Creation House, 1992).

Dempster, Murray W. *et al., The Globalization of Pentecostalism: A Religion Made To Travel,* (Carlisle: Regnum/Paternoster, 1999).

Devlin, Paddy, *Yes, We Have No Bananas,* (Belfast: Blackstaff Press, 1981).

Edsor, Albert W, *George Jeffreys—Man of God: The Story of a Phenomenal Ministry,* (London: Ludgate Press, 1964).

Edsor, Albert W, *'Set Your House In Order': God's Call to George Jeffreys as the Founder of the Elim Pentecostal Movement* , (Chichester: New Wine Press, 1989).

Edwards, Ruth Dudley, *The Faithful Tribe: An Intimate Portrait of the Loyal Institutions,* (London: Harper Collins, 1999).

Epstein, Daniel Mark, *Sister Aimee: The Life of Aimee Semple McPherson,* (New York: Harcourt, Brace, 1993).

Evans, Eifion E., *The Welsh Revival of 1904,* (Bridgend: Evangelical Press of Wales, 1987).

Faupel, D. William, *The Everlasting Gospel: The Significance of Eschatology in the Development of Pentecostal Thought,* (Sheffield: Sheffield Academic Press, 1996).

Fiedler, Klaus, *The Story of the Faith Missions,* (Oxford: Regnum Books, 1994).

Finke, Roger and Stark, Rodney, *The Churching of America 1776-1990,* (New Brunswick: Rutgers University Press, 1997 ed.).

Flegg, C.G., *Gathered Under Apostles: a Study of the Catholic Apostolic Church,* (Oxford: Clarendon Press, 1992).

Ford, Jack, *In the Steps of John Wesley: The Church of the Nazarene in Britain,* (Kansas, KS: Nazarene Publishing House, 1968).

Gardiner, Gordon P., *Out of Zion Into The World,* (Shippensburg, PA: Companion Press, 1990).

Gee, Donald, *Bonnington Poll—And After,* (London: Victory Press, 1943).

Gee, Donald, *Fruitful or Barren?: Studies in the Fruit of the Spirit,* (Springfield, MO: Gospel Publishing House, 1961).

Gee, Donald, *Concerning Spiritual Gifts,* (Springfield, MO: Gospel Publishing House, 1963 ed.).

Gee, Donald, *Wind and Flame,* (Croydon: Heath Press, 1967).

Gee, Donald, *These Men I Knew*, (Nottingham: A.O.G. Publishing House, 1980).

Goff, James R., *Fields White Unto Harvest: Charles F. Parham and Missionary Origins of Pentecostalism*, (Fayetteville, AR: University of Arkansas Press, 1988).

Goff. James R. and Wacker, Grant (eds.), *Portraits of a Generation: Early Pentecostal Leaders*, (Fayetteville, AR: University of Arkansas Press, 2002).

Gold, Malcolm, *The Hybridization of an Assembly of God Church—Proselytism, Retention, and Re-Affiliation*, (New York: Edwin Mellen Press, 2003).

Gordon, A.J., *The Ministry of Healing*, (Camp Hill, PA: Christian Publications, 1992 ed.).

Govan, I.R., *Spirit of Revival: A Biography of J.G. Govan*, (Edinburgh: The Faith Press, 1950 ed.).

Gribbon, Sybil, *Edwardian Belfast: A Social Profile*, (Belfast: Appletree Press, 1982).

Guthrie, Stan, *Missions in the Third Millennium: 21 Key Trends for the 21st Century*, (Carlisle: Paternoster, 2000).

Hamon, Bill, *Apostles, Prophets and the Coming Moves of God*, (Shippenburg, PA: Destiny Image, 1997).

Hardesty, Nancy C., *Faith Cure: Divine Healing in the Holiness and Pentecostal Movements*, (Peabody, MA: Hendrickson, 2003).

Harper, Michael, *This Is The Day*, (London: Hodder & Stoughton, 1979).

Harrell, David E., *All Things Are Possible: The Healing and Charismatic Revivals in Modern America*, (Bloomington, IN: Indiana University Press, 1975).

Hempton, David, *Religion and Culture in Britain and Ireland*, (Cambridge: Cambridge University Press, 1996).

Hempton, David and Hill, Myrtle, *Evangelical Protestantism in Ulster Society 1740-1890*, (London: Routledge, 1992).

Hennessey, Thomas, *A History of Northern Ireland 1920-1996*, (Dublin: Gill & Macmillan, 1997).

Hocken, Peter, *Streams of Renewal*, (Carlisle: Paternoster, 1997 ed.).

Hollenweger, Walter J., *The Pentecostals*, (London: SCM Press, 1972).

Hollenweger, Walter J., *Pentecostalism: Origins and Developments Worldwide*, (Peabody, MA: Hendrickson, 1997).

Holmes, Janice, *Religious Revivals in Britain and Ireland, 1859-1905*, (Dublin: Irish Academic Press, 2000).

Hopkins, Evan H., *The Law of Liberty in the Spiritual Life*, (London: Marshall, Morgan & Scott, 1952 ed).

Horton, Harold, *The Gifts of the Spirit*, (Nottingham: AOG, 1976 ed.).

Hovenden, Gerald, *Speaking in Tongues: The New Testament Evidence in Context*, (Sheffield: Sheffield Academic Press, 2002).

Hughes, R.T. (ed.), *The American Quest for the Primitive Church*, (Chicago, IL: University of Illinois Press, 1988).

Hutchison, James, *Weavers, Miners and the Open Book: A History of Kilsyth, (*published privately, 1986).

Hywel-Davies, Jack, *The Life of Smith Wigglesworth: A Pioneer of the Pentecostal Movement*, (London: Hodder & Stoughton, 1987).

Hywel-Davies, Jack, *The Kensington Temple Story*, (Crowborough: Monarch Books, 1998).

Jeffreys, Edward, *Stephen Jeffreys: The Beloved Evangelist*, (Luton: Redemption Tidings Bookroom, 1946).

Jeffreys, George, *Pentecostal Rays: The Baptism and Gifts of the Holy Spirit,* (Worthing, Henry E. Walter, 1954 ed.).

Jeffreys, George, *Healing Rays*, (Worthing: H.E. Walter,1985 ed.).

Johns, Cheryl Bridges, *Pentecostal Formation: A Pedagogy among the Oppressed,* (Sheffield: Sheffield Academic Press, 1993).

Johnstone, Patrick, *Operation World, (*Carlisle: OM Publishing, 1993).

Jones, Brynmor P., *Voices from the Welsh Revival,* (Bridgend: Evangelical Press of Wales, 1995).

Jones, Brynmor P., *The Trials and Triumphs of Mrs. Jessie Penn-Lewis, (*North Brunswick, NJ: Bridge-Logos, 1997).

Kay, William K., *Inside Story: A History of the British Assemblies of God, (*Mattersey: Mattersey Hall Publishing, 1990).

Kay, William K., *Pentecostals in Britain*, (Carlisle: Paternoster, 2000).

Kennedy, H.C. and Maclean, J.K., *Charles M. Alexander: Romance of Song and Soul Winning*, (London: Marshall Brothers, c.1920).

Kent, John, *Holding The Fort, (*London: Epworth Press, 1978).

Land, Steven J, *Pentecostal Spirituality: A Passion for the Kingdom, (*Sheffield: Sheffield Academic Press, 1993).

Landau, Rom, *God Is My Adventure,* (London: Faber and Faber, 1943).

Lang, G.H., *An Ordered Life: An Autobiography,* (London: Paternoster Press, 1959).

Leonard, Christine, *A Giant in Ghana,* (Chichester: New Wine Press, 1989).

Lindsay, Gordon, *John Alexander Dowie: A Life Story of Trials, Tragedies and Triumphs,* (Dallas, TS: Christ for All Nations, 1986).

Lippy, C.H. and Williams, P.W., *Encyclopaedia of the American Religious Experience: Studies of Traditions and Movement Vol. II,* (New York: Charles Scribner, 1988).

Livingstone, David N. and Wells, Ronald A., *Ulster-American Religion: Episodes in the History of a Cultural Connection,* (Indiana, IN: University of Notre Dame Press, 1999).

Marsden, George M., *Fundamentalism and American Culture: The Shaping of Twentieth-Century Evangelicalism 1870-1925,* (New York: Oxford University Press, 1980 ed.).

Martin, David (ed.), *A Sociological Yearbook of Religion in Britain, No. 2, (*London: SCM Press, 1969).

Massey, Richard, *Another Springtime: Donald Gee: Pentecostal Pioneer,* (Guildford: Highland Books, 1992).

Matthews, David (ed.), *Apostles Today,* (Bradford: Harvestime, 1988).

McDonnell, Kilian, *Charismatic Renewal and the Churches,* (New York: Seabury Press, 1976).

McEwan, A. and Robinson, E., *Evangelical Beliefs and Educational Standards*, (Aldershot: Avebury, 1995).

McGee, Gary.B., *Initial Evidence: Historical and Biblical Perspectives on the Pentecostal Doctrines of Spirit-baptism,* (Peabody, MA: Hendrickson, 1991).

McGrath, Alister, *The Twilight of Atheism: The Rise and Fall of Disbelief in the Modern World*, (Doubleday: New York, 2004).

McKittrick, David et al, *Lost Lives: The Stories of the Men, Women and Children Who Died as a Result of the Northern Ireland Troubles,* (Edinburgh: Mainstream Publishing, 1999).

McLoughlin, William G., *Modern Revivalism: Charles Grandison Finney to Billy Graham,* (New York: Ronald Press Company, 1959).

McPherson, Aimee Semple, *The Story of My Life,* (Waco: Word Books, 1971 ed.).

McWhirter, James, *Every Barrier Swept Away*, (Cardiff: Megiddo Press, 1983).

Metcalf, J.C., *Molded by the Cross: The Biography of Jessie Penn Lewis,* (Fort Washington, PA: Christian Literature Crusade, 1997).

Missen, Alfred F., *The Sound of a Going*, (Nottingham: AOG Publishing House, 1973).

Moloney, Ed. and Pollak, Andy, *Paisley* , (Swords: Poolbeg, 1986).

Montgomery, Samuel, *Elim in Ballymena 1916-1986,* (published privately, 1986).

Mullin, R B., *Miracles and the Modern Imagination,* (New Haven, CT: Yale University Press, 1996).

Murray, Ian H., *Martyn Lloyd-Jones: The Fight of Faith 1939-1981,* (Edinburgh: Banner of Truth, 1990).

Murray, S.W., *W.P. Nicholson: Flame for God in Ulster,* (Belfast: Presbyterian Fellowship, 1973).

Newbigin, Lesslie, *The Household of Faith,* (London: SCM Press, 1955)

Nicholson, W.P., *The Evangelist,* (London: Marshall, Morgan and Scott, n.d.).

Nicholson, W.P., *To Win The Prize: The Spirit-filled Life,* (Belfast: Ambassador, n.d.).

Nienkirchen, C.W., *A.B. Simpson and the Pentecostal Movement,* (Peabody, MA: Hendrickson, 1992).

Oliphant, Mrs, *The Life of Edward Irving, Minister of the National Scotch Church, London,* (London: Hurst and Blackett, 1862 ed.).

Ormsby, Frank (ed.), *The Collected Poems of John Hewitt,* (Belfast: Blackstaff Press, 1991).

Orr, J.Edwin, *The Flaming Tongue: The Impact of Twentieth Century Revivals,* (Chicago, IL: Moody Press, 1973).

Packer, J.I., *Keep in Step in the Spirit*, (Leicester: IVP, 1984).

Paisley, Ian R.K., *The Fifty-Nine Revival,* (Belfast: Martyrs' Memorial Free Presbyterian Church, 1958).

Palmer, Phoebe, *Four Years in the Old World*, (New York, 1866).

Parker, D. and H., *The Secret Sect*, (published privately, 1982).

Patton, Marcus, *Central Belfast,* (Belfast: Ulster Architectural Heritage Society, 1993).

Paulin, Tom, *Writing to the Moment,* (London: Faber, 1996).

Penn-Lewis, Jessie, *War on the Saints,* (Kent: Diasozo Trust, 1987 ed.).

Phoenix, Eamon, *Northern Nationalism: Nationalist Politics, Partition and the Catholic Minority in Northern Ireland, 1890-1920,* (Belfast: Ulster Historical Foundation, 1996).

Pierson, A.T., *Forward Movements in the Last Half Century,* (New York: Funk & Wagnall, 1905).

Pollock, J.C., *The Keswick Story*, (London: Hodder and Stoughton, 1964).

Pollock, John, *The Cambridge Seven,* (Basingstoke: Marshall Pickering, 1985).

Pollock, Vivienne and Parkhill, Trevor, *Britain in Old Photographs: Belfast,* (Stroud: Sutton Publishing, 1997).

Pope, Liston. *Millhands and Preachers; A Study of Gastonia,* (New Haven, CT: Yale University Press, 1942).

Price, Charles and Randall, Ian, *Transforming Keswick,* (Carlisle: OM Publishing, Paternoster, 2000).

Pytches, David, *Prophecy in the Local Church: A Practical Handbook and Historical Overview,* (London: Hodder and Stoughton, 1993).

Quebedeux, Richard, *The New Charismatics II,* (San Francisco: Harper & Row, 1983).

Randall, Ian M, *Evangelical Experiences: A Study of the Spirituality of English Evangelicalism 1918-1939,* (Carlisle: Paternoster, 1999).

Rea, David, *The Life and Labours of David Rea, Evangelist,* (Kilmarnock: John Ritchie, 1917).

Redmond, John, *Church, State, Industry 1827-1929 in East Belfast,* (privately published, 1960).

Richardson, Norman (ed.), *A Tapestry of Beliefs: Christian Traditions in Northern Ireland,* (Belfast: Blackstaff Press, 1998).

Robeck, Cecil M. (ed.), *Charismatic Experiences in History,* (Peabody, MA: Hendrickson, 1985).

Roberts, Keith A,. *Religion in Sociological Perspective,* (Belmont, CA: Wadsworth, 1995).

Rowe, W.A.C., *One Faith, One Lord,* (Penygroes: Apostolic Publications, 1988 ed.).

Samarin, William J., *Tongues of Men and Angels: A Controversial and Sympathetic Analysis of Speaking in Tongues,* (London: Macmillan, 1972).

Sandige, Jerry L., *Roman Catholic/ Pentecostal Dialogue, 1977-1982: A Study in Developing Ecumenism, Vol. II*, (Frankfurt: Peter Lang, 1987).

Schaff, Philip, *History of the Christian Church,* (Edinburgh: T & T Clark, 1884 ed.).

Scotland, Nigel, *Charismatics and the New Millennium,* (Guildford: Eagle, 2000).

Scott, Alfred R., *The Ulster Revival of 1859: Enthusiasm Emanating From Mid-Antrim,* (Mid-Antrim Historical Group, 1962).

Scott, Carolyn, *The Heavenly Witch: The Story of The Maréchale* (London: Hamish Hamilton, 1981).

Scott, O.W., *The Story of the Portstewart Convention,* (Belfast: Portstewart Convention Committee, 1934).

Shaull, Richard and Cesar, Waldo, *Pentecostalism and the Future of the Christian Churches,* (Grand Rapids, MI: Eerdmans, 2000).

Shiels W.J., *The Church and Healing*, (Oxford: Blackwell, 1982).

Smail, Tom, Walker, Andrew and Wright, Nigel, *Charismatic Renewal: the Search for a Theology*, (London: SPCK, 1995).

Smith, Timothy L., *Called Unto Holiness: The Story of the Nazarenes,* (Kansas City, KS: Nazarene Publishing House, 1962).

Stark, Rodney and Finke, Roger, *Acts of Faith: Explaining the Human Side of Religion,* (Berkeley, CA: University of California Press, 2000).

Strachan, Gordon, *The Pentecostal Theology of Edward Irving,* (Peabody, MA: Hendrickson, 1973).

Stunt, Timothy C.F., *From Awakening to Secession: Radical Evangelicals in Switzerland and Britain 1815-35*, (Edinburgh: T. & T. Clark, 2000).

Synan, Vinson, *The Holiness-Pentecostal Movement in the United States,* (Grand Rapids, MI: Eerdmans, 1997).

Synan, Vinson, *Aspects of Pentecostal-Charismatic Origin,* (Plainfield, NJ: Logos, 1975).

Synan, Vinson, *The Century of the Holy Spirit: 100 Years of Pentecostal and Charismatic Renewal,* (Nashville, TN: Thomas Nelson, 2001).

Thistleton, Anthony C., *The First Epistle to the Corinthians,* (Grand Rapids, MI: Eerdmans, 2000).

Thomas, J.C., *The Devil, Disease and Deliverance: Origins of Illness in New Testament Thought*, (Sheffield: Sheffield Academic Press, 1998).

Torrey, R.A., *The Person and Work of the Holy Spirit,* (Springdale, PA: Whitaker House, 1996 ed).

Turnbull, T.N., *Apostle Andrew,* (Bradford: Puritan Press, 1965).

Turnbull, T.N., *What God Hath Wrought*, (Bradford: Puritan Press, 1959).

Turnbull, T.N., *Brothers in Arms,* (Bradford: Puritan Press, 1963).

Van Der Laan, Cornelis, *Sectarian Against His Will: Gerrit Roelof Polman and the Birth of Pentecostalism in the Netherlands,* (London: Scarecrow Press, 1991).

Vulliamy, C.E., *John Wesley*, (New Jersey, NJ: Barbour, 1985 ed.).

Wacker, Grant, *Heaven Below: Early Pentecostals and American Culture* (Cambridge, MA: Harvard University Press, 2001).

Wagner, C. Peter, *Spiritual Power and Church Growth,* (London: Hodder and Stoughton,1986).

Wagner, C. Peter, *Apostles and Prophets: The Foundation of the Church,* (Ventura, CA: Regal, 2000).

Walker, Andrew, *Restoring The Kingdom: The Radical Christianity of the House Church Movement,* (Guildford: Eagle, 1998 ed.).

Walker, Andrew and Aune, Kristin (eds.), *On Revival: A Critical Examination*, (Carlisle: Paternoster, 2003).

Wallis, Arthur, *In The Day Of Thy Power,* (Hampshire: Christian Literature Crusade, 1989 ed.).

Warfield, B.B., *Perfectionism,* (Philadelphia, PA: Presbyterian and Reformed Publishing, 1971 ed.).

Warrington, Keith (ed.)., *Pentecostal Perspectives,* (Carlisle: Paternoster Press, 1998).

Welker, Michael, *God the Spirit,* (Minneapolis, MN: Fortress Press, 1994).

Westerkamp, Marilyn J., *Triumph of the Laity: Scots-Irish Piety and the Great Awakening 1625-1760*, (New York, NY: Oxford University Press, 1988).

Whale, J.S., *The Protestant Tradition,* (Cambridge: Cambridge University Press, 1955).

White, Charles E., *The Beauty of Holiness: Phoebe Palmer, Theologian, Revivalist, Feminist, and Humanitarian,* (Grand Rapids, MI: Zondervan, 1986).

White, Kent, *The Word of God Coming Again,* (Winton: Apostolic Faith Mission, 1919).

Whittaker, Colin, *Seven Pentecostal Pioneers,* (Basingstoke: Marshalls, 1983).

Williams, D.P., *And They Shall Prophesy*, (Penygroes, 1959 ed.).

Williams, Cyril G., *Tongues of the Spirit: A Study of Pentecostal Glossolalia and Related Phenomena,* (Cardiff: University of Wales Press, 1981).

Wilson, Bryan R. (ed.), *Patterns of Sectarianism,* (London: Heinemann, 1967).

Wilson, Bryan R., *Sects and Society: The Sociology of Three Religious Groups in Britain*, (London: Heinemann, 1961).

Wolffe, John, *The Protestant Crusade in Great Britain, 1829-1860,* (Oxford: Clarendon Press, 1991).

Worsfold, James E., *A History of the Charismatic Movements in New Zealand, with a Breviate of the Catholic Apostolic Church in Great Britain,* (Bradford: Julian Literature Trust, 1974).

Worsfold, James E., *The Origins of the Apostolic Church in Great Britain,* (Wellington, NZ: Julian Literature Trust, 1991).

Yong, Amos, *Discerning the Spirit(s): A Pentecostal-Charismatic Contribution to Christian Theology of Religions*, (Sheffield: Sheffield Academic Press, 2000).

Pamphlets

Anon., (Londonderry layman), *Baptism of the Spirit*, 1859.

Anon., *A Local Perspective: W. P. Nicholson, (*published privately, n.d.).

Anon., *Concerning the Ministry and Evangelistic Campaigns of Mrs. Catherine Booth-Clibborn,* (published privately, 1933).

Anon., *St. James' Crinken 1840-1990*, (published privately, n.d.).

Anon., *Bethshan Tabernacle, Belfast: Commemorative Brochure* (1972).

Anon., (Observer), *'Who Are They'?: The Elimites* (Belfast: Sabbath School Society, c.1950).

Anon., *Souvenir exhibiting the Movements of God in The Apostolic Church* (Penygroes, 1933).

Bailie, W.D., *The Six Mile Water Revival of 1625,* (Belfast: Presbyterian Historical Society, 1976).

Booth-Clibborn, Willam, *The Baptism In The Holy Spirit*, (Dallas: Voice of Healing, 1963, 4th edition).

Brown, Terence, *The Whole Protestant Community: The Making of an Historical Myth*, (Derry: Field Day, 1985).

Gee, Donald, *'Apostolic Church' Error,* (London: AOG, n.d.).

Irwin, Archibald, *Lights Along The Way,* (Belfast: Northern Whig, 1941).

Lang, G. H, *The Earlier Years of the Modern Tongues Movement: A Historical Survey And Its Lesson,* (Florida: Conley & Schoettle, 1985).

Leech, John, *Israel in Britain; Point by Point Reply to W.F.P. Burton's ' Why I do not Believe the British-Israel Theory'*, (published privately, 1940).

Long, S.E., *W.P. Nicholson: 'The Rude Evangelist'*, (Dromara: Slieve Croob Press, 1983).

Parr, J. Nelson, *Incredible: The Autobiography of J. Nelson Parr,* (Fleetwood: 1972).

Scroggie, Graham, *The Baptism of the Spirit: Speaking in Tongues,* (London: Marshall, Morgan & Scott, n.d).

Spence, Walter L., *Elim in Cullybackey 1919-1989*, (published privately, n.d.).

Articles

IN JOURNALS

Blumhofer, Edith, 'Alexander Boddy and the Rise of Pentecostalism in Great Britain', *Pneuma*, Vol. 8.1, Spring 1986.

Bundy, David, 'Spiritual Advice to a Seeker: Letters to T.B. Barratt from Azusa Street 1906', *Pneuma*, Vol. 14.2, 1992.

Bundy, David, 'Thomas Ball Barratt: From Methodist to Pentecostal', *JEPTA*, Vol. 13, 1994.

Barfoot, C.H. and Sheppard, G.T., 'Prophetic v Priestly Religion: The Changing Roles of Women Clergy in Classical Pentecostal Churches', *Review of Religious Research*, Vol. 22, 19....

Cartwright, D.W., '"Your Daughters Shall Prophecy": The Contribution of Women in Early Pentecostalism', *SPS Conference paper*, 1985

Cartwright, D W., 'The Real Wigglesworth', *JEPTA*, Vol. 17, 1997.

Creech, Joe, 'Visions of Glory: The Place of the Azusa Street Revival in Pentecostal History', *Church History*, Vol. 65.3, 1996.

Cunningham, R.J., 'From Holiness to Healing: The Faith Cure in America 1872-1892', *Church History*, Vol. 43.4, 1974.

Faupel, D.W., 'Glossolalia as a Foreign Language: Investigations of the Early Twentieth Century Pentecostal Claim', *Wesleyan Theological Journal*, Vol. 31.1, 1996.

Gerlach, Luther P. and Vine, Virginia H., 'Five Factors Crucial to the Spread of a Modern Religious Movement', *Journal of the Scientific Study of Religion*, Vol. 7.1, 1968.

Goff, James R., 'Closing Out the Church Age: Pentecostals Face the Twenty-First Century', *Pneuma*, Vol. 14.1, 1992.

Hathaway, Malcolm R., 'The Role of William Oliver Hutchinson and the Apostolic Faith Church in the formation of British Pentecostal Churches', *JEPTA*, Vol. XVI, 1996.

Hill, Myrtle, 'Ulster Awakened: The '59 Revival Reconsidered', *Journal of Ecclesiastical History*, Vol. 41.3, 1990.

Hocken, Peter, 'Cecil Polhill: Pentecostal Layman', *Pneuma*, Vol. 20.2, 1988.

Hocken, Peter, 'Donald Gee—Pentecostal Ecumenist?', *Papers of the Joint Meeting of SPS and EPCRA*, 1995.

Macchia, Frank D, '"Groans Too Deep for Words": Towards a Theology of Tongues as Initial Evidence', *Asian Journal of Pentecostal Studies*, Vol. 1.2, 1998.

McGee, Gary B., '"Latter Rain" Falling in the East: Early Twentieth-century Pentecostalism in India and the Debate over Speaking in Tongues', *Church History*, Vol. 68.3, 1999.

McGee, Gary B., 'The Debate over "Missionary Tongues" among Radical Evangelicals 1881-97', *SPS Conference Papers*, 1999.

Moore, Rickie D., 'Walter Brueggemann: Prophet to the Critical Establishment and Sage to Pentecostals in the Margin', *SPS Conference Papers*, 1998.

Packer, J.I., '"Keswick" and the Reformed Doctrine of Sanctification', *The Evangelical Quarterly*, July, 1955.

Pinnock, Clark, 'Divine Relationality: A Pentecostal Contribution to the Doctrine of God', *Journal of Pentecostal Theology*, Vol. 16, 2000.

Randall, Ian M, 'Holiness and Pentecostal Movements in Inter-War England', *Papers of the Joint Meeting of SPS and EPCRA*, 1995.

Randall, Ian M, 'Old Time Power: Relationships between Pentecostalism and Evangelical Spirituality in England', *Pneuma*, Vol. 19.1, 1997.

Randall, Ian M, '"Outside the Camp": Brethren Spirituality and Wider Evangelicalism in the 1920s', *Brethren Archivists and Human Network Review*, Vol. 2.1, 2000.

Robinson, James, 'Arthur Booth-Clibborn: Salvationist and Pentecostal Patriarch', *JEPTA*, Vol. 21, 2001.

Taylor, Malcolm, 'A Historical Perspective on the Doctrine of Divine Healing', *JEPTA*, Vol. 24, 1995.

Tierney, David, 'The Catholic Apostolic Church: A Study in Tory Millenarianism', *Historical Research*, Vol. 63, 1990.

Van Der Laan, Cornelis, 'The Proceedings of the Leaders' Meetings (1908-1911) and the International Pentecostal Council (1912-1914)', *JEPTA*, Vol. 6.3, 1987.

Volf, Miroslav, 'Materiality of Salvation: An Investigation in the Soteriologies of Liberation and Pentecostal Theologies', *Journal of Ecumenical Studies*, Vol. 26.3, 1989.

Wacker, Grant, 'Marching to Zion: Religion in a Moden Utopian Community', *Church History*, Vol. 54.4, 1985.

Walker, Andrew G. and Atherton, J.A., 'An Easter Pentecostal Convention: The Successful Management of a "Time of Blessing"', *Sociological Review*, Vol. 19, 1971.

Warrington, Keith, 'Major Aspects of Healing within British Pentecostalism', *JEPTA*, Vol 19, 1999.

Wilhelm, Jared, 'Familiar Ground: Origins of Pentecostal Thought and Belief as seen in the Writings, Life and Ministry of John Alexander Dowie', *SPS Conference Paper*, 1999.

White, Charles E., 'Phoebe Palmer and the Development of Pentecostal Pneumatology', *Wesleyan Theological Journal*, Vol. 23.2, 1988.

Wilson, Bryan R., 'An Analysis of Sect Development', *American Sociological Review*, Vol. 24.1, 1959.

Wyllie, Robert W., 'Pioneers of Ghanaian Pentecostalism: Peter Anim and James McKeown', *Journal of Religion in Africa*, Vol. VI, 1974.

IN BOOKS

Blumhofer, Edith L., 'The Christian Catholic Apostolic Church and the Apostolic Faith: A Study in the 1906 Pentecostal Revival', in Cecil M. Robeck (ed), *Charismatic Experiences in History*, (Peabody, MA: Hendrickson, 1985).

Hathaway, Malcolm R., 'The Elim Pentecostal Church: Origins, Development and Distinctives', in Keith Warrington (ed.), *Pentecostal Perspectives,* (Carlisle: Paternoster Press, 1998).

Holmes, Janice, '"The World Turned Upside Down": Women in the Ulster Revival of 1859', in Holmes, Janice and Urquart, D. (eds.), *'Coming into the Light': The Work, Politics and Religion of Women in Ulster 1840-1940*, (Belfast: Blackstaff, 1994).

Macchia, Frank D., 'The Struggle for Global Witness: Shifting Paradigms in Pentecostal Theology', in Dempster, Murray W., *The Globalization of Pentecostalism,* (Carlisle: Regnum, Paternoster, 1999).

Mews, Stuart, 'The Revival of Spiritual Healing in the Church of England', in Shiels, W.J. (ed.), *The Church and Healing,* (Oxford: Blackwell, 1982).

Wacker, Grant, 'Playing for Keeps: The Primitive Impulse in Early Pentecostalism', in Hughes, R.T. (ed.), *The American Quest for the Primitive Church,* (Urbana, IL: University of Illinois Press, 1988).

Wacker, Grant, 'Searching for Eden with a Satellite Dish', in Hughes, Richard T. (ed.), *The Primitive Church in the Modern World*, (Urbana, IL: University of Illinois Press, 1995).

Walker, Pamela J., 'A Chaste and Fervid Eloquence: Catherine Booth and the Ministry of Women in the Salvation Army', in Kienzle, Beverly Mayne and Walker, Pamela J. (eds.), *Women Preachers and Prophets,* (Berkeley, CA: University of California, 1998).

Wilson, Everett A., 'They Crossed the Red Sea, Didn't They?', in Dempster, Murray W. *et al., The Globalization of Pentecostalism,* (Carlisle: Regnum, Paternoster, 1999).

Internet Sources

Cox, Harvey, 'Age of Miracles, *World Policy Journal*, Vol. 14 (Spring, 1997), pp. 87-95, http://www.dickinson.edu/~ rose/coxrevpqdweb.html

Droogers, Andre, 'Globalization and the Pentecostal Success', http://casnws.scw.vu.nl/publicalities/droogers-globpent.html

Martyn Percy, 'Is there a Modern Charismatic Theology*?'*, www.farmington.ac.uk/documents/ol_docs/mt6.html

Williams, J.Rodman, 'A Theological Pilgrimage', http://forum.regent.edu/rodmwil/tp03.html

Unpublished Theses/Dissertations

Allen, David, 'Signs and Wonders: The Origins, Growth, Development and Significance of Assemblies of God in Great Britain and Ireland 1900-1980', (PhD thesis, London, 1990).

Cartwright, Desmond W., 'Some Evangelists: the Life and Ministry of George Jeffreys and P.S. Brewster in the Formation of the Elim Pentecostal Church', MA diss., Sheffield, n.d).

Cartwright, Desmond W., 'From the Valleys They Came: The Emergence of Pentecostalism in South Wales After the Revival of 1904-5', (MA diss., Sheffield, n.d.).

Darragh, Paul, 'Epidemiological Observations on Episodes of Communicable Psychogenic Illness', (PhD thesis, Queens University Belfast, 1988).

Gibson, Andrew, 'The Charismatic Movement in Northern Ireland against the Background of the Troubles', (MTh thesis, Queens University Belfast, 1987).

Hudson, Neil D., 'A Schism and its Aftermath; An Historical Analysis of Denominational Discerption in the Elim Church 1939-1940', (PhD thesis, London, 1999).

Llewellyn, Henry Byron, 'A Study of the History and Thought of the Apostolic Church in Wales in the Context of Pentecostalism', (MPhil thesis, University of Wales, 1997).

Massey, Richard D., '"A Sound and Scriptural Union": An Examination of the Origins of the Assemblies of God of Great Britain and Ireland during the Years 1920-1925', (PhD thesis, Birmingham, 1987).

Petts, David, 'Healing and the Atonement', (PhD thesis, Nottingham, 1993).

Robinson, Martin, 'The Charismatic Anglican—Historical and Contemporary: A Comparison of the Life and Work of Alexander Boddy (1854-1930) and Michael C. Harper', (MLitt thesis, 1976, University of Birmingham).

Ross, Brian R, 'Donald Gee: In Search of a Church—Sectarian in Transition', (DTh thesis, Toronto, 1974).

Taylor, Malcolm J., 'Publish and Be Blessed', (PhD thesis, Birmingham, 1994).

Thompson, Joseph, ('Geneva'), 'Repercussions in Ulster of the 1904-5 Welsh Revival', (Paul Memorial Prize, Union Theological College, Belfast, n.d.).

Warburton, T.Rennie, 'A Comparative Study of Minority Religious Groups, with Special Reference to Holiness and Related Movements in Britain in the Last 50 Years', (PhD thesis, London, 1966)

General Index

Studies in Evangelical History and Thought

(All titles uniform with this volume)
Dates in bold are of projected publication

Clyde Binfield
The Country a Little Thickened and Congested?
Nonconformity in Eastern England 1840–1885

Studies of Victorian religion and society often concentrate on cities, suburbs, and industrialisation. This study provides a contrast. Victorian Eastern England—Essex, Suffolk, Norfolk, Cambridgeshire, and Huntingdonshire—was rural, traditional, relatively unchanging. That is nonetheless a caricature which discounts the industry in Norwich and Ipswich (as well as in Haverhill, Stowmarket, and Leiston) and ignores the impact of London on Essex, of railways throughout the region, and of an ancient but changing university (Cambridge) on the county town which housed it. It also entirely ignores the political implications of such changes in a region noted for the variety of its religious Dissent since the seventeenth century. This book explores Victorian Eastern England and its Nonconformity. It brings to a wider readership a pioneering thesis which has made a major contribution to a fresh evolution of English religion and society.

2005 */ 1-84227-216-0 / approx. 274pp*

John Brencher
Martyn Lloyd-Jones (1899–1981) and Twentieth-Century Evangelicalism

This study critically demonstrates the significance of the life and ministry of Martyn Lloyd-Jones for post-war British evangelicalism and demonstrates that his preaching was his greatest influence on twentieth-century Christianity. The factors which shaped his view of the church are examined, as is the way his reformed evangelicalism led to a separatist ecclesiology which divided evangelicals.

2002 / 1-84227-051-6 / xvi + 268pp

Jonathan D. Burnham
A Story of Conflict
The Controversial Relationship between Benjamin Wills Newton and John Nelson Darby

Burnham explores the controversial relationship between the two principal leaders of the early Brethren movement. In many ways Newton and Darby were products of their times, and this study of their relationship provides insight not only into the dynamics of early Brethrenism, but also into the progress of nineteenth-century English and Irish evangelicalism.

2004 / 1-84227-191-1 / xxiv + 268pp

J.N. Ian Dickson

Beyond Religious Discourse

Sermons, Preaching and Evangelical Protestants in Nineteenth-Century Irish Society

Drawing extensively on primary sources, this pioneer work in modern religious history explores the training of preachers, the construction of sermons and how Irish evangelicalism and the wider movement in Great Britain and the United States shaped the preaching event. Evangelical preaching and politics, sectarianism, denominations, education, class, social reform, gender, and revival are examined to advance the argument that evangelical sermons and preaching went significantly beyond religious discourse. The result is a book for those with interests in Irish history, culture and belief, popular religion and society, evangelicalism, preaching and communication.

***2005** / 1-84227-217-9 / approx. 324pp*

Neil T.R. Dickson

Brethren in Scotland 1838–2000

A Social Study of an Evangelical Movement

The Brethren were remarkably pervasive throughout Scottish society. This study of the Open Brethren in Scotland places them in their social context and examines their growth, development and relationship to society.

2003 / 1-84227-113-X / xxviii + 510pp

Crawford Gribben and Timothy C.F. Stunt (eds)

Prisoners of Hope?

Aspects of Evangelical Millennialism in Britain and Ireland, 1800–1880

This volume of essays offers a comprehensive account of the impact of evangelical millennialism in nineteenth-century Britain and Ireland.

2004 / 1-84227-224-1 / xiv + 208pp

Khim Harris

Evangelicals and Education

Evangelical Anglicans and Middle-Class Education in Nineteenth-Century England

This ground breaking study investigates the history of English public schools founded by nineteenth-century Evangelicals. It documents the rise of middle-class education and Evangelical societies such as the influential Church Association, and includes a useful biographical survey of prominent Evangelicals of the period.

2004 / 1-84227-250-0 / xviii + 422pp

Mark Hopkins
Nonconformity's Romantic Generation
Evangelical and Liberal Theologies in Victorian England

A study of the theological development of key leaders of the Baptist and Congregational denominations at their period of greatest influence, including C.H. Spurgeon and R.W. Dale, and of the controversies in which those among them who embraced and rejected the liberal transformation of their evangelical heritage opposed each other.

2004 / 1-84227-150-4 / xvi + 284pp

Don Horrocks
Laws of the Spiritual Order
Innovation and Reconstruction in the Soteriology of Thomas Erskine of Linlathen

Don Horrocks argues that Thomas Erskine's unique historical and theological significance as a soteriological innovator has been neglected. This timely reassessment reveals Erskine as a creative, radical theologian of central and enduring importance in Scottish nineteenth-century theology, perhaps equivalent in significance to that of S.T. Coleridge in England.

2004 / 1-84227-192-X / xx + 362pp

Kenneth S. Jeffrey
When the Lord Walked the Land
The 1858–62 Revival in the North East of Scotland

Previous studies of revivals have tended to approach religious movements from either a broad, national or a strictly local level. This study of the multifaceted nature of the 1859 revival as it appeared in three distinct social contexts within a single region reveals the heterogeneous nature of simultaneous religious movements in the same vicinity.

2002 / 1-84227-057-5 / xxiv + 304pp

John Kenneth Lander
Itinerant Temples
Tent Methodism, 1814–1832

Tent preaching began in 1814 and the Tent Methodist sect resulted from disputes with Bristol Wesleyan Methodists in 1820. The movement spread to parts of Gloucestershire, Wiltshire, London and Liverpool, among other places. Its demise started in 1826 after which one leader returned to the Wesleyans and others became ministers in the Congregational and Baptist denominations.

2003 / 1-84227-151-2 / xx + 268pp

Donald M. Lewis
Lighten Their Darkness
The Evangelical Mission to Working-Class London, 1828–1860
This is a comprehensive and compelling study of the Church and the complexities of nineteenth-century London. Challenging our understanding of the culture in working London at this time, Lewis presents a well-structured and illustrated work that contributes substantially to the study of evangelicalism and mission in nineteenth-century Britain.
2001 / 1-84227-074-5 / xviii + 372pp

Herbert McGonigle
'Sufficient Saving Grace'
John Wesley's Evangelical Arminianism
A thorough investigation of the theological roots of John Wesley's evangelical Arminianism and how these convictions were hammered out in controversies on predestination, limited atonement and the perseverance of the saints.
2001 / 1-84227-045-1 / xvi + 350pp

Lisa S. Nolland
A Victorian Feminist Christian
Josephine Butler, the Prostitutes and God
Josephine Butler was an unlikely candidate for taking up the cause of prostitutes, as she did, with a fierce and self-disregarding passion. This book explores the particular mix of perspectives and experiences that came together to envision and empower her remarkable achievements. It highlights the vital role of her spirituality and the tragic loss of her daughter.
2004 / 1-84227-225-X / approx. 360pp

Ian M. Randall
Evangelical Experiences
A Study in the Spirituality of English Evangelicalism 1918–1939
This book makes a detailed historical examination of evangelical spirituality between the First and Second World Wars. It shows how patterns of devotion led to tensions and divisions. In a wide-ranging study, Anglican, Wesleyan, Reformed and Pentecostal-charismatic spiritualities are analysed.
1999 / 0-85364-919-7 / xii + 310pp

Ian M. Randall

Spirituality and Social Change

The Contribution of F.B. Meyer (1847–1929)

This is a fresh appraisal of F.B. Meyer (1847–1929), a leading Free Church minister. Having been deeply affected by holiness spirituality, Meyer became the Keswick Convention's foremost international speaker. He combined spirituality with effective evangelism and socio-political activity. This study shows Meyer's significant contribution to spiritual renewal and social change.

2003 / 1-84227-195-4 / xx + 184pp

James Robinson

Pentecostal Origins (1907–c.1925): A Regional Study

Early Pentecostalism in Ulster within its British Context

Harvey Cox describes Pentecostalism as 'the fascinating spiritual child of our time' that has the potential, at the global scale, to contribute to the 'reshaping of religion in the twenty-first century'. This study grounds such sentiments by examining at the local scale the origin, development and nature of Pentecostalism in the north of Ireland in its first twenty years. Illustrative, in a paradigmatic way, of how Pentecostalism became established within one region of the British Isles, it sets the story within the wider context of formative influences emanating from America, Europe and, in particular, other parts of the British Isles. As a synoptic regional study in Pentecostal history it is the first survey of its kind.

***2005** / 1-84227-329-9 / approx. 424pp*

Geoffrey Robson

Dark Satanic Mills?

Religion and Irreligion in Birmingham and the Black Country

This book analyses and interprets the nature and extent of popular Christian belief and practice in Birmingham and the Black Country during the first half of the nineteenth century, with particular reference to the impact of cholera epidemics and evangelism on church extension programmes.

2002 / 1-84227-102-4 / xiv + 294pp

Roger Shuff

Searching for the True Church

Brethren and Evangelicals in Mid-Twentieth-Century England

Roger Shuff holds that the influence of the Brethren movement on wider evangelical life in England in the twentieth century is often underrated. This book records and accounts for the fact that Brethren reached the peak of their strength at the time when evangelicalism was at it lowest ebb, immediately before World War II. However, the movement then moved into persistent decline as evangelicalism regained ground in the post war period. Accompanying this downward trend has been a sharp accentuation of the contrast between Brethren congregations who engage constructively with the non-Brethren scene and, at the other end of the spectrum, the isolationist group commonly referred to as 'Exclusive Brethren'.

***2005** / 1-84227-254-3 / approx. 318pp*

James H.S. Steven

Worship in the Spirit

Charismatic Worship in the Church of England

This book explores the nature and function of worship in six Church of England churches influenced by the Charismatic Movement, focusing on congregational singing and public prayer ministry. The theological adequacy of such ritual is discussed in relation to pneumatological and christological understandings in Christian worship.

2002 / 1-84227-103-2 / xvi + 238pp

Peter K. Stevenson

God in Our Nature

The Incarnational Theology of John McLeod Campbell

This radical reassessment of Campbell's thought arises from a comprehensive study of his preaching and theology. Previous accounts have overlooked both his sermons and his Christology. This study examines the distinctive Christology evident in his sermons and shows that it sheds new light on Campbell's much debated views about atonement.

2004 / 1-84227-218-7 / xxiv + 458pp

Martin Wellings

Evangelicals Embattled

Responses of Evangelicals in the Church of England to Ritualism, Darwinism and Theological Liberalism 1890–1930

In the closing years of the nineteenth century and the first decades of the twentieth century Anglican Evangelicals faced a series of challenges. In responding to Anglo-Catholicism, liberal theology, Darwinism and biblical criticism, the unity and identity of the Evangelical school were severely tested.

2003 / 1-84227-049-4 / xviii + 352pp

James Whisenant
A Fragile Unity
Anti-Ritualism and the Division of Anglican Evangelicalism in the Nineteenth Century

This book deals with the ritualist controversy (approximately 1850–1900) from the perspective of its evangelical participants and considers the divisive effects it had on the party.

2003 / 1-84227-105-9 / xvi + 530pp

Haddon Willmer
Evangelicalism 1785–1835: An Essay (1962) and Reflections (2004)

Awarded the Hulsean Prize in the University of Cambridge in 1962, this interpretation of a classic period of English Evangelicalism, by a young church historian, is now supplemented by reflections on Evangelicalism from the vantage point of a retired Professor of Theology.

***2005** / 1-84227-219-5*

Linda Wilson
Constrained by Zeal
Female Spirituality amongst Nonconformists 1825–1875

Constrained by Zeal investigates the neglected area of Nonconformist female spirituality. Against the background of separate spheres, it analyses the experience of women from four denominations, and argues that the churches provided a 'third sphere' in which they could find opportunities for participation.

2000 / 0-85364-972-3 / xvi + 294pp

Paternoster
9 Holdom Avenue
Bletchley
Milton Keynes MK1 1QR
United Kingdom

Web: www.authenticmedia.co.uk/paternoster

November 2004

ND - #0052 - 090625 - C0 - 229/152/21 - PB - 9781842273296 - Gloss Lamination